LONGSTREET HIGHROAD GUIDE
TO THE
NORTHWEST COAST

BY ALLAN AND ELIZABETH MAY

FOREWORD BY
THE PUGET SOUND WATER QUALITY ACTION TEAM

LONGSTREET
ATLANTA, GEORGIA

Published by
LONGSTREET PRESS, INC.
2140 Newmarket Parkway
Suite 122
Marietta, Georgia 30067

Great efforts have been made to make the information in this book as accurate as possible. However, over time trails are rerouted and signs and landmarks may change. If you find a change has occurred to a trail in the book, please let us know so we can correct future editions. *A word of caution:* Outdoor recreation by its nature is potentially hazardous. All participants in such activities must assume all responsibility for their own actions and safety. The scope of this book does not cover all potential hazards and risks involved in outdoor recreation activities.

Printed by RR Donnelley & Sons, Harrisonburg, VA

1st printing 2000

Library of Congress Catalog Number 00-104186

ISBN: 1-56352-595-x

Book editing, design, and cartography by Lenz Design & Communications, Inc., Decatur, Georgia. www.lenzdesign.org. Online version: www.sherpaguides.com

Cover illustration by J. Douglas Woodward, *Picturesque America*, 1872

Cover design by Richard J. Lenz, Decatur, Georgia

Illustrations by Danny Woodard, Loganville, Georgia

Photographs by Allan May

The oceans are the planet's last great living wilderness,
man's only remaining frontier on earth,
and perhaps his last chance to prove himself
a rational species.

—John L. Culliney, *Wilderness Conservation, September–October 1990*

Contents

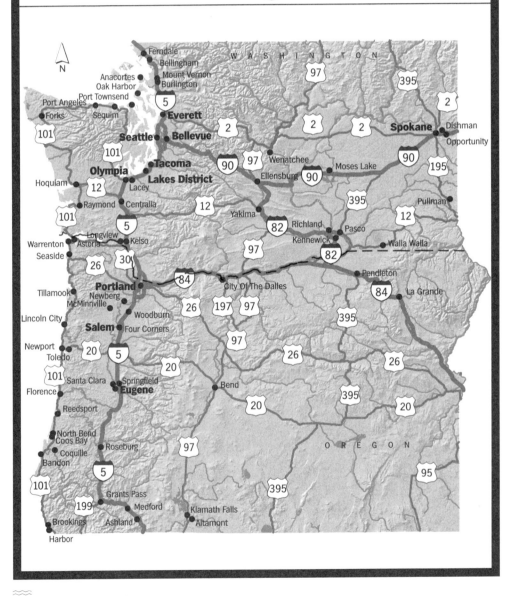

Washington & Oregon

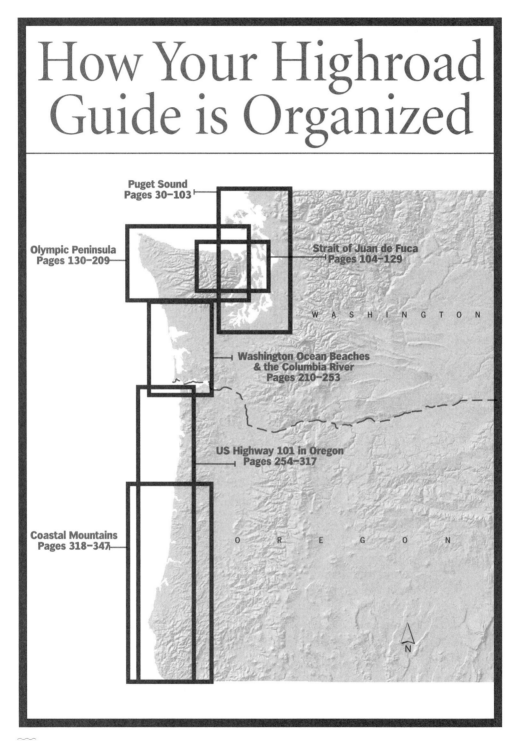

How Your Highroad Guide is Organized

Puget Sound
Pages 30–103

Olympic Peninsula
Pages 130–209

Strait of Juan de Fuca
Pages 104–129

WASHINGTON

Washington Ocean Beaches
& the Columbia River
Pages 210–253

US Highway 101 in Oregon
Pages 254–317

Coastal Mountains
Pages 318–347

OREGON

N

How To Use Your Longstreet Highroad Guide

The *Longstreet Highroad Guide to the Northwest Coast* includes a wealth of detailed information on the best of what the coast has to offer, including hiking, camping, fishing, scenic driving, and boating. The Longstreet Highroad Guide also presents interesting information on the natural history, flora, and fauna of the coast, giving readers a starting point to learn more about what makes the Northwest coast so special.

The coast is divided into six major sections beginning in Washington and moving south to Oregon, and each section is covered in its own chapter. There is also an introduction to the natural history of the Northwest coast.

The maps in the book are keyed by figure numbers and referenced in the text. These maps are intended to help orient both casual and expert coastal enthusiasts. Below is a legend to explain symbols used on the maps. Remember that hiking trails frequently change as they fall into disuse or new trails are created. Serious hikers may want to purchase additional maps from the U.S. Geological Service before they set out on a long hike. Sources are listed on the maps.

For specific information on taking shellfish as well as other fish and wildlife, contact the Washington State Department of Fish and Wildlife, phone (360) 902-2200 or Oregon State Department of Fish and Wildlife, phone (503) 872-5268. Fishing licenses are available from the department offices located in several places through the states and from numerous tackle shops. Oregon does not require a special license for taking shellfish, but Washington does.

A word of caution: Coastal waters can be dangerous for swimming, fishing, and boating. The Northwest coast has powerful and frequently changing tides, and wild animals can act in unexpected ways. Be aware of your surroundings and make safe decisions so all your memories will be happy ones.

Legend

Amphitheater	Camping	Ranger Station
Parking	Bathroom	Misc. Special Areas
Telephone	Wheelchair Accessible	Town or City
Information	First Aid Station	Physiographic Region/ Misc. Boundary
Picnicking	Picnic Shelter	
Dumping Station	Shower	Regular Trail
Swimming	Biking	State Boundary
Fishing	Comfort/Rest Station	70 Interstate
Interpretive Trail	Park Boundary	522 U.S. Route
Good Diving	Good Snorkeling	643 State Highway

Foreword

Welcome to the Northwest, and especially to Puget Sound, where you can have a total sensory experience in just one visit to this amazing place. From rugged mountain ranges to a mosaic of marine and freshwater shorelines, the Puget Sound region is astounding.

Puget Sound is an estuary where salt water from the ocean mixes with fresh water that falls as precipitation or drains from the surrounding land. More than 10,000 streams and rivers drain into Puget Sound. An array of beaches, bluffs, deltas, mud flats, and wetlands teeming with plants, fish, birds, and wildlife surround the sound.

When visiting Puget Sound, breathe in the fresh salty air of the estuary; walk along the beach and listen to a great blue heron squawk if you come too close; stroll along a river and watch spawning salmon; see a bald eagle soar overhead; taste fresh shellfish; feel the mud on your feet when the tide goes out. Enjoy, but please tread lightly in this sacred place.

Estuaries are the richest, most dynamic habitats for fish and wildlife. But they are also among the most sensitive and imperiled. Often called "cradles of the sea," estuaries provide food, breeding and spawning grounds, and protection from predators for many fish, birds, shellfish, and marine animals.

Our quality of life in Puget Sound, our cultural identity, and much of the promise and potential of this region is based on natural resources, and the industries, tourism, and recreation that these resources support.

While much of Puget Sound is healthy, rapid growth and development in the region are stressing the system. A steady loss of habitat, alarming declines in some

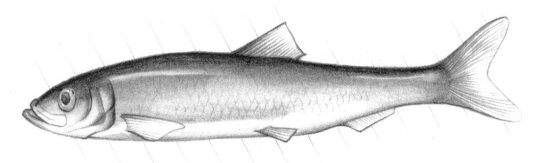

PACIFIC HERRING
(Clupea harengus pallasi)

BLUE MUSSEL
(Mytilus edulis)
Found clinging to the sides and bottoms of tidal pools, mussels have adapted to edure brief periods out of water.

fish and wildlife populations, and closures of shellfish beds are signs that the very best of Puget Sound is threatened.

The Puget Sound Water Quality Action Team was created by the Washington state legislature to enhance the sound and its resources. We partner with federal, state, tribal, and local governments, citizens, and businesses to carry out innovative solutions to the challenges we face in keeping Puget Sound healthy. We're also part of a national network of 28 estuary programs established by Congress in 1987. Together we share information and explore new ways to restore and preserve our nation's estuaries.

We're committed to keeping a strong focus on Puget Sound's health by maintaining the progress we've made and by setting actions in place to protect water quality and enhance habitat for the future.

As you travel through the region, we invite you to join us in our mission to enhance Puget Sound by treading carefully, so that future travelers can also see, smell, taste, feel, and hear the wonders of Puget Sound.

—Nancy McKay, Chair, Puget Sound Water Quality Action Team

Preface

The coastline of Washington and Oregon is characterized as much by its geographical diversity as anything else. Visitors who start at Olympia and move through Puget Sound, out the Strait of Juan de Fuca to the Pacific, down the Washington coast and across the Columbia River, and down the Oregon Coast to the California border will experience an incredible variety of landscapes. The metropolitan cities of Seattle and Portland on one end of the spectrum contrast with wildernesses and rain forests on the other.

There are luxurious, five-star hotels, cozy bed and breakfasts, and primitive campgrounds. Long sandy beaches may be only a few miles from huge wetlands or thick forests. The tidepools of the beaches provide a home for tiny creatures that wait patiently for the next tide to bring them food for nourishment, while a short distance away immense whales cavort in the deep ocean.

A short distance inland, full-scale mountain ranges jut into the air. Icy glaciers creep slowly down the side of the same mountain where hot springs provide a soothing bath. There are sand dunes as high as a 15-story building and trees taller than a 20-story building. Both are near pools and creeks where fish wait to be caught. Elk, cougar, bear, deer, coyote, and innumerable other creatures roam not far from the busy streets of the cities.

This is a country to be experienced, loved, respected, and revered. There is something for everyone here, all within a short distance. Have breakfast in a sophisticated urban restaurant and eat dinner in a primitive camp on the side of a mountain or deep in a forest.

But be careful. This country grows on you. You may not want to leave.

—Allan and Elizabeth May

DEVIL'S CLUB
(Oplopanax horridum)

Acknowledgments

The trouble with mentioning the names of the people whose information, direction, and kind words helped produce a book is that after the book is published and it is too late, the writers will go through the list and suddenly realize that the list is too short by half. Nevertheless, it is necessary to provide the publisher with a list, so with sincere apologies to the half that have been neglected, here is the list for this book. First to be mentioned is Allan's wife and Elizabeth's mother, chief editor and critic, Eleanor May. Then come Richard Lenz and Pam Holliday of Lenz Design, the Longstreet Press editors; and Marge McDonald, the Longstreet Press Project director who originated the project. Thanks to Chip Evans at Lenz Design for

EUROPEAN BUNCHGRASS
(Ammophila arenaria)

his skill in making the best maps possible. We would also like to thank the following people: Mark Nesse, Margaret Riddle, Dave Dilgard, Liz Hawkins, Mary Allen, Marlin Olson, Eileen Simmons, Cameron Johnson, Marge Bodre, Sue Selmer, Scott Condon, and Ellen Chou, the Everett Public Library reference desk people who found sources and information whenever it was needed; Virginia Painter and Linda Burnett of the Washington State Parks and Recreation Commission public affairs office, and Mick Schultz, Port of Tacoma spokesman; Sheila McCartan of the Nisqually National Wildlife Refuge; Betty Ronning of the Everett Parks and Recreation Department; Dave Workman, editor and friend who steered the project to Allan then steered us to valuable information sources; Tim Walsh of the Washington State Department of Natural Resources, Geology and Earth Resources Division; Alan Ramner of the Washington Department of Fish and Wildlife; Helen Lord and Joanne Kartes of the Ocean Shores Visitor Center; Jessica Gonzales, Willapa National Wildlife Refuge; Ken Eldredge of the Olympic National Forest; Karen Loper of the Portland Bureau of Parks and Recreation; Nancy Eaton of the Long Beach Peninsula Visitor Center; Jim Lockwood of the Oregon Parks and Recreation Department; Michael Ronkin of the Oregon Department of Transportation; Randy Peterson, spokesman for the Forest Grove District of the Oregon Department of Forestry; Mary Marrs, Rita Dyer, and Rene Casteran of the Siskiyou National Forest; and Joni Quarnstrom of the Siuslaw National Forest.

Sincere thanks to all.

—Allan and Elizabeth May

Federal Lands of the Northwest Coast

The Natural History
of the Northwest Coast

The 500 miles of rugged Pacific coastline from the Strait of Juan de Fuca south to the Oregon/California border is a dynamic meeting of earth and ocean. Here, the world's largest ocean dramatically meets America's western edge without barrier islands or barrier reefs to buffet the thunderous waves that pound the shore. These primary natural forces produce magnificent results. The waves with loads of grinding sediment and stone work against the mountain ramparts of the Coast Ranges, carving out scalloped tidal pools, undercutting steep cliffs, eroding towers of rock, and strewing beaches with boulders. Huge sand dunes supply evidence of thousands of years of ceaseless erosion by the sea. From the ocean come rain, snow, and fog that feed the rivers, forests, and glaciers that shape and characterize the Pacific Northwest. Rivers wind to the coast where they can, helping to create sounds, harbors, and estuaries that protect and nurture life from the violent effects of the Pacific.

[*Above:* Cannonball Island once served the Makah Indians as a cemetery and lookout site]

Geologic Time Scale

Era	System & Period	Series & Epoch	Some Distinctive Features	Years Before Present
CENOZOIC	Quaternary	Recent	Modern man.	11,000
		Pleistocene	Early man; northern glaciation.	1/2 to 2 million
	Tertiary	Pliocene	Large carnivores.	13 + 1 million
		Miocene	First abundant grazing mammals.	25 + 1 million
		Oligocene	Large running mammals.	36 + 2 million
		Eocene	Many modern types of mammals.	58 + 2 million
		Paleocene	First placental mammals.	63 + 2 million
MESOZOIC	Cretaceous		First flowering plants; climax of dinosaurs and ammonites, followed by Cretaceous-Tertiary extinction.	135 + 5 million
	Jurassic		First birds, first mammals dinosaurs and ammonites abundant.	181 + 5 million
	Triassic		First dinosaurs. Abundant cycads and conifers.	230 + 10 million
PALEOZOIC	Permian		Extinction of most kinds of marine animals, including trilobites. Southern glaciation.	280 + 10 million
	Carboniferous	Pennsylvanian	Great coal forests, conifers. First reptiles.	310 + 10 million
		Mississippian	Sharks and amphibians abundant. Large and numerous scale trees and seed ferns.	345 + 10 million
	Devonian		First amphibians; ammonites; fishes abundant.	405 + 10 million
	Silurian		First terrestrial plants and animals.	425 + 10 million
	Ordovician		First fishes; invertebrates dominant.	500 + 10 million
	Cambrian		First abundant record of marine life; trilobites dominant.	600 + 50 million
	Precambrian		Fossils extremely rare, consisting of primitive aquatic plants. Evidence of glaciation. Oldest dated algae, over 2,600 million years; oldest dated meteorites 4,500 million years.	

Building the Pacific Coastline

Ice, fire, and immense landmasses that float on the molten rock of the earth's mantle have roles in the formation of Washington and Oregon. The story begins with plate tectonics, the process that moves huge plates of the earth's cool, solid, outer layer of rock, called the lithosphere, over the softer, fluid mantle deep within the earth. The plates all move, usually at a rate of about 3 or 4 inches a year, carrying the exposed landmasses with them.

About 200 million years ago, North and South America were part of a supercontinent that also included Europe and Africa. Scientists call it Pangaea. The earth forces caused it to split a number of times, eventually forming the system of oceans and landmasses we know today. The American continents drifted westward creating a water-filled gap we know as the Atlantic Ocean. The Americas' westward movement continues today. At the same time, plates on the bottom of the Pacific were pushed by similar earth forces in roughly easterly directions, toward the Americas.

Two tectonic plates are active off the continent's west coast. The huge Pacific Plate moves in a northwesterly direction. Between the Pacific Plate and the Washington/Oregon portion of the continent, the much smaller Juan de Fuca Plate moves in an easterly direction, flowing toward the western shore of the North American continent. When the plates meet the westerly moving continent, they are forced under the continental landmass in a process called subduction. That creates unimaginable forces under the earth's surface, which result in a variety of phenomena, such as earthquakes, eruptions of lava, and upthrusts that tilt and fold huge landmasses so that the high parts become mountains and the low parts become valleys. But if parts of the plates were buried by subduction, other portions were sheared off to become part of the continent's surface. The result, the Pacific coast, is perhaps the most complex geologic formation in the world. Imagine pulling a tablecloth toward yourself while holding a knife blade flat against the linen to keep peas from falling on the floor. These peas are the west coast. Geologists have identified some 100 places where floating land masses ended up as part of the Pacific Coast.

Similar forces result in ocean floors being raised to become dry land so that rocks high on the mountains may contain the fossils of sea creatures that died many millions of years ago and fell to the bottom of the ocean. They were buried by immense quantities of other creatures and sediments so deeply that the pressure hardened them into rock. Rocks like that may be uplifted out of the ocean to become part of a mountain.

Those earth formation processes began before the supercontinent Pangaea split into today's separate continents over a period of billions of years. They continue today, although geologists believe the pace may be somewhat slower now. The result, on the Washington and Oregon coasts, is a jigsaw puzzle of rocks jumbled and piled together in a huge maze.

A major feature of those formations along the Washington and Oregon coasts is the Coast Range of mountains that run much more than the width of the two states, roughly parallel to and usually a little inland from the beaches.

The range in the northwestern United States is irregular, with the highest portion being in the northwestern corner of Washington, where the Olympic Mountains crown a large peninsula that separates Puget Sound from the ocean. The highest of the Olympic Mountains is glacier-clad Mount Olympus, which rises to 7,950 feet in elevation in the center of the range. Geologists say the Olympics were formed of sedimentary and igneous rock on the bottom of the sea, and became part of the plate that collided with the continent, but instead of entirely subsiding beneath the continent, part of the plate sheared off and became a portion of the mainland. The newly acquired landmass was fractured and folded by the earth forces, creating a jumble of rock formations that were further altered by the erosion forces of wind and rain, and especially by glaciers that even today are carving out valleys that radiate from the center of the range.

South of the Olympics, the Coast Range disappears briefly in the broad lowland of the Chehalis River. The range rises again in Washington a little north of the Columbia River and continues unbroken through Oregon and on into California. The Olympics are higher and more rugged than the Coast Range to the south, but the mountains are closely related to each other in the immensely varied composition of their rock formations.

Some of the rocks of the Coast Range are sedimentary, formed from deposits in the ocean, carried to the continent, and raised out of the sea. Other rocks in the range are igneous, erupted from the earth's interior beneath the seas and exposed by the same forces that brought the sedimentary rock to the surface. And still others of the Coast Range rocks were formed of eruptions on the land.

EROSION AND GLACIATION

Just as the rock-melting heat of the earth's core played an important part in the coastal formations, so did the forces of erosion. In Washington, ice was a major force of erosion. The last of a series of ice ages began about 80,000 years ago during the Pleistocene geological period. Beginning about 28,000 years ago, glacial lobes formed, reaching their maximum size about 18,000 to 20,000 years ago. The glaciers had receded by about 10,000 to 15,000 years ago after leaving marks on the earth's surface that are indelible, at least until the next ice age. The glaciers of that ice age formed in the way all glaciers do. Because the weather was cool, snow that fell in the far northern reaches failed to melt in the summer. The weight of new snow that accumulated over many years squeezed the older snow below and forced it to move away, a little like toothpaste squeezed from a tube. It moved in a southerly direction, scraping and gouging the earth's surface as it moved.

The glaciers of the most recent Ice Age covered much of the North American continent in huge lobes that pushed down through Canada into the United States. One lobe reached down through British Columbia to northern Washington, between the ocean and the Cascade Mountains. The immense sheet of ice was as high as a 400-story building, and, stretched 150 miles into what is now the United States, and spread to about 60 miles wide in the vicinity of today's Seattle. It pushed inexorably southward and changed the face of the surface, including shaping the preexisting structural trough between the mountains of the Cascades and the Coast Range. When the ice receded, the trench filled with seawater and became Puget Sound, America's second largest estuary. A branch of that glacier followed a basin between the mountains of the Olympic Range and those of Canada's Vancouver Island. When that branch receded, the sea flowed into the void and it became the 100-mile-long Strait of Juan de Fuca, which links the ocean and Puget Sound. That lobe of the glacier carried huge boulders, called erratics by geologists. When the glaciers melted, they left the erratics behind. Some of those rocks can still be found as high as 4,000 feet above sea level in the mountains, many miles from where they originated in Canada far to the north.

The weight of the ice pushed the land downward, so parts of the area were covered by the sea, creating new beaches and covering the new sea bottom with sediment. When the ice melted, the unweighted landmass rose, leaving the old beaches and the old sea bottom on dry ground.

Similar forces created the Coast Range Mountains to the south of the Olympics, but with variations that geologists will be studying for many years to come. The southern mountains are smaller than the Olympics, which are themselves not especially high when compared with other ranges in the western states.

Regardless of the differences in height and other characteristics, the mountains along the coastline in Washington and Oregon are rugged and magnificent. Together with beaches, the mountains make this a region of intense interest and charm for visitors and residents alike.

South of the rugged Olympic Mountains in Northwest Washington, the Coast Range Mountains decrease in size. Mary's Peak near Philomath, Oregon, the highest peak, south of the Olympics is 4,097 feet in elevation, compared with Olympus at 7,950 feet. Nearby peaks are only about half as high as the Olympics.

Some of the sedimentary rocks in the Coast Range contain fossils of creatures that have been extinct for millions of years, as well as those of sea lions, whales, seals, and other creatures that have survived into the modern world. Many of the basaltic headlands were formed by lava flows that originated some 300 miles away in what is now Eastern Washington and Oregon and even in Western Idaho. Some of the fluid basalt eruptions flowed through the Columbia River valley to the ocean. Others crossed over the Coast Range.

During the most recent glacial period, glacial lobes periodically dammed the Clark Fork River in Montana, creating a lake as much as 150 miles long. When the ice receded, the dams broke, freeing the lake and causing what have been called the largest floods in the history of earth. The floods carried ice and rubble over the Idaho Panhandle and scoured out the scablands in Eastern Washington, then funneled into the narrow Columbia Gorge. Icebergs, sand, and rock formed another dam near where present-day Rainier, Oregon is now. That downstream dam backed up the flood waters, creating another lake that extended some 100 miles back into the tributary Willamette Valley to the vicinity of present-day Eugene. All of present downtown Portland was covered by as much as 400 feet of water except for a few high spots that existed as islands above the surface. The lake, called Lake Allison by geologists, lasted only a short time before it drained down the Columbia and out to sea, but some of the icebergs carried rocks as large as a house, which were scattered around the Willamette Valley when the lake drained. The rocks—largely granite, quartzite, slate, and gneiss—have been traced back to Montana as their source.

In the far southern coast of Oregon, the mountainous area geologists call the Klamath Mountain Province shows striking differences from the portions of the Coast Mountains to the north. The Klamaths, which extend from the vicinity of Port Orford down into the Humboldt County area of California, appear to have been transported by crustal plates to their present location from undersea areas off Southern California to the south and British Columbia to the north, and possibly as far away as China or Japan. Geologists find evidence for that far-flung wandering in the fossils of a variety of invertebrates and other organisms imbedded in the Klamath rock.

During the most recent Ice Age, much of the earth's water was collected and held in the ice, which caused the sea level to lower and the oceans to recede from the shoreline. Plants and animals inhabited the newly exposed area. When the ice melted, the water flowed to the ocean, flooding the shoreline, drowning the forests and other vegetation along the coast. The ocean flooded into the mouths of rivers, converting the lower valleys into bays and tidewater estuaries so that many large rivers on the coast of the Pacific Northwest empty into large estuaries. Prime examples of the large estuaries are the huge Grays Harbor and Willapa Bays in Southern Washington. Many of the estuaries have become shallow because the ocean waves built sandbars that slowed the water running out of the rivers' mouths. That in turn has caused the rivers to slow near their mouths, and deposit silt that is slowly filling the estuaries.

The harder, tougher volcanic rock that spewed out of the earth and flowed down the valleys formed long, narrow rivers of lava bordered by the sedimentary rock. When the sedimentary rock was smashed to sand, the volcanic rock resisted, and as the softer material wore away, it left fingers of volcanic rock extending into the sea. Eventually they, too, wore down and formed headlands, islands, and sea stacks. The surf now pounds against this sturdy rock in towering, white spray, giving emphasis to the majestic beauty of the beach.

When people who live along the Northwest coast talk about the huge, incessant waves of the surf, they often comment that it is natural for the waves to be huge because they come all the way from Japan and they have a lot of ocean to grow in. Actually the biggest waves come from the Gulf of Alaska in the winter. During the summer, the waves come from the west-southwest and are smaller. Either way, the surf comes a long, unfettered distance before it crashes onto the shore. Soft sedimentary rocks that rose from the sea to become part of the coast have been pounded by that incessant surf for millions of years. They are too soft to stand that kind of punishment and are being ground down to sand, which adds to the sand washed down to the sea by the rivers to become part of the shore and form the beach. That is especially true along the Oregon shoreline, which is well known for its large, sandy beaches. Along the central Oregon beach, wind has blown sand inland from the beach to create immense sand dunes that have been designated the Oregon Dunes National Recreation Area under the management of the U.S. Forest Service. The 14,000-acre recreation area stretches for 40 miles along the coast, and is popular for all kinds of beach and dune recreation (see Oregon Dunes, page 327).

Life in the Sea

Where the Pacific meets the land is a demarcation line between sea and land creatures, both of which abound in their own habitats. Both have evolved to fit their own niches within their habitats, and some have evolved to survive in both.

Many people enjoy walking on the beach and watching the innumerable, often vividly colored little creatures that live in the tiny intertidal pools left in depressions in the sand. The animals wait quietly in the little pools for the tide to return and bring new sustenance, but with a little patience humans can detect the creatures on the sandy or rocky bottom they often resemble.

A little farther out, fish, mammals, and other species find their own habitats in the deeper water. Some are residents of the waters along the beach. For others, the sea off the coast is a highway between the cold waters of the far north and the warmer waters of the south.

MAMMALS OF THE SEA

Mammals, too, are in the waters off the Northwest shores. Several different species of mammals spend all of their lives at sea. Others spend much of their time in the water but also go ashore from time to time. Those mammals that live exclusively at sea include closely related cetaceans such as whales, dolphins, and porpoises. Those mammals that are able to leave the water include the various varieties of seals, such as harbor seals and Steller's sea lions (*Eumetopias jubatus*). Harbor seal populations have been on the rise since the late '70s.

The seagoing mammals were originally land animals, that for one reason or

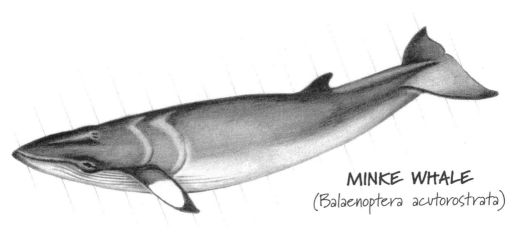

MINKE WHALE
(Balaenoptera acutorostrata)

another, found it difficult to survive there, and migrated to the sea, evolving until they became highly adapted to that environment. Despite that, they are true mammals. Unlike the fish with which they share the ocean, the sea mammals have warm blood and obtain their oxygen from the air. The females bear their young in the womb and the young are given prolonged maternal care after birth. Despite all that, they survive very well in the sea beside the fish, which are cold blooded, get their oxygen from the water, and, in most cases, produce their young as eggs that hatch on their own. Whales also differ from fish in that their flukes are horizontal and are moved up and down for propulsion, while fish tails are vertical and move from side to side.

Mammals of the Sea

Scientists believe the first of the mammals to venture into the ocean was the whale, about 65 million years ago near the beginning of the Tertiary Period. The seals followed about 5 million years later.

Seals often can be seen along the Northwest coast at places where they climb, or "haul," out of the water, often in large groups. Whales and their dolphin and porpoise cousins don't "haul" out of the water and must be seen at sea, which is more difficult but entirely possible. Many of the varieties, however, are similar in appearance and it is not always easy to identify them.

Dolphins may best be seen at the bow of a vessel moving through the water. The vessel creates a positive pressure in the water just ahead of the bow. Dolphins like to position themselves there with their flukes arranged to take advantage of that pressure to be propelled through the water as a kind of aquatic hitchhiker. They may travel for long distances that way. Watching their supple and graceful motions as they glide through the water is a pleasant way to spend time on a voyage, whether it's on an ocean liner or a small pleasure boat.

WHALES

Possibly the most interesting of the cetacea to be found off the Northwest coast are the whales. Some of these huge creatures migrate between the warm waters of the south and the cold waters of the north. The four most common species in Northwestern waters are the orca or killer whales (*Orcinus orca*), (although they are technically the largest members of the dolphin family rather than whales), minke whales (*Balaenoptera acutorostrata*), gray whales (*Eschrichtius robustus*), and humpback whales (*Megaptera novaeangliae*).

Whales are sustained in their long dives underwater by the enormous amounts of air they inhale on the surface. When they come up for another breath, they exhale in a blow that sends vapor, water, or condensation as much as 12 feet in the air. That blow is the telltale sign that there are whales in the vicinity and is the first thing that whale watchers should look for. The first blow will be followed by others from the same whale, and also from any of its companions in the pod. Migrating whales establish blow patterns that may begin with as many as a half dozen shallow and short dives, followed by a longer one that often lasts 3 to 5 minutes, but may last as long as 10 minutes. During the short dives the whales may leave turbulence on the surface that helps track where they will surface the next time. A longer, deeper dive may be indicated if the whale raises its flukes unusually high at the beginning of the dive, but if the flukes remain out of water for several minutes, the animal is performing the maneuver that scientists

The Minke Whale

The minke whale (*Balaenoptera acutorostrata*) is the smallest baleen whale in the North Pacific. It grows to some 33 feet long, with the females growing slightly larger than the males. They tend to live alone and they eat small schooling fish such as herring. Like the humpback and other species, the minke is a rorqual whale. The word "rorqual" is taken from the Norwegian word *rorhval*, which means "furrow" and refers to grooves or folds of skin that run back from the lower jaw to behind the flippers. The grooves are an important part of the rorquals' method of eating. The rorquals swim through the water with their mouths open, taking in large amounts of water containing fish or krill. As the volume of water increases, the folds in the skin distend to accommodate it. When the whale closes its mouth, the folds contract like an accordion and the water is forced out, but the baleen traps the fish and krill.

The minke is the most abundant and smallest of the rorquals. It has a pointed snout, which breaks the surface first when the whale comes up for air. The fins and blowholes become visible at the same time. There is a ridge running back on the head, and the flippers of minke in the Northern Hemisphere have a white band. There are two blowholes side by side and the blow is quick, low, and indistinct. The fluke is somewhat concave on the trailing edge and has a slight notch in the middle, but unlike other species, the flukes do not appear above the surface when the minke dives.

call head standing. That gives whale watchers a great view of the flukes.

With luck, some whales may also head slap, breach, or spyhop giving whale watchers an unexpectedly good show, although it is highly doubtful that the whale has that in mind. Experienced whale watchers learn to distinguish between the blows, as well as the flukes, body shape, and other characteristics of the different species. Some of the distinguishing features to watch for are listed here:

The long white flippers, bumps on the top of the head, sharp angle of the back during the dive, and short dorsal fin of the humpback whale.

The uneven, splotchy, gray color, ridges along the back near the tail, and barnacles on the skin of the gray whale.

The sharply delineated black and white color pattern of the orca or killer whale.

The square head, ridges along the tail, wrinkled skin, and blowhole that leans at a 45-degree angle from the head of the sperm whale.

Whales were exploited for their oil-rich blubber and driven into near extinction by commercial fishing. Protections for the whales were established and today many species are on the rebound. For example, the eastern Pacific gray whale population is estimated at 23,000 individuals, which is believed to be as great or greater than it was prior to the onset of commercial exploitation around 1850.

FISH

Fishing, a mainstay of people of the Pacific Northwest since before Europeans arrived on the coastline, continues to define the area. In 1998, more than 341 million pounds of seafood products were harvested from the waters of Oregon and Washington worth more than $163 million.

SEA NETTLE
(*Chrysaora melanaster*)

There are innumerable species of fish found in the coastal and inlet waters, including the rocky reef denizens— like the red Irish lord (*Itemilepidotus itemillepidotus*) and the buffalo sculpin (*Enophrys bison*), which hums loudly to frighten intruders from its egg masses. One of the fish species found in the sandy, cobbled sea floor is the plainfin midshipman (*Porichth wotatus*), which lives in deep water but moves to shallow water to spawn in the spring. Free-swimming fish include many species of sharks (Class Chondtichthyes), rockfish (*Sebasties* sp.), which tend to stay near rocks and reefs where their colors blend into the background, cod (family Gadidae), and lingcod (*Ophiodon elongatus*).

Better known to many people are the various species of salmon (Salmonidae) that from time immemorial have provided food for humans. They are of abiding interest to both sport and commercial fishermen.

They are anadromous fish that are spawned in fresh water streams, migrate to the sea to become adults, and return to the stream where they were spawned to begin the cycle again.

The salmon stay in the ocean for one to four years, traveling as much as 1,000 or more miles into the northern Pacific. When they mature they swim back to their home stream. They find their way home using the earth's magnetic field and the odor of chemicals unique to their birth stream. The adults stop eating when they get to fresh water, using only stored energy to finish their journey and to spawn.

One of the reasons people like salmon is that they are delicious. Another reason is they provide a challenge for people who indulge in sport fishing, and the mighty salmon is a strong lure for both local Northwesterners and for visitors. Many parks and other recreation spots along the coast have piers where anglers can try their luck, and there are innumerable charter boats that take passengers out to sea to fish. There are serious concerns, however, over depleted salmon runs, and fishing is tightly regulated in both Oregon and Washington. A landmark study in 1992 identified 214 wild spawning stocks that were at risk of extinction or of special concern, including 17 stocks that were already extinct.

The chinook salmon (*Oncorhynchus tshawttscha*) is also known as the king salmon, and that is how many anglers think of it. Twenty-pound specimens have been recorded with fair frequency and there are records of some weighing more than 100 pounds. Chinook migrate farther inland than the other salmon species, some travelling 1,000 to 2,000 miles upstream. That makes them more vulnerable than other species to the dangers of the hydroelectric dams on many of the streams in the Northwest. By 1999, the chinook numbers had fallen so low that the some runs were

Stinging Jellyfish

Jellyfish such as the sea nettle (*Chrysaora melanaster*) are formed of a material called mesoglea that is lighter than the seawater they live in, so they float. When sea nettles are in the water they are pretty, umbrella-like creatures that propel themselves gracefully with a rhythmic contraction of their bodies. However, jellyfish are not especially good swimmers and may be washed up on the beach where they become stranded. Without the water to buoy them, they lose their good looks and become flat blobs of jelly. They look harmless, but jellyfish have stinging cells in their tentacles that cause a painful sting when they are touched, even when they are dead.

The Humpback Whale

Humpback whales (*Megaptera novaeangliae*) are large baleens that grow to about 50 feet long. They often leap out of the water and have been known to corral their tiny prey with walls of bubbles to make them easier to catch. During the mating season the males sing the longest, most complex songs known among animals. The humpback is relatively easy to identify because of the knobs on the top of its head and its long, slender, scalloped, flippers. It is black or dark gray on the upper side. The low, stubby fin has a conspicuous hump in the front. The body is large and stocky. The flukes have irregular, wavy edges, and it has a single blowhole.

declared to be threatened under the Endangered Species Act. Since records have been kept since 1950, Washington and Oregon commercial landings of chinook have trended downward, with a peak of 28.3 million pounds worth $68 million in 1988 compared to 3.7 million pounds worth $3.9 million in 1998.

Fishing for those runs is banned until numbers recover and the threatened classification is lifted. That is likely to take a long time, since in addition to banning fishing for those runs, the recovery of the salmon will require changes in human activities near salmon streams. The 1999 regulations were not the last word. Officials announced that they were continuing to study the situation, and were adjusting and extending protection to other runs and other species. Indeed, the coastal cutthroat trout stocks in one area were also named as threatened under the Endangered Species Act.

The other species of Pacific salmon are depleted in comparison with their original numbers, but are still available during the fishing season for anglers that have the necessary license, skill, and luck. Those species are the sockeye or red (*O. nerka*), coho or silver (*O. kisutch*), pink (*O. gorbuscha*), and chum (*O. keta*). Chinook and coho are probably the most popular with anglers.

Other fish in the waters off the coast include two trout species that are divided into those that go to sea and those that don't. Those that do are called sea run. They include the sea run rainbow trout (*O. mykiss*), which are more commonly called steelhead, and sea run cutthroat trout (*O. clarkii*). The steelhead grow to 45 inches and some 40 pounds with the average being about 24 inches and 5 to 10 pounds. They are a metallic blue-black with silver on the side. There are black spots on the tail and back. The males have a pink or red band on the side during the spawning season. Like the salmon they are hatched in cold, freshwater streams and migrate to the ocean. They migrate far out before returning to their home streams in one to four years to spawn, but unlike their salmon cousins, they may return to the sea for one or two more cycles before they die. Steelhead are a very popular species among fishermen. There are winter and summer runs of steelhead in Northwestern streams, but both runs spawn between February and June.

There are many additional fish in the Northwest's salt waters including varieties such as herring (*Cluped harengus pallasi*) and Pacific halibut (*Hippooglossus stenolepis*), which is a flounder with both eyes on one side of its body. It spends much of its time lying motionless on the sea bottom with its eyes on the upper side. Its coloration makes the halibut nearly invisible against the background until it moves, perhaps in pursuit of a tasty morsel that mistook the halibut for part of the sea bottom. In 1998, more than 4.5 million pounds of Pacific halibut worth $7.2 million were commercially landed in Washington and Oregon. Pacific herring stocks have eroded in numbers and caused concern. In 1998, roughly 1 million pounds of herring were landed.

Another creature off the Northwest shore that is popular with commercial fishermen and diners is the Dungeness crab (*Cancer magister*). They live in quiet estuaries and the open ocean on sandy bottoms. In late winter they shed their outer skeletons, which occasionally wash up on the beach perfectly intact. Sometimes large numbers of the skeletons are found together. The skeletons, however, are empty and the crab is somewhere out on the sandy bottom of the sea. The Dungeness crab is considered to be a prize catch among the many sea creatures that provide food for people, and catching them requires a special technique. They can be caught from structures like docks and piers, and from boats. Special traps, called crab pots, can be bought or rented at stores that handle fishing equipment. The pots are baited with something like a fish carcass and thrown into the water. The crab senses the bait, finds an entry into the crab pot—and then can't find a way out. So it sits, waiting to be pulled out of the water. There are special regulations that change from time to time, and it is highly recommended that crabbers know the current requirements before they begin crabbing. The regulations can be obtained from sporting goods stores throughout both Washington and Oregon. In 1998, more than 7.4 million pounds of Dungeness crab were landed worth $12.5 million.

Intertidal Life

Closer to land, in the tidal area where the bottom is underwater at high tide and exposed at low tide, is a realm where beachcombers become acquainted with the animals of the intertidal area. Some animals live underground and require some digging in soft, sandy, or muddy places. One way to see them is to dig a trench about the width and depth of the blade of a shovel and about 2 feet long, then rub the sides of the trench with the shovel or a stick so that the sides crumble and hidden creatures are unearthed. Many of them will be quite small and require careful watching.

A good way to see creatures that burrow into the sand is by watching for small holes in the surface. Among those creatures are clams that, with fish and crabs, can be taken home for dinner. The rules for harvesting them vary from state to state, from time to time, and from species to species, and should be consulted before launching a fishing expedition.

In addition to the burrowing creatures in the soft beaches, there are innumerable varieties of life in the rocky places. They are found in tidepools that remain on the rocks when the tide recedes, leaving the animals stranded in their pools until the next high tide returns. They can be found any time the tide is going out, but the best time is two hours before and after the lowest tide. That is partly because the exposed beach area is greatest when the tide is out, and partly because the area that is the last place covered by the outgoing tide has less time to dry out, so the creatures' habitat is better in the seaward area.

Most of the creatures beachcombers find in the intertidal areas dwell on or in the bottom when the tide is in. They are referred to as benthic dwellers, which means they are organisms that live on the bottom of a body of water. They differ from the pelagic creatures that drift or swim out to sea when the tide goes out. Those that drift are called planktonic. Those that swim are called nektonic.

The benthic animals remain in place when the tide recedes, but they are dependent on water to avoid dehydration, as well as for food, transportation, and their fertilization process as they release sperm and eggs into the water. Some of them, such as various species of clams, sponges, and sea cucumbers, feed on tiny plankton using filters to trap them. Others, such as the various kinds of crabs, shrimp, and worms, glean organic matter that settles to the bottom when the water above becomes calm. Still others, invertebrate herbivores such as snails and chitons, subsist on marine plants like the algaes and surfgrasses that grow on the bottom.

There are a surprising number of creatures to become acquainted with in the intertidal area. Many are dazzling, with brilliant colors or engaging shapes. Some are drab and ugly, but they all are fascinating, and the better one gets to know them, the more interesting they become. The beaches vary from sandy or muddy to rocky, and that makes for habitat for specific species. One permanent resident of the open, coastal, sandy beach is the mole crab (*Emerita analoga*), which is one of the interesting beach creatures rather than one of the beauties of the beach. With an oval shape that is a little reminiscent of the land moles, this clever creature burrows backward part way into the sand waving its antennae, which are covered with fine hairs. The hairs trap particles of food that wash by in the part of the tidal zone where the waves flow back and forth. Then the mole crab wipes the antennae across its mouth, scraping off the food particles. When the tide moves in or out, the mole crab moves with it to find another place in the new zone where the waves wash back and forth. Mole crabs are not easily seen. The male grows only 0.25 to 0.34 inch long while the females grow to about 2 inches. And they may be absent from some beaches during a period of several years when ocean currents don't suit them.

A little higher on the beach, above the waves, look for the beach hoppers or sand fleas (*Megalorchestia* spp.). They tend to congregate near clumps of seaweed and other material that has been washed up and deposited by receding waves. During the day, they burrow in or beneath the seaweed, but in the evening they come out and look for food, such as the large kelp (*Macrocystis pyrifera*), which seems to be a favorite, although beach hoppers eat anything organic. They are most obvious at dawn or dusk when swarms of them come out to feed.

The razor clam (*Siliqua patula*) is common on the Pacific Northwest ocean beaches. This creature, with a long, thin shell that may be more than 6 inches long, lives in open sandy beaches. It burrows into low tidal areas that have a gentle slope and fine-grained sand, and leaves a dimple in the surface of the sand that clam hunters use to locate it. The dimples are called either keyhole or donut, depending on their appearance. Razor clams are a popular quarry and are hunted by diggers armed with special shovels that have long, narrow, curved blades. When they see the telltale dimple, the hunters dig furiously into the sand, because razor clams are sensitive to any movement on the surface, and when frightened, quickly burrow deeper into the sand to where the hunters can't reach them.

The moon snail (*Polinices* spp.) is a larger mollusk that may be seen on sand and silt beaches of Puget Sound. These snails may grow to 5 or 6 inches in the spiral shape typical of snails. They are carnivores with tongue-like teeth called radulas. The snails use their teeth to bore neat countersunk holes in the shells of other mollusks, then eat the creature inside, leaving the shell on the beach with its strange looking hole to mystify the neophyte beachcomber.

Some sea plants may also find their way to the beach when they are washed up after being torn from their moorings by wave action. One of the common plants found on the Northwest's beaches is the bullwhip or bull kelp (*Nereocystis luetkeana*), an alga that grows up to 70 feet long. It grows attached to a rock on the ocean bottom, and has a branch with a large, air-filled bulb at the end that makes it buoyant. When a storm breaks, the bull kelp whip loose from the rocks. Then it is likely to wash up onto the shore where it looks a little like the huge whips that give it its name. They sometimes are pickled for eating.

ANIMALS OF THE ESTUARIES, BAYS, AND LAGOONS

Many creatures are especially adapted to the quiet waters of estuaries, bays, and lagoons. Among them are numerous species of mud flat creatures such as worms, sea stars, and, crabs such as the pea crab (*Pinnixa faba*), as well as species of shrimps and clams.

In the sand flats of the quiet waters are such creatures as the moonglow anemone (*Anthopleura artemisia*), the ice cream worm (*Pectinaria californiensis*), several kinds of clams such as the Japanese littleneck clam (*Tapes japonica*), and the basket cockle clam (*Clinocardium nuttallii*), and numerous other species.

The rocky places in the quiet waters also are habitats for numerous specific species, such as the Olympia oyster (*Ostrea lurida*) and the Pacific oyster (*Crassostrea gigas*), which has a ruffled, tan or white exterior shell that may have purple streaks. The Pacific oyster shell may be as much as a foot long. It is commercially important, with more than 7 million pounds harvested worth over $18 million.

Probably the most interesting of the creatures in the rocky areas is the singing toadfish or plainfin midshipman (*Porichthys notatus*). This 15-inch-long curiosity is called midshipman because it has two rows of white spots along its underbelly that look like military buttons. It is called the singing toadfish because during the spring the male issues a croaking sound to attract a female. If he is successful, the female lays a cluster of eggs under a rock. The male guards the eggs until they hatch. Sometimes at low tide it is possible to turn over a rock and see the eggs and their guard. The toadfish/plainfin midshipman may not be the most interesting denizen of the rocky places in the quiet water, but it certainly comes close.

Out on the open coast, the rocky intertidal areas form habitats for still more creatures. The rocks may range from dense, hard basalt that resists being eroded by tides and waves to softer sedimentary deposits that erode comparatively swiftly. Innumerable kinds of sea creatures live in the tidepools, depressions in the rocks where pools of water are trapped as the tide goes out. Creatures subsist in the pools until the next incoming tide brings a new supply of the water and nutrients they need to survive.

The creatures of the tidepools are easier to find than those of the surf, sand, and mud because they are trapped in the open where people can easily approach them. Nevertheless, some are tiny and difficult to see. Others hide in the rocks or are well camouflaged. It takes some time and experience to be able to pick them out. Others, however, are comparatively large and brightly colored, and it takes very little effort to see them in their pools. Sometimes people are attracted to the colorful tidepool creatures, but as they look more closely, they begin to discern the less obvious ones. Then the tidepool becomes more and more interesting. Indeed, some people become so involved that they go to the library to learn more, and soon have a new hobby.

Among the creatures people come to know and love are the green spongeweed or dead man's fingers alga (*Codium fragile*), which can grow to be a foot long and have fronds that may be dark green to black. Another of the flashy tidepool creatures is the reddish and purplish Troschel's sea star (*Evasterias troschellii*). Another sea star is the Pacific sea star (*Pissaster ochraceus*), which may be orange, brown, purple, or yellow. Both these creatures can survive being exposed to the air at low tide, and they also may be found in the tidepools. The strawberry anemone (*Corynactis californica*), which usually is pink, red, orange, or scarlet, has tentacles tipped with white club-like appendages. The individuals are only about 1 inch across, but they grow together in colorful masses.

These and the innumerable other tidepool dwellers are well worth devoting an afternoon or a lifetime to watching. What people see depends partly on how they go about it. The recommended way is to approach the tidepool slowly without disturbing the water, then watch quietly until the creatures begin to move about.

Beachcombing For Treasure

In the olden days, beachcombers were rewarded when a shipwreck disgorged things of great value that floated to the beach and became the property of whoever happened to be there. There are stories of people who lighted false beacon fires to lure ships onto reefs to provide the desired flotsam. There isn't much chance of finding great wealth along the beach any more, but there still is the charm of finding pieces of "treasure" from faraway places. One may find broken boxes, for instance, with writing in an unrecognizable language, pieces of rope that may have fallen from a vessel during a storm, pieces of driftwood with strange shapes suitable for a mantle. Perhaps the most sought-after of the flotsam are the glass floats that break loose from the nets of Japanese fishing craft on the other side of the world. They are rare, but some are found from time to time and are highly prized among the beachcombers who look for flotsam. The floats come from the fishing grounds used by Japanese fishing boats and drift eastward on the Japanese current that flows from Asia to North America. That current has been a source of good things for Americans from the beginning. There are records of Indian villages having iron that floated in on parts of wrecked Japanese vessels even before Europeans settled the American West Coast. Even more rare than the fishing floats is a bottle with a note from someone in an exotic, faraway place or perhaps a short distance up the beach.

Beaches and Dunes

But there is more to the coast of the Pacific Northwest than the sea and the tide.

Above the sea and the tidal area are the beaches and dunes built by sand deposited by the waves and currents. The latest deposits are those closest to the sea and are more or less pure sand, containing few nutrients for plants. These deposits tend to contain remnants of sea plants and animals washed up by the waves, and are lined, on the inland side, with driftwood ranging in size from twigs to the logs of full-sized trees. There is little habitat for plant or animal here, and the surface is left to shift and change with the wind and tide. But a few feet inland, on what are called dune hillocks or embryo dunes, are a few hardy plants such as the sea rocket (*Cakile edentula*), which put down quick-growing roots that stabilize the sand. As they die, they add organic material to the sand. That invites other plants such as the dune grasses (*Elymus mollis*), which have extensive underground creepers and roots, to add to the stabilization process. Then come other plants to take advantage of the conditions created by the pioneers. They may include the hardy yellow abronia (*Abronia latifolia*), which has bright yellow flowers and is anchored into the ground with a deep tap root. The abronia may be joined by similar plants such as the beach silvertop (*Glehnia leiocarpa*), which has thick, leather-like leaves, and a rambling low form that traps the blowing sand. Another important early arrival may be the beach pea (*Lathyrus japonicus*), a legume that fixes nitrogen from the air in its roots, and adds to the nutrients in the soil.

As the early plants trap blowing grains of sand, the beach builds up around them, becoming higher, while closer to the sea, waves and wind add to the new beach. The nutrients that decomposing plants add to the soil create an ever-more hospitable environment for new and larger plants. Eventually the sand deposits become mature dunes, supporting larger plants such as shrubs and trees, including the evergreen sitka spruce (*Picea sitchensis*) that may be stunted and misshapen by the constant wind blowing in from the open sea.

The sitka spruce combines with an understory of brushy salal (*Gaultheria shallon*) and other plants to form the final plant community that is exposed to the sea. Inland from that community is the mature coastal forest that has little to do with the sea.

Much of the Northwest Coast, especially in the northern sections of Washington, is rocky. But vast stretches elsewhere are sandy, particularly in Oregon where sand dunes line the coast for some 125 miles, about 45 percent of the state's total coastline. That includes the 40 miles of the Oregon Dunes National Recreation Area in the Siuslaw National Forest, where dunes loom high above the sea (see Siuslaw National Forest, page 325).

Inland Forests

Inland from the sand dunes are forest-clad mountains. When the earliest European explorers sailed their little ships along the coast, into bays, and through the inland sea of Puget Sound, they described the coast and the mountains as being covered with immense forests. The tall, stately evergreen trees have been a major influence on the European culture that followed the explorers. Much of that forest is still here, some of it still in its virgin, old-growth state.

The mountains of the coast are the Coast Range and, in the southern part of the Siskiyou National Forest, the Klamath Mountains. They run in a north and south direction, a little east of the coast and a little west of the higher, more rugged Cascade Mountain Range. Despite their comparative lack of stature, the Coastal Mountains are full-fledged mountains. Some of them, in the Olympic Range for instance, are full-scale challenges to climb, requiring skill and training, as well as endurance. Glacier-covered Mount Olympus, as an example, rises 7,965 feet above the sea, which is only about 40 miles away. Just getting to the base of Olympus can involve a long day's hike through temperate rain forests. And even the lower, less rugged parts of the Coast Range offer awesome places of natural beauty, teeming with luxuriant vegetation and fascinating wildlife.

Protective Doorways

The doors of the Native American cedar-board houses along the Washington coast were low and small with a high threshold. That put an enemy attempting to storm the house at a disadvantage as he entered off balance and in a stooped position. The villages in Washington and Oregon tended to be peaceful, but there were warlike groups to the north that periodically raided for booty and slaves and were a constant threat to the people in present-day coastal Washington. Some villages in the northern section of Washington had palisades for protection.

TREES OF THE COASTAL FOREST

The coastal forest is host to many species of evergreen trees including sitka spruce, western redcedar (*Thuja plicata*), western hemlock (*Tsuga heterophylla*), shore pine (*Pinus contorta*), and Douglas fir (*Pseudotsuga menziesii*) which was named after David Archibald Menzies, an early explorer along the Northwest coast. Sitka spruce and shore pine are the most obvious of the trees near the coast, where they take advantage of the moist sea air, but the inland forest is notable for the straight, wide Douglas fir, an evergreen that is often over 200 feet tall. Technically, the Douglas fir is not a fir tree, but a separate species that is more like the spruce than the fir. It is distinguished from the firs by its cones, which hang down from the branch, while the cones of the true firs stand upright on the branch. The true firs, such as the noble fir, Pacific silver fir, and subalpine fir are classified collectively as members of the Abies family. The coastal forest also is likely to contain deciduous trees such as bigleaf maple and red alder.

The Douglas fir, which dominates much of the forest, is a late comer in the plant succession that begins after a forest has been cleared by fire, disease, insects, wind, or logging. The succession begins with a pioneer plant such as the ubiquitous fireweed (*Epilobium angustifolium*). Other plants such as beargrass (*Xerophyllum tenax*), the pretty blue lupine (*Lupinus latifolius*), and snowbrush (*Ceanothus velutinus*) may join the parade, but the fireweed often comes first and grows thickly. The reason for its early appearance and its thick growth is its seeds, which are small and light and have long, soft hairs that catch the wind and carry the seed for long distances. The plants may find a niche in the dark forest, where, with little sunlight, they grow in a weakened condition. Then, when a fire or another event clears a spot in the forest, the sun reaches the ground and the fireweed bursts into vigorous growth. Those light, flying seeds quickly spread through the newly cleared places.

Within a year or two, a burned and black area of dead trees may burst into purple beauty as masses of fireweed bloom and spread their seeds even farther. Sometimes the fireweed and other pioneers dominate for years after the former forest has been devastated. As the pioneers die, they add nutrients to the soil, inviting other plants to move in.

The new plants may include bracken fern (*Pteridium aquilinum*) and small woody plants, such as the not-very-delicious thimbleberry (*Rubus spectabilis*) and the very delicious Pacific wild blackberry (*Rubus ursinus*), or some of the equally delicious varieties of blueberries (*Vaccinium* spp.). Both the blueberries and blackberries make a fine feast for hikers taking a break from the hot, grueling trail and also can be collected, taken home and transformed into good things such as pies. Bears are also very fond of them, and hikers should make certain there are none working in the same berry patch. If there is a bear present, people should leave. People should also know what kind of berry they are picking. Some of the poisonous ones can look harmless.

The blueberries have an added attraction in the fall when their leaves turn a bright red that becomes brilliant when the sun shines on them, making broad slopes a spectacular red. The blueberry of the west coast is very similar to the huckleberry (*Gaylussacia* spp.) that grows on the East Coast, but it is technically not the same. Nevertheless, the Western blueberry is more commonly called huckleberry. That is true even of the red blueberries.

The succession continues with the small woody plants being crowded out by low growing trees, such as the red alder (*Alnus rubra*), which grows to about 100 feet. Stands of red alder often are thick, and the trees are similar to a legume in that their roots are hosts to bacteria that remove nitrogen from the air and fix it in nodules on the roots in a form that is a fertilizer to plants. That further enriches the forest soil. The wood of freshly cut alder becomes a reddish color, which Native Americans processed to make dye.

Red alder and other deciduous trees in the Pacific Northwest forests such as bigleaf maple (*Acer macrophyllum*), Oregon ash (*Fraxinus latifolia*), and cottonwood (*Populus trichocarpa*) do not do well because of the relatively short, wet summers here. The evergreen coniferous trees are able to use the sunlight year-round, giving them a major advantage over the hardwood deciduous trees that cannot use it while they have no leaves during the winter. As the new forest begins to mature, the deciduous trees are, in their turn, crowded out by the evergreens. That process often makes the tall, straight, majestic Douglas fir dominant, and it may stay dominant for many years, but nature has another step in the succession cycle.

One reason the Douglas fir lives to be about 1,000 years old is its dark brown bark, which is so thick and tough that it withstands the heat of forest fires, leaving the Douglas fir scarred but still standing after even a moderately hot fire. The tree may grow well over 200 feet above the forest floor, becoming a majestic giant reaching for the sun.

But old and tough as it may be, the Douglas fir has a weakness. It needs direct sunlight to prosper. Stands of the stately old firs eventually grow so thick that the branches of neighboring trees join, blocking the sun from the ground below. When their seeds fall to the ground, they may sprout to new young trees, but with little or no sun they soon wither and die. The western red hemlock (*Tsuga heterophylla*), however, can get along just fine without much sunlight. It sprouts from seeds that may be carried in by birds and animals to the floor of the dark Douglas fir forest. It will not grow fast in the shade, but it will grow slowly and in good health. When something

QUAKING ASPEN
(Populus tremuloides)

happens to open a hole in a Douglas fir stand, perhaps a lightning strike that strips branches from a tree, the sunlight reaches the hemlock growing below. That is what the hemlock saplings wait for. They have a head start on any firs that may sprout from seeds on the ground, and they grow quickly in the sun. They have the densest canopy of all western tree species, and that makes the forest floor even shadier, preventing the Douglas fir from getting another start. Eventually the hemlock takes over and establishes itself as the climax tree of the forest succession. But the hemlocks do not have a fire-resistant bark, so they remain only until a hot forest fire kills them off and begins the forest succession anew.

Western redcedars are another of the giants of these forests. These trees sometimes live to be 1,000 years old and grow up to 200 feet high, with a trunk circumference of as much as 60 feet. They may be scattered throughout the forest, but they do well in places that are too moist for other species and may grow in thick stands there.

The western redcedar was a major part of the economy of Native American groups along the coast. It was used for such things as dugout canoes and paddles, boxes, baskets, clothing, hats, dishes, shafts for arrows and harpoons, drums, combs, and fish weirs. Among the reasons for its popularity before Europeans arrived on the scene is the cedar's resistance to rotting. It also is an unusually soft wood that can be carved easily with stone and shell implements. But a major attraction was the cedar's straight grain that made it easily split into boards. The boards were used to form the walls and roofs of the large, wooden houses that characterized pre-European cultures in the coastal Pacific Northwest.

There are many other plants, large and small, in the coastal area. Among them are trees such as the grand fir (*Abies balsamea*), quaking aspen (*Populus tremuloides*),

Pacific dogwood (*Cornus nuttallii*), and Pacific madrone (*Arbutus menziesii*). Shrubs include vine maple (*Acer circinatum*), the leaves of which turn brilliant red in mid summer, devil's club (*Oplopanax horridum*), which is covered by multitudes of very sharp, stinging thorns, and Pacific rhododendron (*Rhododendron macrophyllum*), which bears large, brilliant, pink blossoms and is the state flower of Washington. Herbaceous plants include Western sword fern (*Polystichum munitum*), deer fern (*Blechnum spicant*), bunchberry (*Cornus canadensis*), and many species of moss, liverwort, lichen, and fungus. Among the wildflowers are such beauties as the columbine (*Aquilegia formosa*), Indian paintbrush (*Castilleja angustifolia*), vanilla leaf (*Achlys triphylla*), and enough more to paint entire fields in many hues. All of the plants are part of the ecology of the place where they live, and all of them contribute not only to their own welfare, but also to that of the other species in the habitat, animal as well as vegetable.

FOREST ANIMALS

The animal species of the forest are numerous and varied. There are at least 70 species of mammals along the coast. Possibly the most notable is the native elk (*Cervus canadensis*), which ranges in herds up and down the Northwestern wildlands. Most elk move to the high country in the summer, and back to the valleys where there is more food in the winter. Males may reach 5 feet tall at the shoulder, have a body length of about 10 feet, and weigh more than 1,000 pounds. Females may be about 25 percent smaller than the males. The males have a large antler rack and brown shaggy mane on the throat. Elk favor open meadows and the edges of forests, and they become more active about dusk, tending to forage through the night. They are primarily grazers that feed on grass, but also may eat other plant material. The Roosevelt elk (*Cervus elaphus*) was introduced in the Olympic National Forest early in the twentieth century. It is larger and more shy than the elk found in much of the West. It is rare to catch a glimpse of this elk.

Another of the large animals that may be seen from time to time is the black-tailed deer (*Odocoileus columbianus*), which has a black tail, and large ears that look somewhat like the ears of a mule. The males weigh as much as 475 pounds. The doe may weigh about 160 pounds. During the summer the coats of both sexes are a russet brown, but in winter they turn gray. They are browsers and feed on a variety of plants.

During the winter, deer may find shelter on south-facing forest slopes, where the canopy of trees and southern exposure provide a little heat, and the understory brush is available for browsing. During the summer, they may wander to open ground such as farmland, or open forest where there is good browse. Modern society has decreased the number of wolves that are the deer's natural predators. At the same time civilization's clear-cutting in the forest has increased the browse. State game departments manipulate the hunting seasons to prevent the favorable grazing from causing an overpopulation.

Human visitors rarely see a wild cougar (*Felis concolor*), which may also go under such names as puma or mountain lion. They vary from 4 to 5 feet long, not counting the tail of about 2.5 feet. They are large, solitary, stealthy cats that remain elusive and secretive throughout their lives, hunting alone for game ranging from insects to elk, but most particularly for deer. They locate their prey from a long distance away by smell or sound, then stalk it until they get about 10 yards away. Then they suddenly attack with a rush and a pounce. A large male may eat 20 pounds at a time, then hide whatever remains and return for the rest as much as a week later. There have been reports of cougars stalking humans for days on end, and on very rare occasions, they may attack children, or, even more rarely, a solitary adult.

Another of the large animals is the black bear (*Ursus americanus*), which can weigh as much as 500 pounds and, like most wild animals, has immense strength. Black bears try to avoid contact with humans unless they are injured, or a sow is protecting its cub, or they have had good luck finding food near humans and have lost their respect for two-footed species. Campers should secure their food in a vehicle or hang it in a place bears can't reach, and take whatever other precautions are necessary to avoid attracting bears.

Occasionally a coyote (*Canis latrans*), sometimes called the brush wolf, will allow a human to come close, but usually, if the animal is seen at all, it will be for just a brief instant before the handsome creature disappears behind something or into something. While this slim, gray, cunning, dog-like animal with thick fur is seldom seen, it often is heard in the night when it sings its plaintive howling and yapping song that can carry for long distances.

In a popular animated cartoon, the coyote is consistently outwitted by its intended prey, but in real life this highly intelligent animal does

ROOSEVELT ELK
(*Cervus elaphus*)

Indian Technology

The Northwest coast native's technology produced many items, including various utensils, instruments, and toys. The people even used a few rare pieces of iron that drifted across the ocean from Asia on flotsam, such as derelict Japanese fishing boats. And archeologists have uncovered a few objects made of kinds of stone that occur only in places as far away as the Rocky Mountains, indicating an active long-range trade network. But nearly all of the people's vast possessions came directly from natural resources in their own environment.

just fine. Coyotes eat nearly any kind of animal, run as fast as 40 miles an hour, and jump exceptionally well. But perhaps their major advantage is intelligence. Usually coyotes hunt alone for small game, but they are quite capable of teaming up when they go after larger game. They may even maneuver so that two or more coyotes take turns chasing the intended prey, giving the others a chance to rest. Rabies has been found in some coyotes, and it is wise to avoid the animals if they approach.

A unique feature of West Coast wildlife is the endemic plants and animals of the Olympic Peninsula that are found nowhere else. The peninsula habitat is so isolated that at least eight unique plants and 15 animals have evolved here since the last Ice Age some 15,000 years ago (see Olympic National Park, page 140).

Native Americans and the Pacific Northwest Coast

The modern Pacific Northwest coast is home to many varieties of wild creatures, and also to the people of the cities, towns, and farms that have developed since Europeans arrived in the nineteenth century. But there were people here long before the Europeans arrived.

The native peoples left no record of exactly when they originally arrived, but in the northern area that had been covered by thousands of feet of ice during the last Ice Age, scientists believe they moved in soon after the ice receded some 15,000 years ago.

No one knows where the people came from, but they brought many different languages and dialects, and some neighboring villages could only communicate with a few words that were in general use. Customs and culture also differed among the various peoples, but the basics were the same and were founded on the environment.

Some of the villages developed along the seashore. Other people settled on inland waters, such as Puget Sound and the rivers. All were oriented to the water, but also made use of the wealth of the forest, developing complex economies and customs. The abundance of the Northwest environment gave them the wealth and the leisure to develop arts and crafts to a high degree. They used the soft western redcedar to make large houses that might be home for 20 to 40 persons or more. The houses were built of large posts imbedded in the ground. Beams across the top of the posts provided support for the split cedar board walls. Wooden platforms along the walls provided beds and a place to sit. More boards were laid across supports to create a roof. The roof boards were laid loosely on the supports so one or more could be removed to allow smoke to escape. There would be one or more hearths made of fire rings on the dirt floor.

In at least some villages, each house was led by a chief, who was chosen in part because of his wealth. Everyone else had a specific place in the hierarchy below the chief down, to the slaves who probably had been taken in battle and had no rights.

The native peoples' wealth in part was based on the salmon that returned each year to the streams where they were hatched. It was relatively easy to catch vast numbers as they became concentrated while working their way up the streams. The people used nets, weirs, and hooks for fish. Spears, bows, and arrows for other game came from either land or the sea. To kill a bear, they used elaborate traps that would cause a heavy log to fall when the bear approached. Berries and roots were also a mainstay of their diet.

They believed in spirits, both good and bad, and took steps to avoid those that were bad and attract those that were good. Whale hunters, for instance, spent long days alone in the woods to entice the spirits to help in the hunt.

Possibly their most startling accomplishment was their art work. They produced large quantities of highly stylized and attractive paintings depicting their lives, their persons, their beliefs, and the natural and supernatural world around them. They also produced an immense number of carvings, mostly in cedar and with a practical or ceremonial purpose. Like the paintings, the carvings were highly stylized, but their functions often were more apparent. Items that were acquired by the early European traders, as well as those that have been unearthed in modern archeological digs, show remarkable skill, workmanship, and understanding of artistic methods. Among them are food dishes in the form of hollowed persons, beautiful seal-killing clubs with the face of an owl, a full-sized replica of a whale fin studded with more than 700 bright, shining sea otter teeth, artistically carved combs that could be used both in the hair and to comb berries from a bush, and many others, all beautiful and useful.

The Europeans Arrive

European settlement in Western Washington began in the early 1800s on the southern extreme of Puget Sound and expanded northward along the shores. Within a few decades it had progressed to the point that the Europeans overwhelmed the native culture. In 1853, Congress created the Washington Territory, and Isaac Stevens was named the first governor. One of his first responsibilities was to establish reservations where the Indians could take refuge from the bewilderingly different European culture. He quickly established reservations along the shores of both Puget Sound and Washington's Pacific Ocean. White settlers, however, had not yet moved up the rivers and Indian villages there had not yet been affected, so many of those people refused to move onto the early reservations. In the mid-twentieth century, the government established new reservations and compounds for the upriver people and many of them moved there.

Along the Oregon Coast the Native Americans also were put on reservations. The reservations were terminated, then reestablished, and many of the natives of the area still live on the reservations.

After 150 years of exposure to the new culture, Indians have become educated, industrious people. Some have moved away from the reservations and become part of the mainstream culture. Others have remained on the reservations, which are treated as sovereign nations and part of the federal, rather than state or local jurisdictions. Many of the reservations have established, thriving businesses that function as vital parts of the American economic community.

THE NEW CULTURE

If Juan de Fuca ever actually existed, he may have been the first European to see the coast of the Pacific Northwest. His story was told in 1596 by Michael Lok, an English merchant who told map makers that he had met a Greek sailor named Apostolos Valerianos who had sailed under the Spanish flag, using the alias of Juan de Fuca. Lok said the old seaman told of sailing north from Mexico along the western edge of the North American continent in 1592, and discovering, between 47 and 48 degrees latitude, a strait leading inland. According to Lok, de Fuca said that was the entrance to the Northwest Passage, a waterway through North America, and would provide a means of crossing the continent by ship. Finding such a passage had been a goal of the Europeans since they discovered that the American continents separated them from the lucrative markets of Asia.

Years later, people searched the Spanish records and found no mention of Juan de Fuca, or Apostolos Valerianos, or of the *Caravela* and *Pinace* that Valerianos said were the ships he sailed. On the other hand, the location of his supposed discovery is fairly close to where the Strait of Juan de Fuca is, and the landscape is reminiscent of some of the features Lok described. So nearly 200 years later, when maps of the coast were drawn, the strait was named after de Fuca. The name remains today.

The first sailor to leave an official record of exploring the Northwest coast was a Spaniard named Juan Joseph Perez Hernandez. Spanish authorities in California considered the entire West Coast of America to be theirs, so when they heard that the Russians were beginning to settle in what is now Alaska, they sent Perez north to persuade them to leave. He left Monterey, California on June 11, 1774, and got as far as the Queen Charlotte Islands between Vancouver Island and Alaska. He turned back without finding the Russians.

Perez failed to find the Russians, but he may have dismayed the Haida Indians in the area. One group has a legend that when they saw their first ship the chief thought it was a huge bird. He went out in a canoe to investigate, and when he got a little closer, he saw men in dark clothing and decided they were large birds. Coming closer, he noted they were men, and that when one of them shouted, the others all climbed up the rigging. They stayed there until someone shouted again, and they all came down.

Perez was followed by a succession of sailors who explored the Northwest coast. Some were Spanish, some English, and some American. Some were navy men and some were civilians. The civilians were intent on trading for furs, which they took to China, where they traded the furs for Chinese manufactured goods that they took back to the East Coast of America to sell. Their records, journals, and ships' logs added to the store of knowledge about the new country.

Among the early arrivals was the Spanish sailor Captain Bruno de Heceta, who sailed up the coast in the frigate *Santiago*, accompanied by the schooner *Sonora* in 1775. In 1778, the famous English captain, James Cook, sailed up the coast on the third and last of his epic voyages, but missed seeing many of the important features.

Among the other notable exploring sailors was Captain Robert Gray, an American, who in 1792 named the Columbia River after his ship, the *Columbia Rediva*. Gray was the first American to sail around the world, and he visited the West Coast during voyages he made in 1787-90 and 1790-93, establishing an American claim to the Oregon Territory, which included both Oregon and Washington. In 1787, the English Captain Robert Barkley of the ship *Imperial Eagle* discovered the Strait of Juan de Fuca, possibly for the second time, but did not explore it. Another English captain, John Meares, charted the entrance to the strait and gave it the name it still has.

Perhaps the sailor with the most direct influence on the daily lives of people on the modern Northwest coast was the English Navy Captain George Vancouver. He arrived in Northwestern America in 1792, and meticulously explored the shores of both the Pacific Ocean and Puget Sound, recording in exact detail what he saw. He gave names that are still in common use to innumerable landmarks that are part of people's everyday existence. Vancouver called the land he explored New Albion. He sailed into the Strait of Juan de Fuca, and spent most of the summer of 1792 mapping and recording what he saw in the strait and in Puget Sound, stopping in Possession Sound near where Everett is now, to claim the land for his king. American Captain Robert Gray sailed up the Columbia River the same year.

The succession of sailors left maps and journals that compiled information on the new land, but perhaps the major impetus bringing the European culture to the Pacific Northwest was the Lewis and Clark Expedition. The group travelled across the continent and arrived at the mouth of the Columbia River in the fall of 1805. They stayed for the winter (see Lewis and Clark, page 264). Six years later, John Jacob

Astor, a New York financier, sent a party around Cape Horn to establish a fur business in the new land. Astor's pioneers built the first permanent settlement west of the Mississippi River. That settlement grew into the city of Astoria which still thrives on the bank of the river.

Astoria's early history was troubled. During the War of 1812, a British warship arrived to push out the Americans and install the Canadian Northwest Company in their place. Later, the Canadian Company was absorbed by the British Hudson's Bay Company, which operated from Astoria until 1825, when it established a new headquarters 100 miles up the river in a new settlement called Fort Vancouver (see Fort Vancouver, page 245).

Fort Vancouver was the center of European settlement for a quarter of a century until it was overwhelmed by American settlers who traveled to the Pacific Northwest over the Oregon Trail in the 1840s. Final agreement on the border of Washington and Canada was made with Britain in 1846 and Washington became part of the Oregon Territory in 1848. Both territories attracted more settlers and became states—Oregon in 1859 and Washington in 1889.

At the turn of the nineteenth century, the earliest explorers of the Pacific Northwest coast found a nearly undisturbed land. They were impressed. George Vancouver, the English navy captain who explored much of the coast said in his journal, "The country before us presented a most luxuriant landscape....which made me very solicitous to find a port in the vicinity of a country presenting so delightful a prospect of felicity."

And well they might have been impressed. The forests of magnificent trees stretched as far as they could see to the highest peaks of the mountains in the background. The rivers supported so many fish that in a few days the natives could catch enough to last through the year. The sea abounded with life ranging from tiny invertebrates to immense whales.

Those early explorers must have believed that the environment they saw was eternal. They had no way of knowing that 15,000 years earlier much of the land they were exploring was buried under thousands of feet of ice, and that when the ice receded it left only barren rock where they saw immense forests. Nor did they have any way of knowing that the nearly untouched land they saw would soon be transformed to a new landscape and a changed ecology. The industrious American settlers developed farms, cities, highways, railroads and other marks of a thriving, modern culture. Massive forests were cut and mines were carved out of the mountainsides. The products of the land and the sea were gathered in huge quantities, first to feed just the settlers, then as commerce improved, to be sent around the world on ever larger ships, on trains, and finally, on trucks.

But there was a price to be paid. The conversion of huge segments of land diminished the habitat of wildlife. Fishing and hunting became efficient, adding to the problem. As the human population grew in cities and towns established along the coast and beside the rivers, it began to foul the land, the water and the air.

In the 1870s, a new consciousness slowly began to develop toward America's seemingly inexhaustible nature resources. The westward-moving wave of lumber harvesting that began in the seventeenth century in New England had reached the Pacific Coast. Worries about the depleting national timber supply resulted in the federal government establishing 47 million acres of forest reserves in the 1890s, much of it in the Pacific Northwest. The Forest Reserve Act of 1907 established more than 150 million acres across the country under the management of the U.S. Forest Service under the Department of Agriculture for the "most productive use for the permanent good of the whole people." A debate has raged on since then between those who think the national forests should be treated as a lumber crop and those who believe the forests should be preserved wild areas.

The preservationists have won some battles. Congress passed the Wilderness Act of 1964, which established wilderness areas in the national forests where human activity was limited. With the development of automobile-led recreation in the 1920s, the general public's concept of how the forest should be used was permanently altered. More and more, people started perceiving the national forests more as areas that should be protected for public recreation and wilderness values instead of an agricultural crop. The debate continues today.

The Endangered Species Act, designed to protect species from extinction, became a hot political item when environmentalists used the law to stop industries from destroying important wildlife habitat found in the national forests. Foresters believed their livelihood was under assault by political groups organized to save the Northern spotted owl.

Pollution controls were passed in the 1970s in an attempt to monitor and control the damage done to the nation's water and air supply. Communities large and small were required to treat their sewage before dumping it into waterways. Regulations reduced air pollution from commercial and residential smokestacks as well as auto exhausts. The problems were reduced but not eliminated.

Along the shoreline, in the bays, and off the coast, protections were established, but here too, problems remain. The Puget Sound Water Quality Action Team, a multi-government sub-agency in Washington, is concerned about environmental conditions of the sound's shellfish, water quality, aquatic nuisance species, contaminated sediments, toxic contamination, potential oil spills, fish and wildlife habitat, and fish populations. Other agencies were working on further restrictions in the forests, destruction of power dams to aid endangered salmon species, wildlife habitat restoration, and numerous other issues.

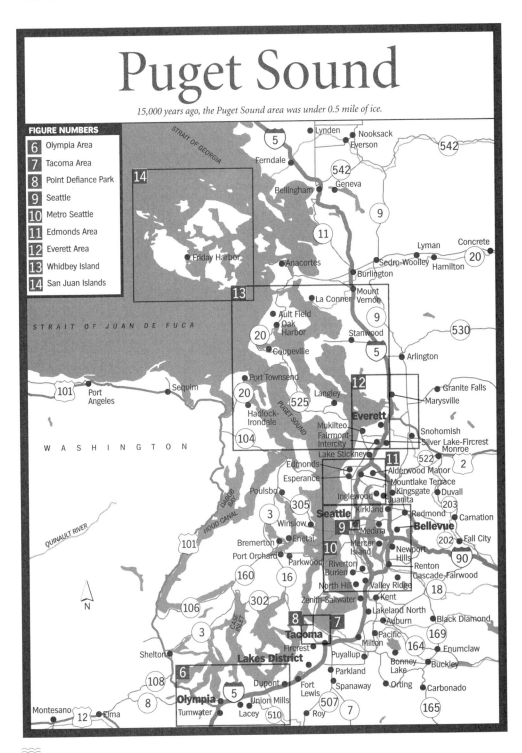

Puget Sound

15,000 years ago, the Puget Sound area was under 0.5 mile of ice.

FIGURE NUMBERS

6 — Olympia Area
7 — Tacoma Area
8 — Point Defiance Park
9 — Seattle
10 — Metro Seattle
11 — Edmonds Area
12 — Everett Area
13 — Whidbey Island
14 — San Juan Islands

Puget Sound

It is difficult to imagine that the land, where bustling cities like Seattle and Tacoma are now, was once buried under an immense ice cap more than 0.5 mile high. That cold hard fact is not only true, but it also has influenced the lives of people in that part of Washington ever since.

The ice cap was the glacier that bulldozed its way down from Canada and halfway through what is now Washington. Along the way it shaped a huge ditch that extends down from the Canadian border more than 130 miles. An arm of the glacier turned almost due west and left a second ditch that extends 100 miles to the Pacific Ocean. When the ice receded about 15,000 years ago, the western ditch filled with sea water and became the Strait of Juan de Fuca that leads to an inland sea. The northern portion of that inland sea is called the Strait of Georgia. The southern portion is named Puget Sound after Peter Puget, one of the British navy officers who accompanied

[*Above:* Rosario Resort on Orcas Island, the largest of the San Juan Islands]

Captain George Vancouver on his epic exploration of the strait and the sound.

Captain Vancouver applied the name only to a small area at the southern tip of the sound. The earliest settlers, however, came across the plains on the Oregon Trail to Oregon, then moved north, settling on the south end of the sound, which they called by the name on the map, Puget Sound. As the population grew, some of them moved northward on the sound, taking Peter Puget's name with them, until it applied to all of the water between the southern tip and the Strait of Juan de Fuca.

The sound is reminiscent of the Scandinavian fjords, arms of the ocean that jut deep into the mountainous land. It lies about midway between two mountain ranges. The Cascades are to the east and the Olympics are to the west. Both are marked by towering peaks and rocky ridges that invite hiking, camping, climbing, and exploring, and both are part of long strings of ranges that parallel the Pacific coast from the extreme north to the extreme south. This part of the Northwest gets more than ample precipitation and both ranges have numerous streams, ranging from tiny rivulets to full-sized rivers, that drain into the sound, making the water a little less salty than the Pacific proper. Nevertheless, Puget Sound is a true saltwater extension of the ocean filled with true salt-water creatures. The tides ebb and flow in the sound, just as they do in the ocean.

All of those geographic characteristics lend themselves to a natural environment rich in plant and animal life, both in the water and on land.

On a map, the sound looks like a roughly scrawled J jutting southward from the much wider Strait of Juan de Fuca and Strait of Georgia. The sound and the two straits are all part of the same body of water despite the names humans have attached to them. A map makes clear what happened during the most recent ice age. The main lobe of the glacier came down from the north, grinding the hard base rock beneath to powder, and shaping the pre-existing basin that eventually filled with water that reaches a width of some 40 miles wide. That now is called the Strait of Georgia. When the glacier got to about where Everett is now, it split into two separate arms. One went west for about 100 miles to the Pacific. That arm filled with water and is called the Strait of Juan de Fuca. The other continued its southward course but shaped a much narrower pre-existing trough. That is called Puget Sound. A short distance south of the place where the Strait of Juan de Fuca arm parted company with Puget Sound, another arm protrudes called Hood Canal. On the map, this long arm looks like a backward J running to the southwest and is even narrower than the sound.

Along the way, the glacier hit some rocky mountains in the bottom of the Puget Sound trough. It smoothed the rock, and lowered it, but when the ice receded and the ocean filled the ditches, the rounded peaks still were so high that they were not completely covered. They are now islands. One cluster, just at the mouth of the Strait of Georgia, includes hundreds of majestically beautiful and largely undeveloped islands called the San Juans. The shape of the islands gives testimony to the power of the ice sheet that once buried them. The glacier forced its way over the north side, grinding away the rock so it is smooth and gently inclined on that side. But when it reached the south side of the rock, it slipped over the top with little resistance, so it ground away much less of the rock. The result is a series of islands that have a north side with a gentle slope and a south side that is also smooth, but more abrupt with a steeper slope.

There are numerous other islands to the south of the San Juans in Puget Sound. They tend to be larger and separate entities rather than part of a group. They are more heavily populated than the San Juans, but also have a majestic beauty. Vancouver Island, in Canada, on the north side of the Strait of Juan de Fuca, is an immense island, some 286 miles long, and it contains its own mountain range dominated by Mount Golden Hine at 7,219 feet in elevation. The island was isolated by the glacier but was out of its main path. It was affected by the flowing ice only in a relatively minor way, much as the Olympic Mountain range to the south.

Indian Habitat

Long before the Europeans arrived, the people of the Northwest were using stone, wood, bone, antler, seashells, hair, tree bark, and other gifts of their environment to produce items of both utility and beauty. The people made many ingenious tools, including elaborate harpoon heads used to hunt whales, and complex looms to make cloth. Aside from the split-cedar houses, the most important product probably was the canoe made by carving, hollowing, and shaping a huge cedar trunk. The canoes ranged in size from big enough for a few people to capable of carrying 20 or more. They were the primary means of transportation, since the forest was so thick that walking was difficult and horses were impractical.

The glacier did not stop at the end of Puget Sound, but continued southward for some 30 more miles to near where the town of Chehalis is now. It smoothed the land there, leaving the ground relatively flat. That relatively level area is part of the Puget Basin that encompasses the land that drains into Puget Sound.

When Captain Vancouver and his crew sailed into Puget Sound they saw a land covered almost completely by huge evergreen trees. The towering giants stretched before their eyes in every direction until they reached the rock and ice of the mountain peaks far in the distance. Vancouver made enthusiastic references to their beauty and their commercial possibilities in the journal of his voyage.

But there was more to the living things of the Puget Sound Basin than trees, as magnificent as those specimens might be. The barren rock and mud landscape that was left when the glacier receded had been transformed into a habitat for innumerable creatures of the land, the sea, and the intertidal places between the land and the sea.

The forests that attracted Vancouver were mostly conifer trees such as Douglas fir, hemlock, cedar, maple, and alder. Nature taught the Indians that fire would clear portions of the forest, making it easier to travel through but also clearing the trees to make way for the forest succession (*see* Inland Forests, page 18). That produced the berry bushes that were an important part of the Indians' diet. It also created a habitat for deer and other game. Beyond that, the forest succession produced innumerable other plants, many of them of use to the natives, before the giant trees again took over the forest. Aside from being useful, many of the succession plants were flowers that painted entire slopes in vivid colors. When Europeans arrived on the scene, they noticed that Indians often started forest fires in the early summer that continued to burn until winter rains extinguished them.

Part of the reason trees and other plants do so well in Puget Sound and other parts of the Northwest coast is the weather. The prevailing winds blow onto the shore from the Pacific, carrying a heavy load of moisture. When the winds hit the Olympic Mountains, they rise. The air cools as it gains altitude, and condenses into rain that nurtures the forests on that side of the mountains. When the air crosses the mountains and descends on the east side, it warms and dries as it loses altitude, resulting in less precipitation. The vegetation must struggle a little harder to survive on that side of the mountains.

These weather patterns result in significant differences in precipitation between places that are only a relatively few miles apart on the Olympic Peninsula. For instance, Sequim, near the northeastern corner of the peninsula, averages about 17 inches of precipitation a year while the rainforests, just 40 miles to the west, may average 140 inches. But the story does not end there. After the air from the Pacific crosses Puget Sound, it hits the shore on the east side and begins to rise again until it reaches the peak of the Cascade Mountains, resulting in heavy precipitation east of Puget Sound.

Temperature changes in the region, however, are less drastic. The Pacific Ocean air is influenced by the temperature of the water over which it passes. The winds from the ocean are warmed in the winter, cooled in the summer. Add to that the cooling effect of the frequent clouds that prevent the sun's heat from reaching the ground, and the result is a relatively minor temperature variation between the seasons. Seattle's average annual temperature, for instance, is 53 degrees Fahrenheit, ranging from about 40 degrees in January to about 65 in July and August. The winter months throughout much of Puget Sound tend to be dull and cloudy. But the clouds seldom produce a hard rain and the average annual rainfall in Seattle, for instance, is only about 35 inches. The vast majority of precipitation in the lower areas is in the form of rain, with snowfall being relatively rare. Much of the precipitation in the high elevations of the mountains, however, is snow. The weather patterns change in the summer months, however, often bringing bright sunshine even though the temperature rarely gets uncomfortably hot.

All that leads to excellent conditions for the land vegetation in the Puget Sound basin. Much has changed since Vancouver wrote about the commercial possibilities of the immense forests he saw on the slopes above the shores of Puget Sound. Much of the forest has been converted to houses, books, newspapers, and the other forest products people use. And many of the trees have been replaced by homes, businesses, roads, schools, playgrounds, and other uses. Indeed, major cities dot the landscape where Vancouver saw very little except trees and an occasional little Indian village.

But not all of the Puget Sound forest is gone. High on the sides of the mountains, far from Puget Sound, one can see vast tracts of forest, some of it second growth, some of it virgin old growth. Closer to the sound, relatively small pieces of the original forest have survived. Some of the forests, mostly second growth, are simply waiting to be harvested. Others, including some old growth, have been set aside in parks and other classifications where they are much like the forests of Vancouver's time. Much of those set-aside forests are on the islands in Puget Sound but some are on the mainland, even within the major cities, where they can be seen and enjoyed.

The trees of the forests are, for the most part, the same species Vancouver saw, largely Douglas fir, hemlock, cedar, maple, and alder. But they are only part of the ecosystem of the forest, and their ecosystem is related to other ecosystems. And the differing ecosystems are interconnected just as the species within an ecosystem are dependent on each other. The trees, shrubs, herbs, and animals, ranging from bears to microbes of the forest, all have a community of interests. When just one community member is diminished or increased, it is likely to have an effect on the other members. If, for instance, something happens to seriously diminish the number of cougars in the forest, the numbers of deer may increase for lack of predators. As the deer become more numerous they will consume more browse, and that may have an effect on other animals that need those plants. And so changes ripple throughout the community. And that process of change is constant. It has been remarked that the only thing that never changes in nature is change itself.

So the trees of the Puget Sound forest do not grow in a vacuum. The floor of a western hemlock forest may be covered with other plants such as sword fern (*Polystichum munitum*), which is often associated with western hemlock. There may also be red huckleberry (*Vaccinium parvifolium*), trailing blackberry (*Rubus ursinus*), Oregon grape (*Berberis nervosa*), and vine maple (*Acer cincinatum*), and near the ground there may well be an assortment of lichens, herbs, and mosses. They all live in harmony with the forest dominated by the western hemlock, which by the way, may also contain other giant conifers such as Douglas fir, and western redcedar.

There are variations in the forest tree species in the southern portion of the sound, where, in addition to the trees in

RACCOON
(*Procyon lotor*)

Whale Watching

All members of the Cetacea are fascinating animals that personify grace in a wild setting, none more so than the whales. And, since some of the whales travel past the Northwest coast twice a year in their migrations between the northern and southern waters while others permanently reside here, the Northwest is one of the easiest places in the world to see whales. Whale watching has become a popular pastime for many people along the shorelines of the Northwest's ocean and inland waters. It also is something of an art. Charter boats in many places take passengers out to locations where there may be whales, and there are numerous places along the shore where whale watching is good.

Scientists and others experienced in whale watching say that the best places on land to watch are on high headlands that jut out to the sea—the higher the better. Whales that migrate between the southern and northern Pacific tend to follow the shoreline as they move. Those that stay in the shallow waters are forced to go around the headlands, thus concentrating close to the shore. Even those that stay in deeper water are closer to the shore as they pass the headlands.

The best time to watch is early morning on a calm day when the winds are light and there are few whitecaps to interfere. If the sky is slightly overcast to eliminate a glare on the surface of the water, so much the better.

the northern section, there are lodgepole pine, paper birch, western white pines, Rocky Mountain juniper, and quaking aspen.

Wildlife in the Puget Sound forest, some of them occasionally even in urban settings, may include grazers such as deer, carnivores such as owls, coyotes, and cougar, omnivores such as black bear and raccoon (*Procyon lotor*), and scavengers such crows. Add to that the insects, worms, fungi, bacteria, and a host of other creatures, and there is a large community of animals dependent on each other and on other communities.

Interspersed in the lowland forests are occasional wetlands, which perform many environmental functions such as cycling nutrients, providing rest areas for migrating waterfowl, acting as nursery areas for fish, and creating permanent homes for numerous birds and animals. Some of the wetlands are in river estuaries where the salt water of the tide meets the fresh water of the river. Others are simply low areas, perhaps left by the retreating glaciers, that collect surface water, which normally keeps the soil wet, inviting the plants and animals that are suited to those conditions. Among the wildlife to be found at the wetlands are young salmon and steelhead, snowgeese (*Chen caerulescens*), Canada geese (*Branta canadensis*), bald eagles (*Haliaeetus leucocephalus*), and many others. Amateur bird watchers also tend to congregate here, sometimes in large numbers.

In a few places Puget Sound is up to about 600 feet deep and, of course, the depth decreases from there to 0 feet at the beachline. The wildlife in the sound, as on the land and estuaries, is similar to that of the ocean coast and extends from the birds above the water surface, to the invertebrates of the tidepools, to the mammals and fish below the surface.

The birds include the ever-present seagulls (*Larus* sp.), which gather in vast numbers wherever there is food available. The gulls may be found on the water, on the beach, or inland in special places like garbage dumps, which seagulls consider to be sources of great treasure. Crows (*Corvus brachyrhynchos*), can also be found nearly anywhere there is something to eat, and sandpipers are among those birds that spend much of their time foraging for whatever is available on the beach and the intertidal zone.

Whale watching is popular and often productive in Puget Sound. Among the whales here are the orcas (*Orcinas orca*), some of which are just visiting but some of which are resident. Gray whales (*Eschrichtius robustus*) are frequently reported in Puget Sound during March and early April when they stop off on their annual migration from their breeding grounds off Mexico to their feeding grounds in the far northern Pacific. Minke whales (*Balaenoptera acutorostrata*) appear during the summer in the Puget Sound waters near the San Juan Islands.

Other sea mammals in the Sound include an estimated 5,000 harbor seals (*Phoca vitulina*) that live here year round. They may be seen especially around the sandbars of estuaries and the mouths of rivers. They are more than a little nervous about humans when they are on land, though, and are likely to return to the water as soon as they see one. On the other hand, when they are in the water they seem to be curious about two-footed creatures and may approach fairly closely. Very young harbor seals don't swim well enough to go hunting with their mothers so they stay on the beach, where sometimes humans mistakenly think they are abandoned and attempt to rescue them.

Male California sea lions (*Zalophus californianus*) are fairly numerous in Puget Sound, where they migrate during the winter while the females stay in the waters off California. The males are very numerous in the Port Gardner area near Everett where nearly 1,000 have been counted. They tend to bask in the sun on log rafts tied up at Jetty Island just off the Everett waterfront, where they serenade the world with loud, barking sounds. They have been known to steal salmon off an angler's hook.

Below the surface are the rocks, sand, and silt that bear undersea plants which provide food and shelter for invertebrates and fish such as thresher sharks (*Alopiidae* sp.), flounders (*Pleuronectidae* sp.), herrings (*Clupeidae*), migrating salmon and steelhead, and many others.

Transportation on and over Puget Sound can be by private vessel or aircraft, but probably the most common way to travel on the sound is by the state ferry system, the largest ferry fleet in the United States. It has 25 vessels that carry 23 million passengers a year to 20 different ports of call. Most of the vessels carry both passengers and vehicles, but a few carry only passengers, mostly commuters who go between their homes and workplaces.

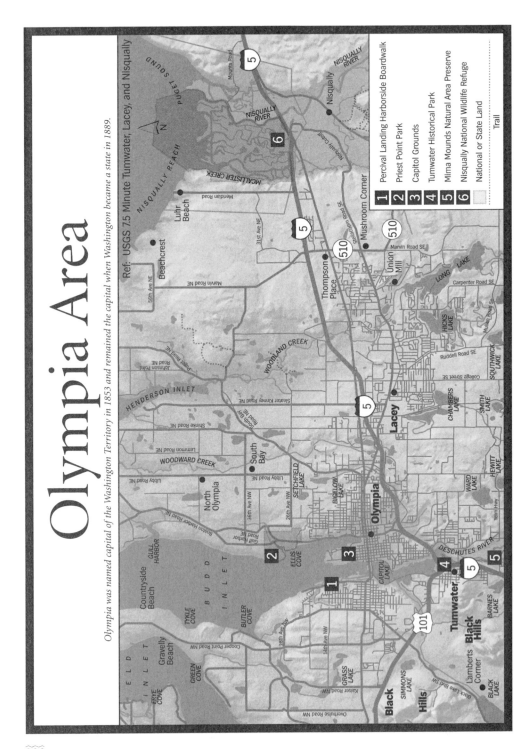

Olympia Area

Olympia was named capital of the Washington Territory in 1853 and remained the capital when Washington became a state in 1889.

Ref: USGS 7.5 Minute Tumwater, Lacey, and Nisqually

1 Percival Landing Harborside Boardwalk
2 Priest Point Park
3 Capitol Grounds
4 Tumwater Historical Park
5 Mima Mounds Natural Area Preserve
6 Nisqually National Wildlife Refuge
National or State Land
Trail

Olympia

[Fig. 6] The southern tip of Puget Sound ends at Olympia, although the Puget Basin continues for miles beyond the shoreline of the sound. While the Olympia area is the end of the sound, it was the beginning of American settlement. Originally, Washington was part of the Oregon Territory. Settlers from the East and Midwest arrived here over the Oregon Trail that has become part of the American story. Early arrivals settled in the Willamette Valley that runs for some 200 miles through Oregon from near Eugene to Portland on the Columbia River. The valley is extremely fertile and offered good land for farming, lumber for housing, wildlife for hunting, and fishing in the Willamette River. It was a good place to stay after the long, hard wagon road from the Midwest.

But some, for various reasons, chose not to stay here. They crossed the Columbia River and made their way by land to the foot of Puget Sound. They were not the first Europeans on the sound. Fur traders had been active in the Northwest since 1811. The English Hudson's Bay Company eventually became dominant and had been established on the Columbia River, first at what is now Astoria, then 100 miles farther up the river at Fort Vancouver where the city of Vancouver is now. In 1833 Chief Factor John McLoughlin established a separate Puget Sound Agricultural Company, which developed a farming settlement near where Tacoma is now (*see* Fort Nisqually, page 50). The company raised crops and exported timber products, and was briefly successful until the 1840s when Americans began to arrive on the sound about the time that a U.S. Navy expedition under Charles Wilkes explored the Oregon Country, including Puget Sound. Hudson's Bay Company was overwhelmed by the American settlers and gradually moved north into Canada, but not until a confrontation over a pig nearly involved England and the United States in a shooting war (*see* San Juan Island National Park, page 93).

The first Americans to settle in the Puget Sound area were a group of pioneers led by George Bush and Michael Simmons. Bush, who was black, was successful in the cattle business in Missouri when he decided to move his family to the new land out west. He led a large wagon train that traveled over the Oregon Trail to the Oregon Territory, but before the train arrived, a provisional government in the territory adopted a law prohibiting black people from owning land. He and some 30 friends decided to move north where the provisional government couldn't reach him. They crossed the Columbia and traveled up the Cowlitz River in 1845 on what is called an extension of the Oregon Trail, and settled near Budd Inlet at the southern tip of Puget Sound. Bush and Simmons built a mill on the Deschutes River. It eventually developed into the small city of Tumwater, adjacent to Olympia. Bush then established a highly successful farm on what is now called Bush Prairie.

In 1846 Edmund Sylvester and Levi Lathrop established a claim near a Native American village, and Sylvester platted the Olympia townsite four years later. In 1853 the Oregon Territory was divided, and Olympia was named the capitol of the new Washington Territory. It remained the capitol when Washington became a state in 1889 and has been the capitol ever since.

In addition to being the political capitol, the city for a long time was the population, economic, and cultural center of Puget Sound, but during the 1870s, the mainline railroads bypassed the city. Citizens built their own 15-mile railroad to connect with the Northern Pacific, but the city never regained is dominance. Now it is a pleasant city of about 37,000 people at the south end of Puget Sound.

PERCIVAL LANDING HARBORSIDE BOARDWALK

[Fig. 6(1)] This popular, pleasant, six-block boardwalk follows the shore of the west bay of Budd Inlet, providing breathtaking views of Puget Sound with the Olympic Mountains in the background. From time to time there are whales in the bay. At the north end of the boardwalk the **Olympia Farmers' Market** offers local produce from 10 to 4 Thursdays through Sundays, from April 1 until Christmas. At the south end of the boardwalk there is a **salmon viewing station** where visitors can watch mature salmon swim past on the way to their spawning grounds in Capital Lake and the Deschutes River.

Directions: Take I-5 exit 105A and turn right on Capital Way. Go to the dead end of Capital Way to the Olympia Farmers' Market and find the end of the boardwalk.

Activities: Harborside walking and scenic views.

Facilities: Restrooms, boat launch and moorage.

Dates: Open year-round.

Fees: Fees are charged for boat launch and moorage.

For more information: State Capitol Visitor Information Center, Fourteenth Avenue and Capitol Way, PO Box, Olympia, WA 98504-1020. Phone (360) 586-3460.

PRIEST POINT PARK

[Fig. 6(2)] This pleasant park displays second-growth forested areas of mostly native trees. The 1.25-mile Ellis Cove Trail goes to a pleasant cove on Puget Sound, where visitors can fish and enjoy nice views.

Directions: From I-5 Exit 105B, go straight onto Plum Street, which leads to the park.

Activities: Picnicking, hiking, fishing.

Facilities: Restrooms.

Dates: Open year-round.

Fees: None.

For more information: State Capitol Visitor Information Center, Fourteenth Avenue and Capitol Way, PO Box, Olympia, WA 98504-1020. Phone (360) 586-3460.

▨ CAPITOL GROUNDS

[Fig. 6(3)] This large, park-like campus features carefully tended lawns, tall trees, and the ornate Legislative Building, which was completed in 1928. The building is 28 stories high, topped by a magnificent dome, and located on a bluff with a splendid view of Puget Sound and the Olympic Mountains. The nearby Capitol Lake in downtown Olympia connects on the lower end with Puget Sound and the upper end with the Deschutes River. A salmon viewing station provides an opportunity to watch mature salmon passing through the lake toward the spawning grounds.

Directions: Take I-5 Exit 105A, which leads to the Capitol Grounds.

Activities: Guided Tours of the Legislative Building and the grounds, which begin at the Legislative Building foyer at the top of the stairs.

Facilities: Government buildings.

Dates: Open year round. Tours of the Legislative Building begin on the hour from 10 to 3 daily. Tours of the Capitol Grounds begin at 10 a.m. daily.

Fees: None.

For more information: State Capitol Visitor Information Center, Fourteenth Avenue and Capitol Way, PO Box, Olympia, WA 98504-1020. Phone (360) 586-3460.

▨ TUMWATER HISTORICAL PARK

[Fig. 6(4)] This neatly landscaped 17-acre park in Tumwater, adjacent to the south side of Olympia on I-5, offers picnic spots and a boat launch on the Deschutes River. On a bluff above the park, is the **Crosby House** (360-943-9884) built in 1860 by Bing Crosby's grandfather, Captain Nathaniel Crosby III, who sailed around the Horn in 1860. The handsome two-story structure is white with green shutters, in the style of middle class, western America in the mid-nineteenth century. The house looks out on a broad, green, tree-rimmed lawn. It is the oldest house in Tumwater and is open for tours on Thursdays.

The park is on the west bank of the Deschutes River where many of the earliest settlers of Tumwater—and the Puget Sound Region—built their homes, mills, and factories. Interpretive signs use words and pictures to tell some of the story of the people who opened the new territory in Western Washington.

Directions: From Olympia, go south on I-5 and take Exit 103. At the end of the exit ramp turn left onto Custer Way and the I-5 overpass. Just past the overpass, turn right onto Boston Street and go to Deschutes Way. Turn right on Deschutes Way. Take the right fork and go to the park at the end of the road.

Activities: Hiking, boating, picnicking.

Facilities: Shelter, picnic tables, restrooms, trails, boat launch.

Dates: Open year-round.

Fees: None.

For more information: Tumwater Park Department, 555 Israel Road, SW, Tumwater, WA 98501. Phone (360) 754-4161.

MIMA MOUNDS NATURAL AREA PRESERVE

[Fig. 6(5)] Curious grassy mounds up to 8 feet high cover this 445-acre area. Science has yet to explain how they came about, but there are many theories, some serious and some just for fun. Local Indians made a practice of burning the vegetation to keep the land productive, but now Douglas fir trees are encroaching on the mounds. An interpretive center describes the area's natural history, and self-guided trails wind through the open area and the forest. From April to June, the mounds support numerous wildflowers.

Directions: On I-5, 10 miles south of Olympia, take I-5 Exit 95 and go 3 miles west on Maytown Road. Go to the Waddell Creek Road then take the northwest fork for 0.7 mile.

Activities: Hiking, picnicking.

Facilities: Visitor center, trails, picnic tables.

Dates: Open year round 8 a.m. to 4:30.

Fees: None.

Closest town: Olympia, 14 miles.

For more information: Mima Mounds Interpretive Center, 1405 Rush Road, Chehalis, WA 98532. Phone (360) 748-2383.

NISQUALLY NATIONAL WILDIFE REFUGE

[Fig. 6(6)] This refuge on the shore of Puget Sound provides nearly 3,000 acres of protected estuary, tidal flats, freshwater marshes, riparian woodlands, grasslands, and upland mixed forest for both resident and migrating wildlife. It also played an early part in the history of Western Washington development.

After the American pioneers established a settlement on the southern tip of Puget Sound, expanding northward became inevitable. Indians had been on the Nisqually Flats for at least 5,000 years, archeologists say. The English came next, but their form of expansion was organized and planned under the auspices of the Hudson's Bay Company. They arrived on the flats in the fall of 1832, when Archibald MacDonald and some companions of the Hudson's Bay Company stopped off here to see if it was suitable for farming. It was, so MacDonald built a storehouse and left three men here to establish both a farm and a fur trade. The post soon acquired 1,800 beaver pelts as well as other furs. The company bought the merchandise at specified rates, such as two hoes for one bear skin, 16 buttons for four raccoon pelts, three buttons for seven trout.

The expansion of the Americans, on the other hand, was on an individual basis. Individuals in the East and Midwest simply decided to go west in search of a better life. They joined with some others of a like mind to form wagon trains that made the long, hard journey across the continent, then they split up and each individual went his own way. The federal government encouraged that, but it did not take a direct part in organizing it. There was not a single organizing force to the American expansion, and no single entity to negotiate questions such as where people would locate and what they would do. That made the American expansion tremendously difficult to control. People just settled where they thought the settling was good, without paying much attention to the rules someone else had established. That happened so often in so many places that it didn't just affect the Hudson's Bay settlements and the native culture; it overwhelmed them to the point that both the English and the natives were no longer able to continue in their accustomed ways.

The Hudson's Bay Company took steps to discourage the American migrations, but in the long run it accepted the inevitable and moved northward to stay ahead of the settlers, eventually establishing its local headquarters in Victoria on Vancouver Island, Canada. It still operates department stores in Canada, and is that country's oldest business organization.

The Puget Sound settlers were dissatisfied with the Oregon Territory government and Congress agreed to divide it, creating a separate territory. Colonel Isaac Stevens was named the territorial governor. One of his first acts was to hold meetings with Indian groups that resulted in establishing a half dozen Indian reservations along the shores of Puget Sound and other places where the natives could find refuge. With the Hudson's Bay Company in Canada and most of the Native Americans on reservations, the way was clear for Americans to complete their stream of settlement.

One of the places from which first the Indians and then the English withdrew was the Nisqually Delta which now is the Nisqually National Wildlife Refuge, one of several that have been established on Washington's inland waters and along the coast.

The refuge provides a wintering area for waterfowl, some that nest there and others just passing through. Some are abundant and others are seen only rarely. Among the 200 species that have been identified are: pied-billed grebes (*Podilymbus podiceps*), which neither fly nor walk very well, but are well adapted to diving for dinner; cormorants (*Phalacrocorax sp.*); great blue herons (*Ardea herodias*) that stand perfectly still in the water waiting for something like a small fish or frog to come by for dinner; brant (*Branta bernicla*); bald eagles (*Haliaeetus leucocephalus*), which eat many things but seem to like salmon best; hawks (*Accipter sp.*); and many others. The refuge is a resting and wintering area for as many as 20,000 migratory waterfowl.

Land mammals include the vagrant shrew (*Sorex vagrans*), which like other varieties of shrew has a metabolism so high that it must eat almost continuously to stay alive. The little animals are super active and live only about one year. There also are Townsend's moles (*Scapanus townsendi*), hoary bats (*Lasiurus cinereus*), Eastern cottontail rabbits (*Sylvilagus floridanus*), and long tailed weasels (*Mustela frenata*). The weasels eat about 40 percent of their body weight a day, but to help out they are equipped with long, thin bodies that can get into holes where thicker creatures go to hide. Not only that, they are fast and fierce enough to take prey twice their size.

Sea mammals in Puget Sound off the refuge shore include killer whales (*Orcinus orca*), harbor seals (*Phoca vitulina*), and California sea lions (*Zalophus californianus*) that can be heard barking as they rest on driftwood in the mud flats. Two creeks on

The Killer Whale

The killer whale (*Orcinus orca*), also commonly called orca, is the smallest of the whales in the Pacific Northwest waters, measuring about 26 feet long and weighing as much as 8 tons. It also is the largest member of the dolphin family. It is jet black with gray and white markings, the white being on the underside from the lower chin to more than halfway to the flukes and extending upward to a white patch on the sides midway back. There also is a relatively small but conspicuous, elliptical white patch behind each eye. The demarcation between the white and black areas is sudden and sharp.

The tall dorsal fin of the male grows to approximately 6 feet high while the female's grows only to about 3 feet. The flippers are paddle shaped and grow to as much as 20 percent of the length of the body. The triangular dorsal fin varies in shape. The flukes, black on top and white on the underside, are slightly concave on the trailing edge and have a distinct notch in the middle. Its blow, often seen in cool air, is bushy and low.

Orcas can reach speeds of 34 miles per hour, and when they move fast, much of the body leaves the water as they come to the surface to breathe. They travel in mixed, matriarchal family groups called pods that usually stay together for life. Occasionally two or more pods may temporarily combine into a superpod of as many as 150 whales. Orcas usually are found within 500 miles of the shoreline and concentrate over the continental shelf, often in bays and inland seas such as Puget Sound.

the refuge, as well as the Nisqually River, are spawning, rearing, and passage areas for anadromous fish.

There are 7 miles of level, gravel trails on the refuge where visitors can see and hear the various creatures. A 1-mile boardwalk covers part of the trail system and is suitable for handicapped persons. A 5.5-mile long dike separates the saltwater habitats from the fresh water, and a trail along the dike provides an opportunity to view the animals in both habitats, as well as riparian woodlands and brush. There are benches along the trails where visitors can rest, eat a sandwich, and watch for wildlife. Bicycles, jogging, pets, firearms, and camping are not allowed on the refuge.

The best time to see the wildlife is in the early morning and late afternoon, or after a storm. Bird migration periods usually run from mid-March to mid-May and from September through December, but bird-watching for other species is good year-round. Binoculars, spotting scopes, and field guides are helpful.

A nearby boat launch gives access to Puget Sound and the water side of the dike.

Directions: Eight miles east of Olympia take I-5 Exit 114 and follow the signs to the refuge.

Activities: Hiking, nature study, fishing.

Facilities: Visitor center, a reservation only education center for educational groups, trails, restrooms.

Dates: Open year-round during daylight hours.
Fees: An entry fee is charged.
Closest town: Olympia 8 miles.
For more information: Nisqually National Wildlife Refuge, 100 Brown Farm Road, Olympia, WA 98516. Phone (360) 753-9467.

RESTAURANTS IN THE OLYMPIA VICINITY

Olympia is the state capital and has a large number of visitors, especially when the legislature is in session, usually during the early months of the year. Because of that, the city is blessed with a number of good places to eat.

KILLER WHALE
(Orcinus orca)

Falls Terrace Restaurant. 106 Deschutes Way Southwest in Tumwater, which is directly south of Olympia. The popular restaurant has an impressive view of the spectacular Tumwater Falls on the Deschutes River. Menu features include chicken, pasta, and seafood. There is a children's menu.

The cocktail lounge has an outside deck. Reservations recommended. *Inexpensive.* *(360) 943-7830.*

La Petite Maison. 101 Divisions Street in Olympia. This restaurant in a converted house features a Northwestern menu of game and seafood with a French influence. Reservations recommended. There is a large wine selection. *Inexpensive. (360) 943-8812.*

Genoas on the Bay. 1525 Washington Street in Olympia. This is a moderately large restaurant with a view of Budd Bay at the southern tip of Puget Sound. It features fresh seafood, prime ribs, chops, pasta, and, on Sunday, a champagne brunch. Reservations recommended. *Inexpensive. (360) 943-7770.*

LODGING IN OLYMPIA

Because the state government attracts a large number of both tourists and business people, Olympia has a large number of places to stay, many of which are chain hotels.

Cavanaughs at Capitol Lake. 2300 Evergreen Park Drive Southwest in Olympia. This full service hotel overlooks Capitol Lake and offers amenities including a restaurant, cocktail lounge, heated swimming pool, spa, and fitness center. There are 185 comfortable rooms. *Expensive. (800) 325-4000 or (360) 943-4000.*

The Harbinger Inn Bed and Breakfast. 1136 East Bay Drive in Olympia. This is a restored mansion built in 1910 and furnished with antiques of that period. A porch, a verandah, and three of the five comfortable guest rooms have views. A complimentary continental breakfast is provided. *Moderate. (360) 754-0389.*

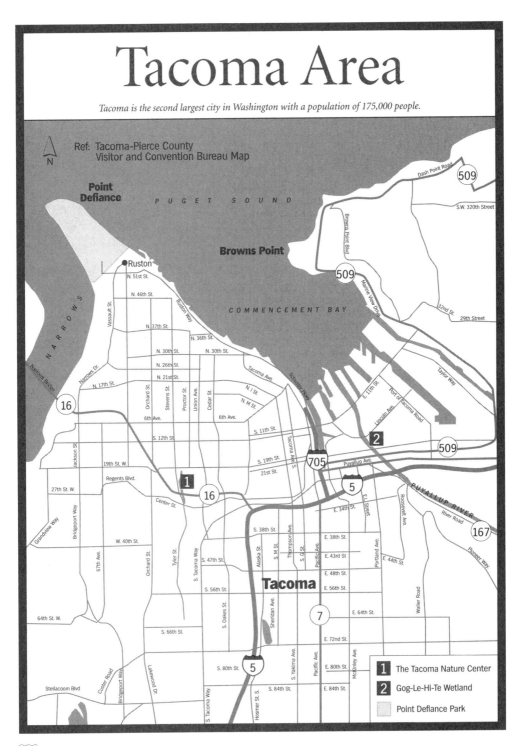

Tacoma Area

Tacoma is the second largest city in Washington with a population of 175,000 people.

Ref: Tacoma-Pierce County
Visitor and Convention Bureau Map

Point Defiance

PUGET SOUND

Browns Point

COMMENCEMENT BAY

NARROWS

1	The Tacoma Nature Center
2	Gog-Le-Hi-Te Wetland
	Point Defiance Park

Tacoma

Tacoma

[Fig. 7] This full-sized city, population 175,000, is the second largest in Washington and was one in the series of communities that developed as the Americans migrated north on Puget Sound from Olympia. The communities were settled, one by one, each by a handful of people who simply camped out in a spot that seemed likely to meet their dreams of a place to put down roots.

In Tacoma's case, the first founder was Nicholas Delin, a cabinetmaker and carpenter from Sweden who had reached Puget Sound by way of Russia, Massachusetts, California, and Portland. He was still restless when he got to Olympia so, in 1852, he pushed on up Puget Sound to Commencement Bay.

He landed here and found two small streams, which he dammed to provide power for a small mill. The brig *George W. Emery* landed here to pick up some lumber for San Francisco. Delin brought in some hired hands to help with the mill. Chauncy Baird set up a shed where he made barrels from lumber supplied by Delin. Two more men arrived to buy barrels they used to pack salmon to ship to San Francisco and Hawaii. An Indian uprising in 1855 drove the people of the little community away. When it ended Delin returned, but didn't stay long. In 1864 Job Carr, who had been wounded twice and discharged from the Union Army, which was fighting the Civil War back east, found a likely spot not far from where Delin had located his mill. He built a cabin and moved in. Part of the cabin still exists where it was moved to Point Defiance. Carr sold all but 5 acres of his claim to Morton M. McCarver who made his living by developing cities. McCarver figured the place was a good site for a railroad terminal. He platted the city, named it Tacoma, the name some Indians used for Mount Rainier. Charles Hanson and his partner, John W. Ackerman, a California businessman, built a mill. Then came more people, more businesses, a post office, a stage line to Olympia, and a school. The Northern Pacific Railroad arrived in 1873 and made its terminus a short distance from the town. Tacoma was on its way.

Growth continued for the next 15 years, and in 1888 four men who had prospered in the timber business in the Midwest saw that the forest there would soon be exhausted and moved west to look for new opportunities. They located in Tacoma and built what would become the largest lumber company in the world, the St. Paul and Tacoma Timber Company.

The city now is comfortable with its place as a major urban center, but it hasn't forgotten its past as part of the natural setting of Puget Sound. For one thing it is a gateway to the wonders of Mount Rainier National Park, the fifth national park to be created and the location of 14,410-foot Mount Rainier. Some Native American groups called the mountain Tacoma and even though it is some 40 miles away, the city maintains a close relationship with the magnificently beautiful giant.

Closer to home, the city has an assortment of nature parks that display plants and animals both native and exotic.

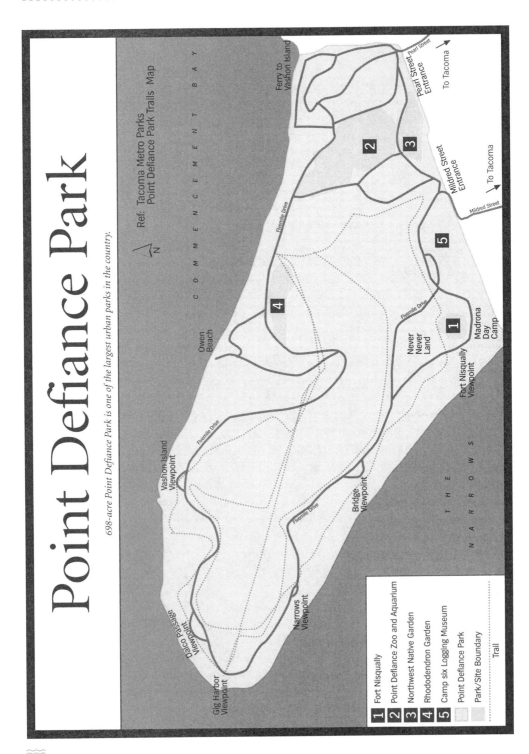

Point Defiance Park

698-acre Point Defiance Park is one of the largest urban parks in the country.

Ref: Tacoma Metro Parks
Point Defiance Park Trails Map

N

COMMENCEMENT BAY

Ferry to Vashon Island

Pearl Street
Pearl Street Entrance

To Tacoma

Mildred Street Entrance

To Tacoma

Mildred Street

Fivemile Drive

Owen Beach

Fivemile Drive

Never Never Land

Madrona Day Camp

Fort Nisqually Viewpoint

Vashon Island Viewpoint

Fivemile Drive

Bridge Viewpoint

THE NARROWS

Dalco Passage Viewpoint

Narrows Viewpoint

Gig Harbor Viewpoint

1 Fort Nisqually
2 Point Defiance Zoo and Aquarium
3 Northwest Native Garden
4 Rhododendron Garden
5 Camp six Logging Museum

Point Defiance Park
Park/Site Boundary
Trail

THE TACOMA NATURE CENTER

[Fig. 7(1)] This 54-acre forested wildlife preserve includes a wetlands display and more then 2 miles of self-guided trails, with shelters where visitors may observe the wildlife.

Directions: From I-5 in Tacoma turn west on State Route 16 to Nineteenth Street. Go east on Nineteenth Street, then turn south on Tyler and immediately turn west into the nature center parking lot at the intersection of Nineteenth and Tyler Streets.

Activities: Nature walks.

Facilities: Visitor center and trails with information and explanations of wetlands and wildlife.

Dates: Open year-round.

Fees: None.

For more information: Tacoma Nature Center, 1919 South Tyler Street, Tacoma, WA 98404. Phone (253) 591-6439.

GOG-LE-HI-TE WETLAND

[Fig. 7(2)] The name means "where the land and the waters meet" in the language of the Puyallup Indians, and it applies to this man-made wetland that demonstrates the nature of wetlands. It is on land owned by the Port of Tacoma, and was created to replace a wetland area the port filled in to build a container terminal. It has a mix of salt and fresh water, and provides habitats for a wide variety of fish, waterfowl, plants, and animals. Some 92 kinds of birds, both resident and migratory, have been identified. There also is a chance visitors will see any number of creatures such as raccoons (*Procyon lotor*), beaver (*Castor canadensis*), muskrats (*Ondatra zibethicus*), rabbits (*Sylvilagus*), and otter (*Lutra canadensis*).

Directions: Take I-5 to the Portland Avenue Exit and go north on Portland Avenue, then turn right on Lincoln Avenue. Cross the Puyallup River and look for the parking lot on the right side.

Activities: Viewing wetlands.

Facilities: Trail, observation deck and interpretive signs.

Dates: Open year-round during daylight hours.

Fees: None.

For more information: Port of Tacoma, PO Box 1837 Tacoma, WA 98401. Phone (253) 383-5841.

POINT DEFIANCE PARK

[Fig. 8] This pleasant, forested park with 698 acres has recreational facilities as well as historical exhibits, a renowned zoo, and an aquarium that features the sea animals of Northwestern

OTTER
(*Lutra canadensis*)

waters, as well as those from other parts of the world.

The park was originally set aside as a military reservation by President Andrew Johnson shortly after the Civil War. Although in modern times the Tacoma area has become home to major installations of the army, the air force, and the national guard, the park land was never used for military operations, and in 1888 Congress and President Grover Cleveland adopted legislation reserving it as a public park. Now it is one of the 20 largest urban parks in the country and is supervised by Metro Parks of Tacoma. Among its features are old-growth forest, numerous gardens that exhibit local and exotic plants, a reconstruction of the Hudson's Bay Fort at Nisqually Flats, and a hands-on, live exhibit of early twentieth century railroad logging. A network of level, easy trails goes through both forested and open areas. The park is on a peninsula that juts into Puget Sound, and there are beaches, boating, fishing, and scenery on three sides. There is a widely recognized zoo and an aquarium with separate exhibits on fish of the Northwestern waters and other places.

The park overlooks the Tacoma Narrows Bridge that crosses the narrow neck of Puget Sound between Tacoma and the Olympic Peninsula. The bridge replaces a 5,939-foot-long bridge that was built in July 1940; it immediately became known internationally because its 2,800-foot center span swayed wildly in the wind. The bridge deck undulated like ocean waves during a storm, so much that drivers lost sight of the car ahead when it went into the trough. Four months after it was built, a 42-mile-an-hour wind collapsed the bridge into the sound, taking a Tacoma newspaper editor's car with it and providing newsreel film that still is shown occasionally on television. A new, safer, 5,979-foot bridge was built over the waters above the Galloping Gerty ruins in 1950. The old span, on the bottom of the sound, has been placed on the National Register of Historic Places to prevent salvagers from disturbing it.

Directions: From I-5 in Tacoma tale Exit 132 and go west on State Route 16 for 3 miles to the Ruston Exit. Turn left at the bottom of the exit ramp and go under State Route 16 then turn right onto Pearl Street. Go 3.6 miles, skirting the western edge of the community of Ruston to the Pearl Street entrance to the Park.

Activities: Hiking, biking, picnicking, educational exhibits, boating, fishing.

Facilities: Trails, boat docks, marina, natural history and human history exhibits, restaurant, restrooms, beaches, picnic tables, rental boats and fishing gear, zoo, aquarium.

Dates: Open year-round.

Fees: The park is free. Fees may be charged at some of the exhibits.

For more information: Tacoma Metro Parks, 4702 South Nineteenth Street, Tacoma, WA 98405. Phone (253) 305-1000.

FORT NISQUALLY

[Fig. 8(1)] This is a reconstruction of the Hudson's Bay Company fort at Nisqually Flats (*see* Nisqually National Wildlife Refuge, page 42) 17 miles from Point

Defiance Park. It includes the old factor's house and granary, both of which were moved from the original location, and both of which are on the National Register of Historic Places.

The factor's house contains exhibits of artifacts from the fur trade of the 1800s. Reconstructions of the fort's blacksmith shop, trade store, workers' dwellings, and defense structures contain furnishings reminiscent of the 1850s era. Staff members and volunteers in period clothing demonstrate activities such as spinning, beadwork, and blacksmithing. Each year in May there is a celebration of the birthday of Queen Victoria, who reigned over England while the Hudson's Bay fort was active.

Directions: Follow the signs for 1.7 miles from Pearl Street Entrance to Point Defiance park.

Facilities: Historical exhibits.

Dates: Open 11 to 6 daily in June, July, and August, on weekends during Apr., May, Sept., and Oct.

Fees: Entrance fees are charged during the summer.

For more information: Tacoma Metro Parks, 4702 South Nineteenth Street, Tacoma, WA 98405. Phone (253) 305-1000.

POINT DEFIANCE ZOO AND AQUARIUM

[Fig. 8(2)] This separate part of the Point Defiance Park complex covers 29 acres devoted to exhibiting wildlife specimens from both the Northwest and other parts of the country and the world. It was founded in 1890 on a small scale, but it has been expanded since into a major educational institution and has become Pierce County's second largest visitor attraction, after the Mount Rainier National Park.

With the Pacific Rim as a theme, the exhibits demonstrate the wildlife that has evolved in the "ring of fire," a series of volcanoes that line the edge of the Pacific Ocean, caused by the plate tectonics that created the shorelands of the Pacific Northwest. There are more than 5,000 animals representing some 350 species.

Among the aquarium's more popular attractions are the 35 cold-water North Pacific exhibits, including a tank that holds 160,000 gallons of water that display marine life species native to the Pacific Northwest. A separate aquarium holds tropical fish from the South Pacific. The Simpson Marine Discovery Lab has a replica of a Pacific Northwest tidepool complete with specimens visitors may find when they investigate tidepools along Northwestern beaches. A visit to the aquarium is a good way for newcomers to become acquainted with the natural science of the Northwest coast. There also are numerous interesting exhibits of creatures from other parts of the world including South America—creatures such as Magellanic penguins, sharks, elephants, whales, and polar bears. The Southeast Asia complex offers settings similar to their native lands of elephants, monkeys, and apes. A replica of the Arctic tundra displays Arctic fox, musk-ox, and native northern waterfowl.

The zoo is an official survival and breeding center for the endangered wild red wolves, and is a good place to learn about conservation programs for species under stress.

Directions: Take the left fork 0.3 mile from Pearl Street entrance to Point Defiance Park and go 0.3 mile. Turn left and go 0.3 mile to the zoo aquarium parking lot.

Activities: Education about wildlife of the Pacific Northwest and other parts of the world.

Facilities: Numerous exhibits of wildlife in habitat similar to their natural settings.

Dates: Open from sunrise to sunset year-round.

Fees: An entrance fee is charged, but entry is free on the third Tuesday of each month.

For more information: Tacoma Metro Parks, 4702 South Nineteenth Street, Tacoma, WA 98405. Phone (253) 305-1000.

NORTHWEST NATIVE GARDEN

[Fig. 8(3)] This expansive, 1.5-acre garden displays indigenous Pacific Northwest plants from six climatic and geographical zones. The exhibit, established in 1964 by the Tacoma Garden Club, is a good place to become acquainted with the plants people may encounter while exploring the coastal areas.

Directions: Take the main road and follow the signs for 2.5 miles from the Pearl Street entrance to the Point Defiance Park.

Activities: Study plants native to the Northwest coast.

Facilities: Trails and interpretative material.

Fees: None.

For more information: Tacoma Metro Parks, 4702 South Nineteenth Street, Tacoma, WA 98405. Phone (253) 305-1000.

RHODODENDRON GARDEN

[Fig. 8(4)] This 5-acre area in a natural setting among native trees is devoted to displaying rhododendrons, Washington's state flower. The 115 cultivated varieties and 29 species make a vivid display when they bloom in the spring. The garden was established in 1968 by the Tacoma chapter of the American Rhododendron Society.

Directions: Follow the signs on the main road from the Pearl Street entrance to the Point Defiance Park for 0.7 mile.

Facilities: Trails through spectacular specimens of one of the Northwest's most beautiful native flowers.

Dates: Open year-round, but the exhibit is most attractive during the spring blooming season.

Fees: None.

For more information: Tacoma Metro Parks, 4702 South Nineteenth Street, Tacoma, WA 98405. Phone (253) 305-1000.

CAMP SIX LOGGING MUSEUM

[Fig. 8(5)] This 14-acre site on the National Register of Historic Places is a replica of one of the early twentieth century logging camps that were the foundation of the settlement and development of not only Tacoma, but also of nearly all communities in the coastal areas of Washington and Oregon. The displays of the Camp Six Museum give visitors a quick and fascinating glimpse into how and why the area was settled.

The museum is operated by the Tacoma chapter of the National Railway Historical Society. Both indoor and outdoor displays exhibit how loggers of 1880 through 1940 lived and worked when muscle, steam, and steel were pitted against the seemingly endless forest of gigantic trees that greeted Vancouver when he explored Puget Sound. A steam-driven logging train carries visitors to various exhibits.

The exhibits can also be visited on foot over a system of trails through the wooded site.

Directions: Follow the signs on the main road from the Pearl Street Entrance of the Point Defiance Park for 1.9 miles.

Activities: Touring historical displays.

Facilities: Educational displays on Northwest coast history.

Dates: The museum is open from 10 to 4 on Wednesdays and Fridays and from 10 to 5 on Saturdays, Sundays, and holidays. The logging train operates on Saturdays, Sundays, and holidays every 30 minutes beginning at noon during the summer and on limited schedules during the winter. Outdoor displays are open from dawn to dusk daily.

Fees: A fee is charged for riding on the railroad.

For more information: Tacoma Metro Parks, 4702 South Nineteenth Street, Tacoma, WA 98405. Phone (253) 305-1000). For recorded information, phone (253) 752-0047.

▨ RESTAURANTS IN TACOMA

Tacoma has an assortment of restaurants catering to Northwestern tastes. Menus often feature specialties that provide shops with a specific reputation.

Antique Sandwich Company. 5102 North Pearl Street. This health-conscious deli-style establishment features sandwiches, soups, and a variety of ethnic dishes such as lasagna and hummus. There is a children's menu. *Inexpensive. (253) 752-4069.*

Harbor Lights. 2761 Ruston Way. This popular seafood restaurant has a lively atmosphere and, among other dishes, tasty fish and chips. Reservations recommended. There is a cocktail lounge, and a children's menu. Dress is casual. *Inexpensive. (253) 752-8600.*

Johnny's Dock Restaurant. 1900 East D Street. A popular restaurant on Tacoma's waterfront this restaurant offers spectacular views of the city and boats docked in the harbor. The menu includes the popular Dock Burger as well as steak and seafood. There is a cocktail lounge and a children's menu. Reservations recommended. *Inexpensive. (253) 627-3186.*

The Lobster Shop. 4013 Ruston Way. This restaurant offers classic seafood dishes and a substantial Sunday brunch. There is a cocktail lounge, outdoor deck, and a children's menu. Reservations recommended. *Inexpensive. (253) 759-2165.*

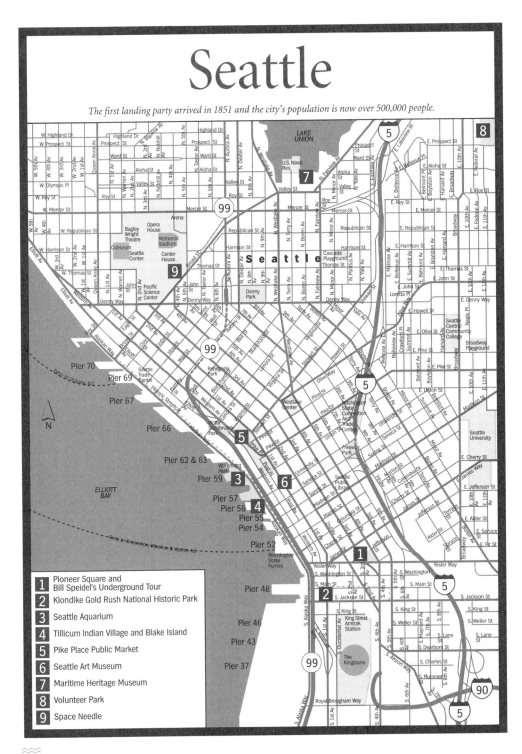

Seattle

The first landing party arrived in 1851 and the city's population is now over 500,000 people.

1. Pioneer Square and Bill Speidel's Underground Tour
2. Klondike Gold Rush National Historic Park
3. Seattle Aquarium
4. Tillicum Indian Village and Blake Island
5. Pike Place Public Market
6. Seattle Art Museum
7. Maritime Heritage Museum
8. Volunteer Park
9. Space Needle

⬚ LODGING IN TACOMA

Commencement Bay Bed and Breakfast. 3312 North Union Avenue. This B&B has three guest rooms in a large, elegant, 1937 home with a view of historic Commencement Bay and the Cascade Mountains. There is a deck, a hot tub, and a game room. Private or shared baths. Complimentary beverages are served in the evening. *Expensive.* *(253) 752-8175.*

Villa Bed and Breakfast. 705 North Fifth Street. With six guest rooms in an elegant, three-story, 1925 Renaissance mansion, this establishment has private baths and most rooms have a verandah and fireplace. All rooms have a spa. There is a view of Tacoma's Commencement Bay and the Olympic Mountains. The hosts offer refreshments in the evening and a full breakfast in the morning. *Expensive.* *(888) 572-1157 or (253) 572-1157.*

King Oscar Motel. 8820 South Hosmer Street. This 107 room, two-story motel has a heated indoor swimming pool and a whirlpool. *Moderate to expensive.* *(253) 539-1153.*

Seattle

[Fig. 9] Seattle is nestled in the midst of snow-capped mountains, masses of greenery, and sparkling bodies of water. It is hard to believe that when the first landing party arrived in 1851, three of the four women who came ashore were in tears.

They can hardly be blamed. They thought they were coming to a town. New York Alki, it was called, *alki* being a word from the native Chinook trade jargon meaning "by and by." Instead, they found themselves standing on a beach with a dozen children, none older than nine, on a gloomy, rainy November day. Waves from the incoming tide lapped at their supplies. The only accommodation was a single, roofless cabin. The idea of this place being like New York City by and by must have seemed like a bad joke.

The very land seemed outlandish and inhospitable to these daughters of Illinois. The forest-clad hills loomed around them, trees creaked and groaned ominously above them, and the sea and tidelands filled the air with strange, unhealthy smells.

In fact, the indigenous peoples had flourished on the bounty from the land and sea, creating one of the richest and most complex cultures in North America. The woods teemed with edible and medicinal plants: lilies such as the common camas *(Camassia quamash)*, varieties of wild onions *(Allium sp.)*, and wild carrots, including Queen Anne's lace *(Daucus carota)*, just to name a few. The sea was also generous. The shoreline alone yielded varieties of barnacles, the blue mussel *(Mytilus edulis)*, littleneck clams *(Protothaca staminea)*, butter clams *(Saxidomus giganteus)*, Pacific oysters *(Crassostrea gigas)*, and rock oysters *(Pododesmus cepio)*. Flounder, grouper,

Coho Salmon

At sea, the coho (*Oncorhynchus kisutch*) has a metallic green/blue back and silver sides and stomach that give it its second name of silver salmon. There are black spots on the back and on the upper part of the tail. In fresh water the adult's appearance is modified to a dark green on the back and bright red on the sides. The mature males become deep red and their snouts become hooked.

The sockeye (*Oncorhynchus nerka*), chum (*Oncorhynchus keta*), and pink (*Oncorhynchus gorbuscha*) salmon are less favored by sports anglers but make up a large proportion of the commercial fisheries.

halibut, and perch, as well as crabs, octopi, and squid were regular food sources.

But it was cedar and salmon that were the main staples of native life. The western redcedar *(Thuja plicata)* could be used for everything from houses and canoes to mats and clothing. King (*Oncorhynchus tshawytscha*), coho *(O. kisutch*), sockeye *(O. nerka*), chum *(O. keta*), pink *(O. gorbuscha*), and steelhead *(O. mykis)* salmon regularly made their way back to the rivers and creeks, returning home to spawn and die in such large numbers that they were the staple food for Pacific Northwest people.

Seattle, which was named after Sealth, an Indian chief who befriended the early settlers, has changed in the years since that first official landing party arrived. The city moved from Alki across to Elliott Bay within a year. The city's population now is well over 500,000. The forest is gone. River courses have changed, and a canal and locks now join Lake Washington to Puget Sound, giving the city both fresh- and salt-water harbors. The hills were re-graded, lowering (and in the case of one, Denny Hill, eliminating) them so the city could expand.

But despite all these changes, some things remain distant: mountains clad with white snow and green trees, the sea, dark and mysterious. What is nice about Seattle is that the green trees and the salt sea beaches can still be found within the city itself.

COHO SALMON
(*Oncorhynchus kisutch*)

ALKI BEACH PARK

[Fig. 10(1)] The site of the first official landing party in Seattle, Alki sits across the bay from the city's downtown area. Alki Beach is a 2-mile-long strip of sandy beach, and is a nice place for a swim, although the water tends to be rather cold. A promenade runs along its length. A monument to the landing party is located at Sixty First Street Southwest.

Directions: From Interstate 5 take the West Seattle Freeway (Exit 163A) westbound for 3 miles. Take the Harbor Avenue Southwest Exit. Turn right at the stop at the end of the ramp and continue about 4 miles.

Activities: Walking, swimming (no lifeguards), fire pits, picnicking, pioneer monument and Statue of Liberty replica, jogging, tennis, basketball.

Facilities: Picnic tables, restrooms, restaurants across the street.

Dates: Open year-round, sunrise to 11 p.m.

Fees: None.

For more information: 1702 Alki Ave Southwest. Seattle Parks Department, Phone (206) 684-4075, or Alki Community Center, phone (206) 684-7430.

PIONEER SQUARE

[Fig. 9(1)] Pioneer Square is historic Seattle. Yesler Way was once called Skid Road because the logs were skidded down along the path to Yesler's Mill, the first power sawmill in the area. Seattle's first and most famous madam, the Great Seattle fire of 1889, and the Klondike Gold Rush all started here.

Directions: From Interstate 5, take James Street Exit 164A. Go west (downhill) on James Street to Yesler Way. The Pioneer Square historic district is irregularly shaped, but the heart of it is located along Yesler Avenue between Alaskan Way South on the west, Fifth Avenue South on the east. The north boundary is Cherry Street and the south is Jackson Street.

For more information: Klondike Gold Rush National Historical Park, (206) 553-7220.

BILL SPEIDEL'S UNDERGROUND TOUR

[Fig. 9(1)] It started life on a tideflat, but Pioneer Square was raised a story, covering the lower parts of the buildings and creating a city underground in the process. The 90-minute guided tour of the underground area examines who benefited—and who lost out—while exploring that forgotten underground city.

Directions: From Interstate 5, take the James Street Exit 164A. Go west downhill on James Street to Yesler Way and First Avenue South intersection. Park anywhere along the way, parking lots are best, and walk, the building is just north of Yesler.

Facilities: Museum, gift shop, and restrooms.

Dates: Tours run daily, times vary.

Fees: There is a charge for admission. Not recommended for children under six.

For more information: Bill Speidel's Underground Tour, 608 First Avenue, Seattle, WA 98104. Phone (206) 682-4646.

KLONDIKE GOLD RUSH NATIONAL HISTORICAL PARK

[Fig. 9(2)] In July 1897, the steamship *Portland* arrived in Seattle with a ton of gold from Alaska in its hold, setting off the Klondike gold rush. Seattle was the closest U.S. port to the gold fields, and thousands of Klondike-bound men rushed to Seattle and bought the ton of supplies that each needed in order to be allowed into the gold fields. The museum tells this story with displays and documentary movies.

Directions: 117 South Main Street. From Interstate 5, take the James Street Exit 164A. Go west downhill on James Street to Yesler Way and First Avenue South intersection. Turn left onto First Avenue South, go two blocks to South Main Street, and turn left on South Main. The building is one-half block on the south side.

Activities: Gold panning demonstrations, ranger programs.

Facilities: Restrooms, wheelchair accessible.

Dates: Open daily, except Thanksgiving, Christmas, and New Year's days.

Fees: None.

For more information: Klondike Gold Rush National Historical Park, 117 South Main Street, Seattle, WA 98104. Phone (206) 553-7220.

SEATTLE AQUARIUM

[Fig. 9(3)] A great way to explore Puget Sound waters in a short amount of time, the aquarium is devoted to local marine life. An underwater dome is filled with local marine creatures such as wolf eels (*Anarrhichthys ocellatus*), halibut (*Hippoglossus stenolepis*), pile perch (*Rhacochelus vacca*), and a Giant Pacific octopus (*Octopus dofleini*).

Directions: From I-5 northbound, take the Madison Street Exit 164A. Go west on Madison to Alaskan Way. Turn right on Alaskan Way, go six blocks to Pier 59. From I-5 southbound, take the James Street Exit 165B. Go west on Columbia to Alaskan Way. Turn right on Alaskan Way, go seven blocks to Pier 59.

Facilities: Rest rooms, gift shop, wheelchair and strollers available.

Dates: Opens daily at 10:00 a.m.

Fees: Admission fees.

For more information: Seattle Aquarium, Pier 54, Alaskan Way, Seattle, WA 98104. Phone (206) 386-4320.

TILLICUM INDIAN VILLAGE AND BLAKE ISLAND

[Fig. 9(4)] This four-hour trip includes a boat trip to and from Blake Island, a salmon dinner, and a 30-minute native dance in an Indian long house. Blake Island is a state marine park.

Directions: Piers 55 and 56. From I-5 northbound, take the Madison Street Exit. Go west on Madison to Alaskan Way. Turn right on Alaskan Way, go about two blocks to Piers 55-56. The ticket office is located between the two piers. From I-5 southbound, take the James Street Exit 165B. Go west on Columbia to Alaskan Way. Turn right on Alaskan Way, go four blocks to Piers 55-56.

Dates: Schedule changes seasonally.

Fees: $60.00 for adults, ages 13-59, $54.00 for those over age 60, and $23.89 for children ages 5-12.

For more information: Tillicum Indian Village and Blake Island, 2200 Sixth Avenue, Seattle, WA 98121. Phone (206) 443-1244.

PIKE PLACE PUBLIC MARKET

[Fig. 9(5)] The Market has been Seattle's favorite grocery store ever since it opened in 1907. Stalls are filled with locally grown seasonal produce, fresh fish, and local crafts. Street performers abound.

Directions: From I-5 southbound, take the Stewart Street Exit 166. Go west on Stewart, which ends at the Pike Place Market. Start looking for parking about Third Avenue; the Bon Marche parking garage is located on the south side of Stewart about four blocks from the Market (Stewart is a one-way street.)

From I-5 northbound, move to the left to take the Seneca Street Exit 165. Go west on Seneca to Western Avenue. Turn right on Western, which goes along the backside of the Market. Start looking for parking around Union Street.

Facilities: Farmers' market and craft stalls, restaurants, restrooms.

Dates: Open from 9 to 6 Monday through Saturday, 11 to 5 on Sundays. Closed Thanksgiving, and Christmas and New Year's days.

Fees: Parking.

For more information: Pike Place Market Preservation and Development Authority (PDA), 85 Pike Street, Suite 500, Seattle, WA 98101. Phone (206) 682-7453.

SEATTLE ART MUSEUM

[Fig. 9(6)] A permanent Pacific Northwest exhibit features Indian artifacts made of indigenous ethnobotanical materials. Included are clothing, boxes, basketry, and exquisite examples of native masks, displayed as they would be seen around a fire at night.

Directions: 100 University Street. From I-5 southbound, take the Union Street Exit. Go straight on Union to First Avenue. Turn left (south) on First Avenue. The Museum is one block south at First Avenue and University Street. From I-5 northbound, bear to the left to take the Seneca Street Exit. Go west on Seneca to First Avenue. Turn right (north) on First Avenue. The Museum is two blocks north at University Street.

Facilities: Restaurant, restrooms, gift shop.

Dates: Closed Mondays and major holidays. Hours are 10 to 5 Tuesday through Saturday, except Thursday, when the hours are extended to 9 p.m.

Fees: There are admission fees, but there are some free days.

For more information: Seattle Art Museum, PO Box 22000, Seattle, WA 98122. Phone (206) 654-3100.

MARITIME HERITAGE MUSEUM

[Fig. 9(7)] This Lake Union park is actually located on the water and has the Center for Wooden Boats as its main occupant at this time; however negotiations are underway to take over the naval reserve pier next door, allowing more occupants. The Center is dedicated to the preservation of small wooden boat crafts of historical significance. Its collection of wooden boats of local, national and global dinghies, prams, sloops, and skiffs and other small crafts reflects this. The center also rents rowboats and sailboats. Free boat rides are available on most Sundays on a first-come, first-served basis. Call the Center to check on times.

The Puget Sound Maritime Historical Society is located near by in a small store-front in Chandler's Cove east of the Maritime Heritage Park. The collection is jam-packed with historic photographs of the Seattle waterfront and miniature replicas of ships, and the volunteer staff is knowledgeable; many of them are retired from the sea.

Directions: From I-5, take the Mercer-Seattle Center Exit 167. At the first traffic light, turn right. At the next traffic light, turn left, but stay in the right lane. The Center for Wooden Boats parking lot is located just past the Burger King; Chandler's Cove is just east of that. Parking can also be found west of the Burger King, at the white Naval Reserve building at Terry Avenue.

Activities: Boat rentals, museum.

Facilities: Restroom, restaurants at Chandler's Cove.

Dates: Varies seasonally. Call for public sail times.

Puget Sound Maritime Museum is open Monday through Saturday from 11 to 7 and Sundays from 12 to 5, except holidays.

Fees: Boat rentals.

For more information: The Center for Wooden Boats, 1010 Valley Street, Seattle, WA 98109. Phone (206) 382-2628.

Puget Sound Maritime Historical Society, 901 Fairview Avenue North, Seattle, WA 98109. Phone (206) 624-3028.

VOLUNTEER PARK

[Fig. 9(8)] Over 170 plants grace this 48-acre park, including a large collection of rhododendrons (*Rhododendron macrophyllum*), the Washington state flower, and azaleas (*Rhododendron albiflorum*), both of which flourish in the wild in the Pacific Northwest. The park is the home of the Volunteer Park Conservatory and the Seattle Art Museum's Asian Art Collection.

Directions: From I-5 southbound, take the Boylston-Roanoke Exit 168A. Turn left on Roanoke (over the freeway). Turn right at Tenth Avenue East. Follow Tenth Avenue East to East Highland Drive. Turn left on East Highland Drive and drive into the park.

From I-5 northbound, take the Olive Way Exit 166. Follow Olive Way (it will change into East John Street) east to Fifteenth Avenue East. Turn left and follow Fifteenth Avenue East to East Prospect Street. Turn left. The entrance is at East Prospect Street and Fourteenth Avenue East.

Facilities: Paths, playground, and restroom.

Dates: Park is open daily, 4:30 a.m. to 11 p.m.

Fees: There is a charge for museum admission.

For more information: Seattle Parks Department, 1247 Fifteen Avenue East, Seattle, WA 98112. Phone (206) 684-4075.

SPACE NEEDLE

[Fig. 9(9)] At 360 degrees around, and 605 feet high, the Space Needle restaurant and observation deck are the best place to get a feel of the city and its surrounding environment. The restaurant takes about an hour to rotate; reservations should be made a week in advance if possible. The observation deck above is stationary but has excellent signage explaining the different landmarks.

Directions: From I-5, take the Mercer-Seattle Center Exit 167. At the first light, turn left onto Fairview Avenue North. Follow Fairview to Denny Way and turn right onto Denny. Follow Denny to the Space Needle.

Facilities: Restaurants, gift shop, restrooms, and wheelchair accessible.

Dates: Open 365 days per year, hours vary.

Fees: There is an observation deck fee for those not visiting the restaurant.

For more information: 219 Fourth Avenue North, Seattle, WA 98109. Phone (206) 443-2100.

WASHINGTON PARK ARBORETUM

[Fig. 10(2)] The wood-lined paths of this 230-acre park connect a series of smaller gardens, designed to display their beauty throughout the seasons. Mountain ash *(Sorbus cashmiriana)*, Japanese maples *(Acer palmatum)*, and Alaskan cedars *(Chamaecyparis nootkatensis)* are just a few of the types of woody plants. Spring brings spectacular displays of rhododendrons (*Rhododendron* sp.) and azaleas. The main garden trail meanders for about 0.7 mile. At the north end of the park Foster Island, a wetland trail, is home to numerous birds and plants. The Japanese Garden is near the south entrance.

Directions: From I-5, take Bellevue-Highway 520 Exit 168A. Move to the right lane; take the University of Washington/Montlake Boulevard Exit (0.75 mile.) At the light at the top of the exit, go straight onto Lake Washington Boulevard. Follow Lake Washington Boulevard to the second stop sign, which is East Foster Island Road. Turn left. The visitor center is at the next right on Arboretum Drive East.

Activities: Free tours at 1 p.m. Saturdays and Sundays; call the center to check.

Facilities: Restrooms, gift shop and maps; parking throughout the park.

Dates: The main park and Foster Island are open 365 days a year, sunrise to

CALIFORNIA SEA LION
(Zalophus californianus)

sunset. The visitor center is open from 10 to 4 daily except for Thanksgiving, Christmas, and New Year's days.

The Japanese Garden opens at 10 daily from Mar. through Nov.; seasonal closing times vary. It is closed Dec., Jan., and, Feb.

Fees: The Japanese Garden has a small fee.

For more information: Graham Visitors Center, 2300 Arboretum Drive E., Seattle, WA 98112. Phone (206) 543-8800.

DISCOVERY PARK

[Fig. 10(3)] A network of trails tangles through second-growth forest, meadowlands, beaches, and wetlands that are features in this 534-acre park. Numerous birds and mammals, including bald eagles *(Haliaeetus leucocephalusu)*, coyotes *(Canis latrans)*, and California sea lions *(Zalophus californianus)* can be found in the park. The beach is a typical Washington State beach, with driftwood, rocks, sand, and a variety of sea creatures, including seaweeds, barnacles, bivalves, chitons, and worms.

Directions: From I-5, take the Forty-fifth Street Northeast Exit 169, turn left onto Forty-fifth Street Northeast. Follow this street west (there will be signs that read either Discovery Park, Fort Lawton or Daybreak Star Center) for about 5.0 miles; it will change names to Midvale. At the end of Midvale is a stop light. Turn left at the light onto North Forty-sixth Street. Move immediately into the right lane and continue for about 0.5 miles. At this point, the road turns into Market Street and goes downhill. Follow Market to Fifteenth Avenue Northwest; turn left and cross the Ballard Bridge. Move right, and take the West Emerson Street overpass, which is the first overpass after the bridge. Follow Emerson to Gilman Avenue West for about 1.0 miles; it turns into Government Way, which leads into the park.

Activities: Hiking, beach exploring.

Facilities: Visitor center, self-guided nature trail, children's playground. Bringing food and drink is recommended.

Dates: The park is open daily, dawn to dusk. The visitor center is open from 8:30 to 5 daily except holidays.

Fees: None.

For more information: 3801 West Government Way, Seattle, WA 98199. Phone (206) 386-4236.

CARL S. ENGLISH BOTANICAL GARDENS, HIRAM M. CHITTENDEN LOCKS AND FISH LADDER

[Fig. 10(4)] The Ballard Locks, as they are locally known, control the flow of water between Lake Washington and Puget Sound, and are engineering and entertainment marvels. Both commercial and pleasure boats—everything from large yachts to kayaks—make use of the two locks, as do some of the salmon returning to spawn. Most of the migrating fish use the fish ladder, which has an indoor viewing area where visitors can watch the different varieties of salmon battle the current to return to their spawning grounds. Each species returns at a different time of the year, but most make the trip during the summer and early fall.

The grounds include a museum with exhibits on the history and construction of the canal and locks, salmon migration, and a small replica that shows how the locks work. The seven-acre garden features an excellent collection of both regional and international botanical specimens suited to the mild Northwest climate. The locks are close to several good restaurants, Shilshole Marina, and Golden Gardens Park beach, which has a small playground, a bathhouse, and a wonderful salt-water beach.

Directions: From I-5, take the Forty-fifth Street Northeast Exit 169, turn left onto Forty-fifth Street Northeast. Follow this street west (there will be signs that read

COYOTE
(Canis latrans)

Metro Seattle

Alki Beach is the site of the first official landing party in Seattle.

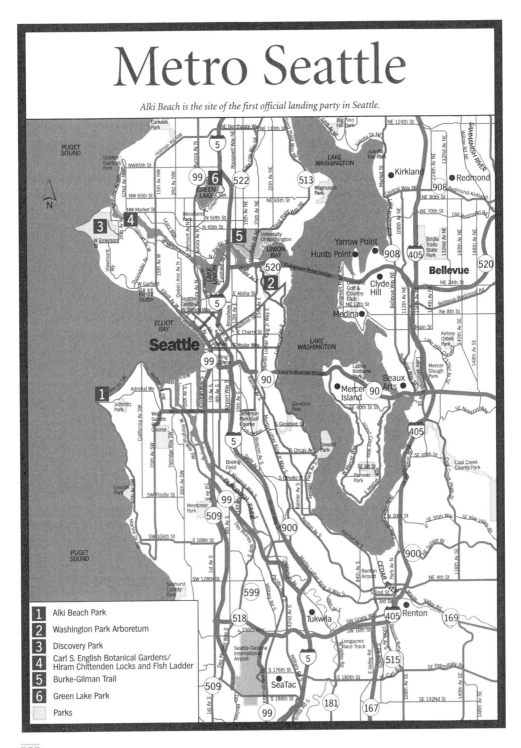

1 Alki Beach Park
2 Washington Park Arboretum
3 Discovery Park
4 Carl S. English Botanical Gardens/ Hiram Chittenden Locks and Fish Ladder
5 Burke-Gilman Trail
6 Green Lake Park
▢ Parks

either Discovery Park, Fort Lawton, or Daybreak Star Center) for about 5.0 miles; it will change names to Midvale. At the end of Midvale is a stop light. Turn left at the light onto North Forty-sixth Street. Move immediately to the right and continue for about 0.5 miles. At this point, the road turns into Market Street and goes downhill. Follow Market Street about 3.0 miles, where the Market Street arterial will branch to the left and become Northwest Fifty-fourth Street. Follow Northwest Fifty-fourth; the

Toxic Seafood

From time to time toxins affect communities of beach creatures and they become dangerous for humans to eat. It is wise to be certain there is no danger. In Washington, contact the State Department of Health marine toxins hotline at (800) 562-5632. In Oregon call the Oregon Department of Agriculture Food Safety Division at (503) 986-4720.

entrance to the locks is just after the branch in the road. Continuing on along Northwest Fifty-fourth leads to Shilshole Marina and Golden Garden Park.

Facilities: Museum, garden, fish ladder with viewing area, locks, restrooms.

Dates: Open daily, 7 a.m. to 9 p.m.

Fees: None.

For more information: Hiram M. Chittenden Locks Visitors Center, 3015 Northwest 54th Street. Phone (206) 783-7059.

BURKE-GILMAN TRAIL

[Fig. 10(5)] Small mammals such as raccoons *(Procyon lotor)*, Douglas squirrels *(Tamiasciurus douglasii)*, and garter snakes *(Thamnophis sirtalis)* live beside this plant-lined, asphalt-covered path where pedestrians, bikers, and skaters speed by. The trail goes 16-miles to join the Sammamish River Trail in King County, which goes to Marymoor Park in Redmond, Washington. It follows Lake Washington for much of the way as it heads east, and follows the Montlake Cut, Lake Union and Ballard Locks that run from Lake Washington to Puget Sound. However, much of this later portion is not well defined. A good destination is the stretch between Gas Works Park on Lake Union, and Magnuson, about 2.6 miles to the east on Lake Washington. Magnuson has a good swimming beach as well as a playground, picnic area, kite-flying hill, public art, boat launch, and walking trails. Gas Works has a kite-flying hill, playground, and picnic areas.

Directions: From I-5, take the Northeast Forty-fifth Street Exit 169. Turn left onto Northeast Forty-fifth Street. Go to Wallingford Avenue North, turn left, follow Wallingford Avenue North to the second light about 0.75 mile to North Thirty-fourth Street. Turn right on North Thirty-fourth Street, go one block and turn left onto Densmore Avenue North. Go to the end of Densmore (one block) and turn left onto North Northlake Way. The park entrance is one block east on the right.

Activities: Pathway for walking, skating, bicycling.

Facilities: The trail passes by parks that have restrooms and picnic tables. In addition, it goes near various business districts where food and restrooms can be found. The trail itself has no facilities.

Dates: The trail is open daily, year around.

Fees: None.

For more information: Seattle City Parks Department, 100 Dexter Avenue North, Seattle, WA 98109. Phone (206) 684-4075. King County Trails, phone (206) 296-4232.

GREEN LAKE PARK

[Fig. 10(6)] Green Lake Park is the most popular park in Seattle, especially on warm, sunny summer days. The sun-starved people of Seattle can't help it. The lake, surrounded by a 2.8-mile path used for walking, skating and biking and people-watching, has two swimming beaches, one of the east side at Green Lake Community Center and Evans Pool, and the other on the west side, at the Bath House, on the lake's west side. Evans Pool is open year-round and is heated; it also has a sauna. A children's playground is located next to Evans Pool and canoes, rowboats, and paddle boats can be rented at the north end of the pool and community center parking lot in the summer months. A children's wading pool is located at the north end of the lake; there is no parking lot there, but the parking lot at the Bath House is only about 0.4 mile away. Green Lake is also a short jaunt to Ravenna Park, which features a heavily wooded ravine complete with a small creek. Nearby Gregg's Bicycle rents bikes and roller blades. The park features many varieties of trees and wetlands, including cattails *(Typha latifolia)* and larches *(Larix sp.)*.

Directions: From I-5 northbound, take Exit 170 Sixty-fifth Northeast. Turn left onto Northeast Ravenna Boulevard. Continue on Northeast Ravenna to Green Lake Drive North. At the five-way stop, continue to the right, following the lakefront to Latona Avenue Northeast. At Latona, turn left into the parking lot.

From I-5 southbound, take Exit 171 Northeast Seventy-first Street. Turn right on Northeast 71st Street. Continue three blocks to Green Lake Drive North. Turn right onto East Green Lake Drive North. Go four blocks to Latona Avenue Northeast; turn left into the parking lot.

Activities: Biking, swimming, wading, boating, walking.

Facilities: Community center, swimming pool, rest rooms, wading pool, rowboat and pedal boat rentals, play ground.

Dates: Open daily, sunrise to 11 p.m.

Fees: There is a charge for admission to Evans Pool, and for boat rentals.

For more information: Green Lake Community Center, 7201 East Green Lake Drive North. Phone (206) 684-0780.

Gregg's Greenlake Cycle, 7007 Woodlawn Northeast. Phone (206) 523-1822.

SEATTLE RESTAURANTS

Seattle has so many good restaurants of so many different ethnicities that selecting just a few is frustrating. Seafood is fresh and plentiful, and plenty of restaurants serve it. But plenty of restaurants serve other things, from Vietnamese pho to prawns, spaghetti to steak, and many of them do so in locations with, thanks to all those hills, spectacular views. Think of the hills as being appetite-whetters. The restaurants listed here are by location, starting with Pioneer and working towards downtown Seattle and the Pike Place Market.

PIONEER SQUARE RESTAURANTS

Merchants Café. 109 Yesler Way, between First Avenue South and Occidental Avenue South. Seattle's oldest restaurant opened in 1890, and is still going strong, with good, reasonably priced lunches and dinners (try the salmon chowder). *Inexpensive. (206) 624-1515.*

FX McRory's. 419 Occidental Avenue S., near the Seahawks Football Stadium. This restaurant's way with seafood has been popular with locals since it opened its doors in 1977. Located in the heart of Pioneer Square, the menu is noted for its seafood, steaks and chops, and includes an oyster bar. Lunch is served Monday through Friday. Dinner starts daily beginning at 5 p.m. There is a full service bar. *Moderate. (206) 623-4800.*

Trattoria Mitchelli. 84 Yesler Way in Seattle. Trattoria Mitchelli serves a variety of central Italian dishes, including clam and salmon linguini. It is one of the few restaurants in Pioneer Square that serve breakfast, including frittas and gypsy toast, French toast made with slices of fried bread pudding. There's no view here, but the ambiance is a kind of sophisticated rustic. The restaurant is open from 7 a.m. to 4 a.m. daily, usually. *Moderate. (206) 623-3885.*

PIKE PLACE MARKET

Now a historical district, the Market has been a local institution for nearly 100 years, complete with rambling old buildings (renovated in the 1970s) and the occasional ghost. This is a great place to browse—and to eat. Be sure to check out the fish market, they occasionally have geoducks for sale. Food ranges from casual eat-as-you-go, to casual sit-down, to fancy. Most of the sit-down restaurants have views of Puget Sound and the Olympic Mountains; watch the ferries glide by on their way to Bremerton. The market is actually made up of several buildings, each with its own name.

Three Girls Bakery. 1514 Pike Place, in the Sanitary Market Building, across the street from the main Pike Place building. A great place to get a pick-up meal, literally, since there are no tables, the bakery opens at 6 a.m. for bakery goods and espresso. Their lunch sandwiches are hearty, the bread's delicious, and the chocolate macaroons are to die for. *Inexpensive. (206) 622-1045.*

Maxmillian's at Pike Place Market. 81A Pike Street, set in the corner of the "L" where Pike Street and Pike Place meet; follow the red neon "Maxmillian" sign. This cozy corner restaurant offers excellent French food for lunches and dinners, complete with white tablecloths, a French maître d', and stunning views from every table. They open for lunch at 11:30, and are usually closed for dinner on Sunday and all day Monday. *Moderate to expensive. (206) 682-7270.*

Place Pigalle. 81 Pike Place, near Maximillian's, follow the neon sign. One of Seattle's most notorious dives has been transformed into a fine Italian restaurant, with excellent views of the Sound and the Olympic Mountains. The window seats have a definite "perch" feeling, as though sitting on an eagle's aerie. *Moderate to expensive. Phone (206) 624-1756.*

WATERFRONT RESTAURANTS

Ivar's Acres of Clams. Pier 54 on Alaskan Way. Restauranteur Ivar Hagland kept Seattle amused for over 30 years with his silly songs and slogans ("Keep clam," is probably the best known). His restaurants reflect the man and his time: the atmosphere is casual, the restaurant sits on the pier, and the seafood, as well as the steaks, hamburgers, salads, are excellent. Reservations are a good idea; this place is popular with locals, too. *Moderate. (206) 624-6852.*

Anthony's Pier 66. Pier 66 on Alaskan Way. Anthony's is actually three restaurants, the inexpensive **Anthony's Fish Bar**, the moderately priced **Anthony's Bell Street Diner**, and the **Anthony's Pier 66**, expensive, but with the best views. These are part of a well-regarded local chain, **Anthony's Home Port Restaurants**, and serve excellent seafood. *(206) 448-6688.*

DOWNTOWN RESTAURANTS

Etta's Seafood. 2020 Western Avenue. Excellent fresh seafood dishes by one of Seattle's leading chefs, Tom Douglas, in a casual atmosphere. Douglas is especially noted for his desserts; the crème brûlèe and coconut cream pie are on the "to die for" list. Lunch and dinner are served, along with breakfast on the weekends. *Expensive. (206) 443-6000.*

Nordstrom's Café. Nordstrom's Department store, fourth floor, 500 Pine. Now nation-wide, Nordstrom's started in Seattle, and this is its new flagship store. Not only that, but the food is good. They are open for breakfast and lunch until the store closes. *Inexpensive to moderate. (206) 628-1610.*

Space Needle. Seattle Center, Fifth Avenue and Denny Way. The food is excellent; the restaurant is high on the Space Needle tower and slowly rotates, providing a full 360-degree view of the city. Diners get free elevator rides and access to the observation deck above. *Expensive. General information, (206) 443-2111. Reservations, (206) 443-2100.*

Seattle Center Food Court. Seattle Center Fifth Avenue and Denny Way. This is a multitude of eateries that share tables in a large common room. Good food, some chain (**Pizza Hut**), some local (**Quincy's, The Magic Dragon**), where each member of the family can find something different to eat, then gather at a table to enjoy it together. Opens at 11 a.m., closing times are seasonal. *Inexpensive. (206) 684-7200.*

SEATTLE LODGING

The good news is that Seattle has many fine hotels; the bad news is that most of them charge for parking. Here's a small sampling.

Pioneer Square Hotel. 77 Yesler Way. This 1914 building sits right in the heart of Pioneer Square, with 72 romantic rooms and a continental breakfast. *Moderate to expensive. Reservations, (800) 458-1227, general information, (206) 340-1234.*

Pensione Nichols. 1923 First Avenue. This urban bed and breakfast has 12 rooms, two suites, and a sitting room with 360-degree views. The inn has a European air, and the amenities include a fainting couch and water fountain for the trek upstairs. *Moderate. (206) 441-7125.*

Inn at the Market. 86 Pine Street. As close to a bed and breakfast as a hotel can get, this gracious contemporary hotel has spacious rooms, a rooftop garden, and a central courtyard. Although it has no restaurant of its own, breakfast and room service are provided by **Campagne**, located across the courtyard. Of course, it is always possible to pick up something in the Market. *Expensive. (800) 446-4484.*

Capitol Hill Inn. 1713 Belmont Avenue. Located eight blocks from downtown, this charmingly restored 1903 home is filled with antiques. One room has a Jacuzzi and fireplace. *Moderate. (206) 323-1955.*

Seattle Inn. 225 Aurora Avenue North. An easy walk to the Seattle Center and the Monorail train to downtown, this hotel offers a pool and hot tub, a continental breakfast, and a children's playground, as well as a laundromat. *Inexpensive. Reservations, (800) 225-7932, general information, (206) 728-766.*

Paramount Hotel. 724 Pine Street. With its peaked roof, "European chateau" describes this hotel, located right downtown. The Paramount has spacious rooms, and there is a gym. **The Blowfish Asian Restaurant**, moderately priced and good, serves an American-style breakfast, as well as lunch and dinner. Children under age 18 stay free, and every room has cable TV and game systems. *Expensive. Reservations, (800) 370-0308, general information, (206) 292-9500.*

Sorrento Hotel. 900 Madison Street. A beautiful fountain patio leading to the entrance of this 1909 Mediterranean-style hotel is just the beginning of the opulence of this hotel, which features well-appointed rooms and excellent restaurants. The Fireside Room offers tea in the afternoon and live jazz in the evening. Board games such as Parcheesi, Monopoly, Cribbage, Pente, and backgammon can be checked out from the concierge. *Expensive. (800) 426-1265 or (206) 622-6400.*

Chelsea Station. 4915 Linden Avenue North. Although located about 4 miles north of downtown, the city is readily accessible from this two-building Federal

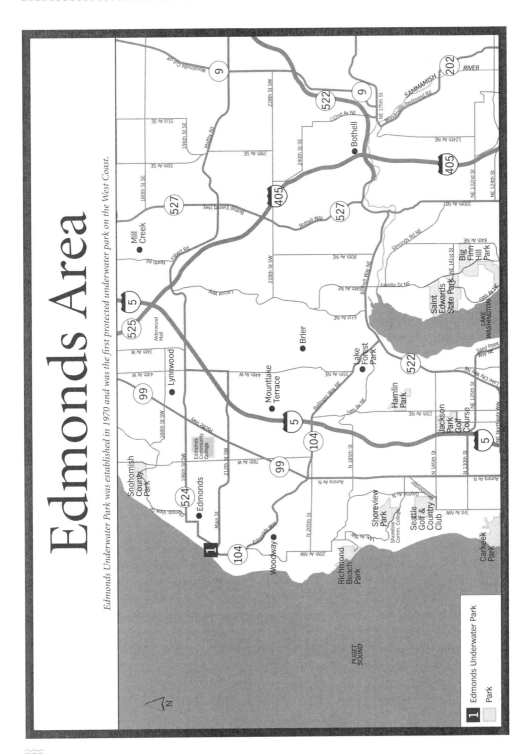

Edmonds Area

Edmonds Underwater Park was established in 1970 and was the first protected underwater park on the West Coast.

	Edmonds Underwater Park
1	
	Park

Colonial-style bed and breakfast, which is located near Green Lake and the Woodland Park Zoo. The breakfast is substantial and tasty, and there are views of the Cascade Mountains from some of the rooms. *Moderate. (800) 400-6077 or (206) 547-6077.*

Edmonds and Edmonds Underwater Park

[Fig. 11(1)] Edmonds was established in 1890 by George Bracket. Legend has it that he needed two more names to make his petition for establishing the town valid, so he added the names of his two oxen. Like most other communities in the Puget Sound area, the economy of Brackett's town was based on logging and lumbering. By the early twentieth century, the waterfront was lined with dozens of small mills that spewed smoke from their boilers into the air. But as happened in other small logging communities, the easy-to-obtain lumber was cut away and the laws of economics required that the small mills give way to larger, more efficient operations elsewhere. By World War II, most of Edmonds' mills had burned or closed and been converted to other uses. The former mill town became an upper-middle class bedroom community for people who commuted to work elsewhere. The downtown area developed an assortment of quaint shops and restaurants. The waterfront evolved into an area of shops, restaurants, a large boat harbor, and parks.

Among the parks, just to the north of the state ferry landing, is the 27-acre Edmonds Underwater Park, which was established in 1970 as a marine preserve and sanctuary, and was the first protected underwater park on the West Coast. Originally, the major feature was the 300-foot dry dock, *Delion,* which had sunk in 1935. Two years later the city arranged for the 94-foot tug *Alitak* to be sunk at the southeast corner of the *Delion.* In 1982, the tug *Fossil* and numerous other objects were added to the underwater site. Rest floats, where divers can catch their breath, dot the surface.

The nutrient-rich water of Puget Sound supports an abundance of sea plants and animals, which find shelter in the sunken vessels and other objects in the park. The combination of seawater and the sheltering objects provides habitats for a rich variety of plants and animals. Plants include eelgrass (*Zostra marina*), bull kelp (*Nereocystis luetkeana*), and Turkish towel (*Gigertina* sp.). Among the numerous varieties of fish are lingcod (*Ophiodon elongatus*), rockfish (*Sebasties* sp.), and Pacific herring (*Clupea harengus*). Invertebrates

EELGRASS
(*Zostra marina*)

include hermit crab (*Pagurus* sp.), Dungeness crab (*Cancer magister*), and octopus. Marine organisms may not be removed from the park.

Scuba-diving equipment and instruction are available at private business establishments south of the park. Parking is in the Brackett's Landing parking lot and is limited to a maximum of four hours. Private parking lots are available nearby. The temperature of the water in the park is consistent year-round at between 48 and 52 degrees Fahrenheit. Depth of the water varies from negligible at the shoreline to 45 feet near the ferry landing. Visibility in the water is from 2 to 40 feet, and divers are required to use a compass and to be guided by a trail system that has been installed. Safety requirements apply to all divers.

Directions: Take Exit 177 from I-5 onto State Route 104 (also called 244 Street) and drive west to Edmonds. Turn west on Main Street, cross the railroad tracks, and turn north to the park. Or take the Edmonds ferry from the end of State Route 104 in Kingston.

Activities: Scuba-diving.

Facilities: Scuba-diving facilities are provided both on the surface and underwater. On the beach, there are showers and foot wash facilities, restrooms, a display with charts, maps, and information that divers can use to prepare a dive plan.

Dates: Open year-round. Night diving is permitted but divers must notify the park department of their plans.

Fees: None.

For more information: Edmonds Park and Recreation Department, 700 Main Street, Edmonds, WA 98020. Phone (425) 771-0230.

RESTAURANTS IN EDMONDS

Edmonds has transformed itself from a timber-and-mill town to an upscale bedroom community and its little downtown district retains some of the flavor of both eras. A few establishments offer food and rest for the hungry and weary.

Cafe de Paris. 109 Main Street. Amidst the early-twentieth century American architecture of downtown Edmonds, this cozy restaurant offers a taste of Paris in decor and cuisine. *Inexpensive. (425) 771-2350.*

Arnies at Edmonds. 300 Admiral Way. This large, busy restaurant on the waterfront offers tremendous views of Puget Sound and the Olympic Mountains, along with a wide array of well-prepared Northwest seafood dishes and a Sunday brunch. There is a cocktail lounge and a children's menu. Reservations recommended. *Inexpensive. (425) 771-5688.*

LODGING IN EDMONDS

Edmonds Harbor Inn. 130 West Dayton Street. The only hotel in downtown Edmonds, this 60-room establishment is near the Port of Edmonds Boat Harbor, ferry landing, and Puget Sound beach. Complimentary breakfast. *Moderate. (425) 771-5021.*

Harrison House Bed and Breakfast. 210 Sunset Avenue. This contemporary home on the bank above Puget Sound has two guest rooms and wide views that include the sound and the Olympic Mountains. Private bath. Continental breakfast. *Moderate. (425) 776-4748.*

Mukilteo and Mukilteo State Park

[Fig. 12(1)] When Isaac Stevens became the first governor of the Washington Territory, one of his responsibilities was to establish reservations where the territory's Indians could go to escape the cultural clash that threatened to destroy them. A little point of land jutting out into Puget Sound was a traditional meeting place among the tribes, and that is where Governor Stevens went to negotiate one of the treaties that created those reservations. The agreement, called the Elliot Point Treaty, was concluded on January 22, 1855, after several days of discussions with members of 22 tribes from the Puget Sound area.

Five years later, after the Indians had gone to the reservations, Morris H. Frost and J. D. Fowler opened a store here. The store became a landing place for passenger and freight boats on Puget Sound. The boats brought settlers who gradually filled the bluff behind the beach with houses and commercial buildings and eventually formed the pleasant suburban city of Mukilteo.

In 1905 the Army Corps of Engineers built a lighthouse here and in 1906 the U.S. Coast Guard established a station that still exists. The station was renovated in 1987 and consists of the lighthouse, two residences, and a pleasantly landscaped garden.

Adjacent to the Coast Guard Station on the north is the state ferry system's Mukilteo landing and downtown Mukilteo, with its shops and restaurants. To the south is the 17-acre Mukilteo State Park. The park has 1,495 feet of mostly rocky saltwater beach on Puget Sound, and a four-lane boat launch with boarding floats.

There is little swimming at the park because of cold water, strong currents, and a steep tidal area, but people wearing wet suits can scuba-dive and wind surf. Strong winds also make the small level area behind the beach popular for kite flying.

The little park attracts more than 1 million visitors a year. Many of them use the 47 fireplace-equipped picnic sites along the beach, while many others simply park their cars in the large parking lot facing the sound and admire the magnificent view that includes busy ferries and lazy sailboats, with the Olympic Mountains in the background.

When the tide goes out, the tidal area may contain interesting creatures, including the 2-inch-long blue mussel (*Mytilus trossulus*), purple, red, or orange starfish, and limpet. There may even be a hermit crab. Hermits are especially adapted to live in an empty snail shell, and that is where they can usually be found.

Directions: The park is just south of the ferry landing at the foot of State Route

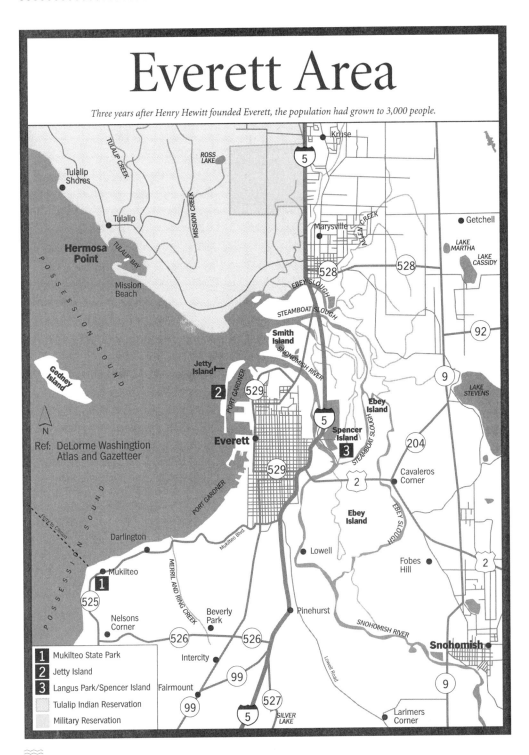

Everett Area

Three years after Henry Hewitt founded Everett, the population had grown to 3,000 people.

Kruse

ROSS LAKE

Tulalip Shores

TULALIP CREEK

MISSION CREEK

Tulalip

Getchell

ALLEN CREEK

Marysville

LAKE MARTHA

Hermosa Point

TULALIP BAY

528

528

LAKE CASSIDY

Mission Beach

EBEY SLOUGH

STEAMBOAT SLOUGH

92

P O S S E S S I O N   S O U N D

Smith Island

SNOHOMISH RIVER

Gedney Island

Jetty Island

PORT GARDNER

2

529

Ebey Island

9

LAKE STEVENS

N

5

Spencer Island

STEAMBOAT SLOUGH

Ref: DeLorme Washingtion Atlas and Gazetteer

Everett

3

204

529

Cavaleros Corner

2

Ebey Island

PORT GARDNER

EBEY SLOUGH

Darlington

Mukilteo Blvd.

Lowell

Fobes Hill

2

P O S S E S S I O N   S O U N D

Ferry to Clinton

Mukilteo

1

MERRIL AND RING CREEK

525

Nelsons Corner

Beverly Park

Pinehurst

SNOHOMISH RIVER

Snohomish

526

526

1 Mukilteo State Park

Intercity

Lowell Road

2 Jetty Island

99

3 Langus Park/Spencer Island

Fairmount

99

527

9

Tulalip Indian Reservation

Military Reservation

5

SILVER LAKE

Larimers Corner

525, also called the Mukilteo Speedway, in Mukilteo.

Activities: Picnicking, beach walking, kite flying, boating, fishing, wind surfing, scuba-diving.

Facilities: Picnic tables with fireplaces, restrooms, boat launch.

Dates: Open year round.

Fees: Fees are charged for parking in part of the parking lot, and for use of the boat launch.

Closest town: Mukilteo.

For more information: Mukilteo State Park, in care of Wenberg State Park, 14430 East Lake Goodwin Road, Stanwood, WA 98292. Phone (425) 353- 2923.

▓ RESTAURANTS IN MUKILTEO

This small, upscale, bedroom community does not have a large business community but it does have some notable restaurants.

Arnies Restaurant. 714 Second Street. This upscale restaurant with a maritime atmosphere is on the bluff above Mukilteo's business district and looks down on the ferry landing, Puget Sound, and beyond to the Olympic Mountains. The menu focuses on Northwestern seafood and there is a Sunday brunch. Cocktail lounge and children's menu are available. Reservations recommended. *Inexpensive. (425) 355-2181.*

Charles at Smugglers Cove. 8310 53 Avenue West. This upscale restaurant gets its name from the 1920s when the building housed a Prohibition-era liquor distillery. The illegal booze was shipped through a tunnel that led to the waterfront. Today Charles at Smugglers Cove offers popular French cuisine in an elegant setting. Reservations recommended. *Inexpensive. (425) 347-2700.*

Everett

[Fig. 12] Tacoma's claim to being a major player in Puget Sound's economy got a big boost when four entrepreneurs from the Midwest founded the St. Paul and Tacoma Timber Company, which became the largest lumber company in the world. One of the four was Henry Hewitt. Son of an English farmer, he immigrated to Wisconsin at age two with his family. With only a few years of schooling, he joined his father in the contracting business, then went out on his own. He became owner or part owner of many businesses, but his expertise and great love was forest cruising, touring a section of forest to ascertain its value and the cost of logging it. When the timber business in Wisconsin began to wane, he sold his interests there and moved west to find new opportunities.

In 1889, after the St. Paul and Tacoma Timber Company was up and running, Hewitt set out to find more timber supplies. One of the places he investigated was the

The Gray Whale

The gray whale (*Eschrichtius robustus*) is a baleen whale that eats by sifting through the mud at the bottom of the sea for food. It has mottled gray skin and no dorsal fin, and usually stays in the open seas rather than venture into the inlets. It grows to about 39 feet long and makes a 12,000-mile round trip each year between its southern breeding grounds off Baja, Mexico and its feeding grounds in the far northern Chuckchi, Beaufort, and Bering seas. It has a low hump rather than a fin and there are from 6 to 12 bumps, or knuckles, between it and the flukes. The flukes are thrust high into the air when it dives. The long, slender head has a long, straight or slightly arched mouth. And the flippers are small and paddle shaped. The skin is a mottled gray and encrusted with barnacles. The blowhole has a V or heart shape. The gray whale frequently breaches where people can see it.

Snohomish River, one of the major streams that empty into Possession Sound, an extension of Puget Sound. The mouth of the Snohomish forms a long peninsula along the south bank. Hewitt found that the peninsula was covered with magnificent Douglas fir forest. E. D. Smith had built a small mill and its accompanying community of Lowell at the upriver end of the peninsula. Wyatt J. Rucker and his brother Bethel J. were in the process of platting a city on the Puget Sound side of the peninsula. Other than that there were only a handful of people with claims or squatters' cabins on the peninsula. Hewitt was impressed with the possibilities of harvesting the forest, but as he investigated, he hit on the idea that the peninsula might be a good place to found a city. He hired some Indians to take him in a canoe to Port Gardner Bay on the west side of the peninsula. He sounded the waters and found they were sufficiently deep to provide for ocean-going ships.

He interested some financial figures from the East, including John D. Rockefeller, reputedly the richest man in America. They formed a coalition that worked with Smith and the Rucker brothers and established the city of Everett. Within a few years they had founded a series of industries around the waterfront of the peninsula that included a pulp and paper plant, a shipbuilding plant, an ore smelter, a sawmill, a nail factory, and an iron works; three years after Hewitt arrived, the forest of the peninsula had given way to a full-scale city with 3,000 people.

Nearly 45 years had passed since George Bush and friends became the first Americans to settle on Puget Sound, and a great many technological changes had taken place. Perhaps the most significant was the advent of steam, which by the time of Henry Hewitt, had pretty much replaced the muscle and sail power of George Bush's day. That brought tremendous changes. For one thing the canoes that had been the main means of travel on the sound had given way to the tiny steamboats that provided a relatively quick and easy way to transport passengers and freight between communities. A multitude of the boats, which local folk called the Mosquito

Fleet, appeared on the sound and continued to make communication easier, until they gave way to railroads and automobiles, making it even more easy. Steam power also made it possible to develop large-scale industries, which supported many more people than the farms and hand industry of George Bush's day could.

Like the other communities on Puget Sound and throughout the country, Everett took full advantage of that change. It was born as an industrial city and soon prided itself on its nickname, City of Smoke Stacks. There were frequent ups and downs; many of the original industries failed soon after they started. During the first half of the century, the industrial base was largely dependent on the vast forests in the vicinity. After World War II that gradually changed: By the end of the century, the forest products industry had been largely replaced by numerous electronics firms, and by a huge Boeing plant that includes the largest building in the world. Henry Hewitt's little city of 3,000 people had grown to well over 80,000.

The downside of that growth was that the magnificent old-growth forest that once covered the peninsula like a tall, green blanket was gone. The upside is that there are places in the city where nature still reigns, and the community keeps them intact.

JETTY ISLAND

[Fig. 12(2)] Probably Everett's most exceptional place where nature is sovereign is Jetty Island, which was created by man, but adopted by wildlife of both land and sea. The island began as a bulkhead built in Port Gardner Bay to create a freshwater harbor, where the wooden ships of the day could escape the saltwater creatures that eat wood. The bulkhead collected silt from the river and became a small island. Over the years, when the harbor was dredged to keep it open for navigation, the spoils were put on the new island. That practice continued until now the island is more than 2 miles long, and protects the city's inner harbor.

The city's parks and recreation department cooperates with the Port of Everett, which owns the island, to maintain its natural beauty. The manmade island has become a haven for numerous wild plants and animals within sight of the busy harbor, which includes a major navy base.

During the summer, the park department provides a free, passenger-only ferry across the narrow waterway from the Tenth Street boat launch and Marine Park to the island, where park rangers conduct nature walks on the trails. There also is a 0.5-mile interpretive trail with signs that describe the wildlife and their habitat. Among the possibilities for animal watching are several gray whales that park naturalists believe may be becoming residents of the waters around the island. They appear, however, during the winter when the free ferry is hibernating. People with canoes, kayaks, or other small craft can get to the island with just a little effort. Some people have been known to swim across the narrow waterway, but the water is very cold and there are no safety provisions.

Other winter creatures on the island include a group of male California sea lions that haul out of the water onto log rafts that often are tied up on the eastern, inner side of the island. The sea lions can easily be seen from the mainland and heard, too. Their loud, wild bark can be heard for a long distance, especially when the animals join together in a chorus. The group consists entirely of males that swim north during the winter while the females remain in California and points south. It is highly unlikely, however, that is what the males are howling about.

During the summer, when the ferry makes a visit easy, there are many other creatures to be seen and admired on the island, including northern harriers (*Circus cyaneus*), which fly over the island looking for voles and other good things to eat. Other birds of prey include bald eagles (*Haliaeetus leucocephalus*) and peregrine falcons (*Falco peregrinus*). The falcons are a Northwestern-shore subspecies of the inland peregrine falcons that have become extremely rare, supposedly in part because chemicals once used as insecticides got into their food chain and caused the walls of egg shells to be so thin and weak that they broke before the chicks could hatch. The shorebirds' prey along the coast has less exposure to the harmful chemicals, so it has less effect on the peregrine eggs. An occasional coyote or deer may visit the island, but they don't stay long because there is no fresh water here.

Vegetation on the island is largely the shore grasses common to the northwestern coast. They provide both food and cover for the creatures that have moved onto what once was a barren island of silt and dredging spoils, only a short distance from a busy port, complete with industry and other human endeavors.

On the western side of Jetty Island, facing the sound, a flat, sandy 2-mile beach offers good walking as well as magnificent views of the sound, some of the sound's islands, and, in the background, the snow-clad peaks of the Olympic Mountains. Put a sailboat in the foreground and the picture becomes a classic, so visitors should take a camera. Shallow water on the west side of the island soaks up the sun, and the beach here becomes one of the few places on Puget Sound where the water is warm enough to be comfortable for wading or even swimming. But keep in mind, there are no lifeguards.

There is no camping on the island, so visitors must be at the boat dock before the last ferry leaves. Ferry hours are posted on both sides of the waterway.

Directions: The five-minute ferry ride begins at the Tenth Street Boat Launch and Marine Park. To reach the boat launch, take Marine View Drive north from downtown Everett to Tenth Street and drive west on Tenth Street to the end of the road.

Activities: Hiking, nature study, swimming.

Facilities: Trails, boat dock, picnic tables, restrooms are provided from Apr. through Oct.

Dates: The island is open year-round, but the ferry and ranger services are available only during the summer.

Fees: None.

Closest town: Everett.

For more information: Everett Parks and Recreation Department, Forest Park, 803 Mukilteo Boulevard, Everett, WA 98201. Phone (425) 257-8300.

LANGUS PARK/SPENCER ISLAND

[Fig. 12(3)] Part of this complex is an abandoned farm that Washington State and Snohomish County have jointly converted to a wild land of forest, wetland, and saltwater marsh where wildlife reign supreme and people may visit—quietly. That part of the complex is on Spencer Island. The other part is on Smith Island and Everett's 96-acre Langus Park. The main trail in that park extends to Spencer Island, following the Steamboat Slough of the Snohomish River. After about 1.5 miles, the wide, paved, bike, skate, pedestrian trail turns sharply to the left and follows Union Slough for another 2.1 miles. It passes, along the way, the footbridge to Spencer Island, where the trail is mostly dirt, wood chips, bark, and sawdust, interspersed here and there by boardwalks and bridges.

The Langus Park Trail, 3.6 miles long, one-way, from the parking lot to the dead end, has deep brush on one side and Snohomish River sloughs on the other side. The Snohomish is a working river, where workboats mingle with pleasure craft and with the shells of rowing teams that make the park their base. On the other side of the river, there are industrial installations. It is a nice walk and interesting, but not terribly natural. The trail has a number of benches where visitors can sit to eat a lunch or just watch the sloughs and their traffic.

That urban outdoors of paved walkway and benches changes abruptly when visitors cross the footbridge to Spencer Island. Bikes and dogs are banned because the island is reserved primarily for wildlife, including some 200 species of waterfowl and shorebirds. A few vestiges of the old farm remain; for instance, a badly deteriorated barn and shed and some remnants of fences and rusted farm machinery. But the island is essentially reclaimed wilderness. The dikes that kept the farmland dry have been breached, so the tide flows through the lowlands, creating salt marshes for many species. Another part of the island has freshwater wetlands fed by the river. The wetlands and marshes provide a haven where young salmon and steelhead hatched far up the Snohomish River can find refuge and ample nutrients while they grow and gain strength to go to Puget Sound and out to sea.

The northern part of the island is owned by the Washington Department of Fish and Wildlife and hunting is allowed in season. The southern part is managed by Snohomish County. There is no hunting here. A circular trail follows the perimeter of the island, allowing easy access between the jurisdictions and a nice walk through interesting country. Another trail, just south of the pedestrian bridge to the island, crosses the island between the east and west banks of the river. The southern trail is a 1.5-mile loop while the northern trail is a 2.5-mile loop.

The old farm, on rich floodplain soil, once supported some 400 head of cattle. Ocean tides affect Possession Sound, which in turn affects the Snohomish River so that it flows backwards at high tide. The farmers built dikes along the rim of the island to prevent the tide from flooding the island. The vegetation that had been on the island originally did not like the new stable water level, and the native plants died back in favor of plants that prefer an erratic water level. To prevent erosion, the farmers planted grass, which became the dominant plant on the island. It likes a stable water table, so the scientists who planned the conversion hope exposing it to tidal influence will eventually eliminate it. The stable water level also brought in deciduous trees that like those conditions. Eventually, the southern tip of the island was covered by a large stand of those trees. Breaching the dike caused the trees to die off and now they stand—dead, gray, and gaunt—along the southern bank of the island. The dead snags provide nesting and perching places for both birds and mammals. Bats, for instance, nest in tree cavities.

The plan for converting the island into wild land was intended to provide habitat for wildlife where the cattle once roamed. It succeeded. Hundreds of species use the island, some as a permanent home, others as a place to stop over during their migrations.

Among the birds are ducks and geese in large numbers. Others include the great horned owl (*Bubo virginianus*), which has large ear tufts that look like horns and give the owl its name; the American bittern (*Botaurus lenpiginosus*); the bald eagle; the red-tailed hawk (*Buteo jamaicensis*); the great blue heron (*Ardea herodias*); and innumerable songbirds, such as the robin (*Turdinae migratorius*) and American goldfinch (*Carduelis tristis*). The island also attracts large numbers of bird watchers who set up their spotting scopes along the trails.

Mammals on Spencer Island include deer, coyote, and busy beavers that spend their nights chewing through the trunks of trees until the trees fall. Then they eat the tender twigs and haul the branches to build dams and lodges on the streams.

The trail has overlooks here and there to give a view over the ponds, wetlands, and marshes. Included in the vegetation are vast fields of cattails (*Typha latifolia*) that Indians once used to weave into thick, spongy sleeping pads and other soft things.

GREAT BLUE HERON
(*Ardea herodias*)

Some also ate the rhizomes and inner basal stalks, raw or baked, or ground as flour. Now, on the island, the thick maze of stalks serves as protection for hatchlings of ducks and other birds that nest here. Other vegetation includes a vast multitude of mostly young western red alder (*Alnus rubra*), blackberry (*Rubus* sp.), and sedges (*Carex* sp.). Rushes on the shallow edge of the pond provide security for breeding birds, fish, frogs, salamanders, and insects. Mammals taking advantage of the cattails may include raccoons (*Procyon lotor*) and muskrats (*Ondatra zibethicus*). Butterflies and dragonflies may well be part of the cattail scenery, too.

Directions: Drive north on Everett's Broadway, crossing the Snohomish River Bridge where the road becomes State Route 529. A short distance from the bridge, turn right and follow the Langus Park signs on Ross Avenue, turning east on Smith Island Road. Pass the boat haven, then veer right and go a short distance to the park. The trail to Spencer Island is at the far end of the park, past the boat launch.

Activities: Hiking, nature study, and bird-watching.

Facilities: Langus Park has restrooms, extensive parking, a boat launch and picnic tables. Spencer Island has portable toilets and a bike rack just off the pedestrian bridge.

Dates: Open year-round.

Fees: There is a fee to use the Langus Park boat launch.

Closest town: Everett.

For more information: Everett Parks and Recreation Department, Forest Park, 803 Mukilteo Boulevard, Everett, WA 98201. Phone (425) 257-8300.

🌿 RESTAURANTS IN EVERETT

Restaurants in Everett run the full sweep from small to large and offbeat to upscale.

The Sisters Restaurant. 2804 Grand Avenue. This popular restaurant operates in a building that was a livery stable in early Everett, became a factory where the Boeing Company made bomber parts during World War II, and now is the Everett Public Market Building. The decor is plain, with mismatched furniture and bare brick walls hung with rough paintings. The menu varies with specials for breakfast and lunch, including delicious homemade soups, salads, quiche, veggie burgers, and espresso coffee. *Inexpensive. (425) 252-0480.*

Emory's Lake House Restaurant. 11830 19 Avenue Southeast. This upscale restaurant's tables look out on spacious Silver Lake. The menu features seafood, steaks, and pastas. There is a deck above the lake, a cocktail lounge, and a children's menu. *Inexpensive. (425) 337-7772.*

Trendy's by the Bay Restaurant. 1728 West Marine View Drive. This is a restaurant on the bay in the true sense. The windows look out on an outside dining area. Beyond that are a pedestrian walkway, a dock where large yachts may be tied up, the Snohomish River busy with boat traffic, Everett's Jetty island, Puget Sound, Hat Island, Whidbey Island, and the Olympic Mountains. On or above the water there may be geese, ducks, shorebirds, and there certainly will be seagulls. If someone throws out something edible, there will be hoards of seagulls. Inside, the menu includes a large assortment of luncheon platters, dinners of seafood, steak, chicken, pastas and daily specials. There is a piano lounge for cocktails. *Inexpensive. (425) 339-2233.*

Camas Restaurant. 1509 Wall Street. This gourmet restaurant is in a 1925 building that served as Everett's posh hotel for many decades. It eventually was replaced by modern facilities, but the heavy concrete walls and floors were so rugged that it was not feasible to demolish the building, so the city acquired it and converted the upper floors to senior citizen housing. The ground floor contains the Everett Cultural Commission's Center for

Whidbey Island

Whidbey Island is the longest island on the West Coast at 45 miles long.

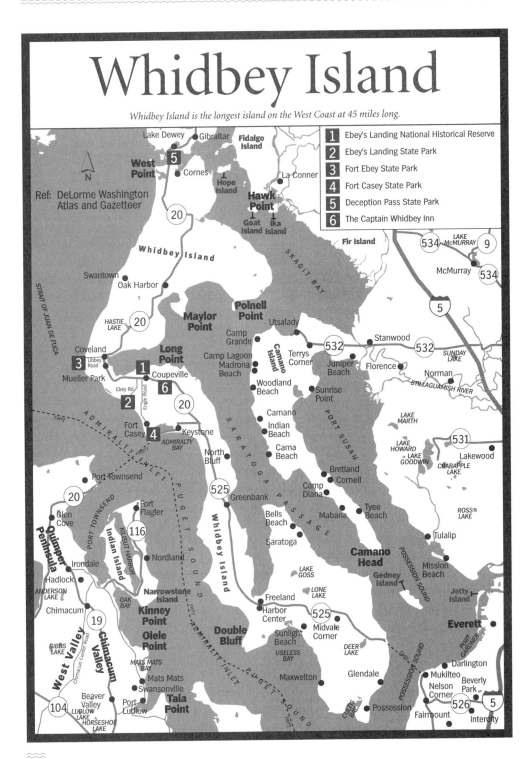

1	Ebey's Landing National Historical Reserve
2	Ebey's Landing State Park
3	Fort Ebey State Park
4	Fort Casey State Park
5	Deception Pass State Park
6	The Captain Whidbey Inn

Ref: DeLorme Washington Atlas and Gazetteer

N

Lake Dewey · Gibraltar · **Fidalgo Island**
West Point · Cornes · Hope Island · La Conner
Hawk Point · Goat Island · Ika Island
Fir Island
LAKE McMURRAY · 9
McMurray · 534
Whidbey Island
Swantown · Oak Harbor
STRAIT OF JUAN DE FUCA
HASTIE LAKE · 20
Maylor Point
Polnell Point · Utsalady
Camp Grande
Stanwood
532
532
SUNDAY LAKE
Coveland · **Long Point**
Camano Island
Terrys Corner
Juniper Beach
Florence
Norman
STILLAGUAMISH RIVER
Libbey Road · Coupeville
Camp Lagoon · Madrona Beach
Woodland Beach
Sunrise Point
Mueller Park
Ebey Rd · Engle Road
20
Camano
LAKE MARTH
531
Lakewood
Fort Casey · Keystone
ADMIRALTY BAY
Indian Beach
Cama Beach
PORT SUSAN
LAKE HOWARD · LAKE GOODWIN
CRABAPPLE LAKE
North Bluff
Bretland
Cornell
Port Townsend
525
Greenbank
Camp Diana
ROSS LAKE
20
Glen Cove
Quimper Peninsula
Fort Flagler
116
Indian Island
Nordland
Bells Beach
Saratoga
Mabana
Tyee Beach
Tulalip
Camano Head
Mission Beach
Gedney Island
Jetty Island
Irondale
Hadlock
ANDERSON LAKE
OAK BAY
Narrowstone Island
LAKE GOSS
LONE LAKE
Freeland
Everett
Chimacum
19
Kinney Point
Harbor Center
525
Midvale Corner
Olele Point
Double Bluff
Sunlight Beach
DEER LAKE
Darlington
GIBBS LAKE
West Valley · **Chimacum Valley**
MATS MATS BAY
USELESS BAY
Maxwelton
Glendale
Mukilteo
Nelson Corner
Beverly Park
Mats Mats
Swansonville
104
Beaver Valley
LUDLOW LAKE
Port Ludlow
Tala Point
Possession
Fairmount
526
5
Intercity
HORSESHOE LAKE
SKAGIT BAY
SARATOGA PASSAGE
ADMIRALTY INLET
PUGET SOUND
PORT TOWNSEND
KILISUT HARBOR
Whidbey Island
POSSESSION SOUND
PORT GARDNER
CULTUS BAY
20
534
5

the Arts, including rooms full of art objects. Adjacent to the arts center, the former ballroom still houses large social functions, and, in a corner with a separate entrance, the Camas Restaurant maintains the original, early twentieth century decor, including lots of marble. It offers gourmet soups, salads, chicken, prawns, seafood, steaks, pasta, and a delicious Thai veggie wrap. There is a cocktail lounge. *Inexpensive.* (425) 347-6995.

LODGING IN EVERETT

As in many of the communities on the eastern shore of Puget Sound, hotel chains along I-5 provide most of the lodging possibilities, but there still are some nice places elsewhere in the city.

Marina Village Inn. 1728 West Marine View Drive. This is a deluxe, waterfront motel that caters to guests who arrive by car or by boats that dock in the nearby harbor. Rooms facing west have bay windows that look out on the busy harbor and Jetty Island, as well as Puget Sound and the Olympic Mountains. Those rooms are equipped with telescopes. The rooms facing east have a view of the upscale Marina Village waterfront mall. Some rooms have whirlpools. Complimentary breakfast. Reservations recommended. *Moderate to expensive.* (425) 259-4040.

Everett Inn. 12619 Fourth Avenue West. This three-story motel with 72 rooms is near I-5 Exit 186 and caters largely to highway traffic. Some rooms have whirlpools. All rooms have refrigerators and coffee makers. *Moderate.* (425) 347-9099.

Gaylord House. 3301 Grand Avenue in Everett. With five guest rooms, this bed and breakfast is on a tree-lined residential street within walking distance of downtown Everett. The handsome two-story building dates from 1910, but the rooms have telephones and baths, and one room has a gas fireplace. A full hot breakfast is served. *Moderate to expensive.* (425) 339-9153.

Farwest Motel. 6030 Evergreen Way. This motel in a business area has 20 rooms, including a two-bedroom unit. Some units have kitchenettes and weekly rates are available. *Inexpensive.* (425) 355-3007.

Whidbey Island

[Fig. 13] This pleasant, rural island is the longest on the West Coast and is situated about halfway up Puget Sound from Olympia, across from the mouth of the Strait of Juan de Fuca. The second longest island in the United States, behind Long Island in New York State, it is 45 miles long, but no place on the island is more than 5 miles from salt water. Whidbey Island totals some 208 square miles.

The island was first noted by Spanish explorers but was actually explored by Joseph Whidbey, an officer with George Vancouver's exhibition in 1792. Whidbey discovered Deception Pass on the north end, establishing that it was an island, and Vancouver named it after him.

Colonel Isaac Ebey was the first permanent settler on the island. He led a wagon train to the Oregon Territory, located in Olympia for a time, and then, in 1850, wandered up to the island in a canoe. A lawyer, he served in numerous governmental offices, including the territorial legislature, and as the commander of a company of volunteers during an Indian uprising in 1855. His 640-acre land claim, 2 miles southwest of where Coupeville is now, was on a broad, sloping lowland with a magnificent view of the Strait of Juan de Fuca and the Olympic Peninsula. His land is now a state park (*see* Ebey's Landing State Park, page 86), and part of the Ebey's Landing National Historical Reserve. He and others developed farms here.

The Indians of what now is Washington State were generally peaceful, but groups from Canada periodically raided them for booty and slaves. In August 1854, a group from the north was camped on the Olympic Peninsula and a U.S. Navy ship was dispatched to send them home. The Indians refused to leave and the ship fired on them, killing a chief. The survivors went home, but they returned the following year seeking revenge on any eminent white man they could find. They went to Ebey's home at night, and when he opened the door they shot him, beheaded him, and took his head home to Canada. The head eventually was returned to be buried with his body in a cemetery near his home.

The island population grew considerably during the eighteenth and nineteenth centuries, but it remains largely rural with a handful of small towns scattered here and there. The largest of the towns is Oak Harbor, with 20,500 residents near the north end of the island. It is the home of the Whidbey Island Naval Air Station, and many of the residents in the north part of the island are active duty or retired navy people. The other towns have less than 2,000 residents each, but there are numerous lodging places ranging from hotels and motels to quaint bed and breakfasts.

There are patches of towering old growth forests of Douglas fir and western redcedar, tall second-growth forest, wetlands, meadows of wildflowers, lakes, cattail marshes, rocky and sandy beaches, a sheltered lagoon, prairies, and brackish lakes. All of these provide habitat for innumerable kinds of wildlife, including waterfowl, raptors, fish, whales, songbirds, mammals, tidepool creatures, and many others.

The island lies in the rain shadow of the Olympic Mountains and tends to get less rain than other parts of the Puget Sound trough. Temperature variation from winter to summer is minimal.

Directions: To reach the south end, take the Mukilteo/Clinton ferry from Mukilteo. To reach the west central area, take the Port Townsend/Keystone ferry from Port Townsend on the Olympic Peninsula. To reach the north end, drive cross the Deception Pass Bridge, which is about 12 miles west of I-5 Exit 230 on State Route 20.

Activities: Camping, hiking, beach walking, wildlife watching, crabbing, fishing, picnicking, kite flying, wind surfing, scuba-diving, bicycling, boating.

Facilities: Eight state parks, lodging, dining, historical sites, lighthouses.

EBEY'S LANDING NATIONAL HISTORICAL RESERVE

[Fig. 13(1)] This 20-square-mile reserve is the first of its kind in the nation. It was created by Congress in 1978 and is managed by the National Park Service to maintain the natural and cultural appearance of the community, which is reminiscent of the 1800s. It extends to the shores on both sides of the island and includes farms, prairies, forests, the sheltered bay of Penn Cove, three state parks, and the quaint town of Coupeville. Much of the reserve is private property, and some 9,000 people live there.

The people who settled the area built five log blockhouses for protection. Four of them still exist in the reserve, although only one is still in its original location. That one is on private property. The others, however, are open to the public.

Directions: The reserve lies on both sides of State Route 20 about 30 miles from the ferry landing in Clinton.

Activities: Hiking, biking, camping, beach walking, nature study, fishing, boating.

Facilities: State parks, shops, restaurants, lodging, beaches, historical places.

Dates: Open year-round.

Fees: None.

Closest town: Coupeville.

For more information: Ebey's Landing National Historical Reserve, PO Box 774, Coupeville, WA 98239. Phone (360) 678-6084.

COUPEVILLE

[Fig. 13] Looking down the main business street of this little town of 1,600 persons, you could imagine you are in a Victorian era American village. This is the second oldest town in Washington, after Olympia, and the attractive, wooden, false-front buildings have the look and flavor of times past.

Thomas Coupe, a sea captain from New England who registered a claim for 320 acres, founded the town in 1852. The town lies on the sheltered Penn Cove, and Coupe recognized the location's potential as a deep-water port for the sailing ships of the time. Puget Sound was the main route of travel for both freight and passengers, and Coupeville was a central location with easy access to the other parts of the sound. Soon the town was a thriving moorage for as many as a dozen ocean-going, square-rigged ships that transferred their freight and passengers to the smaller vessels that sailed the sound.

Around the end of the nineteenth century, railroads arrived in the Puget Sound region and a few years later, highways and automobiles followed. Sea traffic moved to the mainland and Coupeville became a pleasant backwater that remains much like it was in the past. Now there are some 100 buildings in the vicinity on the National Register of Historic Places.

The quaint, wooden buildings of the little business district are adjacent to Penn Cove and offer a variety of goods and services such as books, food, collectibles, woodcrafts, and jewelry. Visitors mainly browse through the shops and enjoy the slower, quieter atmosphere of long ago times.

Directions: Just north of State Route 20 in the Ebey's Landing National Historical Reserve.

Activities: Beach walking, nature study, fishing, boating, shopping.

Facilities: Shops, restaurants, wharf, historic places.

For more information: Ebey's Landing National Historical Reserve, PO Box 774, Coupeville, WA 98239. Phone (360) 678-6084.

THE CAPTAIN WHIDBEY INN

[Fig. 13(6)] This is one of some 20 places that offer accommodations in the Coupeville area. The main building of the pleasant, old-American Captain Whidbey Inn was built in 1907 and is on the National Register of Historic Places, but the accommodations are modern and comfortable and the setting is ideal. There are 25 rooms in the quaint lodge as well as rustic cottages and conference facilities for up to 25 persons. There are outstanding views of Penn Cove from the wooded grounds. Room prices are moderate to expensive. A restaurant in the main building offers three-course and five-course dinners, reservations required. Restaurant prices are moderate.

Directions: From Coupeville go 3.5 miles east on State Route 20. Turn south on Madrone Way for 0.8 mile to Captain Whidbey Road.

Activities: Beach walking, kayaking, sailing charters, boating, golf, horseback riding, carriage rides.

Facilities: Lodge, cabins, restaurant.

Dates: Open year round. Food service is on weekends only from October until June.

Closest town: Coupeville, 3.5 miles.

For more information: Captain Whidbey Inn, 2072 W. Captain Whidbey Road, Coupeville, WA 98239. Phone (360) 678-4097 or (800) 366-4097.

EBEY'S LANDING STATE PARK

[Fig. 13(2)] This 45-acre park has 120 feet of beach on the Strait of Juan de Fuca, on land that once belonged to Isaac Ebey and includes the site of the home where he was killed by Indians raiding from far north in Canada. A mildly steep loop trail climbs to a pleasant bluff just off the state park and onto Ebey's Landing National Historical Reserve. The trail follows the bluff for 1 mile before leading down a series of switchbacks to the beach and past the Perego Lagoon and back to the park. Another trail leads from the parking lot for 1 mile up the slope through Ebey's property to the cemetery where he is buried. Near the cemetery is one of the blockhouses settlers built for protection from Indian raiders.

Directions: Go 0.2 mile west of Coupeville on State Route 20, turn south on Ebey Road and go about 2.7 miles.

Activities: Beach walking, hiking, surf fishing.

Facilities: Trails, restroom.

Dates: Open year round.

Fees: None.

Closest town: Coupeville, 3 miles.

For more information: Contact Fort Ebey State Park, 395 North Fort Ebey Road, Coupeville, WA 98239. Phone (360) 678-4636.

FORT EBEY STATE PARK

[Fig. 13(3)] This 644-acre park began as an addition to the Puget Sound coastal defenses during World War II era. After the Japanese bombed Pearl Harbor, they went on to numerous conquests for the first year of the war in the Pacific. The American military worried that they could slip a few ships through the Strait of Juan de Fuca and cause havoc with the exposed facilities in Puget Sound. Three Spanish-American War-era forts on Whidbey Island and the Olympic Peninsula had been largely dismantled during World War I, so the Army built this fort to reinforce the defense system. During World War II, experience showed that aircraft and carrier ships had made coastal forts obsolete and the forts were abandoned to become state parks.

The heavy, concrete fortifications are still here, providing an eerie echo of the days when soldiers and construction people swarmed over the grounds. They are interesting places to explore for people with flashlights.

The park is on a bluff above the beach, but trails lead down to more than 1.5 miles of beach on the Strait of Juan de Fuca. There is camping in the park with reservations accepted during the summer. Phone (800) 452-5687 for reservations.

Hiker/biker trails in the park lead to various interesting places, including a series of land depressions east of the park left 15,000 years ago when the Ice Age glaciers receded. The depressions are called Ebey's Kettles and the route here is also a horse trail. One of the beach trails goes to the Point Partridge Lighthouse, which is interesting from the outside but is not open to the public. Another beach trail goes to a campground on the Cascadia Marine Trail used by kayakers to paddle to numerous similar campgrounds in the sound. Another trail goes along the bluff above the beach, affording magnificent views and leading to the campground, gun battery, and forested areas.

Bald eagles roost in snags near Lake Pondilla in the northern section of the park. Both eagles and anglers go after bass in the lake. Much of the park is covered by second-growth forest and has mammals such as deer, squirrels, and otters living here. Birds reside here as well, including pileated woodpeckers (*Dryocopus pileatus*), kinglets (*Regulus calendula*), and brown creepers (*Certhia americana*), which climb trees, starting at the bottom and working upward while probing the bark with their thin bills in search of tasty insects.

Directions: Take State Route 20 south from Oak Harbor for 5.8 miles then turn west on Libbey Road. Go about 1 mile, then turn south on Hill Valley Drive for about 0.5 mile.

Activities: Camping, hiking, picnicking, biking, beach walking, fishing, paragliding, horseback riding, kayaking.

Facilities: 42-two standard campsites, 3 primitive campsites, Cascadia Marine Trail campsites, group campsite, picnic sites, restrooms, showers, 3 miles of trails, lighthouse, abandoned fortifications.

Dates: The day-use area is open year-round. Campgrounds are open from Mar. to Nov.

Fees: Fees are charged for camping.

Closest town: Oak Harbor, about 7 miles.

For more information: Fort Ebey State Park, 395 North Fort Ebey Road, Coupeville, WA 98239. Phone (360) 678-4636.

FORT CASEY STATE PARK

[Fig. 13(4)] This 142-acre complex of coastal artillery fortifications was built about the time of the Spanish-American War and equipped with huge artillery guns designed to sink any enemy ships that might try to slip into Puget Sound. Forts Worden and Flagler were positioned on the Olympic Peninsula to provide triangular fire against the invaders. By World War I, the heavy guns at the forts were declared obsolete for use against modern, heavily armored war ships, and the main guns were removed and converted to railway guns. Fort Casey remained in operation as a training ground for troops, and as an anti-aircraft base through World War II, then it was given to the state as a park. After the war, some guns similar to the original armament were brought to Camp Casey from abandoned forts in the Philippines and installed in the Fort Casey emplacements, complete with the scars from the Japanese bombs that put them out of action.

The battery emplacements, concrete fire control stations, and underground rooms with thin slits that allowed the troops to track targets sailing past, are all fascinating reminders of days long gone. They also are great places for youngsters to play. Altogether, there are nine battery emplacements, as well as the underground facilities for troops, ammunition, and equipment. There are lights in the interior of Battery Worth, but flashlights are needed in the total darkness behind the heavy steel doors of the other underground places.

The park has an interpretive trail, campgrounds, picnic sites, 8,000 feet of beach on Admiralty Inlet, and an underwater park for scuba-diving along an offshore reef. The handsome Admiralty Head Lighthouse near the north end of the park is now an interpretive center, with displays on the history of the fort and natural history of Whidbey Island. The original lighthouse was built in 1861, and relocated a short distance inland when the fort was established. The lighthouse is open for irregular hours during the summer months.

The old barracks, officers' quarters, and warehouses on the north end of the fort are now used as an extension campus by Seattle Pacific University. The landing for the Keystone/Port Townsend ferry is just east of the park and there is a boat ramp nearby. Crocket Lake, located just north of the ferry landing, is a 250-acre shallow marsh that serves as a rest stop for multitudes of migrating waterfowl, including ducks and geese. A spit at the ferry landing has fresh water on one side, salt water on the other side, and fresh winds on both sides. It is a good place for kite flying.

Directions: Turn south onto Engle Road from State Route 20 at Coupeville and go 3 miles to the park. Or take the Port Townsend/Keystone ferry.

Activities: Camping, hiking, picnicking, beach walking, scuba-diving, fishing, boating.

Facilities: Historic coastal fortifications, campgrounds, trails, lighthouse, picnic sites, boat launch, underwater park.

Dates: Open year-round.

Fees: None

Closest town: Coupeville, 3 miles.

For more information: Fort Casey State Park, 1280 Engle Road, Coupeville, WA 98239. Phone (360) 678-4519.

DECEPTION PASS STATE PARK

[Fig. 13(5)] This 3,158-acre park is a conglomeration of campgrounds, day-use areas, trails, lakes, forests, offshore islands, and saltwater beaches.

A major attraction to the park is the Deception Pass Bridge that leads to it. The high, graceful bridge looks down on the narrow passage between Rosario Strait on the Strait of Juan de Fuca and Skagit Bay on Puget Sound. The scene from the bridge is of the sea with the rocky, forested land on both sides. When the tide changes, the sea rushes through the constricted passage at great speed. Often motorboats try to buck the current at full speed, sending up a large bow wave, but making almost no headway. Under-powered boats find shelter in nearby Bowman Bay or Coronet Bay to wait for slack tide.

There are cabins, Adirondack shelters, campsites, and kitchen shelters throughout the park. The saltwater shoreline stretches for some 15 miles, offering ample place for beachcombing and exploring. There is fishing and boating in the lakes and the sea. Gasoline motors are banned from the lakes. Some 25 miles of trails wander through the park, taking visitors to and from campgrounds, forests, lakes, beaches, and other attractions. This is not a place to go to be alone; as many as 3.5 million people a year visit the park. Campsite reservations are recommended.

The park is divided into eight separate areas based on lakes, beaches, and other natural centers. Trails and/or roads give access between those on land. Several are on islands and require boats for access.

Northwest Island and Urchin Rocks on Rosario Bay in the northwest section of the park has an underwater park and tidepools where visitors may see but not remove the creatures that live there.

Much of the original preparation of the park was done by the federal Civilian Conservation Corps, which gave young men jobs during the Depression of the 1930s. One of the structures the corps built now contains information on the CCC program. Another is used as an environmental learning center. Despite the number of human visitors, there are many kinds of wildlife in the park, including deer, shorebirds, songbirds, fish, and tidepool creatures. Heart Lake is stocked with rainbow trout and is popular with anglers.

Directions: Turn off I-5 at exit 230 and drive west on State Route 20 about 19 miles to the north entrance to the park. Or take the Mukilteo/Clinton ferry and follow State Route 525, which becomes State Route 20 for 44 miles to the south entrance.

Activities: Camping, hiking, beach walking, boating, picnicking, paragliding, scuba-diving, biking, fishing.

Facilities: Individual and group campgrounds with standard, primitive, and RV sites, pumpout stations, picnic sites, interpretive center, trails, restrooms, showers, cabins, kitchen shelters, boat launches.

Dates: Open year round, but some facilities may be closed during the winter.

Fees: Fees are charged for camping and some services.

Closest town: Oak Harbor, about 10 miles.

For more information: Deception Pass State Park, 5175 North State Highway 20, Oak Harbor, WA 98277. Phone (360) 675-2417.

RESTAURANTS ON WHIDBEY ISLAND

Whidbey is a long, narrow island with sparse population. Unlike the mainland a few miles away, it does not have major highways that attract large chains to offer food and drink to hungry, weary travelers. As a result, there is a multitude of small, independent places to eat and rest that, for now at least, have not been driven away by larger competitors with national or international reputations. Some are listed here in geographical order, starting from the bridge to the mainland on the north end of the island.

Island Grill. 41020 State Route 20. This restaurant near Deception Pass north of Oak Harbor offers several versions of burger, steak and seafood dishes, salad, and pasta. There are menus for children and senior citizens. *Inexpensive.* (360) 679-3194.

Kasteel Franssen Restaurant. 33575 Highway 20 in the Auld Holland Inn. This restaurant with a cultivated Dutch ambiance offers classic Northwestern, French, American, and Dutch cuisine. There is a cocktail lounge. Reservations recommended. *Inexpensive.* (360) 675-0724.

Captain's Galley. 10 Front Street in Coupeville. With a view of Penn Cove, this establishment serves poultry, pasta, seafood, and beef. There is a cocktail lounge. Reservations recommended. *Inexpensive. (360) 678-0241.*

LODGING ON WHIDBEY ISLAND

As with the restaurants, lack of a major highway tends discourage large hotels on Whidbey Island, and results in a majority of the lodging places being independent small motels or bed and breakfasts.

The Auld Holland Inn. 33575 State Route 20 north of Oak Harbor. This two-story, 34-room motel with attractive European ornamentation has antique furnishings in the rooms, including the suite in a windmill. Some rooms have fireplaces. There is a heated swimming pool, a steam room, a whirlpool, a playground, a tennis court, and a dining room. *Inexpensive to moderate. (360) 675-2288.*

Acorn Motor Inn. 31530 State Route 20 in Oak Harbor. This motel is close to the beach, and it has 26 clean comfortable rooms. There is a restaurant nearby. *Inexpensive to moderate. (360) 675-6646.*

Queen Ann Motel. 450 Southeast Pioneer Way in Oak Harbor. With 21 rooms, this motel offers a variety of lodging, including two-bedroom units and kitchens. There are a heated indoor pool, a whirlpool, and a restaurant with a cocktail lounge. *Moderate. (360) 675-2209.*

Compass Rose. 508 South Main Street in Coupeville. This 1890 two-story Victorian-style home is on the National Register of Historical Places. It has impressive woodwork and is furnished with art and antiques from around the world. *Moderate. (800) 237-3881 or (360) 678-5318.*

The Victorian Bed and Breakfast. 602 North Main Street in Coupeville. A restored, 1889 Italianate Victorian Home that is listed on the National Registry of Historical Places, this bed and breakfast has three units, one with two bedrooms. All units have baths. A complimentary breakfast is served. *Moderate. (360) 678-5305.*

Garden Isle Guest Cottages. 207 Northwest Coveland Street in Coupeville. This establishment has two guest cottages, one with a fireplace. There is a hot tub and the view includes snow-clad Mount Baker. The rooms have shower baths and kitchens. *Moderate. (360) 678-5641.*

The Coupeville Inn. 200 Coveland Street in Coupeville. This motel has 24 rooms, many with a balcony looking down on downtown Coupeville and Penn Cove. All rooms have baths and there is a restaurant nearby. *Moderate. (360) 678-6668.*

Old Morris Farm Inn. 105 West Morris Road, near Coupeville. This two-story home started as a farmhouse built in 1909. It still has a country setting. There are four guest rooms, all with baths. The public rooms are elegantly bedecked. There are a gift shop and hiking trails. *Moderate. (360) 678-6586.*

The Inn at Penn Cove. 702 North Main in Coupeville. This bed and breakfast is in two side-by-side homes, one built in 1887, the other in 1891. Each home has three comfortable guest rooms. *Moderate. Phone (360) 678-8000.*

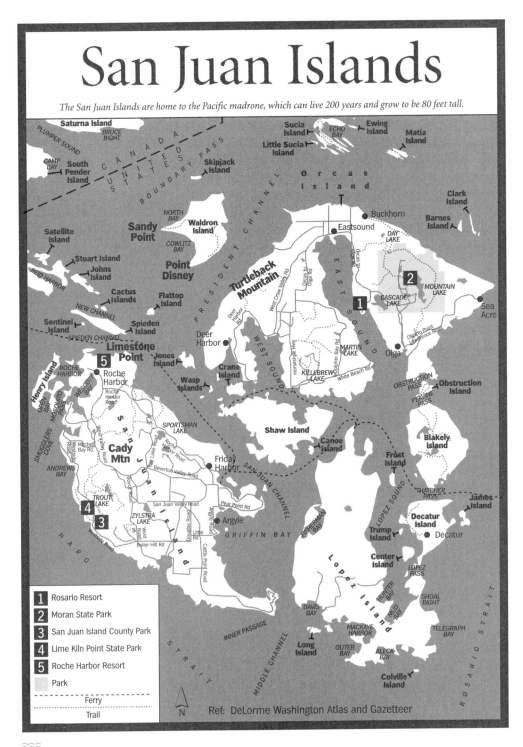

San Juan Islands

The San Juan Islands are home to the Pacific madrone, which can live 200 years and grow to be 80 feet tall.

Legend:

1 Rosario Resort
2 Moran State Park
3 San Juan Island County Park
4 Lime Kiln Point State Park
5 Roche Harbor Resort
Park
Ferry
Trail

Ref: DeLorme Washington Atlas and Gazetteer

Guest House Bed and Breakfast. 24371 State Route 525, near Greenbank. This facility on 25 acres of forest and meadow has six cottages and a lodge. All rooms have a kitchen, and a fireplace, and some have porches. There are a heated pool and a whirlpool. *Expensive. (360) 678-3115.*

Harbour Inn Motel. 1606 Main Street in Freeland. This motel has 20 rooms, ranging from small to spacious. The lawn has both picnic tables and horseshoe pits. *Moderate. Phone (360) 331-6900.*

San Juan Islands

[Fig. 14] When the glaciers of the most recent Ice Age gouged out the trough that forms the Strait of Georgia and Puget Sound, they collided with some formidable, rocky mountains. That didn't stop them. They rode over the top, scraping, grinding, and polishing the hard rock as they pushed on pressing with the weight of 0.5 mile of ice. Even the highest of the mountains in the trough, Mount Constitution on Orcas Island, was smoothed by ice skidding over its peak, some 0.5 mile above today's sea level.

The ice lowered and changed the mountains, but it failed to eliminate them. When it receded and the trough filled with water from the Pacific Ocean, the mountain peak remained as the magnificently beautiful San Juan Islands in the Strait of Georgia, just north of where it meets Puget Sound.

There is still considerable discussion of how many islands there are. Some are simply rocks that jut out of the water at low tide, and there is a question about whether they are islands at all. Others are one island at low tide, but become two or more when the tide rises, covering low channels to divide the single island into several. So, at low tide some count 768 islands, reefs, and rocks. At high tide, they say, there are only 457, but some don't have names. And 84 of them have been set aside as the San Juan Islands National Wildlife Refuge, where wildlife is protected from unnatural disturbance and human visitors are not allowed. Other islands have state parks. Some are marine parks, accessible only by private boat. Others have drive-in parks on islands accessible by state ferries. Still others are undeveloped property of the State Parks and Recreation Commission where people can go for a very primitive visit.

The islands with marine parks are Sucia, James, Patos, Turn, Matia, Clark, Jones, Stuart, Doe, Posey, and Blind. They are popular for activities such as scuba-diving, exploring, camping, picnicking, bird-watching, hiking, swimming, fishing, and crabbing.

Some islands are occupied permanently by residents who come and go by private boat. Other larger islands are occupied permanently and are accessible by state ferries. They are places where people have homes, farms, and businesses, mostly tourist related. The primary means of travel between the larger islands are airplane, boat, and ferry, with ferries probably being the most popular. The terminal for the San Juan ferry is Anacortes on the mainland. The ferries travel to four of the larger islands with daily extensions to Sidney on Vancouver Island in British Columbia. The trip between Anacortes and Sidney takes about 3 hours and 15 minutes, one way. There are numerous runs through the day but the ferries do not stop at all the islands on any run and there are special requirements for loading at the different ferry landings. Call Washington State Ferry System for specific information. Two of the islands, Orcas and San Juan, are oriented toward visitors and have moderately ample lodging and food options. The facilities, however, are often filled, so visitors who do not have reservations and miss the last ferry may spend the night in their car. Lopez and Shaw have few amenities for visitors, although Lopez is relatively flat and has few cars, so it attracts some people on bicycles.

The San Juans have Spanish names because unlike Puget Sound to the south, the Strait of Georgia was explored by the Spanish who had a settlement at Nootka on the west side of Vancouver Island. The Spanish, however, eventually drew back to their permanent settlements far to the south, but the Spanish names stuck.

The islands have large stands of evergreen forest dominated by Douglas fir similar to the forests of the rest of Western Washington. But in the lowlands, they also have numerous Pacific madrone (*Arbutus menziesii*), which has a paper-like bark that it sheds in ragged, crisp strips. The bark is greenish on younger trees but becomes orange, then brownish as the tree grows. The colorful madrone has large, shiny leaves and pink flowers. They may live for 200 years and reach as much as 80 feet tall. Their pea-sized fruit is a favorite for birds, which drop the seeds and spread the trees wherever they go. Other plants of the islands include wild roses (*Rosa sp.*), salal (*Gaultheria shallon*) and Oregon grape (*Berbis nervosa*). The Oregon grape berries were pounded into cakes by the Lummi Indians, who frequented the islands. Now the berries are used to make jellies.

There are hawks on the islands, and bald eagles sit patiently, aware that the common European rabbit (*Oryctolagus cuniculi*) is available when needed for a meal. Along the shore there are cormorants (*Phalacrocorax* sp.), clams, sea anemones, and starfish. Harbor seals and sea lions may be resting on rocks near the shore, and three pods of orca whales ply these waters. Those who study whales say each of the pods has its own dialect that members use to communicate with each other. Mink and gray whales may also be seen from time to time.

Directions: The ferry leaves from the terminal at Anacortes. Take exit 230 from I-5 and go about 10 miles west on State Route 20, then turn right on March Road and immediately turn right again onto South March Road. Park in the free park and ride lot and take the shuttle to the ferry. To take a car onto the ferry, drive 8.3 miles past the park and ride lot to the terminal. There also is a small, pay parking lot at the terminal but it often is full long before the ferry leaves. Note: There are few facilities for pedestrians at the island ferry landings, except on San Juan Island where the town of Friday Harbor is adjacent to the landing.

Activities: Camping, picnicking, beach walking, crabbing, fishing, bird-watching, whale watching, kayaking, canoeing, motorboating, sailing.

Facilities: Campgrounds, trails, picnic tables. San Juan and Orcas islands have extensive lodging and restaurants. Other islands have visitor facilities ranging from a simple state park to nothing at all.

Closest town: Anacortes in Washington, Sidney in British Columbia.

For more information: Washington State Ferries, phone (800) 833-6388.

ORCAS ISLAND

[Fig. 14] With some 56 square miles, this is the largest of the San Juan Islands, although it has a little smaller population than San Juan Island. It is U shaped with West Sound cutting deeply into the south shore to nearly divide the island in two. There are several small villages on the island with lodging and restaurants.

ROSARIO RESORT

[Fig. 14(1)] A major attraction on Orcas Island is the Rosario Resort. Rosario was built as a mansion during the first decade of the twentieth century by millionaire Robert Moran, who had arrived in Seattle in 1874 at the age of 17 with 10 cents in his pocket. He worked on steamboats, started a marine repair shop and parlayed it into a major shipyard, and served as mayor of Seattle at the same time. In 1904, while the shipyard was building the navy battleship *Nebraska*, he developed health problems and retired to build Rosario on a point of land that juts into the island's Eastsound.

He lived in the mansion until he sold it in 1939. It went through several hands, until it was converted into a resort after 1960. Moran built the 54-room mansion with concrete walls set 16 feet into solid rock. The solid Honduran mahogany doors are so heavy Moran invented a special hinge for them. The windows are nearly 1-inch-thick plate glass, and the roofing consists of 6 tons of copper sheeting. There is a music room with a stained-glass window and a pipe organ with 1,972 pipes. The music room is part of a second floor museum that includes the library, photographs, and furnishings from the early 1900s.

The resort has an inexpensive restaurant overlooking the bay and a cocktail lounge. There is a marina with a separate restaurant, and there are newer lodging buildings separate from the mansion. Pricing for lodging is moderate to expensive. There is a golf course and a major state park nearby. A horse stable and other attractions are available on and near the grounds. The *Morning Star*, a two-masted sailing ship takes guests on short cruises.

Directions: By private boat, sail to the marina on Orcas Island's Eastsound village. By car, take the Horseshoe Highway 3 miles from Eastsound. The resort is at 1400 Rosario Road.

Activities: Lodging, dining, golf, bicycling, lawn games, sailing, shopping, fishing, whale watching, tennis, horseback riding, health spa activities.

Dates: Open year-round.

Closest town: Eastsound, 3 miles.

For more information: Rosario Resort, 1400 Rosario Road, Eastsound, WA 98245. Phone (800) 562-8820 or (360) 376-2222.

MORAN STATE PARK

[Fig. 14(2)] This 5,252-acre park is part of the land Robert Moran gave to the state when he built his nearby mansion. The main feature of the park is 2,400-foot Mount Constitution, the highest spot in the San Juans. A stone view tower at the peak adds to the elevation and the interest. It is a replica of a feudal fortress from medieval Eastern Europe, and provides a view of the San Juans in every direction.

The park's saltwater shoreline is difficult to get to, but there are several lakes with a total of 45,000 feet of shore. Two of the lakes are stocked with trout. There are boat ramps, but gasoline motors are banned. The park is largely covered by Douglas fir forest, and there are 45 miles of trails interwoven through the park, ranging from level to steep. Some of the trails are open to horses and bicycles, but that varies with the season.

There are campgrounds with a total of 136 standard campsites and 15 hiker/biker campsites, but the park is very popular. It is often filled to capacity and reservations are highly recommended. An environmental learning center has cabins and other buildings for up to 150 persons. Phone (800) 452-5687 for reservations.

Directions: From the Orcas Island ferry landing take the Horseshoe Highway to Eastsound, and then go east and south to the park entrance, distance about 13 miles.

Activities: Camping, hiking, picnicking, swimming, fishing, boating, bird-watching.

Facilities: Campgrounds, beaches, food service, boat rentals, trails, mountaintop observation tower, restrooms, showers, boat ramp, and docks.

Dates: Open year-round.

Fees: Fees are charged for camping, boat rental, and for use of a group facility with a swimming beach and dock.

Closest town: Eastsound, 3 miles.

For more information: Moran State Park, 3572 Olga Road, Eastsound, WA 98252. Phone (360) 376-2326.

RESTAURANTS ON ORCAS ISLAND

Being isolated from the outside world means that places to eat tend to be small and highly individualistic. But that doesn't mean that good food is not available.

Bilbos' Festivo. On North Beach Road in Eastsound. This restaurant with a Mexican influence features grilling on a mesquite fire. All menu items are home made. A specialty cocktail is margaritas made with freshly squeezed lime juice. Children's menu. Reservations recommended. *Inexpensive.* (360) 376-4728.

Christina's. 1 Main Street in Eastsound. This restaurant has tremendous views of Puget Sound. Inside, the menu offerings include northwestern style seafood and steak in an elegant setting. There is a cocktail lounge. Reservations recommended. *Inexpensive to moderate.* (360) 376-4904.

Orcas Hotel Fireside Lounge. This restaurant in the Orcas Hotel above the island's ferry landing serves fresh seafood prepared with local ingredients. The dining room has an attractive Victorian ambiance. There is a cocktail lounge and a children's menu. Reservations recommended. *Inexpensive. (360) 376-4300.*

LODGING ON ORCAS ISLAND

Lodging on the island is offered primarily by a multitude of bed and breakfast establishments but there are a few larger places. It is a good idea to make reservations in advance because if all the rooms are full and the last ferry has left, there literally will be no place to stay.

The Orcas Hotel. Located above the island's ferry landing. This three story Victorian structure dates from the early 1900s and is on the National Register of Historic Places. There are nice views of Harney Channel and nearby Shaw Island. The building has been extensively restored and includes both older rooms with shared baths and larger, more luxurious rooms with a whirlpool in the private bath. *Moderate to expensive. (360) 376-4300.*

Deer Harbor Inn. On Deer Harbor Road, 8 miles southwest of the Ferry Landing. This lodge with early American furnishings overlooks Deer Harbor Bay. It has 8 guest rooms in a modern log building. There also are three cottages with gas fireplaces and an outdoor whirlpool. There is a restaurant on the property. Private baths. *Moderate to expensive. (360) 376-4110*

Cascade Harbor Inn. 1800 Rosario Way in Eastsound. The 45 rooms in this two-story motel all have a view of the harbor. Some rooms have kitchens. There is a heated swimming pool. *Moderate to expensive. (360) 376-6350.*

Outlook Inn on Orcas Island. On Main Street in Downtown Eastsound. This is a two-story, early twentieth century motor inn with a Victorian flavor. There are 45 rooms. Those in the original building have shared baths. There also are luxury suites with private baths, bay views, and private balconies. Some rooms have whirlpools. There is a dining room with a cocktail lounge. *Moderate to expensive. (360) 376-2200.*

BED AND BREAKFASTS ON ORCAS ISLAND

Kangaroo House Bed and Breakfast. On North Beach Road, 1 mile north of Eastsound Village. This establishment has 5 guest rooms in a two-story, 1907 home that reflects an early twentieth century atmosphere. *Moderate to expensive. Phone (888) 371-2175 or (360) 376-2175.*

Windsong Bed and Breakfast. 213 Deer Harbor Road. Four large, elegant rooms with private baths mark this B&B. *Moderate to expensive. Phone (800) 669-3984 or (360) 376-2500.*

Chestnut Hill Inn. 5157 Victorian Valley Road. This two-story establishment in a pleasant valley has 5 rooms with a rural atmosphere in a two-story Victorian farmhouse.

From November to April private dinners are available with 24-hour notice. *Expensive. Phone (360) 376-5157.*

Turtleback Farm Inn. 6 miles north of the Ferry Landing on Crow Valley Road. This facility has 7 rooms in a restored, two-story, 1890s farmhouse, and 4 more rooms in the upscale Orchard House. The two structures are surrounded by 80 acres of forest and farmland. All rooms have private baths. *Moderate to expensive. Phone (800) 376-4914 or (360) 376-4914.*

Otters Pond B&B of Orcas Island. 100 Tomihi Drive in Eastsound. This is a two-story bed and breakfast with 5 guest rooms and an attractive setting that overlooks Otters Pond and is in walking distance of Moran State Park. There is a tree house with a hot tub. *Moderate to expensive. Phone (888) 893-9680 (360) 376-8844.*

SAN JUAN ISLAND

[Fig. 14] This is the westernmost of the large San Juan Islands, and it is only about 20 miles from Canada's Vancouver Island. It is not quite as large as Orcas, but, with a population of 6,500, it has more people and its main town, Friday Harbor, has considerable amenities.

The island's main claim on history is the Pig War, which lasted for some 14 years and nearly embroiled the U.S. and Britain in their third war against each other. Fortunately, the opposing troops never got beyond inviting each other to parties, and the only casualty was the pig that gave the war its name.

The war was the outcome of the 1846 Treaty of Washington, which set the boundaries between the U.S. and Canada. The treaty said the boundary would go through the main channel of the Strait of Georgia. The trouble was that there were two main channels. One, on the east side of San Juan Island, put the island in Canada. The other, on the west side of the archipelago, put it in the United States. The result was that the British Hudson's Bay Company developed a farm on the island while about 25 individual U.S. citizens were settling there. The neighbors got along tolerably well until 1859, when Lyman Cutlar found a British pig rooting in his American potato patch. He shot the pig. The British threatened to arrest him. The American authorities in the area sent a company of soldiers to protect him. The American troops were commanded by Captain George E. Picket, who a few years later would be a general in the Confederate Army, and who gained fame as the commander of the Confederate troops that made the futile last charge during the Battle of Gettysburg. The British sent war ships. The Americans sent more troops. Within two months the situation mushroomed to the point that the Americans had a redoubt with 461 troops and 14 cannon to face off the British who had five warships with 2,140 troops and 167 cannons. It looked like the pig had started a real war, but cooler heads prevailed, and it was agreed that both sides would maintain a token force on the island until the situation could be straightened out.

The British built an elaborate camp on the north end of the island, and the

Americans built an elaborate camp on the south end of the island. There wasn't much work to do while they waited for someone to resolve the situation, so they attended each other's parties and dances.

Twelve years later the matter was turned over to Kaiser Wilhelm I of Germany to arbitrate. On October 21, 1872, he found for the Americans, and the troops on both sides went home.

They left their camps and fortifications, which were largely ignored for the next century, when Congress created the San Juan Island National Historical Park, which includes the two camps.

The **British Camp** lies on the tree-lined Garrison Bay, where the Pig War-era hospital, barracks, commissary, and guardhouse, as well as the formal British garden, have been restored. The barracks presents an audio-visual program depicting the period of the occupation. The buildings are open every day during the summer, but are often closed during the winter. There are several trails within the English Camp site, including a 2-mile, level loop trail that follows the shoreline north to Bell Point and back. Another steeper, 4-mile round-trip trail goes 1.25 miles to the English Camp Cemetery then zigzags to the top of Young Hill, which at 650 feet in elevation gives a good view of the territory. Clam digging is permitted, but check with the ranger for where to go and limits.

The central feature of the **American Camp** on the other end of the island is the redoubt, which still stands much as it did 150 years ago when the troops built the high, thick walls with little more than shovels, wheelbarrows, and muscle. It was here they manned their posts through the long, dreary years of their non-combat war.

About 0.5 mile to the northwest of the redoubt, the buildings of the officers' quarters and the laundress' quarters still stand, and the sites of some of the other buildings have been located. A visitor center near the parking lot tells the story of the camp and there is a self-guided interpretive trail to the historic sites. The trail extends from the American installations to the nearby site of the Hudson's Bay Company farm. It then goes south to Grandma's Cove, and turns east to follow the south shore of the island for about 2 miles to South Beach, the longest public beach on the island.

The beach is a good place to see shore birds such as plovers (*Pluvialis squatarola*), turnstones (*Arenaria* sp.), yellowlegs (*Tringa melanolevca*), lesser yellowlegs (*Tringa flavipes*), and terns (*Sterna hiundo*). Bald eagles are among the raptors that visit the island and some 200 other species of birds have also been identified here. Tidepool creatures emerge during low tide, and occasionally, one or more whales may swim by. Porpoises, sea lions, and harbor seals may also be seen in the vicinity.

A network of trails at the eastern end of the park wanders through Douglas fir forest and goes 1.5 mile to Jake's Lagoon where deer and birds can be seen. The 3-mile loop Mount Finlayson Trail goes to the top of that mountain, where, at 290 feet in elevation, there are views of the Strait of Georgia, with Mount Baker to the east,

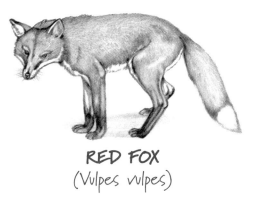

RED FOX
(Vulpes vulpes)

Mount Rainier to the southeast, the Olympic Mountains to the south, and the Canadian mountains to the west (assuming, of course, that the weather is clear).

The American Camp is a good place to see the remnants of a population of European rabbits (*Oryctolagus cuniculi*) that apparently descended from pet rabbits brought to the island early in the twentieth century. Some escaped or were released and became wild. The population increased over the decades until the rabbits seemed to overrun the island, destroying crops and gardens and changing the natural environment for many years. Natural diseases and a population of red foxes (*Vulpes vulpes*) eventually culled the rabbits to a manageable number. But they still appear in large numbers. This breed of rabbits finds protection from predators by digging deep burrows that can become dangerous to people who don't watch where they are walking.

Access to the two camps, as well as to other facilities on the island can be by private autos, by autos rented in Friday Harbor, by motor bikes rented in Friday Harbor, or by the San Juan Transit shuttle buses that visit the camps from time to time. For schedules and information, phone (360) 378-8887.

Directions: The park headquarters is located at 125 Spring Street, near the ferry landing in Friday Harbor.

Activities: Historical tours, hiking, bird-watching, whale watching.

Facilities: An information desk at the park headquarters in Friday Harbor, and separate visitor centers at both camps. More than 8 miles of trails.

Dates: The grounds at the American and English camps are open from dawn until 11 p.m. year round, but the buildings in the camps are closed in winter. The visitor center in Friday Harbor is open daily from 8:30 until 5 during the summer, and from 8:30 to 4:30 Thursday through Sundays during the other seasons.

Fees: None.

Closest town: Friday Harbor.

For more information: San Juan National Historical Park, PO Box 429, Friday Harbor, WA 98250. Phone (360) 378-2240.

FRIDAY HARBOR

[Fig. 14] This pleasant town of 1,500 people is where the ferry lands on the island and is the headquarters for many of the attractions throughout the island. Features include the headquarters of the island's national historical park, and the whale museum, which has displays on the natural history of whales and the history of whaling.

The downtown area, adjacent to the ferry landing, has shops, restaurants, lodgings, car and motor bike rentals, and the terminal for the San Juan Transit shuttle buses that visit the national historical park's camps from time to time. For schedules and information, phone (360) 378-8887. The waterfront includes picturesque scenery and charter boat services for fishing and sight-seeing.

For more information: San Juan Island Chamber of Commerce, PO Box 98, Friday Harbor, WA 98250. Phone (360) 378-5240.

SAN JUAN ISLAND COUNTY PARK

[Fig. 14(3)] This little park is the only public place on the island with camping, and it has only 20 spaces, which are almost always full during the summer. Reservations are highly recommended. The campground has restrooms and piped water. Recreation vehicles up to 25 feet long can be accommodated. The park is home to black-tailed deer, European rabbits, red fox, and numerous birds, including bald eagles. There also are tidepool creatures, harbor seals, sea lions, orca whales, and gray whales in the water.

Directions: Take Spring Street from the ferry dock for approximately 2 miles and turn left onto Douglas Road, which changes names to become first Bailer Hill Road, then West Side Road. Follow that road along the west shore of the island to the park.

Activities: Camping, boating, kayaking, beach walking, and hiking.

Facilities: 20 standard camping units plus unorganized camping for hikers/bikers, restrooms, water, beach, trails, boat ramp.

Dates: Open year round.

Closest town: Friday Harbor, about 16 miles.

For more information: San Juan County Park Department, 350 Court Street, Number Eight, Friday Harbor, WA 98250. Phone (360) 378-8420. For reservations, phone (360) 378-1842.

LIME KILN POINT STATE PARK

[Fig. 14(4)] This 32-acre park is a good place for whale watching and history. The park is adjacent to a lighthouse that has been operating since 1914, although it now is automated rather than manned. There is 0.5 mile of saltwater beach and trails to overlooks, where visitors can search the waters for whales and other sea creatures, not to mention some magnificent scenery. Volunteers from the whale museum in Friday Harbor often are available to provide information about the whales during the late summer and fall, when they are most likely to be in the waters off the island. At the north end of the park, there are two ancient lime kilns that once contributed to the economy of the island.

Directions: Go west from the ferry landing in Friday Harbor on Spring Street, then north on Second Street, west on Guard Street, and north on Tucker Street. Veer to the left at a Y onto Roche Harbor Road. Go 9 miles, then head south on West Valley Road, and west on Mitchell Bay Road. Go to the West Side Road, turn south, and go 6.5 miles to the parking lot in the park.

Activities: Beach walking, whale watching, sight-seeing, picnicking.

Facilities: Picnic sites, restrooms, whale-watching lookout.

Dates: Open year-round.

Fees: None.

Closest town: Friday Harbor, 20 miles.

For more information: Lime Kiln Point State Park, 6158 Lighthouse Road, Friday Harbor, WA 98250. Phone (360) 378-2044.

ROCHE HARBOR RESORT

[Fig. 14(5)] This is probably the most picturesque of San Juan Island's picturesque places of lodging, in large part because its history goes back to the early days of settlement. The original building, the Hotel de Haro, is listed on the National Register of Historic Places. It was built by John S. McMillan in 1886 at the site of a Hudson's Bay Company Post. McMillan was the head of the Roche Harbor Lime Company, which became one of the nation's major producers of lime. He built a company town which at its peak had a population of 800. That town has become the basis of the 8,000-acre resort.

The Hotel de Haro offers a taste of living as it once was. President Teddy Roosevelt visited the hotel twice, and the hotel proudly displays his signature on the register. The structure is ancient. The walls are thin and some rooms have shared baths, but there is an old-time atmosphere that is augmented by some of the original furnishings.

For more modern accommodations, the resort also offers condominiums and renovated company town cottages at moderate to expensive rates. There is a popular marina, shops, a swimming pool, tennis courts, and trails that take visitors into the places where men and women once worked.

Directions: The resort is located at 4950 Tarte Memorial Drive, in Roche Harbor, San Juan Island.

Activities: Boating, swimming, hiking, tennis, beach walking, water sports.

Facilities: Food, lodging, marina, swimming pool, trails, tennis courts, historical sites.

Dates: Open year-round.

Closest town: Friday Harbor, 16 miles.

For more information: Roche Harbor Resort, PO Box 4001, Roche Harbor, WA 98250. Phone (360) 378-2155 or (800) 451-8910.

RESTAURANTS ON SAN JUAN ISLAND

Most of San Juan Island's restaurants are in Friday Harbor, the town where the ferry lands.

Friday Harbor House Restaurant. 130 West Street. This is a casual, candlelight, fine dining restaurant with a harbor view and an a la carte menu of dishes prepared with ingredients from the San Juan Islands. Cocktails are available. Reservations recommended. *Moderate. (360) 378-8455.*

Downrigger. 10 Front Street. With views of the harbor, this restaurant's menu offers steak and a large variety of seafood a la carte. There is a Sunday brunch, a cocktail lounge and a children's menu. Reservations recommended. *Inexpensive. Phone (360) 378-2700.*

LODGING ON SAN JUAN ISLAND

Most lodging on San Juan Island is in Friday Harbor where the ferries land, and much of it is the bed and breakfast variety. Reservations are highly recommended, because if the rooms are all rented after the last ferry leaves, there is no alternative.

The Inn at Friday Harbor. 410 Spring Street in Friday Harbor. This is a two-story motel with 72 rooms. There is a heated swimming pool, sauna, and whirlpool, a gift shop, and game room. Rental cars are available for exploring the island. All rooms have private baths. *Moderate to expensive. Phone (800) 752-8752 or (360) 378-4000.*

Inn at Friday Harbor Suites. 680 Spring Street in Friday Harbor. This two-story motor inn has 64 guest units, 6 with two bedrooms. It offers island tours as well as rental cars. There is a restaurant with a cocktail lounge. *Moderate to expensive. Phone (800) 752-5752 or (360) 378-3031.*

Friday Harbor House. 130 West Street in Friday Harbor. This three-story inn has 20 upscale guest rooms and many of them have harbor views. *Expensive. Phone (360) 378-8455.*

BED AND BREAKFASTS ON SAN JUAN ISLAND

States Inn. 2039 West Valley Road, 7 miles northwest of Friday Harbor. This is a bed and breakfast on a working ranch in a rural valley. There are 9 guest rooms, each named after a state, in a two-story building. There also is a two-bedroom apartment in a separate building. The apartment includes a kitchen with a washer and dryer. *Moderate to expensive. Phone (360) 378-6240.* **The Meadows.** 1557 Cattle Point Road, 3 miles south of Friday Harbor. There are two large rooms in a guest house, which is separate from the 100-year-old farm house where breakfast is served and where there are a sun room and deck for guests. The rooms have walk-in closets, contemporary furnishings, and a shared bath. The surroundings include ancient oaks, firs and open fields. *Moderate. Phone (360) 378-4004.* **Argyle House.** 685 Argyle Street in Friday Harbor. This B&B has guest rooms in an appealing home built in 1910, and in a nearby cottage. There are private baths and a hot tub. *Moderate to expensive. (360) 378-4084.* **Duffy House.** 4214 Pear Point Road on a peninsula 1.7 miles southeast of Friday Harbor. This two-story, 1926, Tudor Home in a quiet, rural setting offers excellent views of Griffin Bay and has 5 guest rooms with baths. *Moderate. Phone (800) 972-2089 or (360) 378-5604.* **Trumpeter Inn.** 318 Trumpeter Way, 2 miles west of Friday Harbor. With five pleasant guest rooms and contemporary decoration, this two-story B&B nestles in a rural setting. Most rooms have views of the country or, in the distance, False Bay and the Olympic Mountains. *Moderate to expensive. Phone (800) 826-7926 or (360) 378-3884.* **Hillside House.** 365 Carter Avenue in Friday Harbor. This large contemporary home in a forested location has 7 guest rooms. Some have views of the harbor. Others overlook a charming atrium. *Moderate to expensive. Phone (800) 232-4730 or (360) 378-4730.*

Strait of Juan de Fuca

The Strait of Juan de Fuca was formed 13,000 years ago when the last Ice Age ended.

FIGURE NUMBERS

16 Getting to the Olympic Peninsula
17 Port Townsend Area
18 Fort Worden State Park
19 Sequim/Dungeness Area

The Strait of Juan de Fuca

When the last ice age finally ended 13,000 years ago, its receding fingers revealed a narrow, straight, water-filled gorge that today is called the Strait of Juan de Fuca. This strait separates Washington State's Olympic Peninsula from Vancouver Island in British Columbia, Canada. The channel flows due east for about 100 miles before bumping into the mainland of the continental United States. The water then runs either south into Puget Sound or north between Vancouver Island and the mainland of Washington State and British Columbia.

On the United States side, the strip of land that lies between the Strait of Juan de Fuca on the north and the Olympic Mountains on the south has a drier, warmer climate than the rest of the Olympic Peninsula. The reason for this is that the area is in a rain shadow. Rain shadows are created when moisture-laden clouds from the Pacific rise as they meet the Olympics, causing the moisture in them to cool,

[*Above:* The Rector's Castle at Fort Worden State Park is designed around a water tower]

condense, and precipitate. As the clouds drop back down to sea level on the other side of the mountains they continue to release moisture. By the time they reach sea level they are dry. One town, Sequim, has an average annual rainfall of 16 inches and is known as Western Washington's sunbelt. Its dry, sunny weather has attracted many retirees.

Sequim is also where of some of the earliest signs of human occupation on the peninsula were found. No one is sure when the first humans arrived in the Olympics, but strong evidence seems to indicate that it was probably about 12,000 years ago. In 1977 the remains of an old, arthritic mastodon *(Mamut americanum)* were uncovered near Sequim. The evidence indicates that between 10,000 to 11,000 years ago the animal became mired in a mud pit. It apparently struggled so frantically to get free that it broke its pelvis. Even more intriguing to the archeologists, however, was the mastodon's skull, which had been smashed into hundreds of pieces and turned 180 degrees, toward the tail. Bones of both right legs had been scattered uphill from the skeleton and bore marks as if the animal had been butchered with primitive knives of chipped stone. Pieces of bone found at the site appeared to have been worked into tools, and a piece of antler or bone was imbedded in one of the animal's ribs. This wound had partially healed before the animal died. It is possible the mastodon was simply gored by another animal. It is also possible that this foreign object once had been fitted on a spear or dart and thrust into the rib by a human hand.

These early butchers were undoubtedly the ancestors of the tribes, such as the Makah and the C'lallam, who were living along the coast and rivers when the first Europeans arrived. The drier climate, along with easy access to food and transportation provided by the nearby water, made the Strait a good location to settle. The native peoples built longhouses, often 40 feet or longer, which several families, related by either blood or clan ties, shared. They lived in permanent villages,

CHINOOK SALMON
(Oncorhynchus tshawttscha)

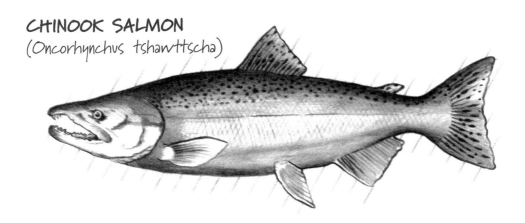

although they would move inland temporarily in the summer to gather plants for food and medicine, and to use in making clothes, baskets, and tools.

The sea and the forest were the basis of Indian life. The waterways were the main means of transportation, important in a land where the vegetation is so dense that it is often virtually im-passable and easy to become lost. Many tribes told stories of *tamanowis,* a kind of bogeyman; children were regularly warned not to wander into the woods for fear that the *tamanowis* would grab them and they would never be seen again.

Even *more* important than transportation was the food the rivers and sea provided. An abundance of sea life, from shellfish to salmon, seals to sea

Salmon Life Cycle

The cycle of the Pacific salmon (genus *Oncorhynchus*) begins when the female chooses a gravel bed in the stream near where she was spawned and digs a nest by flailing her tail to displace the pebbles. That attracts the males who battle each other for the privilege of spawning. The winner joins the female over the nest and releases his sperm at the same time she releases her eggs. The eggs fall into the nest and the female moves a short distance away and flails her tail to dislodge pebbles into the nest and bury the fertilized eggs. She then moves upstream a short distance and repeats the operation, continuing that process until she depletes her supply of eggs. The exhausted salmon die when they finish spawning, while their eggs mature into alevin, tiny young fish that get their nourishment from a yolk sac that is attached to their abdomens. When the yolk sac is absorbed the young fish are known as parrs and travel downstream to an estuary where they feed, gain in size and energy, and become acclimated to salt water so they can migrate into the ocean where they are called smolts. They usually spend from one to four years at sea, ranging as much as 1,000 miles to the north Pacific Ocean and growing until they become adults. Then, using the earth's magnetic field and odors specific to their home stream, they navigate back to the place where they were born. After spawning they die and the life cycle begins anew as the eggs hatch.

otters, was used for food and furs. Mussels, scallops, grouper, rockfish, and halibut were found along the coast. One group, the Makah, even put to sea in canoes to hunt whale, the only native group outside of Alaska to do so. This custom was renewed, amidst much publicity, in the summer of 1999.

Of all this sea life, though, it was the salmon that was the backbone of Indian life. Magnificent runs of various salmon species—Chinook, chum, coho, humpback (or pink), and sockeye—returned each year to the rivers and streams of their birth to spawn and die. On their way up the streams, they were caught; their flesh was eaten fresh or dried for winter use.

So important were these fish that they were regarded as gods who assumed fish form each year in order to sacrifice themselves so that humans could live. The first catch was ceremonial, and the bones of the fish were carefully returned to the water so that the fish gods could find them and return the next year.

The salmon runs occur in the spring, summer, and fall months and that was the time when most of the food gathering was done. Deer, elk, bear, and other animals roamed the forests. Their meat made a change from the primarily fish diet. Numerous varieties of edible berries grow throughout this area and were gathered by the Indians. What wasn't eaten fresh was dried and preserved for a sweet treat in the winter.

Common camas (Camassia quamashi), the principle source of starch in native diets, was harvested and stored for winter use. Water-resistant western redcedar, as essential to native life as salmon and nearly as revered, was cut for building and repairing the longhouses and making canoes. Its bark was stripped, soaked to soften it, then beaten to make it pliable for weaving into items such as baskets, clothing, and sleeping mats.

Winter was a more leisurely time. Sacred ceremonies, with the participants dancing and in many tribes, wearing elaborate masks, were held. Winter, too, was a great time for storytelling, passing along tribal and family histories and lore while gathered around the fires. This was the time to weave baskets, work at looms, carve tools, repair fishing equipment, and make boxes. Life was good. And then the change came.

There had been rumors, of course. Neighboring villages visited each other, holding potlatches, great feasts at which guests would be given gifts in accordance with their rank, until the host village had literally given away all its accumulated wealth. Aside from redistributing property and accumulating status, the potlatches also provided a time for people to gossip and share news. This was not always as easy as it may seem, as native peoples spoke several unrelated languages. Still, despite these linguistic drawbacks, the Indians had heard rumors of strange, pale-skinned men, of their winged canoes and shooting sticks, of their willingness to trade for pelts, and of the mysterious sicknesses that often followed in their wake, leaving whole villages dead and dying.

These strangers had been slowly edging their way to the peninsula for years. Spain, from its holdings in California, had been the earliest visitor; in 1543, the Captains Juan Cabrillo and Bartolome Ferrelo sailed as far north as the Umpqua River in Oregon.

This expedition was just the beginning of European exploration. By the middle of the eighteenth century, Spain, Russia, England, and France were all laying claim to some portion of this area. The Spanish were after gold; the Russians, sea otter pelts. The British and French wanted to protect their lucrative trade in beaver pelts. After its successful revolution in 1776, the newly formed United States of America joined the lists of claimants, desiring a hold on these potentially profitable lands, which would also secure their back door at the same time.

All these competing countries wished to take title to any potential wealth in this remote part of the world, although no one knew quite what that wealth might be. But there was another pressing reason to claim the area: the Northwest Passage. This route would allow European ships to sail through the North American continent, saving them the long, expensive trip around South America's Cape Horn or Africa's Cape of Good Hope to reach the Far East.

The most famous—or infamous—claim was the dubious story told by a sailor that many scholars consider mythological. The sailor, a Greek by the name of Apostolos Valerianos, told an English geographer that, in 1592, while sailing for Spain under the name Juan de Fuca, he sighted a large channel of water heading towards the east, which he claimed was the Strait of Anian, the fabled Northwest Passage. This tale was spread by the geographer and led to two centuries of exploration for something that didn't exist. It did, however, accom-

Vancouver's Maps

In addition to naming places in the Northwest after English things and people, Vancouver left maps that put his own name on Vancouver Island on the north side of the Strait of Juan de Fuca, on a major city in southern British Columbia, and on a smaller city in southern Washington. He also published maps and journals that Lewis and Clark used in 1805, when they neared the end of their epic overland journey from St. Louis to the mouth of the Columbia River.

plish the charting of North America's western coast. Part of Lewis and Clark's mission was to find this passage. Their discovery of the Rocky and Cascade mountain ranges ended the dream forever. It wasn't until the completion of the Panama Canal in 1914 that a shorter route was achieved.

Although Europeans had been sailing in Northwest waters for years, it wasn't until 1775 that the first contact with the native populations was recorded. That meeting was with the Quinault Indians. In July of that year, the Spanish ship *Sonora*, after trading with the Quinaults the previous day, sent a party of seven men ashore to get water. The men were attacked and killed by the Indians, and as canoes of armed native men were paddling out towards the ship, the Spaniards hastily weighed anchor and set sail. The Spanish captain named a nearby island *Isla de Dolores*, Isle of Sorrows.

In 1778, Captain James Cook, exploring and charting the local waters, spotted what he described as a large bay, and passed it by as too dangerous to sail, thus missing his chance to find the Strait. He sailed on, and eventually left the region to sail to the Sandwich Islands, now known as Hawaii, where he met his death. One of Cook's officers was a young midshipman, George Vancouver, who later would return and explore much of the area.

It wasn't until 1787 that the Strait was discovered—or rediscovered, if de Fuca is to be believed. Certainly it seems Captain Charles Barkley believed de Fuca's story. It was Barkley, sailing the *Imperial Eagle*, who finally recognized the waters as a strait and not just a bay.

On board the ship, Barkley's 17-year-old bride, Jane, probably the first white woman in the area, wrote in her journal that Barkley immediately recorded the discovery in the ship's log and that he had named it the Strait of Juan de Fuca. On this same voyage, Barkley landed a party on the beach in the area of *Isla de Dolores*, only to have his men meet the same fate as the Spanish party had 12 years earlier. He named the river Destruction, a name that eventually came to be applied to nearby Destruction Island.

At the time of Barkley's discovery, the Spanish were still furthering their claims in the area. In 1790, Manuel Quimper spent the summer sailing along the Strait's waters. He named the Canal De Haro after his pilot. This canal, between Vancouver Island and San Juan Island, is where the U.S./Canadian boundary line is drawn. Quimper also named *Porto de Nuestra Señora de Los Angeles*, which was eventually shortened to Port Angeles.

The Quimper Peninsula, where the city of Port Townsend is located, is named after this last of the Spanish explorers in the Northwest. By 1793, Spain was bowing out of the race for the Pacific Northwest. Revilla Gigedo, the Spanish Viceroy in California, sent a secret report to the Spanish government. In it he said that the Pacific Northwest had nothing worth having except sea otter pelts, which hardly constituted a reliable source of wealth. Gigedo was correct; the fur trade would decimate the sea otter colonies almost to extinction, from which they would not recover until the last half of the twentieth century. By then, Spain was long gone from the region, having signed a treaty in 1819 relinquishing all claims north of 42° latitude, which is the northern border of California.

In 1792, George Vancouver, that young midshipman who had sailed with Cook in 1778, now a captain himself, sailed back into Pacific Northwest waters. His mission was to strengthen the British claim to the area and to explore the area in search of the Northwest Passage. It was Vancouver who actually sailed up the Strait to its end. He and his men explored Puget Sound to the south and the Strait of Georgia to the north. In the process, he adorned the area with his name, as well as the names of his officers, friends, family, and mentors. Puget Sound bears the name of his subaltern, Peter Puget; Admiralty Inlet was named after the British Admiralty. Hood Canal (as well as Mount Hood in Oregon), Mount Baker, Mount Rainier, and Port Townsend are just a few of the place names left behind by Vancouver. Even English plants were honored. Vancouver, sailing past some bluffs of what is now Seattle, mistook the indigenous madrones for English magnolias, and called the area Magnolia, a misnomer that it bears to this day.

Vancouver spent several years sailing the local sea, greatly enhancing Britain's claim that the land belonged to them and not the Americans, Russians, or Spanish— or for that matter, to the native peoples who had been living here for millennia. However, it was during Vancouver's stay that an American sea captain, Robert Gray, made an important discovery that would, along with the successful completion of Lewis and Clark's Expedition of 1804 to 1806, strengthen the United States' claim to the Oregon Territory.

Gray, a merchant rather than a naval seaman, was searching for fur hunting grounds when he managed to navigate the mouth of the Columbia River—some of the most treacherous water in the world. Interestingly enough, it was Vancouver who would make known the discovery and the discoverer to the world. Gray never mentioned it outside of his log, apparently preferring to keep his hunting locations secret.

The contenders for the Oregon Territory were now winnowed down to two, the United States and Britain. In 1846, the matter was settled with the establishment of the 49° parallel as the mainland's boundary line. Everything north belonged to the British; everything south went to the United States. The exception was Vancouver Island, which went to Britain, with the border running down the middle of the Canal De Haro and the Strait of Juan de Fuca.

The United States was interested in the peninsula mainly because Puget Sound was considered militarily strategic for the defense of the country. The peninsula was deemed a wet, worthless wilderness of trees, which made farming almost impossible.

This perception of a damp, dismal land, with only trees for company, would last well into the twentieth century. Most of the peninsula's pioneers settled along the Strait of Juan de Fuca. The Strait had good harbors and, thanks to the rain shadows, kinder weather than the rest of the peninsula. As the trees were cut, farming became at least feasible. Most importantly, traffic into Puget Sound funneled through the Strait, giving towns there, especially if they had a customs house, a shot at shipping out merchandise.

Until the last 20 years, lumber was the economic backbone of the area, just as salmon had been the backbone for native cultures. The first two settlers arrived in Port Townsend in 1850 and had established the town by 1851. By 1853 a crude sawmill began turning the giant trees into lumber. By 1854 a total of 3,673,797 board feet of lumber, plus ship spars, masts, and house shingles were exported. By 1878, less than 25 years later, the mills were cutting approximately 335,000 board feet a day, over a billion board feet a year.

Today, lumber remains a part of the peninsula's culture. Mills still pepper the landscape and mill company tree farms and clear cuts are plentiful. Ships continue hauling cut timber to distant ports. But lumber is not the only use for forests today. The vast majority of the peninsula, nearly 85 percent, is owned and managed by the United States National Park System and the United States Forest Service. Much of the Strait of Juan de Fuca's mountain areas are under the jurisdiction of the National Park System. The Strait also has state and county parks; parts of its shorelines are under the jurisdictions of the National Wildlife Refuge and Marine Sanctuaries systems. For those seeking quaint historic towns to stroll in, beaches and mountains to explore, or a combination of experiences, the Strait of Juan de Fuca has it all.

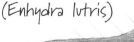

SEA OTTER
(Enhydra lutris)

Getting to the Olympic Peninsula

Three ferries provide quick access to the Olympic Peninsula.

Ref: DeLorme Washington Atlas and Gazetteer

Getting To The Olympic Peninsula

[Fig. 16] US 101 is the only highway around the Olympic Peninsula, but there are several ways to get there, all of which include either circumnavigating or crossing Puget Sound and Hood Canal. The routes listed here are the easiest ways, but not the only ones.

▩ SEATTLE-BAINBRIDGE ISLAND FERRY

[Fig. 16] This 25-minute ferry ride leaves from the Seattle Ferry terminal on Colman Dock, Pier 52, Alaskan Way. The ferry lands at Winslow on Bainbridge Island. From there, it is about 8 miles by road across Bainbridge Island to the Kitsap Peninsula, then another 4 miles to the town of Poulsbo (which was originally called Paulsbo and is still pronounced that way. Anyone saying "Pullsbo" or "Poolsbo" is not a native). A small, scenic town with strong Scandinavian influences, Poulsbo has plenty of restaurants and shops, and is worth a look. It is about 6 miles from the Hood Canal Bridge, which connects the Kitsap and Olympic peninsulas.

Directions: The ferry to Bainbridge Island departs from the downtown Seattle terminal at Colman Dock, 801 Alaskan Way, Pier 52. There are two ferries leaving from this dock, one to Bremerton, and the other to Winslow on Bainbridge Island. Take the Bainbridge Island ferry.

From I-5 northbound, take Fourth Avenue Exit 164B. There are ferries and stadium signs. From I-5 southbound, take the Fourth Avenue/Airport Way Exit 164. Follow the exit ramp loop, turning south onto Fourth Avenue. Go 1 block on Fourth to Royal Brougham Way. Turn right on Royal Brougham and go about 5 blocks to Alaskan Way on the waterfront. (Royal Brougham goes past both the Seahawks and Mariners stadiums.) Turn right on Alaskan Way and go about 1.2 miles. There is a special left-hand turn lane for ferry traffic; watch for the overhead signs.

From the Bainbridge Island ferry terminal, follow the State Route 305 signs about 12 miles to Poulsbo. Continue to follow State Route 305 through Poulsbo until it joins State Route 3 North. Follow State Route 3 North for about 6 miles; it will turn left onto the Hood Canal floating bridge, which is part of State Route 104.

Activities: Boat ride, viewing decks.

Facilities: Cafeteria, restrooms, viewing decks.

Dates: The ferries run year-round.

Fees: There are fees for boarding the ferries.

Closest town: Seattle, Winslow.

For more information: Washington State Ferries, 2911 Second Avenue, Seattle, 98121-1012. In state only phone (800) 843-3779 (automated) or (888) 808-7977. Phone (206) 464-6400. Web site www.wsdot.wa.gov/ferries.

▩ EDMONDS-KINGSTON FERRY

[Fig. 16] The easiest, and therefore recommended, route to get to the Olympic

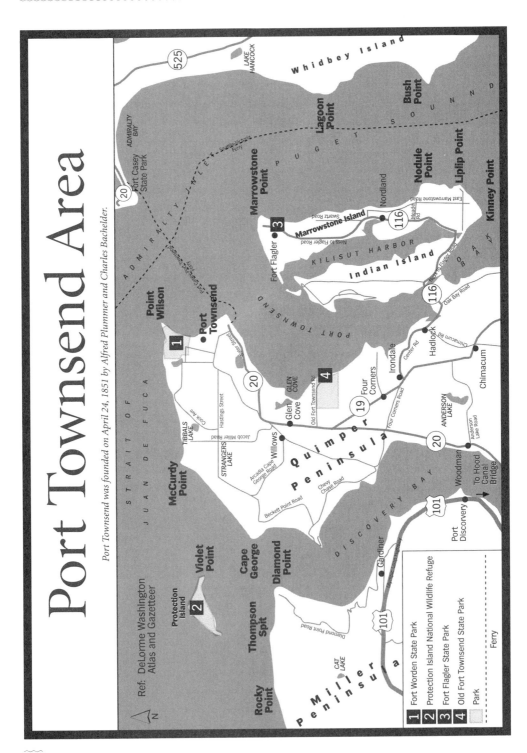

Port Townsend Area

Port Townsend was founded on April 24, 1851 by Alfred Plummer and Charles Bachelder.

Ref: DeLorme Washington Atlas and Gazetteer.

1 Fort Worden State Park
2 Protection Island National Wildlife Refuge
3 Fort Flagler State Park
4 Old Fort Townsend State Park

Park

Ferry

Peninsula is to take the Edmonds-Kingston ferry. This 20-minute ferry ride allows barely enough time for a snack at the ferry cafeteria. Kingston is located near the northeastern tip of the Kitsap Peninsula, which is the stretch of land between Puget Sound and Hood Canal. The Hood Canal Bridge connects the Kitsap and Olympic peninsulas. The Hood Canal Bridge is one of Washington's three floating bridges. A Trident nuclear submarine may occasionally be sighted passing through the draw-span en route to or from the nearby base. The road to the bridge, State Route 104, passes through historic Port Gamble, a company-owned milltown from 1853 until 1995 when it was closed. It's worth a quick stop.

Directions: To reach the Edmonds ferry, take I-5 northbound from Seattle to the Edmonds/Kingston Ferry Exit 177. Use the left lane when exiting the freeway. Follow the "Ferry" signs and State Route 104 westbound to the Edmonds ferry dock to Kingston.

From the Kingston ferry dock, follow State Route 104, which is the main road, for 8.5 miles. Watch for the Hood Canal and the Hood Canal Bridge signs along the way.

From Port Gamble continue on State Route 104 for another 1.5 miles, to the Hood Canal Bridge. Cross the bridge onto the Olympic Peninsula.

Activities: Boat ride.

Facilities: Cafeteria, restrooms.

Dates: The ferries run year-round.

Fees: There is a charge for boarding the ferries.

Closest towns: Edmonds, Kingston.

For more information: Washington State Ferries, 2911 Second Avenue, Seattle, 98121-1012. In state only phone (800) 843-3779 (automated) or (888) 808-7977. Phone (206) 464-6400. Web site www.wsdot.wa.gov/ferries.

Port Townsend

[Fig. 17] This picturesque Victorian seaport on Quimper Peninsula is about 25 miles north off US 101, but it's a worthwhile drive. The oldest city on the peninsula, Port Townsend was founded April 24, 1851, by two enterprising gentlemen, Alfred Plummer and Charles Bachelder. A deep-water bay located near the mouth of Puget Sound seemed a logical place to build a city and possibly to make some money.

Quimper Peninsula actually has two bays. Captain George Vancouver named the one on the west side Discovery Bay, after his ship. Vancouver had deliberately grounded the ship, *Discovery*, to repair the hull. A later entry in his journal indicates that he may have regretted that he had not waited until he had reached the bay on Quimper's east side. It is, he wrote, "a very safe and more capacious harbor than Port Discovery, and rendered more pleasant by the high land being a greater distance from the water-side." Vancouver named the bay Townshend after his friend, the Marquis of Townshend. The spelling eventually was changed to the present "Townsend."

Although they never may have read Vancouver's passage, Plummer and Bachelder also found Port Townsend Bay alluring. The deep bay and its location near the mouth into Puget Sound at Admiralty Inlet made it an ideal site for an U.S. customs house. Unfortunately for Plummer and Bachelder's dream, there was already a customs office located far south in Puget Sound at Steilacoom, near present-day Olympia.

Luckily, the customs agent stationed there had already decided that Steilacoom was not a wise site for an office that was to supposed to cover all of the Oregon Territory, an area which included the coasts of present-day Washington and Oregon. In fact, he said the territory was too large for one man to cover and not only should the customs house be moved to an area closer to the trade, but an additional customs house should be established south of the Columbia River.

In 1852, the U.S. government in Washington, DC, decided that its customs man was right. The Oregon Territory was divided into two areas, and a new customs house was established closer to the Columbia. The Steilacoom office was also moved farther south in Puget Sound, into what is now Olympia. Port Townsend was thwarted again. But not for long. In 1854, the city's lobbying finally paid off, and the customs office was moved again, this time to Port Townsend. Plummer and Bachelder's dream was realized. Their town had the first crack at commerce, sailors, and the money that came with them before any of it reached Puget Sound.

In the 1870s Port Townsend hoped for even greater fortunes when it tried to become the terminus for the Northern Pacific railroad. Competition was fierce, with Seattle, Tacoma, Olympia, Everett, and Bellingham all sure they would become "the end of the line." But logic had prevailed for the town before, and officials were sure it would again.

The city experienced a building boom as speculators invested fortunes, real or hoped for, in these prospective railroad towns. Many of the Victorian-style houses found throughout Port Townsend were built during the frenzy of this time to impress the railroad impresarios, in an attempt to convince them that Port Townsend was the end of the railroad rainbow.

But it was not to be. The terminus went to Tacoma in 1878, and later was extended to Seattle. Although the lumber industry continued to flourish, Port Townsend never achieved its dream of having a population of 25,000 people, let alone of being the region's hub, an honor that belongs to Seattle. Eventually the customs house was moved to Port Angeles. Port Townsend became a sleepy backwater, suffering with the rest of the Olympic Peninsula from the nagging question, "Why bother?" Why bother to lay railroad line all the way to the northeast corner of the peninsula when boats can bring goods much more economically all the way to Puget Sound? Why bother with the peninsula when other places were so much closer?

Port Townsend has remained a small town filled with charming Victorian houses, a paper and pulp mill, and a small port to provide an economic base. Around the turn of the nineteenth century, the U.S. government built three coast artillery forts around Admiralty Inlet to prevent enemies from entering Puget Sound. Two of these forts were located on the Quimper Peninsula. In 1899, work was begun on the first fort, Fort Flagler, located on Marrowstone Island on Port Townsend Bay. Construction of Fort Worden, right next door to the city limits, was started in 1902. That same year the third fort, Fort Casey, was begun across Admiralty Inlet on Whidbey Island (named for one of George Vancouver's officers). All three forts are now popular state parks. The Keystone-Port Townsend ferry carries traffic between Whidbey Island and Port Townsend.

With a population of around 8,300 people, Port Townsend is once again a growing, thriving community and is truly, as it likes to call itself, the gateway to the Olympic Peninsula. Many of the Victorian gingerbread houses have been converted to bed and breakfasts, and the town hosts a variety of cultural events and festivals, creating a laid-back, sophisticated atmosphere of ease and activity. This combination makes it a favorite weekend getaway for neighbors from more heavily populated areas seeking relaxation, as well as out-of-state visitors. It is a small city of great charm, and worth leaving the main road to visit.

Directions: From the Hood Canal Bridge, continue on State Route 104 westbound for about 16 miles where it joins US 101. Follow US 101 about 2 miles to the junction with State Route 20. Turn right onto State Route 20 and follow it into Port Townsend.

Activities: Art galleries, antique shops, beaches, boat tours, and over 75 festivals and events every year, including historic Victorian home tours, jazz and bluegrass festivals, a sailing regatta, and the Wooden Boat Festival.

For more information: Port Townsend Chamber of Commerce, 2437 East Sims Way, Port Townsend, WA 98368. Phone (360) 385-2722. Web site www.ptchamber.olympus.net.

BLACK OYSTERCATCHER
(Haematopus bachmani)

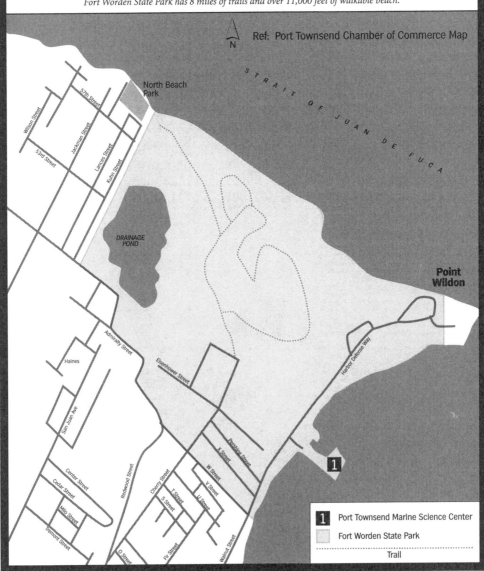

Fort Worden State Park

Fort Worden State Park has 8 miles of trails and over 11,000 feet of walkable beach.

Ref: Port Townsend Chamber of Commerce Map

North Beach Park

STRAIT OF JUAN DE FUCA

Wilson Street

57th Street

Jackman Street

53rd Street

Lances Street

Kuhn Street

DRAINAGE POND

Point Wildon

Admiralty Street

Haines

Eisenhower Street

Harbor Defense Way

San Juan Ave

Center Street

Cedar Street

Redwood Street

Cherry Street

T Street

S Street

W Street

V Street

U Street

Fanshine Street

X Street

Milo Street

Tremont Street

O Street

Fir Street

Walnut Street

1

1	Port Townsend Marine Science Center
	Fort Worden State Park
·······	Trail

FORT WORDEN STATE PARK

[Fig. 17(1), Fig. 18] Fort Worden is one of three coast artillery forts that were built at the main inlet leading into Puget Sound at the turn of the century by the U.S. government. Its 14 massive gun batteries became obsolete almost as soon as they were put in and are now long gone, although their concrete revetments remain and many can be explored. Fort Worden is now a calm, beautiful, historic state park. It is also a lot of fun. In 1982, the movie *An Officer and A Gentleman* was filmed on location at Fort Worden.

In addition to the revetments, Fort Worden's grounds also include the Puget Sound Coast Artillery Museum, the Commanding Officer's House, and the Port Townsend Marine Science Center (*see* Port Townsend Marine Science Center, page 120). Be sure to check out the Centennial Rhododendron Garden at the main gate, especially in the spring when the rhodies are blooming.

The park grounds surround Point Wilson where the U.S. Coast Guard runs the Port Townsend lighthouse. South of Point Wilson is a marine underwater park where scuba divers can observe, but not hunt, local sea creatures in their natural environment. Be forewarned, however, that waters in this part of the world tend to be dark and murky, and the currents swift and treacherous.

This 443-acre state park has 8 miles of hiking trails and over 11,000 feet of walkable beach. The trails go through forests and open fields, with views of the Strait. The hardy can even swim. The park grounds also include a wealth of recreational activities, from basketball hoops to bike trails, as well as such amenities as a laundry facility and showers. Fiddle, country blues, jazz, and classical musical festivals are among the many cultural events held at the park throughout the summer. Contact the Port Townsend Chamber of Commerce for a complete list of events.

The campground also includes facilities for recreational vehicles and tents. For those in need of a respite from the latter, the old military housing has been turned into lodging, including dormitories, single family rentals, and a youth hostel. Calling ahead for reservations is recommended.

Directions: From the Hood Canal Bridge, follow State Route 104 about 16 miles to its juncture with US 101 West. US 101 West then bears right. Follow US 101 West for 3 miles to State Route 20, then turn right. Follow this road into Port Townsend for about 26 miles. It will turn into Sims Way. (Keep an eye out for the brown Washington State Park signs that will say Fort Worden.) Follow Sims Way one block past the Port Townsend Visitors' Information Center to the Kearney Street stoplight; turn left onto Kearney. Next, follow Kearney to Blaine Street, turning right on Blaine and continuing onto Walker Street. Turn left onto Walker. Walker turns into Cherry Street, which runs into the fort's main entrance.

Activities: Beach walks, camping, picnicking, Coast Guard station tours, touring military museums and historical sites, touch tanks, scuba-diving, tennis, volleyball, basketball, fishing, boating, kite flying, hiking, and biking.

Facilities: RV and tent campgrounds, swimmers' changing facility, marine underwater park, picnic tables, boat moorage and ramp, grocery store and snack bar, restaurant and cafeteria, laundry facility, restrooms and showers. Ball fields; tennis, basketball, and volleyball courts; hiking and biking trails; museums; marine science center; historical sites; and lodging.

Dates: The fort and campground are open year-round. Museums and the marine science center hours are seasonal; tours can be arranged.

Fees: There are fees for camping and the museums.

Closest town: Port Townsend, 0.5 mile.

For more information: Fort Worden State Park, 200 Battery Way, Port Townsend, WA 98368. Fort Warden State Park, 200 Battery Way, Port Townsend, WA 98369. Phone (360) 385-4730. Fax (360) 385-7248. E-mail fwadmin@olympus.net. Web site www.olympus.net/ftworden.

This is the only state park that takes reservations year-round. It has its own reservation system and does not use Washington State's Reservations Northwest toll-free number. Reservations can be made in several different ways; all require the name, address, phone number, number of vehicles and people, and a major credit card; checks are not accepted except by arrangement with the park. In-person reservations can be made two months prior to the reservation date.

PORT TOWNSEND MARINE SCIENCE CENTER

[Fig. 18(1)] The marine center consists of a building housing four large touch tanks and eight viewing tanks. The touch tanks are almost as good as real tidepools and are filled with an excellent array of sea fauna. Cards identify the animals, and the very knowledgeable staff and volunteers stand ready to answer questions.

The touch tank animals are gathered from and returned to local waters on a regular basis, so the animals on display vary. Past holdings included rose and plumed anemones *(Urticina piscivora and Mitridium sp.)*, green shore crabs *(Hermigruphus oregonsensis)*, sea worms, including calcareous tube worms *(Serpula vermicularis)*, purple hinged rock scallops *(Hinnites giganteus)*, and sea cucumbers *(Parastichopcis californius)*, as well as chitons, sea stars, and numerous other offerings.

Directions: Follow the directions to

BALD EAGLE
(Haliaeetus leucocephalus)

Fort Worden on page 119. Once on Fort Worden, follow the Marine Science Center signs.

Activities: Touch tanks and touch tank tours, guided beach walks, daily marine interpretive programs, and natural history boat tours.

Facilities: Exhibits, restrooms, beach, picnic tables, mini-grocery story with snack bar, moorage buoys, docks.

Dates: The center is open year-round, but in the winter by appointment only. From June 15 through Labor Day, it is open Tuesday through Sunday, noon to 6. Spring and fall hours are Saturdays and Sundays, noon to 4.

Fees: There is a fee for admission.

Closest town: Port Townsend, 0.2 mile.

For more information: Port Townsend Marine Science Center, Fort Worden State Park, 532 Battery Way, Port Townsend, WA 98368. Phone (360) 385-5582. Fax (360) 385-7248. E-mail ptmsc@olympus.net. Web site www.olympus.net/ftworden/ptmsc.html.

PROTECTION ISLAND NATIONAL WILDLIFE REFUGE

[Fig. 17(2)] Sitting just outside the mouth of Discovery Bay on the west side of Port Townsend and the Quimper Peninsula, this 364-acre island serves as a breeding site and rest area for seabirds and marine mammals. An estimated 70 percent of the Strait of Juan de Fuca and Puget Sound's nesting seabirds raise their young on this island. Half of the rhinoceros auklet *(Cerorhinca monocerata)* population in the contiguous United States nests here, and the other half nests at Destruction Island near La Push (*see* Ruby Beach to Queets River, page 174.) The island is also the largest nesting ground for glaucous-winged gulls *(Larus glaucescens)* in Washington State, as well as the last nesting site for tufted puffins *(Fratercula cirrhata)*

Bald Eagle

Bald eagles (*Haliaeetus leucocephalus*), the nation's symbol, were long considered dangerous predators of livestock, and in the past many states offered bounties for killing them. Bounty hunting, loss of habitat, loss of prey, and widespread use of the pesticide DDT, which got into the birds' food chain and weakened the shells of their eggs and prevented hatching, resulted in bald eagle numbers being reduced. The bald eagle was declared an endangered species in 1973. Since then, DDT was banned and habitat improved to the point that in 1999 bald eagle numbers in the U.S. increased from 417 breeding pairs in 1963 to 5,800 in 1999, and they were upgraded from endangered status to threatened.

Bald eagles are plentiful on the West Coast from Alaska to the Columbia River, but are somewhat less numerous in Oregon. They tend to congregate in places where fish are available such as the ocean shore and along riverbanks. Bald eagles are especially fond of salmon breeding grounds where the exhausted fish die when they finish spawning. The carcasses float to the shore and become a free meal for the eagles. The majestic birds breed in mid to late winter and both parents take turns incubating the eggs until they hatch. The chicks stay in the nest for another 10 to 12 weeks before being able to survive alone.

in the Puget Sound area. Scores of other species can be spotted; these include species of pigeon guillemots *(Cepphus columba)*, oystercatchers, mergansers, murrelets, and ducks, such as harlequin ducks *(Histrionicus histrionicus)*, peregrine falcons *(Falco peregrinus)*, and bald eagles *(Haliaeetus leucocephalus)*. Double-crested and pelagic cormorants' nests can be seen from boats. A reminder, however: To protect the creatures living here from disturbance, no one is allowed within 200 yards of the island.

Mammals found on the island include California *(Zalophus califorianus)* and Northern or Steller's *(Eumetopias jubatus)* sea lions and harbor seals *(Phoca vitulina)*. Minke *(Balaenoptera acutorostrata)* and gray *(Eschrictius robustus)* whales are often sighted around the island. The Port Townsend Marine Science Center organizes cruises around the island in the spring and fall.

Directions: Contact Port Townsend Marine Science Center for information on boat tours and departure locations.

Activities: Tours of offshore island wildlife.

Dates: Boat tours are scheduled during the spring, summer, and fall, dates and times vary yearly.

Fees: There are charges for the boat tours.

Closest town: Port Townsend, 8 miles.

For more information: Port Townsend Marine Science Center, Fort Worden State Park, 532 Battery Way, Port Townsend, WA 98368. Phone (360) 385-5582. E-mail ptmsc@olympus.net.

🦅 FORT FLAGLER STATE PARK

[Fig. 17(3)] Deer graze the parade grounds where ranks of soldiers once stood at attention and children play in the open fields where men were trained for war. Visitors gawk at the massive bunkers and batteries that once were filled with gigantic guns installed to protect Admiralty Inlet from enemy invasion. The fort was the first of the three built to protect Puget Sound from enemy forces. Construction of Fort Flagler, located on Marrowstone Island southeast of Port Townsend, started in 1899. Like Fort Worden (*see* page 119) and Fort Casey (*see* page 88), Flagler was obsolete almost as soon as it was built, in large part due to its susceptibility to enemy fire, even with massive emplacements protecting the fixed mount guns. Two more batteries with movable carriages were added in

PEREGRINE
FALCON
(Falco peregrinus)

1907, but most of the fort's guns were removed and shipped to Europe during World War I. Soldiers were trained at the fort during both world wars, but the fort was not considered strategically important and was taken out of service in 1953.

As with Forts Worden and Casey, it is somehow fitting that Flagler, once a bastion of war, is now a place of peace, where nature and humanity coincide in harmony. The 783-acre fort fronts three bodies of water for a total of over 19,000 feet of beach. Admiralty Inlet is on the east side. Port Townsend Bay rolls in on the north, and Kilisut Harbor is on the western side of the park grounds. The park features two main camping areas, plus walk-in bicycle campsites located at the west end. One of the two main campgrounds is located on a wooded bluff at the southwest section of the park; the other, lower campground is on more open ground above the northwestern beach. Four of the old fort's living quarters have been turned into rentals and a youth hostel.

The fort grounds offer a surfeit of activities. Hiking and biking trails run through the park. The Roots of the Forest interpretive trail is a self-guided walk. Five of the fort's batteries and emplacements are open to the public; four of the main batteries are unsafe and closed.

The beaches and tideland environments within the park grounds vary. At low tide, Scow Bay Spit, a 0.25-mile sand hook across the front of Kilisut Bay, is a tideflat, offering opportunities to dig clams and search for crabs hiding in the seaweed. Kilisut Bay is also the site of one of the park's two boat ramps, as well as its moorage. The other boat ramp is located on the north side of the island on Townsend Bay. The north beach runs all the way to Marrowstone Point lighthouse, which is a working navigational lighthouse, but closed to the public. Beachcombers making their way from Marrowstone Point along the east beach will find the decaying remains of the old wharf originally used to bring supplies and building materials into the fort. The pilings are rotted out and the pier is closed to visitors. However, marine life flourishes in the old pilings that now harbor an underwater park for scuba divers.

Directions: From the Hood Canal Bridge, follow State Route 104 to State Route 19 for about 9 miles. Turn right onto State Route 19. Go 9 miles to Chimacum. At the four-way stop sign, turn right onto Chimacum Road. Follow this road 1.5 miles to Port Hadlock. At Port Hadlock turn right onto Oak Bay Road. Take Oak Bay Road for about 0.75 mile to the second major turn. The sign here is confusing, as it is placed before the first turn. Continue past the sign and first turn for about 100 feet to the next left turn. Turn left onto State Route 116 (Old Fort Flagler Road) and travel 7.5 miles. The road leads into the park.

Activities: Camping, picnicking, beachcombing, clamming, crabbing and fishing, scuba-diving, biking, hiking, and exploring historical sites.

Facilities: RV, tent, and bicycle campsites. Boat ramps, float moorage (summers only), buoys, picnic tables, bathrooms with showers, snack stand, grocery store, RV dump station, interpretative displays, nature trails, and deactivated coast artillery fortifications.

Dates: Open from the last weekend in Feb. to Nov. 1. Summer reservations accepted. Open year-round for day use.

Fees: There are fees for camping and moorage.

Closest town: Port Hadlock, 11 miles.

For more information: Fort Flagler State Park, 10541 Flagler Road, Nordland, WA 98358. Phone (360) 385-1259 or (800) 233-0321. For campground reservations, contact Washington State's Reservations Northwest, 7150 Clearwater Lane, PO Box 42650, Olympia, WA 98504. Phone (800) 452-5687 or (360) 902-8500.

░ OLD FORT TOWNSEND STATE PARK

[Fig. 17(4)] Construction of this army fort located on Port Townsend Bay was begun in 1856 in response to the fears of white settlers following the Indian War of 1855-56. This war was Western Washington's largest and only Indian uprising, and frightened the European population, even though they won. The fort's company was relocated to Fort Steilacoom in 1858. Unlike Forts Worden, Flagler and Casey, Fort Townsend's abandonment was not due to obsolescence, but to bad location. After losing its custom house ultimately to Port Townsend, one can only assume that Steilacoom must have felt pleased to get Port Townsend's fort.

No matter. After 18 years of lobbying, Port Townsend got the fort reopened. Despite the army's protests it remained open until 1895, when the barracks were destroyed in a fire. It remained out of service until World War II, when it was used as a defusing station for enemy munitions; the group campground now is located on the old defusing site. The fort was turned over to the Washington State Park's department in 1953.

Today, the 368-acre park has nearly 4,000 feet of rock-and-cobblestone shoreline, as well as 0.25 mile of nature trails, and another 0.25 mile of historical trails. The nature trail wanders through patches of Douglas firs, salal, ferns, and rhododendrons, while the historical trail features displays of the fort as it was in 1877, shortly after it reopened. There are over 6 miles of hiking trails in the park. The beach is suitable for fishing and kayaking. The fort's old disintegrating pilings are ideal for scuba-diving.

Directions: From the Hood Canal Bridge, follow State Route 104 about 16 miles west to its juncture with US 101 West, which bears right. Follow US 101 West for 3 miles to State Route 19, then turn right. Follow State Route 19 toward Port Townsend for about 20 miles; then turn right on Old Fort Townsend Road; watch for the watch for the brown Old Fort Townsend State Park State Park sign. It is about 0.5 mile to the park entrance.

Activities: RV, tent, walk-in, and group camping; picnicking, hiking, paddling, fishing, boating, history and nature interpretive trails.

Facilities: Tent, RV, group, and walk-in campsites, restrooms, one with a shower, picnic tables, ball fields and playground, kitchen shelters, and RV dump site.

Dates: Open from mid-Apr. to mid-Sept.

Fees: There are fees for camping and showers.

Closest town: Port Townsend, 7 miles.

For more information: Fort Worden State Park, 532 Battery Way, Port Townsend, WA 98368. Phone (360) 385-4730. Fax (360) 385-7248.

PORT TOWNSEND LODGING

Port Townsend is a favorite tourist destination, and lodging is available.

Manresa Castle. Seventh and Sheridan in Port Townsend. Port Townsend is filled with Victorian-style lodgings, many of them excellent. Manresa Castle is one of the most romantic. Built in 1892 by the town's first mayor, it was sold in the 1920s and served as a vacation home, first for nuns, then for the Jesuits, who named it after the Spanish town, Manresa, in which their founder, Ignatius Loyola, established the Jesuit order. Now the castle has been converted into a luxury hotel, complete with an excellent restaurant. *Moderate to very expensive. Phone (360) 385-5750.*

Bishop Victorian Hotel. 714 Washington Street in Port Townsend. Centrally located right in the city's Downtown Historic District, this building once housed a cigar factory and a seamen's hotel. All of its 14 guest suites have at least one bedroom, as well as full baths, sitting rooms, and kitchenettes. Some include fireplaces, soaking tubs, and views of Admiralty Inlet. The hotel is filled with antique furniture, and guests can use the facilities at the nearby Port Townsend Athletic club, including steam rooms and a Jacuzzi. *Moderate to expensive. Phone (800) 824-4738. E-mail bishop@waypt.com.*

PORT TOWNSEND RESTAURANTS

Food is available in this favorite tourist haunt.

The Public House. 1038 Water Street. The Public House is located on the main street in a brightly lit old storefront with a neat tin ceiling, and it serves excellent Dungeness crab chowder, as well as tasty salads. The French fries are hand-cut and not overly greasy, and the large hamburgers are cooked to your specification. Tasty, generously sized lunches and dinners make this restaurant a good choice. *Moderate. Phone (360) 385-9708.*

DUNGENESS CRAB
(Cancer magister)

Sequim/Dungeness Area

The Dungeness National Wildlife Refuge is located on the Dungeness Spit, the longest spit in the world.

Ref: Sequim Chamber of Commerce Map

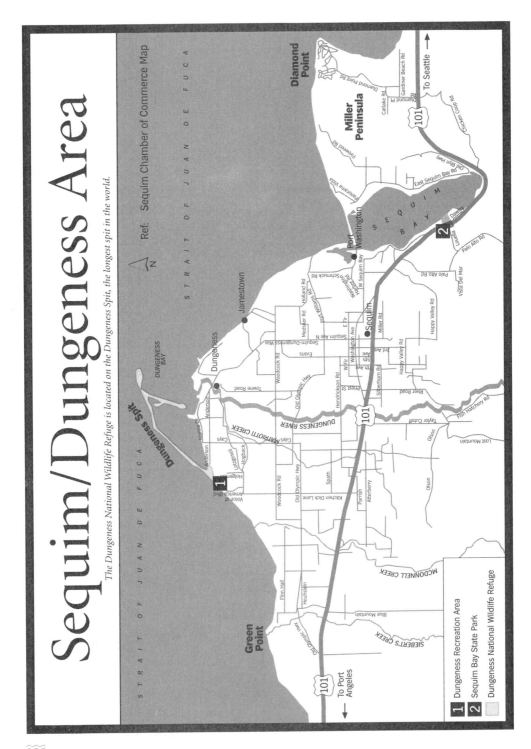

1 Dungeness Recreation Area
2 Sequim Bay State Park
☐ Dungeness National Wildlife Refuge

Sequim/Dungeness

[Fig. 19] The next stop along US 101 is the town of Sequim, pronounced "Squim." The road bypasses downtown, which is nice for those in a hurry, but unfortunate for visitors with more time. The town has a nice mix of businesses, tourist shops, and antiques. It also has the lowest average annual rainfall in Western Washington, barely managing 16 inches a year. When early settlers arrived, they thought nearby prairies would be suitable to farming. They were, but only after irrigation was introduced. The town still celebrates this event with a yearly Irrigation Festival. The community of Dungeness, where the Dungeness Spit is located, has become a part of Sequim. The spit, the longest in the world, is a national wildlife refuge (*see* Dungeness National Wildlife Refuge, below) located just west of Sequim. It is home to one of the Northwest's favorite seafood delicacies, Dungeness crab *(Cancer magister)*.

▓ DUNGENESS NATIONAL WILDLIFE REFUGE

[Fig. 19] This low, sandy hook juts out into the Strait of Juan de Fuca from the mainland to which, unlike a shoal or barrier reef, it is attached. Its 5.5-mile length makes it the longest natural sand spit in the world, according to the U.S. Fish and Wildlife Service. The entrance to the 631-acre spit is located approximately 6 miles west of Sequim, as the crow flies. It was established as a refuge for waterfowl to rest, feed, and rear their young, with special concern for a small, sweet sea goose called the black brant *(Brant bernicla)*. The black brant has plenty of company. As many as 270 species of birds visit the spit yearly, making the refuge a haven for birds and a paradise for bird watchers. Birding is best in the winter, but the spit is worth exploring at any time. During the course of a year, mallard and pintail ducks, sandpipers, common loon *(Gavia immer)*, red-necked grebe *(Podiceps grisegena)*, double-crested cormorant *(Phalacrocorax auritus)*, pelagic cormorant *(Phalacrocorax pelagicus)*, great blue heron *(Ardea herodias)*, black oystercatcher *(Haematopus bachmani)*, black-bellied plover *(Pluvialis squatarola)*, northern harrier *(Circus cyaneus)*, and bald eagle *(Haliaeetus leucocephalus)* are just a few of the species that have been spotted. A number of other animals can also be seen, including harbor seals, river otters, and on rare occasions, red fox *(Vulpes vulpes)*.

The west side of the spit, except for the tip beyond the lighthouse, is open to visitors year-round. The inner, eastern side along Dungeness Harbor plus all of Graveyard Spit (the Dungeness Spit's north-south dogleg), are closed to visitors. Fishing and shellfishing are allowed on the spit during their respective seasons and with the proper licenses. Oysters are privately owned and cannot be harvested. For further information, check with the rangers.

The New Dungeness light station, run by the New Dungeness Chapter of the U.S. Lighthouse Society, is open for tours. The end of the spit has an artesian well, so fresh, sweet water is available, as are restrooms and picnic tables. There are free guided tours of the lighthouse from 9 a.m. to two hours before sunset every day.

Pets, bicycles, fires, camping, firearms, and kites are not allowed in the refuge; plants, animals, fossils, artifacts, and driftwood may not be removed. Allow four hours minimum round-trip from the trailhead at the parking lot to the lighthouse and back. The 0.3-mile trail to the spit is easy, but it drops steeply for the last 100 feet.

Directions: On US 101, turn north onto Kitchen-Dick Road. Go 3 miles to the Dungeness Recreation Area. Continue driving through the recreation area grounds to reach the wildlife refuge parking lot.

Activities: Beach hiking, birding, wildlife viewing, lighthouse tours, fishing, shellfishing, jogging, swimming, picnicking, and other recreational beach activities.

Facilities: Trail to the beach, restrooms, water, and picnic tables at both parking lot and lighthouse.

Dates: The main spit trail and light station are open daily, from sunrise to sunset, year-round. Fishing, shellfishing, boating, and access to some portions of the spit are subject to seasonal restrictions.

Fees: There is a fee to access the beach. Children under 16 are free.

Closest town: Sequim, 6 miles.

For more information: Dungeness National Wildlife Refuge, 33 South Barr Road, Port Angeles, WA 98362. Phone (360) 457-8451.

DUNGENESS RECREATION AREA

[Fig. 19(1)] The chief attraction to this shrubby campground is accessibility to Dungeness Spit National Wildlife Refuge, which is right next door. Clallam County operates this 65-site campground.

Directions: *See* Dungeness National Wildlife Refuge, page 127.

Activities: Camping, picnicking, access to Dungeness Wildlife Refuge and its activities.

Facilities: Campsites, children's playground, bathroom and showers, picnic area. No reservations.

Dates: Open Feb. 1 to Oct. 1.

Fees: There is a fee for campsites and showers.

Closest town: Sequim, 6 miles.

For more information: Dungeness Recreation Area, 554 Voice of America Road, Sequim, WA 98382. Phone (360) 683-5847.

SEQUIM BAY STATE PARK

[Fig. 19(2)] Located on the southwest end of Sequim Bay, this state park offers both forested campsites and the "quiet waters" for which the Indians named the bay. Swimming is allowed; however, there are no lifeguards. The 92-acre park also features an interpretive center with displays. A few of the campsites closest to the water have views, but the campground is mostly forested, with stands of Douglas fir, grand fir, and western redcedar. The upper loop is near the highway. A series of short trails connect the different areas, encompassing about 1 mile of trails. A baseball field, tennis court, and a basketball half-court are located near the ranger station. They are accessed through the US 101 underpass located at the picnic grounds.

The park has moorage and buoys for boaters who wish to brave the narrow, shallow channel into the bay. The channel is well marked for those willing to make the effort. The water on the landward side of the dock can be shallow and the bay's entrance is obscure; Europeans exploring the Strait did not discover it until 1841.

Directions: The park is 4 miles southwest of Sequim on US 101. Watch for the brown state park signs.

Activities: Tent and RV camping, picnicking, beach walks, hikes, shellfish harvesting, fishing, baseball, tennis, basketball, and interpretive learning center.

Facilities: Float (summer only), dock, and boat ramp; restrooms (3 with showers); mooring buoys; baseball field, tennis courts, and basketball half-courts; interpretive center.

Dates: Open year-round.

Fees: There are fees for camping and showers.

Closest town: Sequim, 4 miles.

For more information: Sequim Bay State Park, 269035 Highway 101, Sequim, WA 98382. Local phone (360) 683-4235 or (800) 233-0321. For campground reservations, call Washington State's Reservations Northwest, 7150 Clearwater Lane, PO Box 42650, Olympia, WA 98504. Phone (800) 452-5687 or (360) 902-8500.

SEQUIM/DUNGENESS LODGING

Sequim's warm climate make it a popular destination and lodging is available.

Groveland Cottage. 4861 Sequim-Dungeness Way in Sequim. This early nineteenth century farmhouse bed and breakfast is set in a 1.25-acre garden 5 miles north of Sequim on Dungeness Bay. The five rooms all have private baths, two with Jacuzzis. The guest's beverage of choice is left outside the room about 7 a.m. A multi-course breakfast is served at a later hour in the dining room. *Moderate to expensive. Phone (800) 879-8859.*

SEQUIM/DUNGENESS RESTAURANT

Choices of restaurants in Sequim are limited, but food can be found.

The Three Crabs Restaurant. 11 Three Crabs Road in Sequim. This restaurant has been serving locals and tourists fresh seafood for over 40 years. Most of the seafood is purchased directly from local fishermen. The restaurant sits right on the Strait of Juan de Fuca, and regular fare includes salmon, halibut, and sole, as well as steaks, salads, and sandwiches. The location is out of the way, but worth the trip. The atmosphere is casual and hours vary according to the season. The restaurant serves both lunch and dinner. *Moderate to expensive. Phone (360) 683-4264.*

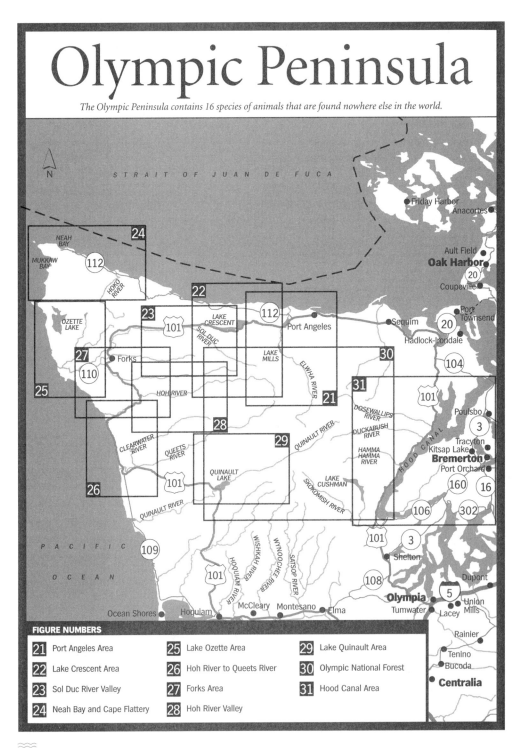

Olympic Peninsula

The Olympic Peninsula contains 16 species of animals that are found nowhere else in the world.

FIGURE NUMBERS

21 Port Angeles Area	**25** Lake Ozette Area	**29** Lake Quinault Area
22 Lake Crescent Area	**26** Hoh River to Queets River	**30** Olympic National Forest
23 Sol Duc River Valley	**27** Forks Area	**31** Hood Canal Area
24 Neah Bay and Cape Flattery	**28** Hoh River Valley	

The Olympic Peninsula

Some of the Olympic Peninsula is privately owned, some is owned by state and local governments, and some is owned by five Indian reservations. But by far the largest portion, a total of more than 2 million acres, is the Olympic National Forest, under the jurisdiction of the U.S. Forest Service, and the Olympic National Park, under the jurisdiction of the National Park Service.

Generally speaking, the park is in the central section of the peninsula where the highest mountains of the Olympic Mountain Range are, but it also extends to long stretches of the Pacific Ocean shoreline and the rain forests of the valleys on the west side of the mountains. The national forest borders most of the outer perimeter of the park but in the northern section, paralleling the Strait of Juan de Fuca, most of the land is in the park with only relatively small portions in the national forest.

Most of the Olympic National Forest is in a large block bordering nearly all the

[*Above:* Symbiotic lichen hang from the trees in an Olympic Peninsula rainforest]

Sitka Spruce Shape

The odd, lop-sided shape of many sitka spruce trees along the seashore is caused by the wind and salt spray killing the buds on the windward side of the tree, forcing most of the growth to the leeward side. The sitka spruce, however, also absorbs nutrients from the sea spray, and it grows best within several hundred yards of the shore.

southern and eastern segments of the park and in a large area of the northwestern corner of the park. Only a small portion of the forest, on the eastern edge, along Hood Canal, touches salt water. The national forest's mountains are smaller than the park's but still offer a challenge for hikers and climbers. It also has large rain forest areas, and Congress has set aside nearly 90,000 acres of the forest in five wilderness areas.

The first glimpses of the Olympic Peninsula are of masses of dense green forests sweeping up from the banks of the gray ocean and disappearing in the barren peaks of the Olympic Mountain Range, dark brown in summer, but snow-covered white in winter. It is hard to imagine that once the whole of this greenery-draped, bountiful land lay at the bottom of the sea.

Yet it was so. About 55 million years ago the land that would rest on the highest peaks of the Olympic Mountain Range was lying on the ocean floor. But as lava from the earth's core pushed its way up through cracks in the ocean floor, the floor moved. The Pacific Plate was pushing its way westward until it collided with the eastward-bound Juan de Fuca Plate. The Pacific Plate, being lighter, floated upward while the heavier Juan de Fuca Plate sank beneath it. Deposits of sediment and debris collected in the troughs where the two plates met. As the Juan de Fuca Plate slid by, the Pacific Plate skimmed off the high places, so that this huge floating chunk of real estate was lifted up. This real estate is today the Olympic Mountains.

The Olympic Mountains have 7,965-foot Mount Olympus at their apex. Considering that the Olympics start at near sea level, the range is as high as the Rocky Mountains, which get a height boost from the 5,000-foot plateau they sit on. Geologists believe the Olympics are still growing. There are fault lines along the coast, and two hot springs on the northern end indicate geologic activity.

About 2 million years ago, the Juan de Fuca lobe of the Corderillian Glacier reached its icy fingers all the way across the Olympic Peninsula and to the Pacific Coast. It began to recede about 13,000 years ago. The peninsula was isolated by the waters that surround it—the narrow, deep channels of the Strait of Juan de Fuca on the north, of Puget Sound and Hood Canal on the east, and of the Pacific Ocean to the west. So intense was this isolation that the peninsula contains species of animals and plants that are found no other place in the world. The short-tailed weasel (*Mustela erminea*), the Olympic marmot (*Marmota olympus*), and the red-legged frog (*Rana aurora*) are among the 16 species of animals that are found only on the Olympic Peninsula. In addition, there are eight endemic plants: Piper's bellflower

(*Campanula piperi*), Flett's violet *(Viola flettii)*, Henderson's rock spirea *(Petrophytum hendersonii)*, Olympic Mountain milkvetch *(Astragalus australis var. olympicus)*, Flett's fleabane *(Erigeron flettii)*, Webster's senecio *(Senecio neowebsteri)*, Thompson's wandering fleabane *(Engeron peregrinus peregrinus var. Thompsonii)*, and Olympic Mountain synthyris *(Synthyris pinnatifida var. lanuginosa)*.

But this took time. Initially, the glaciers' retreat left behind a scoured and barren land. The devastation was as immense as that found on Mount St. Helens following its 1980 eruption. As with St. Helens, the barren peninsula soon started to regenerate. First, seeds carried by winds or deposited by birds found footholds in which to grow. As soil was created by the death of the early plant colonizers, other, larger plants were able to find growing space. Trees and insects, small animals, and then larger ones, made their way up the wide stretch of land. Life returned.

At some point humans arrived. Archeologists believe this probably occurred not long after the last of the ice retreated about 12,000 years ago. Archeological sites contain evidence showing that humans arrived shortly after the grasses and shrubs appeared. These plants attracted grazing animals, which, in turn, attracted humans.

Archeologists have uncovered evidence of early human habitation. The oldest find on the peninsula was at Sequim and dates to about 12,000 years ago. At this site, a mastodon skeleton apparently was butchered by humans (see Sequim mastodon, page 106). There is also good carbon-dated evidence that about 5,000 years ago, 7,000 years after the mastodon died at Sequim, hunters ventured up into the Olympic Range to at least the 5,000 foot level. There, archeologists found a layer of charcoal with pieces of animal bone mixed in, indicating a cooking fire. Still another find, a burden basket over 2,900 years old, was found several years ago at Obstruction Point near Hurricane Ridge, at an elevation of 5,000 feet. Other, relatively recent sites have also been discovered and archeologists are still working to piece together the story of early people.

As the climate warmed over the millennia, the peninsula changed. Forests replaced pioneer plants. Eventually Douglas fir *(Pseudotsuga menziesii)* and western hemlock *(Tsuga heterophylla)* came to dominate the slightly drier (or perhaps it would be better to say, less wet) east side of the range. Sitka spruce *(Picea sitchensis)*, western redcedar *(Thuja plicata)*, and western hemlock interspersed with smatterings of Douglas fir are found on the western mountain

SITKA SPRUCE
(Picea sitchensis)

OLYMPIC MARMOT
(Marmota olympus)

slopes. It is along these slopes, where the moisture-laden ocean breezes blow up the river valleys, that the most magnificent of the temperate rain forests, for which the peninsula is famous, are located.

The unique circumstances that go into the creation of rain forests are not yet perfectly understood. Rain forests are found along the valleys of such mountain-fed rivers as the Bogachiel, the Hoh, and the Quinault. But just as important as the rivers are the moist air masses blowing in from the Pacific Ocean. These forests are the wettest spots in the contiguous United States. The average rainfall in the Hoh River valley is 140 inches; the Quinault River valley receives about the same amount of rain. It is estimated that some forest areas in these valleys may receive over 200 inches of rain every year.

The rain forests are distinguished by other traits besides abundant rain. One of the most notable is the long strands of moss that hang like hanks of hair from the trees. These mosses, along with licorice ferns, lichens, and liverworts, are members of the epiphyte family. They are not parasites, since they are primarily nourished by decaying bark, and so do no harm to the trees.

Another characteristic feature of the rain forests is the dense tangles of undergrowth that makes them virtually impenetrable, except along the trails and paths created by passing animals such as deer, elk, and probably, long ago, mammoths. This understory is thick with ferns, wildflowers, and shrubs, all struggling for a foothold and quite literally a spot in the sun.

Seen throughout the forest are straight, orderly lines of trees. Sitka spruce *(Picea sitchensis)* and western hemlock seem to march along the forest floor in straight lines called colonnades. The trees seem to be standing on their toes like ballerinas reaching for the light. Colonnades are created when seedlings grow on the straight lengths of fallen trees, called nurse logs. Nutrients from the decaying nurse logs nourish the seedlings even as the nurses rot out from under the new crop of baby trees. The young trees continue to reach their roots down towards the ground around the disintegrating girths of their fallen nurses until finally—now scores of years old—the new growth is left alone, standing straight and stranded on exposed roots. Other trees, such as Douglas fir, bigleaf maple *(Acer macrophyllum)*, and vine maple *(Acer circinatum)* struggle to grow among these colonnades.

The Olympics do not consist only of rain forests. Several ecosystems are found as the forests sweep up from sea level into the high mountains. As the rain forests ascend the mountain valleys, they give way to lowland forests, where stands of grand fir *(Abies grandis)* and western hemlock predominate. At 2,000 to 3,000 feet, the montane forest begins to take over. Here are found Pacific silver fir *(Abies amabili),* named for the color of its bark, along with Douglas fir on the range's east side. The undergrowth here is less dense, and flora species begin to disappear.

Higher up, at about 3,600 feet, the subalpine forests, dominated by skirted subalpine firs *(Abies lasiocarpa),* are found. Still higher, in the short growing season of the alpine meadows, ground-hugging plants scramble for a hold amidst exposed rocks. Beyond that are the mountain peaks, some snow-covered year-round; others are uncovered for only a few weeks and remain as barren as if the last ice age had ended yesterday.

By 3,000 years ago, conditions on the peninsula had stabilized. The forests were in place. Salmon were running in the rivers, and humans were fishing for them. At a site on the Hoko River, on the road to Neah Bay at the northwest tip of the peninsula, archeologists uncovered an old fishing camp. People on the peninsula were fishing for salmon, halibut, and cod, harvesting mussels and clams from the beaches, and hunting seals, dolphins, and otters in the coastal waters. For 700 years, this camp was used seasonally by people of this evolving culture. Indications are that these people fished both in the river and offshore in canoes. Artifacts were buried along the Hoko's muddy bank. It was this mud, archeologists believe, that preserved the artifacts, sealing off oxygen and preserving numerous items that ordinarily would have rotted away.

The Hoko site shows that the indigenous people were also using cedar extensively. The western redcedar was, like the salmon, at the heart of Indian culture. Cedar is water-resistant, easily cut, and has a straight, even grain ideal for myriad uses, including house siding and roof shingles, canoes, tools, and such items as masks and beautifully decorated cedar boxes, which are found among every coastal tribe in the region.

Trunks of the cedar were hollowed out and shaped into canoes, the main form of transportation in the densely forested region. The soft inner bark was made into blankets, mats, and rain resistant hats and clothing. Cedar, along with grasses found in the prairies that dot the forest, was used to make baskets. Knives were made of small, sharp, quartzite chips, wedged into a cedar handle and lashed around the end of a stick with bark. The people who used the camp had advanced considerably from the people who may have butchered the Sequim mastodon many thousands of years earlier.

These civilizations continued to advance over the millennia. By the time the first Europeans reached the peninsula, the native people had developed a strong maritime culture based on fish (especially salmon), cedar, and sea mammals. One group, the Makah at Neah Bay, even hunted whales (*see* Neah Bay, page 157). They built sturdy houses, traveled great distances in canoes and on foot, harvested food and other materials from the forests, and had leisure in which to develop magnificent arts and crafts.

Things changed with the coming of the Europeans. Columbus landed in the New World in 1492. In 1592, a story circulated that a sailor named Juan de Fuca had reached a body of water on the Northwest Coast of North America in the vicinity of the channel now known as the Strait of Juan de Fuca. It was said that de Fuca claimed the channel was the mouth of the fabled Strait of Anian, a water route across North America that would provide an easy passage between the Atlantic and Pacific Oceans.

Today, many scholars are skeptical that de Fuca even existed, let alone reached the strait, and regard the tale as nothing more than a sailor's boast. However, the de Fuca story set off a 200-year search for the fabled "Northwest Passage." It was not until 1787 that Captain Charles Barkley, sailing by, realized that the uncharted expanse of water was not a large bay, as other explorers had thought, but indeed a strait. He promptly dubbed it the Strait of Juan de Fuca.

While Europeans were plying the waters around the peninsula looking for the Northwest Passage and bickering about who owned the land, the Indians were left in relative peace. It wasn't until 1792, five years after Barkley "found" the Strait of Juan de Fuca, that the first European colony was established. That year, 300 years after Columbus landed in the New World, the Spanish established an all-male colony at Neah Bay. It lasted for five months. Apparently, the men did not like the weather.

By the seventeenth century, Spain, Russia, and England all had laid claim to the area. When the American Revolution ended, the newly formed United States entered the ever-so-polite fray. Ships plied the waters, exploring for the Northwest Passage, charting the coast, and laying claim to it as they went.

By the mid-nineteenth century, the feuding was over. Russia and Spain had given up their claims. Treaties had established the borders between the United States and Canada that exist to this day. In the 1850s, Isaac Stevens, the first governor of the Washington Territory, established a series of Indian reservations, and the people of the nine tribes that lived on the peninsula moved onto them. These reservations still exist.

White settlers began to enter the area, and they brought towns, roads, and technology that continued to overwhelm the indigenous Indian cultures developed over 12 millennia. The town of Port Townsend was established in 1851. The brothers Will and Grant Humes were among the homesteaders. They settled in Geyser Valley above the Elwha River. The Humes cabin still remains some 2.5 miles up the trail from the Whiskey Bend trailhead above Lake Mills. This was part of the area the Press Party, financed by the *Seattle Press* newspaper to explore the Olympics, passed through in 1889-90 as it made its way into the interior mountain range.

The Press Party was just one of the groups attempting to explore the interior of the Olympic range. This land was the subject of much speculation and myth, which generally described it as a Shangri-La filled with warm, lush green valleys enclosed within the formidable circle of mountains. No such paradise was found, but explorers spent a great deal of energy searching for it. The Press Party was one of the more interesting. Its members spent six months and nearly starved doing it, but they did manage to make their way from the Elwha Valley in the north of the peninsula to Aberdeen in the south. Since it was winter and they all survived, they are generally credited with not having done not too badly. Unfortunately, they came out of the wilderness only to learn that C.S. Gilman, and his son, S.C. Gilman, had already transversed the mountains. But the Gilmans didn't have a newspaper sponsorship, so the Press Party got most of the publicity.

The Gilmans and the Press Party were not the first explorers in the area. Although there were some amateur attempts previously, it was in 1885 that the first official party was sent out. It was led by Lieutenant Joseph O'Neil. He, too, underestimated the terrain just as the Press Party would. O'Neil apparently thought he could penetrate to the interior in 2 to 3 days. It took the group close to 10 days just to reach the top of the foothills. Much to their consternation, they were greeted not by mountain valleys, but by another series of foothills that they would have to cross before they even reached the mountain bases. They decided it was time to go home.

O'Neil wasn't through, however. He came back in 1890, after the Press Party, and set out again. This time he was more successful, and he and his party managed to explore much of the interior. Three of them claimed to have climbed Mount Olympus, the highest peak in the Olympic range, but the copper box they said they left on the summit has never been found. However, most folks give them the benefit of the doubt. Exploration fever died down after the 1890 push.

Jack McGlone made the first substantiated climb of Mount Olympus in 1902. In 1910, a group of mountaineers made the climb, thinking they would be the first to reach the summit. Instead they found McGlone's rock cairn.

At the same time that the Indians were moved onto reservations, the lumber industry was beginning to make headway into the forests. Lumber production climbed steadily from its beginning in 1853, when the peninsula's first mill was built at Port Gamble. That year, 3,500,000 board feet of lumber were cut. By 1877, Port Gamble mills were cutting 335,000 board feet *a day*. By the 1880s, the forests along the Hood Canal and Strait of Juan de Fuca coasts were largely gone, and serious incursions were being made into the mountain forests.

These vast inroads on what had been considered a virtually limitless resource aroused some local citizens to call for some protection of at least part of the forest. In 1897, the U.S. government responded when President Grover Cleveland set aside land in the Olympics for a forest reserve. In 1909 Theodore Roosevelt used his presidential power to establish the Mount Olympus National Monument. President Franklin D. Roosevelt visited the peninsula in 1937, and in 1938 signed the Olympic National Park into being. In 1984, Congress passed the Wilderness Act.

Because of this legislation, vast tracks of the Olympic Peninsula look, at least from afar, much as they did before Europeans came to this region. Towns have developed along the edges, and both the U.S. Forest Service and private companies harvest the trees. Hikers, fishermen, campers, and other tourists come in multitudes to enjoy the parks and forests.

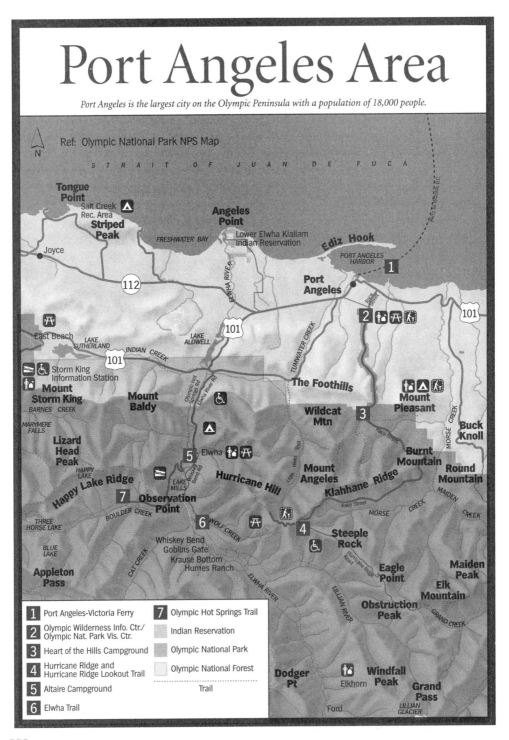

Port Angeles Area

Port Angeles is the largest city on the Olympic Peninsula with a population of 18,000 people.

Ref: Olympic National Park NPS Map

N

STRAIT OF JUAN DE FUCA

Ferry to Victoria, B.C.

Tongue Point

Salt Creek Rec. Area

Striped Peak

Joyce

FRESHWATER BAY

Angeles Point

Lower Elwha Klallam Indian Reservation

Ediz Hook

PORT ANGELES HARBOR

1

112

ELWHA RIVER

Port Angeles

Rook Street

2

101

101

East Beach

LAKE SUTHERLAND

INDIAN CREEK

LAKE ALDWELL

101

TUMWATER CREEK

Storm King Information Station

Mount Storm King

BARNES CREEK

Mount Baldy

Olympic Hot Springs Rd

Elwha River Rd

The Foothills

Wildcat Mtn

3

Mount Pleasant

Buck Knoll

MORSE CREEK

MARYMERE FALLS

Lizard Head Peak

HAPPY LAKE

Happy Lake Ridge

Elwha

5

Little River Trail

Mount Angeles

Klahhane Ridge

Burnt Mountain

Round Mountain

MAIDEN CREEK

LAKE MILLS

Whiskey Bend Rd

Hurricane Hill

7 Observation Point

BOULDER CREEK

THREE HORSE LAKE

BLUE LAKE

Appleton Pass

CAT CREEK

6

WOLF CREEK

Whiskey Bend
Goblins Gate
Krause Bottom
Humes Ranch

ELWHA RIVER

Race Street

MORSE CREEK

4

Steeple Rock

Hurricane Ridge Road

Eagle Point

LILLIAN RIVER

Obstruction Peak

Elk Mountain

Maiden Peak

GRAND CREEK

Dodger Pt

Elkhorn

Windfall Peak

Grand Pass

Ford

LILLIAN GLACIER

1 Port Angeles-Victoria Ferry	7	Olympic Hot Springs Trail
2 Olympic Wilderness Info. Ctr./ Olympic Nat. Park Vis. Ctr.		Indian Reservation
3 Heart of the Hills Campground		Olympic National Park
4 Hurricane Ridge and Hurricane Ridge Lookout Trail		Olympic National Forest
5 Altaire Campground		Trail
6 Elwha Trail		

Port Angeles

[Fig. 21] At nearly 18,000 people, this is the largest city on the peninsula. Established in the 1850s, the town's economic base has been logs, lumber, and fish. It also has a customs crossing, once the proud possession of Port Townsend. The crossing is most frequently used for traffic between Port Angeles and the city of Victoria, the capitol of British Columbia, located on Vancouver Island. The economic hub of the peninsula, Port Angeles is situated in an absolutely beautiful setting, with the Strait of Juan de Fuca on the north, the Olympics on the south, and the Elwha River valley and Lake Crescent to the west less than an hour away. The Strait of Juan de Fuca offers a wealth of both commercial and recreational activities, as well as providing easy access to Canada.

PORT ANGELES-VICTORIA FERRY

Port Angeles is home to a commercial, open-sea ferryboat, *Coho*, run by the Black Ball Transport Corporation. The ferry travels daily to Victoria, British Columbia, on Vancouver Island, and back. The round trip to Victoria can be done either in a day or overnight; the trip takes about 90 minutes.

Directions: In Port Angeles, follow the ferry signs on US Highway 101 to Lincoln Street. Turn right on Lincoln. The ferry dock is 1 block straight ahead at 101 East Railroad Avenue, Port Angeles.

Facilities: Snack bar, restrooms, open decks.

Dates: The ferry runs year-round.

Fees: Fees are charged for both cars and passengers, and for walk-on passengers.

Closest towns: Port Angeles and Victoria, B.C.

For more information: Black Ball Transport Corporation, 10777 Main, Bellevue, WA 98004. Phone (206) 622-2222. Tourism Victoria, Travel Info Center, 812 Wharf Street, Victoria, BC V8W 1T3. Phone (250) 953-2033.

PORT ANGELES RESTAURANTS

Port Angeles is large enough to have many of the fast-food franchises, but it also has some excellent full-service restaurants.

Chestnut Cottage Grove. 929 East Front Street. An opportunity to sample English charm without going to Victoria to do it, the Chestnut Cottage Grove is open for breakfast and lunch. The menu features fresh seafood, pasta, steaks, and sandwiches served either in the restaurant or on the patio. There is children's menu. *Moderate. Phone (360) 452-8344.*

The Bushwhacker. 527 East First Street. Seafood and prime rib are served in a relaxed, informal setting for dinner only. There is also a salad bar and a children's menu. *Moderate. Phone (360) 452-4113.*

C'est Si Bon. 23 Cedar Park Drive Road. A local favorite, this restaurant serves traditional French cuisine. The restaurant has gardens and views. *Moderate to expensive. Phone (360) 452-8888.*

PORT ANGELES LODGING

There are many good lodgings, including bed and breakfasts, in Port Angeles, but here are two that are well regarded.

The Tudor Inn. 1108 South Oak. There is no need to go to Victoria, British Columbia to soak up English atmosphere. This bed and breakfast, located a mere 12 blocks from the Blackball Ferry terminal, is crowded with English and American antiques, and has a library that is open to guests. All five bedrooms have private baths; one has a fireplace and balcony. They all have views, too, of either the Strait or the Olympic Mountains. The breakfast is opulent. Typical offerings include chicken crepes and fresh baguettes. *Moderate to expensive. Phone (360) 452-3138.*

Best Western Olympic Lodge. 140 Del Guzzi Drive. Although this is a chain, it has a hometown feel and is well regarded among travelers to the area. Its features include 105 units, a heated pool, and a rustic atmosphere. Many of the rooms have golf course or mountain views, and a continental breakfast is served. *Expensive. Phone (800) 600-2993.*

Northern Olympic Peninsula and Olympic National Park

[Fig. 21] Most of the northern section of the Olympic Peninsula, paralleling the Strait of Juan de Fuca, in the vicinity of Port Angeles, is in the Olympic National Park. The northern section of the peninsula is by far the most urban, but still there are numerous mountains, lakes, streams, campgrounds, trails, and other places of interest and beauty. Perhaps the best place to begin a visit to the backcountry is to take the drive over a smooth paved road with numerous viewpoints to Hurricane Ridge. That is partly because the ridge offers a large, immensely beautiful meadow where deer browse and chipmunks play, with mountain panoramas in the background, but also because the road passes a visitor center, which provides information about the park, and a wilderness information center, which provides information about both park and Forest Service areas. Visitors can obtain maps, literature, and advice at those places.

Hurricane Ridge is a high meadow with sweeping views of the Strait of Juan de Fuca and the Cascade Mountains, including Mount Baker to the north, and the peaks of the Olympic Mountains to the south. The ridge is located about 20 miles from downtown Port Angeles. At over 5,000 feet in elevation, Hurricane Ridge is a wonderful introduction to the park, and the only place in the park where visitors can reach subalpine areas by car. The ridge also offers a downhill ski run, complete with a poma lift and two tow ropes, as well as cross-country skiing.

The Olympic National Park Wilderness Information Center and Visitor Center is located at the beginning of the road to Hurricane Ridge. The park's main headquarters is located in Port Angeles. Elsewhere in the northern section of the peninsula, the park has lakes such as Lake Crescent, where there are fresh water beaches, lodges, and a campground. Nearby valleys have hot springs, resorts, campgrounds, and forested trails.

The National Park Service, under the jurisdiction of the Department of Interior, manages the park lands. Their preservation efforts are reflected in the park's regulations. Nothing is to be disturbed or removed. Hiking is permitted on existing trails; camping and fires are allowed only in designated sites. In the backcountry, food must be hung or carried in animal resistant containers. Hunting and firearms are not permitted in the park. Fishing regulations vary with locations and seasons. Pets are not permitted in the backcountry.

Quotas and reservations for overnight backpacking are in effect in some areas, including the Lake Ozette Loop, Badger and Grand valleys, Lake Constance, Hoh River Trail, and Sol Duc Trail. Permits and fees are required for all backcountry overnight hiking, but not for day use. Reservations in quota areas are available no more than 30 days in advance, and may be obtained by calling the wilderness center.

The Olympic National Park is one entity, but it has two portions. One portion is the mountains of the peninsula's interior. The other is the ocean beaches. US Highway 101 lies between the mountains and the beaches, snaking its way around the edge of the peninsula. Although the highway is not part of the park's boundary, it provides a psychological boundary for Olympic Parks two areas.

Directions: The park covers much of the interior of the Olympic Mountains as well as 57 miles of saltwater beaches. Access is provided by US Highway 101, which runs along the east, north, and west sides of the Olympic Peninsula. The major access into the park is in Port Angeles, 90 miles west of Seattle.

Activities: Beach and mountain hiking, camping, picnicking, fishing, river rafting, nature trail hikes, bird and wild life viewing.

Facilities: Campgrounds, trails, picnic grounds, lodging, ranger stations, wilderness center, interpretative centers, nature trails, restrooms, water, RV dumps and hook-ups at some of the park concessions.

Dates: The park is open year-round. Individual campground openings vary somewhat from year to year, especially in the winter, depending on the weather.

Fees: Fees are charged for entering the park and for backpacking permits, campgrounds, and for Sol Duc Hot Springs pools.

Closest town: Port Angeles, 1.5 miles.

For more information: Olympic National Park, Wilderness Information Center, 600 East Park Avenue, Port Angeles, WA 98362. Phone (360) 452-0330.

OLYMPIC WILDERNESS INFORMATION CENTER/OLYMPIC NATIONAL PARK VISITOR CENTER

[Fig. 21(2)] A quick hop from Port Angeles, the visitor center has a great museum and interpretative center, as well as guidebooks, maps, park activity information, and a very knowledgeable staff. In addition to the visitor center, the national forest and national park also have a wilderness information center, which is located in a trailer behind the visitor center. The Olympic Wilderness Information Center has the most up-to-date information on what trails and campgrounds are open, as well as practical advice on how to deal with obstacles that might be encountered on trails. The *Olympic Wilderness Trip Planner* offers comprehensive information on everything from mountain lions to hypothermia to dehydration. The guide is a must-have for every visitor and can be obtained ahead of time by calling or writing the wilderness center. The wilderness center also issues backcountry overnight permits, rents animal-resistant buckets and canisters, and hands out wilderness trip planners, which contain pertinent information and tips, and outline the park's rules and regulations.

Directions: Continuing on US Highway 101 from Port Townsend and Sequim, enter Port Angeles. Continue on Highway 101 for about 1 mile. Turn south on Race Street, following the Olympic National Park/Hurricane Ridge signs. The wilderness information center is located behind the Port Angeles Visitor Center.

Facilities: Museum, picnic tables, restroom, information and permit station.

Dates: Both centers are open year-round.

Fees: Fees are charged for overnight backcountry permits, maps, guide books, and rentals.

Closest town: Port Angeles, 0.5 mile.

For more information: Olympic National Park, Wilderness Information Center, 600 East Park Avenue, Port Angeles, WA 98362. Phone (360) 452-0330.

HEART OF THE HILLS CAMPGROUND

[Fig. 21(3)] This lovely campground is heavily wooded with conifers, predominately Douglas fir *(Pseudotsuga menziesii)*. It is close to numerous trails as well as Hurricane Ridge. Heart of the Forest Trail, an easy 2-mile forest-lined hike, starts right in the campground. It ends at a clear-cut on private property adjoining the park.

Directions: On US Highway 101 in Port Angeles, turn south on Race Street, following the Olympic National Park/Hurricane Ridge signs. Continue on that road for 2 miles past the park entrance.

Activities: Tent and RV camping, hiking, naturalist talks in the summer, picnicking.

Facilities: Campsites, restrooms, drinking water, garbage service.

Dates: Open year-round. During periods of snow, it is necessary to walk in, a distance of 100 yards.

Fees: Fees are charged for camping.

Closest town: Port Angeles, 2.3 miles.

For more information: Olympic National Park, Wilderness Information Center, 600 East Park Avenue, Port Angeles, WA 98362. Phone (360) 452-0330.

⬛ HURRICANE RIDGE

[Fig. 21(4)] The road up Hurricane Ridge passes from lowland forests to subalpine meadows. Turnouts along the way offer (weather permitting) spectacular views of the Strait of Juan de Fuca, Dungeness Spit, Vancouver Island, and snow-capped Mount Baker, a volcano near Bellingham in the Cascade Mountain Range. The road, starting from Port Angeles, climbs from sea level to 5,225 feet in 17 miles. The ridge's highest point, Klahhane Ridge, is 6,454 feet high.

From June through August the alpine meadow trails at Hurricane Ridge wander through fields of wildflowers such as avalanche lily (*Erythronium montanum*), fan-leafed cinquefoil (*Potentilla flabellifolia*), spreading phlox (*Phlox diffusa*), common harebell (*Campanula rotundifolia*), and American bistort (*Polygonum bistortoides*). When covered with snow in the winter, these same meadows become cross-country ski areas, suitable for everyone from beginners to intermediate and advanced skiers. Check at the ranger station to see what is open. A downhill ski run, with a poma lift and two rope tows, runs down the steep back cliffs on the south side of the meadows. There are numerous hikes in the area. Check at the visitor centers for a complete list. Meadow areas are suitable for novice cross-country skiers.

Directions: From US Highway 101 in Port Angeles, turn south on Race Street, following the Olympic National Park/Hurricane Ridge signs. Continue on the road 17 miles to Hurricane Ridge.

Activities: Hiking, cross-country and downhill skiing, scenic and nature viewing.

Facilities: Visitor center and museum, restaurant, restrooms, gift shop, poma lift and two rope tows, cross-country ski trails.

Dates: Open year-round, weather permitting.

Fees: Fees are charged for downhill skiing.

Closest town: Port Angeles, 20 miles.

For more information: Olympic National Park, Wilderness Information Center, 600 East Park Avenue, Port Angeles, WA 98362. Phone (360) 452-0330.

HURRICANE HILL LOOKOUT TRAIL

[Fig. 21(4)] This 1.4-mile-long hike offers views of the Elwha River and Mount Olympus, as well as views of the Strait of Juan de Fuca, Vancouver Island, and Mount Baker. It is graced with a great selection of wildflowers, including Indian paintbrush (*Castilleja miniata*) and large-leafed lupine (*Lupinus polyphyllus*). Several Douglas fir trees, growing above their normal climatic zone, are struggling to survive.

Directions: From the Hurricane Ridge Visitor Center on the Hurricane Ridge Road, go northeast another 1.4 miles to the parking lot at the end of the road.

Trail: 1.4 miles, one-way.

Elevation: 757-foot elevation gain.

Degree of difficulty: Moderate.

For more information: Olympic National Park, Wilderness Information Center, 600 East Park Avenue, Port Angeles, WA 98362. Phone (360) 452-0330.

ELWHA RIVER VALLEY

Next door neighbor to Hurricane Ridge, the glacier-fed Elwha River tumbles down from the mountain peaks above. Its lower reaches spill happily to the sea, but two dams, the Elwha and the Glines, rein in the higher waters. Both Lake Mills, created by the Elwha Dam, and the river provide good fishing, and there is a boat ramp on the lake. The valley was the focus of much of the early exploration of the interior of the Olympics. The 1885 party led by Lieutenant Joseph O'Neil started its explorations of the interior of the Olympic Mountain Range from here, and the Seattle Press Party spent months trying to get out of the Elwha Valley in the winter of 1889-90. The cabin of early pioneer brothers Will and Grant Humes is located in this area.

Directions: From Port Angeles, continue to follow US Highway 101 another 8.5 miles west to the Olympic Hot Springs Road (also called the Elwha River Road). Turn left on the Elwha River Road which runs along the river valley.

Activities: Camping, hiking, fishing, and boating.

Facilities: Boat ramp, campgrounds.

Dates: Open year-round, except when winter weather cause road closure. Fees are charged for camping and park entrance.

Closest town: Port Angeles, 8.5 miles.

For more information: Olympic National Park, Wilderness Information Center, 600 East Park Avenue, Port Angeles, WA 98362. Phone (360) 452-0330.

ALTAIRE CAMPGROUND

[Fig. 21(5)] This spacious, shady campground, with dappled sunlight filtering through the trees, is nestled between a tree-covered hill and the Elwha River.

INDIAN
PAINTBRUSH
(Castilleja miniata)

Directions: From Port Angeles, follow US Highway 101 8.5 miles west and turn south on to the Olympic Hot Springs Road (also called the Elwha River Road). Altaire is 2.6 miles further on the right.

Activities: Camping, hiking.

Facilities: Campsites, restrooms, picnic tables.

Dates: Open spring to early fall, exact dates are dependent on the weather.

Fees: Fees are charged for camping.

Closest town: Port Angeles, about 11 miles.

For more information: Olympic National Park, Wilderness Information Center, 600 East Park Avenue, Port Angeles, WA 98362. Phone (360) 452-0330.

ELWHA TRAIL

[Fig. 21(6)] The Press Party blazed much of this trail. In fact, it is possible to still spot some of the party's characteristic blaze marks—three axe cuts, one above the next—between Antelope and Idaho Creeks as the trail goes above Geyser Valley. The trail passes through both second growth and the darker green old-growth forests. There are several good destinations along the way. A side trail, Lillian River Trail, intersects with the Elwha Trail at 4.1 miles; go 0.5 mile down this side trail (it drops about 300 feet in elevation). At the bottom of the canyon is Lillian Campground, which is pretty, but can be cold even in summer. There also is camping at Mary's Falls (8.8 miles) and Camp Baltimore (9.0). Chicago Camp is located at 25.8 miles. The Elwha Trail is 27.8-miles-long. Check with the Olympic Wilderness Information Center for a complete trail guide.

Directions: From Port Angeles, follow US Highway 101 another 8.5 miles west to the Olympic Hot Springs Road (also called the Elwha River Road). Turn south. Continue 4 miles on the Elwha Road to Lake Mills, where the road branches. Take the left branch, Whiskey Bend Road, and follow it along the eastern side of Lake Mills to its end.

Trail: 27.8 miles, one-way.

Elevation: The elevation gain is 2,200 feet.

Degree of difficulty: Moderate.

For more information: Olympic National Park, Wilderness Information Center, 600 East Park Avenue, Port Angeles, WA 98362. Phone (360) 452-0330.

OLYMPIC HOT SPRINGS TRAIL

[Fig. 21(7)] This is one of the Olympic Mountains' two hot springs. The other is at Sol Duc (*see* Sol Duc River Valley, page 149). The native peoples used both Olympic and Sol Duc for medicinal soaking. Olympic Hot Springs was discovered in 1892 by Andrew Jacobsen, but it remained a hidden jewel due to lack of access until the early 1900s, when a trail was created. In the 1930s, the U.S. Forest Service built a road, and a lodge was constructed. The lodge is long since gone, but there is still a trail. People come to the springs to soak, but at their own risk since the water quality is not monitored. This is a clothing-optional area. This spring is not particularly

Lake Crescent Area

9-mile-long Lake Crescent is at an elevation of 200 feet and is over 600 feet deep.

1 Log Cabin Resort

2 Lake Crescent Lodge

3 Fairholm Campground

4 Spruce Railroad Trail

5 Sol Duc Hot Springs Resort/ RV Campground/Sol Duc Campground

6 Canyon Creek Trail

Olympic National Forest

Olympic National Park

Trail

Ref: Olympic National Park Nps Map

N

S T R A I T   O F

J U A N   D E   F U C A

Tongue Point

Salt Creek

Striped Peak

FRESHWATER BAY

Lyre River

Joyce

112

EAST TWIN RIVER

WEST TWIN RIVER

SUSIE CREEK

LYRE RIVER

112

East Beach

1

LAKE SUTHERLAND

INDIAN CREEK

Mt Muller

North Shore

Pyramid Mtn

101

101

3

4

Sol Duc Valley

LAKE CRESCENT

Storm King Information Station

101

Mount Baldy

CAMP CREEK

EAGLE LAKES

Sol Duc Hot Springs Road

La Poel

2

Mount Storm King

CREEK

Mount Baldy

NORTH

Sourdough Mountain

Aurora Pk

MARYMERE FALLS

BARNES

Lizard Head Peak

HAPPY LAKE

Altaire

Salmon Cascades

Aurora Ridge Trail

Happy Lake Ridge

LAKE MILLS

SOL DUC

FORK

RIVER

Sol Duc Hot Springs Road

5

6

Boulder Peak

THREE HORSE LAKE

BOULDER CREEK

Observation Point

MUNDEN CREEK

MINK LAKE

SOL DUC FALLS

BLUE LAKE

Mount Appleton

Appleton Pass

CAT CREEK

Rugged Ridge

CAMP CREEK

Slide Pass

Slide Pk

HIDDEN LAKE

RING LAKE

BLACKWOOD LAKE

BOGACHIEL LAKE

DEER LAKE

Seven Lakes Basin

CLEAR LAKE

SOL DUC LAKE

LONG LAKE

HEART LAKE

Mount Fitzhenry

NORTH FORK

Sugarloaf Mountain

BOGACHIEL RIVER

Green Peak

Bogachiel Peak

High Divide

Cat Peak

Mount Carrie

attractive; however, the relatively short distance and low elevation gain make a nice hike for families.

Directions: From Port Angeles, go 8.5 miles west on US Highway 101, and turn south onto the Olympic Hot Springs Road (also called the Elwha River Road). Go 4 miles to Lake Mills. Take the right branch. Follow the road for 7 miles along the west side of Lake Mills to its end.

For more information: Olympic National Park, Wilderness Information Center, 600 East Park Avenue, Port Angeles, WA 98362. Phone (360) 452-0330.

Trail: 2.4 miles, one-way.

Elevation: 220-foot elevation gain.

Degree of difficulty: Easy.

LAKE CRESCENT

[Fig. 22] Sitting in a deep glacier-gouged bed, Lake Crescent's waters are over 600 feet deep. With an elevation of 200 feet at the water's top surface, this means the floor of the lake is below the level of the sea, only 4 miles away at the Strait of Juan de Fuca. The lake is so clear that on a cloudless night a diver can see the moon and stars from a depth of 100 feet. There is good trout fishing here. Native trout species interbred with introduced trout species used to stock the lake and can no longer be found in pure form. Although much of the lake is under the jurisdiction of the National Park Service, there are privately owned homes around the lake, and Clallam County has a group facility on the northwest side. Highway 101 runs along the south side of the 9-mile-long lake.

Boats can be rented from the park's concessionaires at Log Cabin Resort, and Fairholm. Log Cabin Resort, on the north side of the lake, is rustic and very family oriented. Lake Crescent Lodge, located on the southeast corner of the lake, offers some good day hiking and is a splendid, old-fashion resort. Fairholm has a campground, a picnic area, and a small grocery-deli where boats are rented.

LOG CABIN RESORT

[Fig. 22(1)] This resort, operated by a park concessionaire, features 24 very rustic cabins and motel units, and 12 chalets. Set far up the lake's north shore, it is nestled in the lake's basin with the forest surrounding it. A high ridge backs the north side. The resort is a short car trip to trails at Storm King Ranger Station by Lake Crescent Lodge. The Spruce Railroad Trail ends close by and is a good day hike before taking a dip in the lake. Boat rentals are available to the general public as well as resort guests.

Directions: From Port Angeles, go west on US Highway 101 for 16 miles to Piedmont Road at Lake Crescent's east end. Turn right, and follow the road about 3 miles to the resort.

Activities: Lodging, swimming, fishing, boating, hiking.

Facilities: Lodge, cabins, restaurant, RV campgrounds, boat rentals, boat launch, beach, playground, gift shop.

Dates: Open from Mar. through Oct.

Fees: Fees are charged for lodging and boat rentals.

Closest town: Port Angeles, 16 miles.

For more information: Log Cabin Resort, 3183 East Beach Road, Port Angeles, WA 98362. Phone (360) 928-3325.

LAKE CRESCENT LODGE

[Fig. 22(2)] Located next to the Storm King Ranger Station, the main building of this fine old lodge was built in 1916 and hosted President Franklin Roosevelt on his information gathering visit in 1937. He signed Olympic National Park into existence the next year. The lodge is quaint and old-fashioned, with loads of wooden beams and charming features. In addition to the old lodge, there are both modern and rustic cabins, and a restaurant. Visitors can rent rowboats to paddle around or fish.

Directions: From Port Angeles, follow US Highway 101 for 21 miles to the east end of Lake Crescent. Turn right at the Storm King Ranger/Lake Crescent Lodge signs.

Activities: Lodging, fishing, boating, hiking.

Facilities: Lodge and cabin accommodations, boat rentals, restaurant, and gift shop.

Fees: Fees are charged for lodging and rentals.

Dates: Late Apr. through late Oct.

Closest town: Port Angeles, 21 miles.

For more information: Lake Crescent Lodge, HC 62, PO Box 11, Port Angeles, WA 98362. Phone (360) 928-3211.

FAIRHOLM CAMPGROUND

[Fig. 22(3)] This woodsy campground sits amid towering Douglas firs and western hemlocks on the western tip of Lake Crescent; it has an unguarded swimming beach and there are trails in the campground and nearby.

Directions: From Port Angeles, go west on US Highway 101 for 26 miles, to the west end of Lake Crescent. Turn right at the Fairholm Campground signs.

Activities: Camping, picnicking, fishing, boating, swimming, hiking.

Facilities: Campground, nature trail, boat launch, RV dump. Fairholm General Store and Café, groceries, deli, and boat rentals.

Dates: Open from spring through fall, depending on weather.

Fees: Fees are charged for camping and rentals.

Closest town: Port Angeles, 26 miles.

For more information: Olympic National Park, Wilderness Information Center, 600 East Park Avenue, Port Angeles, WA 98362. Phone (360) 452-0330.

SPRUCE RAILROAD TRAIL

[Fig. 22(4)] During World War I a unique branch of the U.S. Army, the Spruce Production Division, built a railroad line here to provide spruce wood used to build airplanes. Unfortunately, the line was completed 19 days after the war's end and was never used. But its old bed makes a good trail, especially since this north side is the only stretch of Lake Crescent without a road along it. There are two derelict and unsafe tunnels, but safe trails bypass them. The trail offers wonderful views of the lake, and passes by some interesting geological formations, including pillow basalt. This trail can be done as a round trip; it is also possible for hikers to be picked up on the other end, near Log Cabin Resort (*see* Log Cabin Resort, page 147).

Directions: From Port Angeles, go west on US Highway 101 for 26 miles to the west end of Lake Crescent. Turn right at the Fairholm Campground signs. Continue past the campground, and follow the road 5 miles to the end.

Trail: 4 miles, one way.

Elevation: Elevation gain is 600 feet.

Degree of difficulty: Moderate.

For more information: Olympic National Park, Wilderness Information Center, 600 East Park Avenue, Port Angeles, WA 98362. Phone (360) 452-0330.

SOL DUC RIVER VALLEY

[Fig. 23] Sol Duc Valley has one of two hot springs in the Olympic National Park, the other being Olympic Hot Springs in the Elwha Valley (*see* Olympic Hot Springs Trail, page 145). *Sol Duc* (also spelled—and always pronounced—Sole duck) is the Indian word for "sparkling waters." It is possible to hike from the Elwha and Hoh Valleys to the Sol Duc River valley—an excellent way to earn a good, long soak in the hot spring pools at Sol Duc Resort. There are also a number of good short hikes.

Water from the now capped hot springs is piped into two soaking pools and a swimming pool; a long soak is a wonderful treat after a hike (or several days of camping). Although there has been a resort at Sol Duc since the early twentieth century, the ambiance in the more recently constructed cabins would best be called "modern rustic." Sol Duc Hot Springs RV Campground, which is part of the resort, is for RVs only, not tents.

Directions: From Port Angeles, go west on US Highway 101 for 27 miles and turn south on Sol Duc Hot Springs Road. Watch for the Sol Duc National Park road signs. Go about 11 miles to the resort.

Activities: Two hot springs-fed soaking pools and one swimming pool, hiking.

Facilities: Suit and towel rentals, shampoo and other items may be purchased. Restaurant, cabin rentals, RV campground with electrical, sewage, and water hook-ups, hiking trails, ranger station, grocery store, gift shop.

Dates: Open from late May to early Oct.

Fees: Fees are charged for lodging, for RV camping, and for the hot springs pool facilities, including towels, bathing suits, shampoos, etc.

Closest town: Port Angeles, 40 miles.

For more information: Sol Duc Hot Springs Resort, PO Box 2169, Port Angeles, WA 98362. Phone (360) 327-3583.

SOL DUC CAMPGROUND

[Fig. 22(5)] The Sol Duc River babbles along the western side of this shady

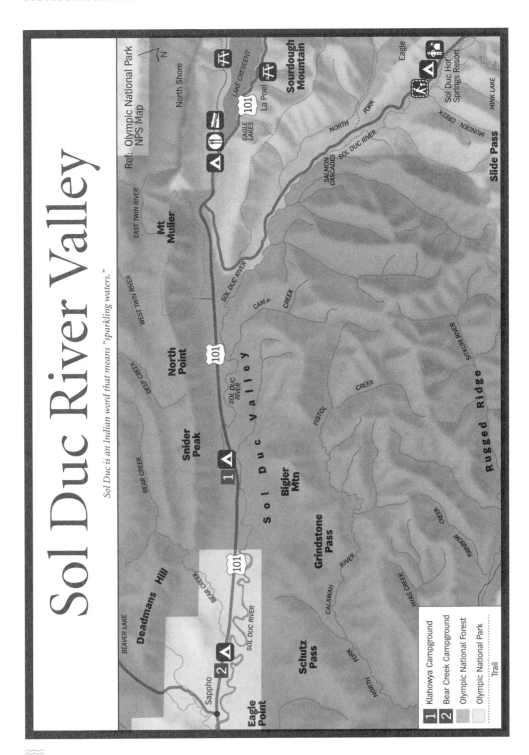

Sol Duc River Valley

Sol Duc is an Indian word that means "sparkling waters."

Ref: Olympic National Park
NPS Map

Klahowya Campground
Bear Creek Campground
Olympic National Forest
Olympic National Park
Trail

campground set amidst groves of Douglas fir and hemlocks. This campground is not operated by a park concessionaire, but is a regular Olympic National Park campground and should not be confused with the resort and the resort's RV campground. The campground is located about 200 feet beyond Sol Duc Resort.

Directions: From Port Angeles, go west on US Highway 101 for 27 miles. Turn south on Sol Duc Hot Springs Road, and watch for the Sol Duc National Park road signs. Go about 11 miles to the resort. The campground is located about 200 feet past the hot springs.

Activities: Camping, fishing, hiking, ranger programs, picnicking, swimming and soaking in the resort's hot spring pools.

Facilities: RV and tent sites, drinking water, restrooms and garbage pick-up, resort soaking and swimming pools.

Dates: Open spring through fall, depending on weather and funding.

Fees: Fees are charged for overnight camping and for use of the resort pools.

Closest town: Port Angeles, 40 miles.

For more information: Olympic National Park, Wilderness Information Center, 600 East Park Avenue, Port Angeles, WA 98362. Phone (360) 452-0330.

CANYON CREEK TRAIL

[Fig. 22(6)] This well-maintained trail climbs steadily for nearly 1,600 feet, from misty Sol Duc Falls (elevation 2,000 feet) to Deer Lake (elevation 3,600) following along the deep waters of Canyon Creek. The trail goes through forests of mostly Douglas fir and hemlock, but other plants abound, too. Be careful of the thickets of devil's club, which is aptly named for its devilish thorny spines. Fishermen will find rainbow and Eastern brook trout in Deer Lake. The lake is popular, and camping is restricted to designated spots to protect the vegetation. The trail extends all the way to the Bogachiel River (*see* Bogachiel Trail, page 179).

Whale Antics

Whales live much of their lives underwater, but they are mammals and must come to the surface to breathe. They break the surface rolling in a graceful, curving motion. During that process they expel used air from their lungs in a process called blowing, which differs from species to species. The mist of the blow can often be seen from long distances, and its form is one method for identifying the different species. After expelling the air, they take in a new supply and, without interrupting their motion, slide back into the water.

More rarely, whales come to the surface when they breach, head slap, or spyhop. In breaching they rise up out of the water, either head first or, rarely, tail first, going straight up and falling back on the water in a spectacular, splashing display. Head slapping is similar to breaching but the animal lifts only its head and the top of its body from the water then slaps them onto the surface. Spyhopping consists of poking the head straight up out of the water until the eyes emerge. Sometimes the whales turn in a circle before easing back into the water as if they are just looking around, which may be exactly what they are doing.

Directions: From Port Angeles, go west on US Highway 101 for 27 miles, turn south on Sol Duc Hot Springs Road, and watch for the Sol Duc national park road signs. Go about 11 miles to the resort. Continue 2 miles past the resort and Sol Duc Campground on the Sol Duc Hot Springs Road to the trailhead.

For more information: Olympic National Park, Wilderness Information Center, 600 East Park Avenue, Port Angeles, WA 98362. Phone (360) 452-0330.

Trail: 4 miles, one-way.

Elevation: 1,595-foot elevation gain.

Degree of difficulty: Moderate.

KLAHOWYA CAMPGROUND

[Fig. 23(1)] This U.S. Forest Service campground, located near the Sol Duc River, is rather close to the road and road noise. However, with its lovely grounds and relatively private campsites, this drawback is fairly easy to forgive. The grounds are covered with Oregon wood sorrel *(Oxalis oregana)*, salal *(Gaultheria shallon)*, and ferns. Lacy vine maples reach towards the sun as they try to grow beneath the towering Douglas firs and hemlocks. Pioneer Path Natural Trail is located at the western loop's south end. Although the trail mostly wanders through second-growth rather than virgin forest, it is interesting and pleasant. Be sure to look for the notches on some of the old stumps. These held the springboards that loggers stood on in order to attain enough height to reach the narrow portion of the trunks, making their work with arm-powered axes and saws easier. The campground is close to hiking trails in the Elwha and Sol Duc valleys.

Directions: From Port Angeles, follow US Highway 101 west for 35 miles. Watch for the state park signs. The campground is on the north side of the road.

Activities: Camping, hiking, fishing, picnicking.

Facilities: Campsites, nature trail, restrooms, picnic tables.

Dates: Open from late spring to mid-Nov., depending on demand and funding.

Fees: Fees are charged for overnight camping.

Closest town: Forks, 27 miles.

For more information: Olympic National Forest Headquarters, 1835 Black Lake Road Southwest, Olympia, WA 98512. Phone (360) 374-7566.

BEAR CREEK CAMPGROUND

[Fig. 23(2)] This Washington State Department of Natural Resources campground is primitive, but popular. It is located right off US 101, about 6 miles west of Klahowya. The wooded grounds contain 15 campsites, including one that is wheelchair accessible. Some of the sites have views of Bear Creek 100 feet below the campground. There are outhouses, but there have been water purity problems, so bring water.

Directions: From Port Angeles, follow US Highway 101 west for 42 miles, and watch for the signs. The campground is on the north side of the road.

Activities: Camping.

Facilities: Campsites, outhouses.

Dates: Open year-round.

Fees: None.

Closest town: Forks, 21 miles.

For more information: Washington State Department of Natural Resources, Olympic Regional Headquarters, 411 Tillicum Lane, Forks, WA 98331. Phone (360) 374-6131.

Western Olympic Peninsula

[Fig. 24] The 57 miles of saltwater beaches in Olympic National Park offer some of the most beautiful and, frequently, remote ocean hiking in the contiguous United States. Visitors will encounter some rugged terrain but will be well rewarded with sweeping views, tidepools, wildlife, remnants of old-growth forest, and solitude. It is possible to hike 35 miles from Shi Shi Beach at Cape Flattery to Rialto Beach at La Push and barely brush against civilization along the way. Many shorter hikes capture much of this same magic.

The beaches along this coast are varied as to terrain. The beaches south of the Hoh River to the park's boundary at the Queets River are easily accessible and are designated for day-use only. Beaches north of the Hoh River to Shi Shi, over 45 miles, are wilderness. While there are stretches of sand, much of this coastline consists of rocks deposited by glacial fingers that once reached down from the mountains, or cobblestones washed smooth by rivers. Some beaches are strewn with large boulders that turn a hike into something more closely resembling a rock scramble. The beach south of Point of the Arches is one such beach.

The coast is punctuated by headlands, high-banked points of land that jut out into the ocean, impeding passage along the beach. Hikers can easily walk around a few of these headlands, but others can only be rounded at low tides. A few of them are impassable and the only way for the traveler to conquer them is by climbing over them. Fortunately, there are usually ropes, ladders, or trails to aid the climb.

Backpacking on this coastline requires careful planning. Some areas are restricted and reservations for overnight backpacking trips are required. A tide table, available at the ranger stations, and a watch are essential for rounding points and headlands. Getting caught halfway around a point with an incoming tide can be uncomfortable and possibly deadly. Weather can turn cool quickly, and hypothermia is a real threat even in summer. Warm clothing and jackets are other essential items.

Trips can last for one night or several weeks. Shi Shi, Cape Alava, South Beach, Third Beach, and Rialto Beach, for instance, are all suitable for an overnight trip, or to set up camp for several nights. On the other hand, the trip from Shi Shi to Cape

Alava will require at least three days, because the two headlands must be tackled at low tides and it is not possible to get from one to the other in a single day. The Lake Ozette Loop Trail offers an alternative for those who want to hike without covering the same beaches twice. The trail offers a 9-mile triangle of hiking between Lake Ozette, Cape Alava, and Sand Point and back to Lake Ozette.

These coastal waters, tidelands, and beaches almost overwhelm the senses with their startling features. Geology, wildlife, and weather have created a distinct environment here. Sea stacks (rock monoliths that stand alone in the sea), islands, and rocks often sprout trees and other vegetation. On some stretches of beach these geological features take astonishing forms, while around the next point, the coast, bereft of any salient obstacles for the incoming waters to beat against, is as open and mellow as a duck pond.

Most of the rocky promontories were once part of the mainland. These remnants were left behind when the constantly pounding waves ate away the softer rocks from around the headlands. Eventually, holes, then arches, tunnels, canyons, and caves would appear, then fall into the sea as the land crumbled around them. Finally the remaining isolated sea stacks fell into jumbled piles of rock. The waters off these shores are filled with the bones of dead ships that ran afoul on these rocks. Small pebbles with holes through them can frequently be found. The holes are the work of boring clams, not geological forces or a drill bit.

The rocky shores are home to a huge variety of sea creatures. Birds, mammals, and tidepool creatures can be seen and heard. Over 250 species of birds roam these coasts, some calling it home, others just passing through, making these waters a birder's heaven. Auklets, cormorants, puffins, and members of the shearwater family, such as the northern fulmar *(Puffinus creatopus)* and the sooty shearwater *(Puffinus griseus)* are found here. The pigeon guillemot *(Cepphus columba)*, common murre *(Uria aalge)*, marbled murrelet *(Brachyramphus marmoratus)*, brown pelican *(Pelecanus occidentalis)*, and occasional bald eagle *(Haliaeetus leucocephalus)* may also be seen.

Many intertidal sea animals also find sanctuary in the tidepools found at the bases of these same rocks. Visitors should watch for shallow pools that lie in the crevasses of the rocks, sea stacks, islands, points, and headlands. Sea stars *(Piaster ochraceous)*, mussels *(Mytilus californianus)*, a variety of small crabs, including hermit crabs *(Pagurus samuelis)*, and gastropods such as fingered limpets *(Collisella digitalis)*, as well as barnacles and chitons make their homes in the quiet, protected pools, or cling to the side of rocks that are exposed at low tides. Shellfish can be harvested in season; check with the ranger. While exploring the tidepools, keep an eye out on the water for whales and Dall porpoises that swim offshore on their migrations or while hunting for food. Sea lions and seals can occasionally be spotted on the beaches or heard above the surf as they rest on offshore rocks.

Twisted, stunted trees are some of the most distinctive features found along the coast. Although some areas are sheltered enough for vegetation to thrive, in other areas vegetation has a more tenuous hold. In these areas plants cling to precarious rootholds among the rocks and islands found along the coast, leading tortured lives and being buffeted by continuous winds and seawater spray. A tree only several feet high can be 300 years old. Sitka spruce (*Picea sitchensis)* are easily identified by the bulbous knobs, called burls, that grow on their trunks. The cause of these knobs is unknown. Some theorize viruses are the cause, others think it is salt water.

Permanent stacks of drift logs are slung just above the tide line. Only extreme high tides and the fiercest winter storms are strong enough to move these fallen giants. The next storm will toss up similar stacks in a never-ending cycle. Be careful when walking on them. They can move unexpectedly.

Many of the beaches along the Washington coast are high-banked. At times the land is 100 feet or more above the beach. Those beaches are accessible only at specific points where trails have been cut. Orange and black targets mark the trailheads. Keep a close look out because in bad weather they are easily missed.

Drinking water can be a problem. It is not available on some beaches, and even when it is, it should be purified before it is used. What water there is comes from streams. However, only streams large enough to have names can be counted on to flow all summer. The water is often a brownish color from the tannins and sediments leached out of the soil; tannin is not harmful.

A protozoan, *Giardia lamblia,* found in untreated water is another matter. Although not fatal, this little protozoan can be extremely unpleasant, causing severe stomach cramps and diarrhea, usually two weeks after it is ingested. A full minute at a rolling boil kills it. There are also tablets that treat the water and filters that will strain out giardia protozoa.

Except for a very few outhouses, this is cathole country. Holes should be dug in organic soil, not the beach. Sticks work, shovels are better. Go as far back into the woods as possible, and bury the results; however, pack out toilet paper. All other garbage must be packed out, too. Unfortunately, some beaches, because of the way ocean currents run, are littered with jetsam from ships illegally dumping their garbage. Most things in the park are not supposed to be removed; this is an exception, so feel free to pack it out.

There are no designated campgrounds per se, but fire rings, makeshift driftwood "furnishings," and bear wires indicate established campsites. Campfires are allowed on most beaches, but not all. One beach where fires are prohibited is the stretch between Wedding Rocks and Yellow Banks at the end of the Sand Point leg of the Lake Ozette Trail. At beaches where fires are allowed; only driftwood may be used. Cutting or burning live vegetation is not allowed.

Beach fires should be 10 feet away from beach logs, as the logs will smolder and burn for weeks once the logs catch fire. Chainsaws are not allowed; axes and cutting implements are discouraged. Use smaller pieces of driftwood (wrist size or less) that don't need to be cut.

Raccoons have become especially aggressive and very smart about getting into food.

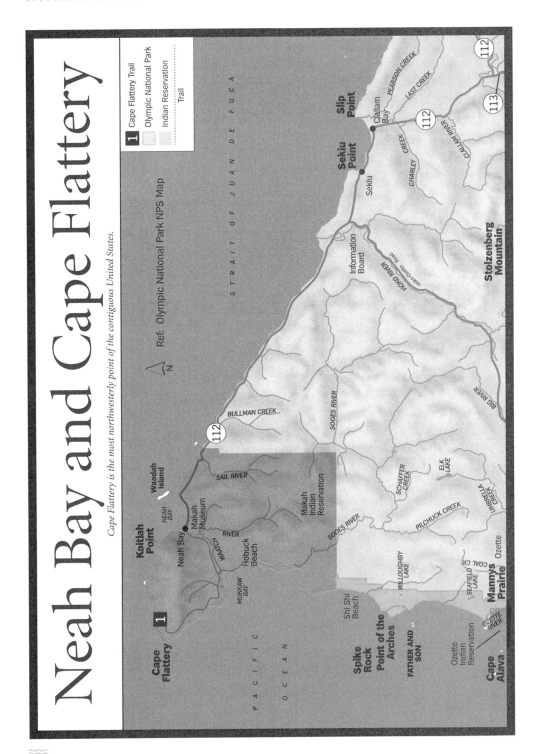

Neah Bay and Cape Flattery

Cape Flattery is the most northwesterly point of the contiguous United States.

Ref: Olympic National Park NPS Map

N

| Cape Flattery Trail |
| Olympic National Park |
| Indian Reservation |
| Trail |

STRAIT OF JUAN DE FUCA

PACIFIC OCEAN

Koitlah Point

Waadah Island

Cape Flattery

1

Neah Bay

NEAH BAY

Makah Museum

WHATCH RIVER

Hobuck Beach

MUKKAW BAY

SAIL RIVER

Makah Indian Reservation

SOOES RIVER

BULLMAN CREEK

112

Information Board

HOKO RIVER

Hoko-Ozette Road

Sekiu

Sekiu Point

Clallam Bay

Slip Point

112

113

112

PEARSON CREEK

LAST CREEK

CLALLAM RIVER

CHARLEY CREEK

Stolzenberg Mountain

BIG RIVER

SCHAFFER CREEK

ELK LAKE

UMBRELLA CREEK

PILCHUCK CREEK

Ozette

WILLOUGHBY LAKE

SEAFIELD LAKE

COAL CR

Mannys Prairie

OZETTE RIVER

Ozette Indian Reservation

Cape Alava

FATHER AND SON

Point of the Arches

Spike Rock

Shi Shi Beach

SOOES RIVER

They have figured out how to climb down the ropes used to hang food from trees and are even having some success at opening buckets with lids. Bears also sometimes find their way to the beaches and are willing to scrounge a free meal. As a result, animal-resistant buckets and canisters are required for carrying all items that have an odor. This includes all food, candy, medicines, lip balms, bug repellants, and make-up.

The large, plastic buckets with animal-resistant lids can be rented or purchased at various locations, including ranger stations and outdoor stores. The Lost Resort at Lake Ozette rents buckets. The buckets can be carried empty while hiking, and the food can be placed in them at camp.

Bear-proof canisters are a better choice. These cylindrical containers have smooth surfaces and animals are unable to get a good hold to break them open. They fit into many backpacks, and they don't need to be hung. They are designed so that even a bear will be frustrated and go away—hungry. Raccoons are completely baffled by them, at least so far. The canisters hold enough food for two people for two or three days. They can be rented at the Olympic Wilderness Information Center in Port Angeles, as well as some camping suppliers. Many campsites have bear wires; Cape Alava for instance, has a series of bear wires near the creek just north of the beach trailhead. Several camping parties can share them. Bring rope in case wires aren't available—unless you have bear canisters, of course. Keeping food in a tent is for the foolhardy, or for those who don't mind four-footed visitors chewing holes in their tents in the middle of the night.

The main ethic of hiking the coast is simple: Leave no trace. The ranger stations have free wilderness trip planners to help hikers pass through the wilderness as lightly as possible, leaving it feeling clean and untouched. Call or send for a trip planner ahead of time.

For more information: Olympic National Park, Wilderness Information Center, 600 East Park Avenue, Port Angeles, WA 98362. Phone (360) 452-0330.

NEAH BAY AND CAPE FLATTERY

[Fig. 24] Looking at a map of the United States, Cape Flattery is the most north-westerly point of the contiguous United States, the West Coast counterpart to the East Coast's Quoddy Head, Maine. Cape Alava is more westerly, and the Canadian Border is the most northerly. But Cape Flattery is the spot on the map where the land ends.

Located at Neah Bay on the Makah Indian Reservation, and owned by the tribe, Cape Flattery may seem a little like the end of the world, but it is worth the trip to see such a wild, beautiful piece of the coast. The cape marks the end of the Strait of Juan de Fuca. Once ships round the cape, they are in the Pacific Ocean. The Makah have occupied this area for at least 2,000 years. They are related to the Nootka Makah on Vancouver Island and were the only group of indigenous people outside of Alaska to hunt whales, a custom they revived in late summer 1999, amidst much controversy.

At one time the Makah had five villages, including the one at Cape Alava to the south of Neah Bay. Neah Bay is the only one left. Fishing and tourism are now the principle industries of the Makah, as the new marina built on the reservation in 1997 attests. It holds over 200 sport-fishing and commercial boats, as well as pleasure boats. Boats can be chartered for those wishing to try deep-sea fishing for salmon, steelhead, and an assortment of bottom-dwelling fish. Ecological tours are also available. Rainbow and cutthroat trout are caught regularly in the Sooes and Waatch Rivers and Hobuck Lake, all located on the reservation.

At different times of the year different whale species can be seen swimming offshore. The rocky coast provides good perches where birds can roost. The shoreline is part of the Olympic National Marine Sanctuary and the Flattery Rocks National Wildlife Refuge. Sandy beaches suitable for a variety of activities, including beach-combing and swimming, can be found around the area. Numerous lodgings are available in town; there is also a private campground at Hobucks, near the trailhead for Shi Shi Beach.

On the coast, about 15 miles south of Neah Bay (*see* Lake Ozette-Cape Alava-Sand Point Triangle, page 161) at Cape Alava, the Makah village known as Ozette was the location of an internationally known archeology site, and many of the artifacts found there are now on display at the Makah Museum. The village had several hundred people living there until it was abandoned in 1917, when the children were required to go to school at Neah Bay.

The Ozette site, called so because the Cape Alava trailhead is located at Lake Ozette, was rediscovered in 1970 when artifacts were found in the eroding bank of the beach. The Makah had long told stories of houses buried there by slides. No one is sure exactly how long people lived at Cape Alava, but carbon dating confirmed that artifacts found in the slide were around 500 years old.

Thousands of rare wooden artifacts were taken from the site. Cedar bark hats and mats, loom parts, hunting and fishing gear made with antler or bone fixed to wood, baskets with oil and paint still in them, a fragment of a blanket made from cedar bark, woodpecker feathers, cattail fluff, and dog hair were unearthed. Such items generally disintegrate quickly in the wet Northwest climate. It is believed these ordinarily highly perishable artifacts survived because the heavy clay soil in the slide sealed out the air, preventing decay.

The Makah Museum in Neah Bay opened in 1979. This excellent museum is arranged to display the daily life of the village throughout the seasons of the year. It has a full-size replica of a longhouse at the Cape Alava site as it might have looked before the slide destroyed it. It is fascinating to walk around in this longhouse and see from the small door towards the back wall a diorama of the geographical features one sees from the site at Cape Alava. There are Cannonball Island and the Boteltah Islands to the right. A small chimney-like sea stack sits in its usual position almost directly in front of the door, and the largest island, Ozette, fills the skyline to the left, just as it does at the Cape.

Every August, usually the weekend closest to August 24, the tribe holds the Makah

Days celebration. This date, August 24, is the anniversary of the day that Indians on reservations were given the right to vote. A parade and street fair, canoe races, traditional shell games, dancing, singing, and feasting are climaxed by a fireworks display.

Directions: There are two routes to the Cape. The first, along State Route 112 from Port Angeles, follows the Strait of Juan de Fuca along a curvaceous road that runs through hills and skirts along the water's edge, often close enough to pull over and dip a toe into the water. In Port Angeles, follow the State Route 112 signs to Joyce and Pysht.

The other route to Neah Bay follows US Highway 101 from Port Angeles for 40 miles to the town of Sappho. Turn north at Sappho onto State Route 113. From Sappho on, the route is less scenic, but it is shorter than State Route 112. Both routes lead towards the town of Clallam Bay, and just before Clallam Bay State Route 113 joins with State Route 112. The road wanders through Clallam Bay and past Sekiu, and past the Hoko-Ozette Road before making its way another 18 miles to Neah Bay.

Activities: Hiking, views, boating, birding, whaling, fishing, beach activities, and museum.

Facilities: Lodging, private RV and tent camps, restaurants, marina, charter boats, and ecological boat tours.

Dates: Open year-round. The museum is open from Memorial Day to Sept.15 daily from 10 to 5. From Sept. 15 to Memorial Day it is closed Mondays and Tuesdays.

Fees: There is a charge for museum admission.

For more information: Makah Tribal Council, PO Box 115, Neah Bay, WA 98357. Phone (360) 645-2201. Makah Museum, PO Box 160, Neah Bay, WA 98375. Phone (360) 645-2711.

CAPE FLATTERY TRAIL

[Fig. 24(1)] The Cape Flattery Trail goes to land's end for the lower 48 states. The viewpoint sits on a high bank looking out to the Pacific, and Tatoosh Island and its lighthouse. The 0.7-mile-long trail has interpretive signs at several observation sites along the way. Sit quietly and feel the waves pounding below. Look straight down and see the caves and tunnels formed as the sea eats away at the softer rocks underneath the cape. Sea otters, seals, seabirds, as well as humpback, gray, and orca whales can be spotted along the coast. The trail was recently renovated, and the cedar boardwalks and groomed earth make it an easy walk. The drive to the trailhead is short, but the road is not good, so it takes awhile.

Directions: From the Makah Museum continue west on State Route 112, which is the main road through town. The road makes a sharp left turn. The whole route to this point is about 1.5 miles. Go to the Health and Indian Services Clinic building, and take a right turn. Go 1 block. The road goes in several directions; take the left turn (don't go up the hill), following the Tribal Center signs, and travel approximately

6 miles. The road changes to dirt and gravel for the last 4 miles. Turn left at the Cape Trail sign, the parking lot for the trailhead is about 70 feet from the turn.

Trail: 0.75 miles, one-way.
Elevation: No elevation change.
Degree of difficulty: Easy.

NEAH BAY RESTAURANT

There are only a couple of restaurants in Neah Bay, and none of them are fancy.

The Makah Maiden. Bayview Avenue, right across from the Cape Motel. Freshly caught seafood is standard on this menu, and the cook personally knows the fishermen. For those who don't care for fish, items such as fettuccine and steak are offered. Be sure to check out the photographs of Indians from the Indian agency days to more recent times; the one of the beautiful Indian woman is known as the Indian Mona Lisa. *Inexpensive to moderate. Phone (360) 645-2924.*

NEAH BAY LODGING

There are a number of motels and resorts in Neah Bay. Most of them are located on State Route 112 just outside the main part of town, and many are located right on the water. Most have kitchens, as restaurants are few.

The Cape Motel and RV Park. Bayview Avenue. Old and funky, but comfortable. This place sits right snug up to the beach and has views of the Strait of Juan de Fuca that don't stop until they reach Vancouver Island on the far side of the Strait. There are eight rooms and two cabins. Five of the units, including the cabins, have fully equipped kitchens. The RV park has 54 units with complete hookups, and there is also a RV dump. In the summer, there are 3 acres of land open for tenting, complete with restrooms, showers, and a laundry. *Moderate. Phone (360) 645-2250*

SEKIU

[Fig. 24] Sekiu (pronounced Sea-cue) is a destination resort town for fishermen, which seems appropriate since the town started as a salmon cannery in 1870. Fishermen today come for halibut, lingcod, and a variety of rockfish, as well as coho and chinook salmon. But this charming village also has humpback and pilot whales, Steller's and California sea lions, harbor seals, dolphins, and, in winter, sea otters off its shores, and a number of good bird-watching locations. Lodging and RV camping are plentiful. Boats and kayaks can be rented, and the town also offers charters for both fishing and sea mammal watching.

SEKIU RESTAURANT

Sekiu is quite small, and has only one restaurant.

The Breakwater Inn. 15560 Highway 112, Clallam Bay. Located halfway between Clallam Bay and Sekiu on the south side of the road, it is open for breakfast, lunch, and dinner. Although it's called an inn, it's a restaurant only. The specialty is seafood, but the restaurant offers an assortment of American-style dishes. *Moderate. Phone (360) 963-2428.*

SEKIU LODGING
Most visitors to this tiny town are fisherman, and they can find a place to stay near the water.

Van Riper's Resort and Charters. 280 Front Street, Sekiu. This modern, two-story resort sits 50 feet from the beach, and 7 of its 16 rooms have spectacular views of the Strait and Vancouver Island. Two of the units have full kitchens. There are also RV hookups and tent sites with restrooms and showers. The resort has a boat launch and rents 16-foot fishing boats. There is a small grocery store and a bait and tackle shop. *Moderate to expensive. Phone (360) 963-2334 or (888) 462-0803.*

LAKE OZETTE-CAPE ALAVA-SAND POINT TRIANGLE
[Fig. 25] Lake Ozette is a good fishing lake; it is also the location of the trailhead for two easy hikes to two ocean beaches. The trails form a triangle, two of them starting at the Ozette ranger station. The north leg goes from Lake Ozette to Cape Alava, the south leg goes from the lake to Sand Point, and they are both about 3 miles long. The 2.8-mile stretch of beach between Cape Alava and Sand Point forms the third side of the triangle. The whole 8.8-mile loop can be done in a day.

The beach camping is good at Sand Point and Cape Alava. Both trails from Lake Ozette are mostly boardwalks and have no real elevation gain. The boardwalks are slippery when wet, and the park recommends lightweight hikers wear tennis shoes rather than stiff hiking boots to enable them to feel the boardwalk better.

The trails meander through beautiful forests of Douglas fir and cedar typical of the region. Although not rain forest, the woods have a rich feel to them. Huckleberries are found along the trail in late summer. Whether they are bitter or sweet depends on the summer weather. There is only one way to find out.

Bald eagles, river otters, and raccoons frequent the beaches. Beware of the raccoons. This is definitely bucket and bear canister territory. The raccoons are pernicious pests and will steal anything remotely edible. Day packs, bottles, and jars with screw-on lids are fair game. Do not leave food in tents, keep gear odor free, and store garbage away from food.

A highlight of the 2.8-mile beach between Cape Alava and Sand Point is the petroglyphs at Wedding Rocks. The Makah carved whales, fish, masks, and a European ship in full sail into the rocks. The Wedding Rocks are believed to ensure fertility. They are located about 1 mile from the Cape Alava beach trailhead and 1.8 miles from Sand Point beach trailhead.

Although the area is quite popular and quotas are in effect from May through September, there is no sense of being crowded. The beaches seem to absorb the

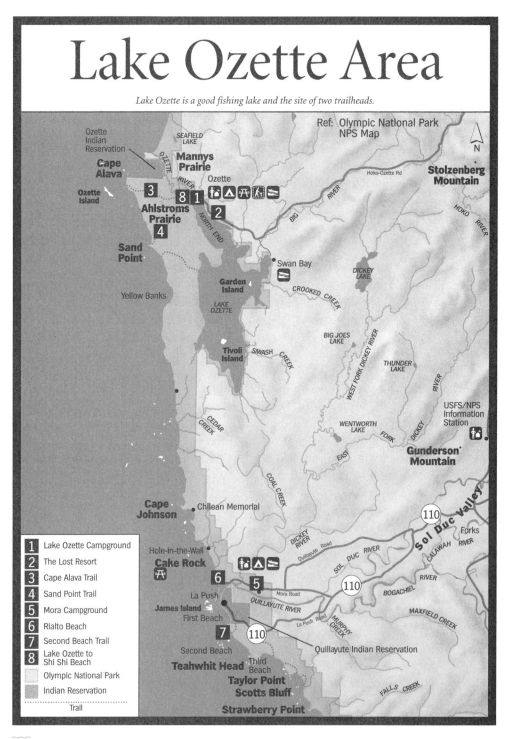

Lake Ozette Area

Lake Ozette is a good fishing lake and the site of two trailheads.

Ref: Olympic National Park NPS Map

N

Ozette Indian Reservation

SEAFIELD LAKE

Cape Alava

Mannys Prairie

Ozette

OZETTE RIVER

Hoko–Ozette Rd

Stolzenberg Mountain

Ozette Island

[3] [8][1] 🏕️🔺⛲🚻

[2]

Ahlstroms Prairie

[4]

NORTH END

BIG RIVER

HOKO RIVER

Sand Point

Swan Bay

DICKEY LAKE

Yellow Banks

Garden Island

LAKE OZETTE

CROOKED CREEK

BIG JOES LAKE

WEST FORK DICKEY RIVER

Tivoli Island

SIWASH CREEK

THUNDER LAKE

RIVER

CEDAR CREEK

WENTWORTH LAKE

FORK

DICKEY

USFS/NPS Information Station

Gunderson Mountain

EAST

COAL CREEK

Cape Johnson

Chilean Memorial

110

Sol Duc Valley

Forks

DICKEY RIVER

Quillayute Road

SOL DUC RIVER

CALAWAH RIVER

Hole-in-the-Wall

Cake Rock

🅿️

[6]

[5]

110

RIVER

BOGACHIEL

La Push

James Island

First Beach

Mora Road

QUILLAYUTE RIVER

La Push Road

MURPHY CREEK

MAXFIELD CREEK

[7] 110

Second Beach

Teahwhit Head Third Beach

Taylor Point

Scotts Bluff

Strawberry Point

Quillayute Indian Reservation

FALLS CREEK

[1]	Lake Ozette Campground
[2]	The Lost Resort
[3]	Cape Alava Trail
[4]	Sand Point Trail
[5]	Mora Campground
[6]	Rialto Beach
[7]	Second Beach Trail
[8]	Lake Ozette to Shi Shi Beach
	Olympic National Park
	Indian Reservation
....	Trail

people effortlessly, leaving a feeling of spaciousness and seclusion. Call the wilderness center no more than 30 days in advance to make reservations.

Directions: On State Route 112 approximately 4 miles west of Sekiu, turn south on the Hoko-Ozette Road. Go 22 miles to the end of the road.

Activities: Camping, beach hiking and backpacking, fishing.

Facilities: Campground, ranger station, The Lost Resort (*see* below). No garbage pickup.

Dates: Open year-round.

Fees: Fees are charged for overnight camping at the lake, overnight backpacking permits, and trailhead parking.

Closest town: Sekiu, 26 miles.

For more information: Olympic National Park, Wilderness Information Center, 600 East Park Avenue, Port Angeles, WA 98362. Phone (360) 452-0330.

LAKE OZETTE CAMPGROUND

[Fig. 25(1)] Lake Ozette offers good fishing, and access to the beaches at Cape Alava and Sand Point. The campground's 15 sites are in the open with few trees. The campground sits right on the shore of the lake, and drainage is poor, which is why there is only one water spigot, and the only restroom is the one located at the ranger station about 100 feet up the road. Mosquitoes are plentiful in the summer. The campground is part of the Olympic National Park.

Overflow camping is allowed in the picnic area. The privately owned Lost Resort also has campsites and showers.

Directions: On State Route 112 approximately 4 miles west of Sekiu, turn south on the Hoko-Ozette Road. Go 22 miles to the end of the road.

Activities: Fishing, forest and beach hikes.

Facilities: Ranger station, campground with water and restroom, boat ramp. Lost Resort general store and deli-restaurant; animal-proof 5-gallon containers can be rented.

Dates: Open year-round.

Fees: Fees are charged for overnight camping.

Closest town: Clallam Bay, 26 miles.

For more information: Olympic National Park, Wilderness Information Center, 600 East Park Avenue, Port Angeles, WA 98362. Phone (360) 452-0330.

THE LOST RESORT

[Fig. 25(2)] Lost Resort has the only store for 26 miles. The store features a small selection of groceries and a deli that serves 80 kinds of beer. The resort also has primitive campsites and a shower.

Directions: On State Route 112 approximately 4 miles west of Sekiu, turn south on the Hoko-Lake Ozette Road. Continue on the Hoko-Lake Ozette Road for 22 miles. The turn off for Lost Resort is up the hill on the right, about 200 feet before Lake Ozette Campground.

Activities: Fishing, hiking, boating, camping.

Facilities: Campsites, showers, garbage service, grocery, and deli.

Dates: Open year-round.

Fees: Fees are charged for camping, showers, animal-resistant container retails, and garbage service.

Closest town: Sekiu, 26 miles.

For more information: Lost Resort, 20860 Hoko-Ozette Road, Clallam Bay, WA 98326. Phone (360) 950-2899 or (800) 950-2899.

CAPE ALAVA TRAIL

[Fig. 25(3)] About 2.3-miles from the trailhead at Lake Ozette, the mostly board-walk trail emerges from lush forest into Ahlstrom's Prairie, named after the Scandinavian settler who homesteaded here around the turn of the nineteenth century. A number of Scandinavians settled here, but most left after President Grover Cleveland made the area part of the National Forest Reserve in 1897. Ahlstrom's cabin burned in the 1980s. All that remains at the old cabin site is a bench, itself rapidly disappearing beneath encroaching vegetation. In fact, the whole prairie, which is a natural occurrence, is slowly giving way to the forest.

Once hikers reach the beach, it is another 0.5 mile north to Cape Alava, and the rock and loose sand beach makes for tiring walking. The cape is the site of the old Makah village, Ozette (*see* Neah Bay, page 157). A ranger station is located at the old archeology site, which has been completely reclaimed by low-growing shrubs and grasses. The longhouse replica is open to the public. Looking at the area, it is hard to believe that there was ever an archeology site here, let alone a village. Actually, there was a succession of houses built on this spot, each buried in turn by mud slides from the slopes behind the village.

To the north of the site, just off the cape, Cannonball Island looms. Joined to the mainland when the tide is out, the island was used as a lookout for raiding tribes and as a burial site. Because of the latter activity, it is off limits for non-Indian visitors to climb it. It is perfectly acceptable to explore the island's rocky base, however. Be sure to look for the rusting anchor of the *Austria* which low tides leave exposed at the foot of the island. This ship sank in 1887, one of innumerable shipwrecks along the coast.

The beach on the other side of the cape is a complete surprise after the rough southern beach. Rocks give way to smooth, dark sand, and the low banks adjoining the beach offer excellent camping amidst the trees. Whale spouts, and sometimes the whales themselves, can occasionally be seen far off in the sea, and the barking of sea lions resting on distant rocks on the north side of the cape can be heard over the sea's roar. There is good tidepooling along the rocky shore, or at the headland by the mouth of the Ozette River. Campfires are allowed; use driftwood only. Beach fires must be 10 feet from drift logs.

Reservations for camping can be made by calling the wilderness center, (360) 452-0300, no more than 30 days in advance.

Fees: Fees are charged for overnight permits and trailhead parking.

Trail: 3.1 miles to beach, 0.5 miles north to Cape Alava, one-way.

Elevation: Trail drops about 150 feet to the beach.

Degree of difficulty: Easy.

For more information: Olympic National Park, Wilderness Information Center, 600 East Park Avenue, Port Angeles, WA 98362. Phone (360) 452-0330.

SAND POINT TRAIL

[Fig. 25(4)] This trail to Sand Point is a favorite of families with small children who like to play in the sand. The mostly boardwalk trail to Sand Point is flat and easy, and there is no headland at the beach as there is at Cape Alava. The beach offers good campsites, water, and tidepools. Raccoons are frequent guests, so animal-resistant buckets and canisters are required. The water needs to be purified. Reservations can be made by calling the wilderness center no more than 30 days in advance.

Fees: Fees are charged for overnight permits and trailhead parking.

For more information: Olympic National Park, Wilderness Information Center, 600 East Park Avenue, Port Angeles, WA 98362. Phone (360) 452-0330.

Trail: 2.8 miles, one-way.

Elevation: Elevation gain is about 150 feet.

Degree of difficulty: Easy.

LAKE OZETTE TO SHI SHI BEACH

[Fig. 25(8)] Although the Ozette loop trails are a destination in themselves, Lake Ozette is also the jump-off spot for a 15.4-mile-hike to Shi Shi Beach, the most northern of the park's beaches. Shi Shi Beach's other border is the Makah Reservation at Neah Bay. With its golden sands and wave-lapped beaches, Shi Shi is considered by many to be the most beautiful beach in the state. Good water sources, nature hikes, and campsites nestled in the surrounding forest add to Shi Shi's pleasures.

Before reaching Shi Shi, however, visitors cross through one of the most spectacular coastlines in Washington State, Point of the Arches, a 1-mile stretch of sea-carved arches and rock sculptures, all that remains of a headland ground down by the surf over the millennia.

This trip requires a minimum of three days one-way, five days round-trip, as there are two obstacles, the Ozette River and the headland before Point of the Arches, that need to be passed at low tide. They can't both be reached in a single day. The Ozette can be forded only in the summer, at low tide, and at its estuary. Walking sticks are helpful in fording the Ozette River and for negotiating the boulders at the beach just south of Point of the Arches. Bring water or refill at streams along the way because water is not available at some beaches. What water there is should be purified.

The hike starts at Lake Ozette, take the trail to Cape Alava, which is about 3.0 miles long (*see* Cape Alava Trail, page 164). Those who want a longer hike can take the trail from Lake Ozette to Sand Point. This adds the nearly 3 mile long stretch of beach lying between Sand Point and Cape Alava to the distance, making the hike 18.4 miles total.

Once at Cape Alava, continue north along the shore. The 2-mile length of beach north of Cape Alava is flat and sandy, with good camping for those who want to go no farther. Except for streams that may dry up in the summer, the nearest sources of water are the river or the Cape Alava trailhead. There are tidepools when the tide is out, and sea lion rocks are located off the south end, too far away to see the animals without binoculars. This beach ends at the north end at a headland about 0.5 mile before the Ozette River, but the headland is easy to round at low tide. There is also a trail over it. Look for the trail target.

The river itself is the biggest obstacle at this point. It must be crossed at its estuary at low tide, and then with some caution. Link arms with a partner, and use each other for support. Be sure to unfasten all backpack harnesses so the backpack can be easily removed in case the hiker falls in the water. Use a walking stick for balance and to feel for secure footing in the water. There is good camping on the north side of the river.

Several more headlands and points need to be negotiated to reach Point of the Arches and Shi Shi. The most difficult part of the hike is the beach just south of Point of the Arches. "Beach" is a misnomer; a 2.2-mile boulder dump is more like it, and crossing it more resembles a horizontal rock climb than a hike. This is strenuous work, and there is that other headland, which can be traversed only at low tide. It is necessary to watch the time and tide tables at this stretch, and leave enough time to negotiate the boulder beach and round the headland. The effort is worth it, with golden-sanded Shi Shi as the reward.

Reservations and permits for overnight camping are required and may be obtained through Olympic National Park Wilderness Information Center. Fires are allowed. Use driftwood, and build fires only on the beach below the high tide line or in fire rings in existing campsites.

Directions: On State Route 112 approximately 4 miles west of Sekiu, turn south on the Hoko-Ozette Road. Go 22 miles to the end of the road.

For more information: Olympic National Park, Wilderness Information Center, 600 East Park Avenue, Port Angeles, WA 98362. Phone (360) 452-0330.

Trail: 15.4 miles, one-way.

Elevation: Sea level, except headlands, which are around 15 to 30 feet high.

Degree of difficulty: Moderate to strenuous.

LAKE OZETTE TO RIALTO BEACH

This 22.8-mile hike along this beautiful, rugged coast is full of beaches, wildlife, and adventure. The trail starts at Lake Ozette; from there it is possible to get to the beach along the Sand Point or Cape Alava trails. It adds only 2.8 miles to use the Cape Alava trail, and that route goes by the petroglyphs at Wedding Rocks (*see* Cape Alava Trail, page 164).

Sand Point beach offers plentiful camping and water (*see* Sand Point Trail, page

165). The next beach, Yellow Banks, is 2 miles farther, about 5 miles from Lake Ozette, and has limited tent space. The beach is sandy and open; there are tidepools at its south end. Despite being unprotected from the sea, Yellow Banks is so popular that it has to be reforested. No campfires are allowed while that process is going on. The small point at the beach's south end has a natural tunnel that is fun to explore and can be used to get past the point at most high tides.

The 2.5-mile section of beach past Yellow Banks is rough and there are streams to cross. A headland at the end of this stretch of beach has no high tide trail. Missing low tide here means waiting until the next outgoing tide. This is one of those times when a watch and tide table are necessities.

A 2-mile stretch of cobblestone waits on the other side of this headland before sandy Kayostla Beach is reached. It is much more protected than Yellow Banks and has plenty of water and camping space. A path through the forest leads to the Norwegian Memorial, dedicated to the sailors lost aboard the bark *Prince Arthur* in 1903.

The next, unnamed beach, about 11 miles from Lake Ozette, contains quite a few marks of civilization along its pleasant 1-mile length, including some campsites and outhouses. Equipment from the old, defunct Starbuch Mine rusts along Cedar Creek.

The next headland can be walked around, but a World War II Coast Lookout Post at the top of it deserves a look. The whole coast was off limits to visitors during the war. A military branch called the Coast Lookout System was established, and men were stationed at these little cabins to scan the waters off the coast for enemies. Only this cabin and two concrete bunkers at Portage Head on Shi Shi Beach remain as solitary reminders of this band of lonely watchers. There is tent space and water.

This coast lookout beach is followed by 1 mile of sandy beach. There is water here but no tent spaces, and high tides and storms could block access and egress. The south end headland is the only one on this section of the coast that must be crossed overland, but its low banks are easy to climb. Once on the other side of the headland, there is a 1.25-mile stretch of beach with good water and some pretty camping. However, a storm a few years ago left trees blown across the beach at odd angles, making passage slow and difficult until the next storm removes them.

Cape Johnson's northern point follows this beach, which begins with a boulder-filled beach that requires some rock-jumping to navigate. The beach that follows this has several campsites, but no water. The actual cape requires some more rock-jumping to round. Both of these last two points are closed by more than medium high tides, and there is no overland crossing. Watch and tide tables are necessary to time passage to avoid long waits for the next low tide.

Now 15 miles from Lake Ozette, hikers are within 6 miles of their destination, Rialto Beach. A good camping beach and the Chilean Memorial immediately follows Cape Johnson. The memorial honors Chilean sailors lost in shipwrecks in 1883 and 1920. Several of them are buried beneath the beach's sands, and there are some who say the beach is haunted. Sleep well.

The point south of the Chilean Memorial can only be passed at low tide. From here, there are only 3.5 miles to go to Rialto Beach trailhead, about half of them through rough rocks. Be sure to check out the tidepools and to look for Hole-in-the-Wall. Wave action has eroded a hole through this large sea stack, and it makes a good frame for photographers. It is located about 1.5 miles from Rialto Beach.

The final destination, Rialto Beach, is one of the most popular beaches on the coast. It has no bank between its smooth, flat expanses of beach and the parking lot. Don't be concerned about beach access being too easy. There are still piles of driftwood to overcome to get from the beach to the parking lot, although the rangers do use chainsaws to cut a path through the piles of sea-bleached, silver-gray timber. Camping is allowed on the north side of Ellen Creek, but not the south. Mora Campground is located 2 miles east (see Mora Campground, below.) The Quillayute River is not fordable, and it is necessary to leave the beach and take the road to the next beach at La Push.

Trail: 22.8 miles, one-way.

Elevation: Elevation gain is about 150 feet.

Degree of difficulty: Moderate.

For more information: Olympic National Park, Wilderness Information Center, 600 East Park Avenue, Port Angeles, WA 98362. Phone (360) 452-0330.

MORA CAMPGROUND

[Fig. 25(5)] Although the campground is located right next to it, Mora Road is very quiet, especially at night. The only sounds are the pounding of the waves and, if weather conditions make it necessary, the foghorn from the lighthouse at James Island, offshore from La Push.

Mora is located 1.9 miles from Rialto Beach. There are no reservations at Mora. It is strictly first come, first served, and on summer weekends and in nice weather all 94 sites are often full. The best time to get a camping place is in the morning. Ranger programs are offered in the amphitheater on Friday, Saturday, and Sunday evenings from late June through Labor Day. Programs are sometimes added as staffing permits. Naturalists lead tidepool walks daily. Check at the ranger station and at the bulletin boards near the restrooms for times.

Directions: From Sappho, follow US Highway 101 west for 11 miles to State Route 110 (also called La Push Road), and watch for the La Push/Olympic Park road sign. Follow La Push Road 8 miles to Mora Road and turn right onto Mora Road. Go 3 miles to the campground. Rialto Beach is another 1.9 miles farther.

Activities: Camping, hiking, fishing, beach walking, wildlife viewing, picnicking, ranger programs, and tidepool walks.

Facilities: Campground with restrooms, RV dump, garbage pick-up, ranger station

Dates: Open year-round.

Fees: Fees are charged for overnight camping.

Closest town: Forks, 14 miles.

For more information: Olympic National Park, Wilderness Information Center, 600 East Park Avenue, Port Angeles, WA 98362. Phone (360) 452-0330.

RIALTO BEACH

[Fig. 25(6)] Rialto Beach is 1.9 miles from Mora Campground. There is a picnic area, somewhat sheltered from the ocean winds, with camp grills and picnic tables. The driftwood piles are high, but a path to the beach is generally sawn through them. Just before the headland at the north end of Rialto is a sea stack known as Hole-In-The-Wall, which offers interesting photo opportunities.

Directions: 1.9 miles beyond Mora Campground (*see* page 168).

Activities: Beach walking, hiking, tide pools, sand castle building, picnicking.

Facilities: Picnic tables with grills, restrooms, drinking water.

Dates: Open year-round.

Fees: None.

For more information: Olympic National Park, Wilderness Information Center, 600 East Park Avenue, Port Angeles, WA 98362. Phone (360) 452-0330.

LA PUSH

[Fig. 25] La Push is located on the 814-acre Quillayute Indian Reservation on the south side of the Quillayute River. It has been a village here for 800 years. The only developed harbor located directly on the Pacific Ocean of Washington, the town has a small marina, a few rustic motels and resorts, some with fully equipped kitchens, and a small store.

The town, the headquarters of the Quillayute Tribe, has its own beach, First Beach, which is open to the public. First Beach sits on the south side of the Quillayute River, across from Rialto Beach, which is part of the Olympic National Park. The beaches share many similar features: They are sandy and driftwood-laden, with sea stacks and islands jutting just offshore. A plethora of wildlife comes through this area. Brown pelicans, cormorants, and bald eagles are among the 70 species of birds spotted here and whales can be seen off the coast at times. Surfers and kayakers find the waves at La Push challenging. Wet suits are necessary as the water temperature hovers around 45 degrees Fahrenheit. Mora Campground is on the north side of the Quillayute River, near Rialto Beach (*see* Mora Campground page 168).

Directions: From Sappho, follow US Highway 101 west for 11 miles to State Route 110 (also called La Push Road), and watch for the La Push/Olympic Park sign. Turn right on La Push Road, and follow it for 13 miles to La Push.

For more information: Quillayute Tribal Council, La Push, WA 98350. Phone (360) 374-6163.

LA PUSH LODGING

La Push Ocean Park and Shoreline Resorts. 770 Main Street. La Push has only two resorts, and the same company operates them both. They are quite large, with about 50 rooms and cabins each, as well as RV sites with hookups. There are also some tent sites. The town has no restaurant, but the resorts have kitchens. *Moderate to expensive. Phone (800) 487-1267.*

SECOND BEACH TRAIL

[Fig. 25(7)] This 0.75-mile trail is a gentle, forested hike to a high-cliffed, sandy, 1.5 mile-long beach. Sea stacks dot the seascape. One of them is the 85-foot-high Quillayute Needle. Tidepools lie at the base of both headlands.

Directions: The trailhead is located 11.5 miles from La Push Road junction with US Highway 101, about 0.5 mile before La Push.

Facilities: There is an outhouse at the road.

For more information: Olympic National Park, Wilderness Information Center, 600 East Park Avenue, Port Angeles, WA 98362. Phone (360) 452-0330.

Trail: 0.75, one-way.

Elevation: 200-foot elevation gain.

Degree of difficulty: Easy.

THIRD BEACH TO OIL CITY

[Fig. 25] This rugged 17.1-mile length of the coast is nearly as much headland as beach. The hike starts with a 1.5-mile-long trail that leads through a shady forest before making a steep descent from the high bank down to the beach. Driftwood piles at the trail's end can make passage onto the beach difficult. On the other side of that obstacle, a sandy beach with good camping and water runs towards the south and makes a fine stopping point for day hikers and backpacking families with young children.

Taylor Point, at Third Beach's south end, past Strawberry Bay, is one of the most difficult headlands hikers will encounter on this part of the coast. A series of steep ladders has been put in place on both sides of the headland to aid climbing. There are campsites on top of the headland if the tide is too high to go farther.

Only a few streams run between Scott's Bluff and Toleak Point, 6.4 miles from the Third Beach trailhead. The Giant's Graveyard, a group of a dozen or so sea stacks that have claimed countless ships, stands offshore.

Toleak once was a Quillayute Indian fishing village and the old village midden can still be seen. It should not be disturbed. The beach south of Toleak is sheltered and provides limited but good camping as well as water. Seals can occasionally be spotted here. There is a headland which must be crossed. Goodman Creek, which is a river, crosses the headland, and must be forded. Although usually shallow in the summer, storms can cause Goodman's banks to fill and make the river quite dangerous to ford. If the water seems too high, hikers should wait for it to go down before fording it. There are some good campsites to spend the night. Hikers should cross with caution and be sure their backpacks are unbuckled so they can be shrugged off easily if you fall in the water. Link arms with a partner, and use walking sticks for stability and balance; the sticks also help hikers feel for secure footing in the water. Once past the river, there is a sand ladder to climb down to the next beach.

Past Goodman Creek, the hiker is closer to Oil City than La Push. A 1-mile sand beach is the reward for all this work. The state's largest population of Cassin's auklets (*Ptychoramphus aleuticus*) can be spotted on one of their favorite haunts, Alexander Island, distinguishable by its flat top. Mosquito Creek, near the south end of this beach, has tent sites.

With only 6 miles left, probably the hardest stretch lies ahead. A choice has to be made here. A 3.5-mile-long trail goes through the forest and over the headland. It is rough, but safe.

The other possibility is to wait for low tide and go around the headland between Mosquito Creek and Hoh Head. This 0.5-mile route can be dangerous. The slippery boulders make this slow, rough going and getting caught by an incoming tide could be fatal. The experience is similar to walking on slippery boulders on a mountain peak, with the added danger of drowning thrown in. This route does offer hikers a chance to explore deep canyons carved under the headland, but be sure not to get trapped by an incoming tide. Check the tide table, not only for the time of high tide but also for the height, and watch the weather.

Those taking the low route around the headland will find a kindly 1-mile-long beach with campsites and water. The beach continues on to a short, steep bank, where the beach and overland routes merge back together again. The trail continues through the woods and over Hoh Head.

The trail drops back down to the beach at Jefferson Cove, with 3 miles to Oil City remaining. The beaches from here on are rocky but accessible at all tides. Two small points that can be rounded only at low tide are the only obstacles on the home stretch. North of the Oil City trailhead are campsites on the bank amidst the trees, and there is a creek for water. The trail up to the road sometimes washes out, so believe the trail target and scramble up the side of the bank.

Oil City is on the north bank of the Hoh River. It is located at the end of 15 miles of mostly dirt road. Oil companies have attempted to find oil in the area over the years, starting around the beginning of the twentieth century. Oil City was the most promising spot, but came to nothing. In fact, Oil City is nothing but a turnaround and a park bulletin board. So far the area has remained free from industrial intrusions.

The Hoh River is not fordable, so leave the beach at Oil City and take a car to Highway 101. The next accessible park beach to the south is Ruby Beach.

Directions: The Third Beach trailhead is located about 10.7 miles west of the La Push Road junction with US Highway 101, about 0.7 mile before La Push.

Trail: 17.5 miles, one-way.

Elevation: 150-foot elevation gain.

Degree of difficulty: Moderate.

Hoh River to Queets River

The coast from Hoh River to Queets River is 15 miles of sandy beach.

Hoh Head

Oil City Road

RIVER

Oil City

HOH

NOLAN CREEK

Mt Octopus

Hoh Indian Reservation

BRADEN CREEK

101

CEDAR CREEK

Abbey Island
Ruby Beach

CHRISTMAS CREEK

SNAHAPISH RIVER

CLEARWATER RIVER

Beach 6   Big Cedar Tree

Upper Clearwater

Destruction Island

KALALOCH CREEK

Beach 4

Copper Mine Bottom

Beach 3

CLEARWATER RIVER

Kalaloch Rocks

Kalaloch Information Station

P A C I F I C

HURST CREEK

BOULDER CREEK

TACOMA CREEK

Beach 2

MCKINNON CREEK

Beach 1

South Beach

O C E A N

N

Queets   RIVER

QUEETS

Ref: Olympic National Park NPS Map

SALMON   RIVER

Quinault Indian Reservation

101

1 Kalaloch Campground and Ranger Station

2 Kalaloch Lodge

   Olympic National Park

   Indian Reservation

   Olympic National Forest

Tunnel Island

   Trail

COTTONWOOD DNR CAMPGROUND

[Fig. 27(1)] This Washington State Department of Natural Resources campground is located on the Oil City Road, 6 miles from US Highway 101. It is situated on the Hoh River. Although primitive and secluded, it is a pretty, wooded campground and is a good jumping off place for hiking this stretch of beach. There are nine campsites, some large enough for RVs. There are no RV hookups. There is a hand boat launch. Water should be brought in.

Directions: From Forks, go 14 miles south on US Highway 101. Watch for the small Oil City sign. Turn right onto Oil City Road. Go about 6 miles; the campground is on the left. The beach entrance is at the end of the road, about 9 miles.

Activities: Camping, fishing, hiking.

Facilities: Campsites, hand boat launch, outhouses.

Dates: Open year-round.

Fees: None.

Closest town: Forks, 14 miles.

For more information: Washington State Department of Natural Resources Olympic Regional Headquarters, 411 Tillicum Lane, Forks, WA 98331. Phone (360) 374-6131.

HOH RIVER TO QUEETS RIVER

[Fig. 26] This is 15 miles of straightforward, uncomplicated beach, a great place for strolling or for letting the kids frolic in the sand and waves. Even the beach names are uncomplicated; most of them are numbered, south through north, one through six. However, so things won't be too easy, Beach 5 is closed, and there are a few extra access roads that are not marked. Just to keep everyone on their toes, the stretch contains two named beaches, including the most northern beach, Ruby Beach. The other one, Kalaloch, is located north of Beach 2.

Unlike the beach accesses along the northern coastlines, from Oil City to Shi Shi Beach, the beaches between the Hoh and Queets rivers are easy to reach. All the beaches have access roads, with broad, well-kept trails right at the parking lots. (They have restrooms, too.) Some of these walkways are high, and a little steep, and heaps of driftwood piled in front of the path are the norm. But the beaches are flat and can be walked in all but the highest tides. Check the tide tables. They are available at Kalaloch Ranger Station.

The water is cold, but hardy souls swim in it anyway. Watch out for rough waves and rip tides and stay away from drift logs in the surf. Unsuspecting swimmers have been crushed to death when they were pinned by logs thrown up by waves.

There are a couple of trade-offs for this easy life. One is that there is no camping along this section of beach. Another is that the sea stacks, islands, and rock-ridden shorelines that make the beaches north of here so spectacular and forbidding are missing here. Except for Destruction Island, the seascape along this portion of coast is water, water everywhere, with barely a sea stack in sight.

RUBY BEACH TO QUEETS RIVER

[Fig. 26] The Olympic National Park beaches actually start at Ruby Beach rather than the Hoh River's south side, which is part of the Hoh Indian Reservation and has no tourist facilities. The access to Ruby Beach is right off US Highway 101 about 27 miles south of Forks. This is a "blink and you'll miss it" situation, so watch for the signs along the highway. The trail to the beach is short, but steep. Ruby Beach gets its name for the claret-colored garnet flecks found in its sands. A huge, cathedral-size volcanic rock lies north past Cedar Creek, near Abbey Island, which was named in honor of the rock.

To the south, a small point requires a fairly low tide to get around it without getting wet. Beach 6 lies beyond this point. Look for the quickly vanishing remains of an old shipwreck. Destruction Island looms 3 miles offshore. In 1775, the Spanish named it *Isla de Delores*, Isle of Sorrow, after losing seven men to an Indian attack in the area. In 1787, Captain Charles Barkley anchored his ship *Imperial Eagle* off the island, and sent a small crew of men to explore the river. They, too, were killed. Barkley called the island Destruction. Although the latter name stuck, either seems appropriate, for there is something enigmatic about this mist-shrouded, wave-washed island. In the fog, its foghorn wails mournfully, as though calling to the mainland. Only seabirds and the ocean waves visit its 60-acre, table-flat top. It is the largest refuge in the Olympic Coast National Marine Sanctuary.

Continuing south, the next 3.5-mile stretch requires hikers to negotiate several small creeks and Star Fish Point. The latter is an interesting bit of geology. It consists of sandstone rock layers pushed onto their sides by the movement of the earth's crust over the eons. Beach Trails 4 and 3 lie just beyond. From Beach 3 it is an easy 2.5-mile walk to Kalaloch (*see* Kalaloch Campground and Lodge, page 175).

The beach continues on another 3 miles beyond Kalaloch, becoming narrower and rockier, although still accessible except in very high tides. It passes Beaches 1 and 2 before bumping into the Quinault Indian Reservation where the national park ends. The South Beach Campground, near the south border, has no water, although it does have a toilet. Although the water is cold, swimming is possible, but be careful of driftwood logs in the water as well as rip tides and outgoing tides.

Directions: From Forks, go 20 miles south on US Highway 101. Watch for the Ruby Beach/Olympic National Park sign on the west side of the road.

Facilities: Outhouse.

Trail: 14.7 miles, one-way.

Elevation: There is no change in elevation.

Degree of difficulty: Moderate.

KALALOCH CAMPGROUND AND LODGE

Kalaloch (pronounced Clay-lock) is actually two entities, Kalaloch Campground, with its attending national park ranger station, and Kalaloch Lodge.

KALALOCH CAMPGROUND AND RANGER STATION

[Fig. 26(1)] One of the most popular campgrounds in Olympic National Park, Kalaloch has 129 campsites running along an approximately 1-mile strip of cliffs above Kalaloch beach. In the summer the campground is usually full. To get a site, plan on arriving at the campground by midmorning and circling like a buzzard. The east side of the campground is next to the highway, with its attending road noises. The sites are close together, although many of them are still remarkably private. There are several stairways to the sandy beaches below. Kalaloch Lodge, next door, has both a grocery store and deli, as well as a notable restaurant. Although the water is cold, swimming is possible, but be careful of driftwood logs in the water as well as rip tides and outgoing tides.

Directions: From Forks, go south on US Highway 101 f or 33 miles. Watch for the signs.

Activities: Tent and RV camping, sandy beach suitable for swimming, kite flying, sand castles, hiking, nature walks, ranger program, and sea mammal and bird viewing.

Facilities: RV and tent sites, restrooms, water, firewood sales. A grocery store and restaurant are located at neighboring Kalaloch Lodge.

Dates: Open year-round

Fees: Fees are charged for camping and for firewood.

Closest town: Amanda Park, 30 miles.

For more information: Olympic National Park, Wilderness Information Center, 600 East Park Avenue, Port Angeles, WA 98362. Phone (360) 452-0330.

KALALOCH LODGE

[Fig. 26(2)] Perched right on the cliff edge, the lodge and its cabins overlook the beach, and here visitors are well situated for spotting the whales, dolphins, and sea birds that pass offshore. The first lodge was built in the late 1920s. Wood for the earliest buildings was cut from beach logs. Sadly the original lodge burned down in 1941 while under the jurisdiction of the U.S. Coast Guard, which used it as a base during World War II. The lodge and house were rebuilt in the 1950s. The property was sold to Olympic National Park in 1978. This is one of the five concessionaire-run lodges in the park. It is tremendously popular, and it's wise to make reservations far in advance. Besides the lodging, it has a restaurant, snack bar, and grocery store.

Swimming is possible along these beaches, but be careful of driftwood logs in the water, and of rip tides and outgoing tides.

Directions: On US Highway 101, just south of Kalaloch Campground.

Activities: Beach walking, sand castle building, swimming, kite flying, sea mammal and bird viewing, nature walk, and ranger program at Kalaloch Campground.

Facilities: Lodging, restaurant, gift shop, snack bar, and grocery store.

Dates: Open year-round.

Fees: Fees are charged for lodging.

Closest town: Amanda Park, 30 miles

For more information: Kalaloch Lodge, 157151 US Highway 101, Forks, WA 98331. Phone (360) 962-2271.

Forks Area

Forks is named for the confluence of the Sol Duc, Calawah, and Bogachiel rivers.

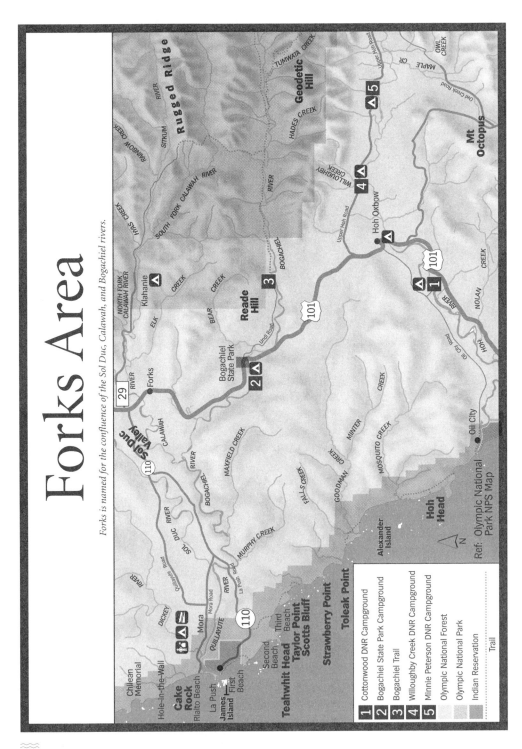

Legend:

1 Cottonwood DNR Campground
2 Bogachiel State Park Campground
3 Bogachiel Trail
4 Willoughby Creek DNR Campground
5 Minnie Peterson DNR Campground

Olympic National Forest
Olympic National Park
Indian Reservation
Trail

Ref: Olympic National Park NPS Map

Inland Western Olympic Peninsula

Visitors will find true rain forest land here, complete with dense understory plants, towering, moss-draped evergreen trees, and an amount of rainfall that can't be beaten anywhere in the continental U.S. Three rivers and their valleys, the Bogachiel, the Hoh, and the Quinault Rivers, are the wettest places in the lower 48 states. The official record is 140 inches average rainfall, but there are places in the valleys that easily top 240 inches.

The forests in all three valleys are filled with Douglas fir, western hemlock, and western redcedar. They all have trails that lead into the interior mountain regions, where Pacific silver fir and sitka spruce reign tall and proud. Along these trails visitors will find vine maples, bigleaf maples, black cottonwood *(Populus balsamifera)*, huckleberries, salmonberry *(Rubus spectabilis)*, horsetails, ferns, fungus, mosses and liverworts. The ground is covered with oxalis and salal, vanilla leaf *(Achlys triphylla)*, Scouler's corydalis *(Corydalis scouleri)*, and Pacific bleeding heart *(Dicentra formosa)*. In the spring, skunk cabbage *(Lysichiton americanum)* makes its presence known by its odor and bright yellow flowers. This is the home of Roosevelt elk, and mountain goat can sometimes be spotted in the mountains.

Bogachiel Valley is the least known, and therefore least frequented, of the rain forest river valleys. Its trails pass through perhaps the most pristine of the rain forests. The Hoh is one of the most visited sections of the park, and the name Hoh is almost synonymous with the Olympic rain forest. This popularity is due in part to the Trail of Mosses and the Spruce Nature Trail, two short hikes located next to the Hoh Campground visitor center. But equally appealing is the Hoh River Trail. Leading up to Mount Olympus, the trail follows the Hoh River's course through a variety of climatic zones, and is outstanding for its lush beauty. The lower section of the trail is easy hiking. On the south side of the Hoh Valley is the Hoh River's major tributary, the South Fork River, which offers less frequented trails and camping.

The most southern of the river valleys is the Quinault, and it is nearly as popular as the Hoh. It is also closer to US Highway 101, and offers a variety of campgrounds and lodging, as well as nature trails. There are also trails that access the deep interior of the Olympic Mountain Range and provide challenges for experienced hikers.

All of these valleys are worthy of the traveler's time and attention. The reward will be memories as lush as a rain forest.

▓ FORKS

[Fig. 25, Fig. 27] This is the main town in this region. Named for the confluence of the Sol Duc, Calawah, and Bogachiel rivers, Forks (population 2,700) is a timber and tourist town, and it is ideally situated for visitors to Rialto Beach and the Bogachiel and Hoh river valleys. The Forks Timber Museum, located in town on US 101, features a pioneer kitchen and an old fire lookout, as well as old lumber equipment.

Directions: Follow US Highway 101 for 55 miles west from Port Angeles.
Activities: Lodging, shopping, hiking, beaches.
Facilities: Lodging, restaurants, museum, stores.
For more information: Forks Chamber of Commerce, PO Box 1249, Forks, WA 98331. Phone (800) 443-6757.

RESTAURANT IN FORKS

Because it's a small town, Forks doesn't have a huge number of restaurants to chose from.

The Smokehouse Restaurant. 1606 Main Street. A steak and seafood restaurant, the fresh salmon is good. They make their own smoked salmon. The menu also features traditional American food, and there is carry-out food for those preferring to picnic. *Moderate. Phone (360) 374-6258.*

LODGING IN FORKS

Forks is small but has places to stay.

Miller Tree Inn. 654 East Division. Refurbished in 1995, this bed and breakfast offers a pre-dawn breakfast from April to October to accommodate the fishing crowd, and the hosts are knowledgeable about fishing spots and day hikes in the area. Miller Tree Inn has three guest rooms with full baths, two with half-bath (sink and toilet), and two that share a bath. *Moderate. Phone (360) 374-6806.*

BOGACHIEL RIVER VALLEY

The Bogachiel River flows from its headwaters at Bogachiel Peak almost to the Pacific Ocean. It joins the Sol Duc River and the two rivers become the 5-mile-long Quillayute River, which flows into the Pacific. The Quillayute runs through the Quillayute Indian Reservation at La Push, which is on the river's south side. Rialto Beach and Mora Campground lie on its north side.

BLACK BEAR
(*Ursus americanus*)

Unlike its southern neighbor, the Hoh River, the Bogachiel runs clear, a small irony since its name means "muddy waters." Although this river lies right next to the highway on the edge of the national park, it contains some of the best-preserved and most isolated rain forest areas on the peninsula. Two of its trails, Rugged Ridge and Indian Pass (*see* Bogachiel Trail, page 179) provide the only access into the even more remote Calawah Valley to the north.

BOGACHIEL STATE PARK CAMPGROUND

[Fig. 27(2)] This 123-acre park is close to the highway, and road noise can be a bit of a problem, but stands of western hemlock and spruce make this a lovely park to visit. It has 42 camping spaces, including 2 walk-in sites. There is a 0.5-mile nature trail in the park. The north end of the campground is near the river, which is noted for its fine salmon and steelhead runs.

Directions: From Forks, follow US Highway 101 south for 5 miles. The campground is on the west side of the road; watch for the signs.

Hungry Black Bears

During the summer, black bears are almost always ravenously hungry. In the winter they find a den where they enter a deep sleep. They maintain a nearly normal body temperature and a normal respiratory and heart rate, so scientists don't consider them to be in a state of true hibernation. Nevertheless, they stay asleep through the winter, except possibly for an occasional short break. When they awaken in the spring they are thin and hungry, and they have only until the following fall to eat enough to put on the fat they will need to carry them through the next winter. So food is constantly on their minds, and they eat any animal or vegetable material.

Activities: Camping, hiking, picnicking, fishing.

Facilities: RV, tent, and primitive campsites, restrooms and running water, shower, picnic tables, nature trail.

Dates: Open year-round, weather permitting.

Fees: Fees are charged for camping.

Closest town: Forks, 4.5 miles.

For more information: Bogachiel State Park, 185983 Highway 101, Forks, WA 98331. Phone (360) 374-6356 or (800) 233-0321. For campground reservations, call Washington State's Reservations Northwest phone (800) 452-5687.

BOGACHIEL TRAIL

[Fig. 27(3)] Except for the first 2 miles, which are managed by the U.S. Forest Service, the Bogachiel Trail is part of the Olympic National Park. The trail follows the Bogachiel River for over 30 miles to its source, passing through clear-cuts, virgin forest, and luxurious rain forest.

From the trailhead at the end of Bogachiel River Forest Road (Road 2932), the trail runs through stands of second growth alder and crosses several small creeks for 2 miles before entering the rain forest and the national park. The vegetation continues to grow more dense and opulent as the hiker continues along the trail, with large stands of western hemlock, Douglas fir, and spruce. The first campsite is 6 miles from the trailhead. The next campground is another 6 miles past the first. The largest known silver fir, with a diameter of nearly 7 feet, is located 8.5 miles from the trailhead. There are also campsites at Flapjack Camp (10.3 miles), Fifteen Mile Shelter (14.4 miles), Hyak Shelter (17 miles), and at 21 Mile Shelter (20.6 miles). As the trail

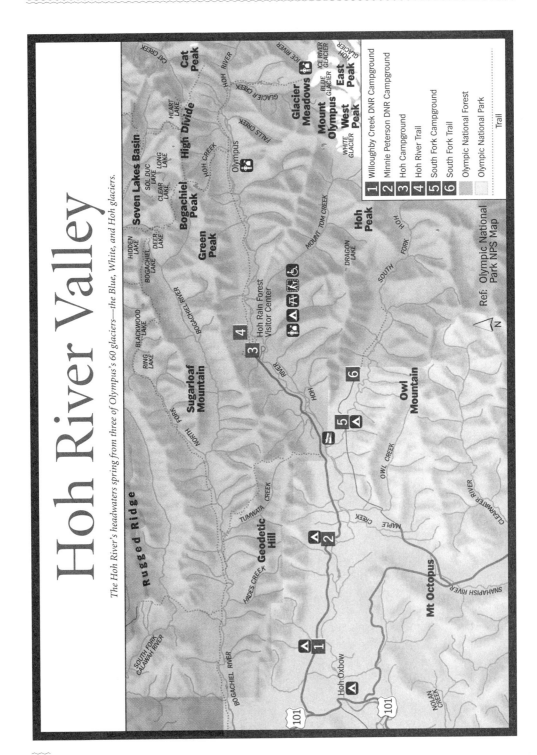

Hoh River Valley

The Hoh River's headwaters spring from three of Olympus's 60 glaciers—the Blue, White, and Hoh glaciers.

Rugged Ridge

Seven Lakes Basin

Cat Peak

High Divide

Heart Lake

Hoh Creek

Glacier Meadows

Mount Olympus

West Peak

East Peak

Blue Glacier

Ice River Glacier

Hoh Glacier

White Glacier

Sol Duc Lake

Long Lake

Clear Lake

Bogachiel Peak

Green Peak

Hidden Lake

Deer Lake

Bogachiel Lake

Blackwood Lake

Ring Lake

Sugarloaf Mountain

Bogachiel River

North Fork

Hoh River

Mount Tom Creek

Hoh Peak

Dragon Lake

South Fork

Hoh Rain Forest Visitor Center

Owl Mountain

Owl Creek

Maple Creek

Tumwata Creek

Geodetic Hill

Hoes Creek

Mt Octopus

Clearwater River

Snahapish River

South Fork Calawah River

Bogachiel River

Hoh Oxbow

Nolan Creek

1	Willoughby Creek DNR Campground
2	Minnie Peterson DNR Campground
3	Hoh Campground
4	Hoh River Trail
5	South Fork Campground
6	South Fork Trail
	Olympic National Forest
	Olympic National Park
	Trail

Ref: Olympic National Park NPS Map

N

101

101

takes the hiker up the mountain, it is possible to see plants from the different climatic zones. Mountain hemlock, silver fir, and western redcedar are represented along the route, as are such plants such as vanilla leaf *(Achlys triphylla)* and bracken fern *(Pteridium aquilinum)*.

Directions: From Forks, follow US Highway 101 south for 5 miles. Turn east on Undie Road (U.S. Forest Service Road 2932 on some maps). Follow Undie Road to the trailhead, about another 5 miles.

Dates: Open seasonally, depending on weather and funding.

Fees: Fees are charged for overnight backpacking permits.

Closest town: Forks, 5 miles.

For more information: Olympic National Park, Wilderness Information Center, 600 East Park Avenue, Port Angeles, WA 98362. Phone (360) 452-0330.

Trail: 30 miles, one-way.

Elevation: 3.954-foot elevation gain.

Degree of difficulty: Strenuous.

HOH RIVER VALLEY

[Fig. 28] Usually referred to as "The Hoh" by Pacific Northwesteners, this is a large, rough river, and its waters are clouded with "rock flour." Glaciers grind rocks on Mount Olympus to make this glacial silt. The river's headwaters spring from three of Olympus's 60 glaciers, the Blue, White, and Hoh glaciers. In addition to the glacier waters, tributaries add to the river's volume.

The river is often referred to as the steelhead capital of the world. Fishermen come from all over the world to fish for steelhead as well as coho and chinook salmon.

The Hoh River Road runs through lands of the Olympic National Park, private parties, and the Washington State Department of Natural Resources (DNR). There are two DNR campgrounds located along the road. A visitor center, Hoh Campground, and Hoh River Trail are located at the end of this road.

Directions: From Forks, go 15 miles on US Highway 101 south to the Hoh River Road. Turn left and follow the road 19 miles to its end.

Activities: Camping, hiking, interpretative trails, fishing, wildlife and plant viewing, ranger programs.

Facilities: Tent and RV sites, museum

MOUNTAIN GOAT
(Oreamnos americanus)

and visitor center, ranger station, drinking water, garbage service, restrooms, picnic area, phone, RV dump.

Dates: Open year-round, weather and funding permitting.

Fees: Fees are charged for camping and overnight backpacking permits.

Closest town: Forks, 32 miles.

For more information: Olympic National Park, Wilderness Information Center, 600 East Park Avenue, Port Angeles, WA 98362. Phone (360) 452-0330.

WILLOUGHBY CREEK AND MINNIE PETERSON DEPARTMENT OF NATURAL RESOURCES CAMPGROUNDS

Two DNR campgrounds are located within a few miles of each other along the Hoh River Road. They are the Willoughby Creek and Minnie Peterson campgrounds. Both are in attractive forest settings but are close to the road. Like most DNR campgrounds, they are undeveloped, with outhouses and not much else. Even the water must be purified, so come prepared.

WILLOUGHBY CREEK DEPARTMENT OF NATURAL RESOURCES CAMPGROUND

[Fig. 27(4), Fig. 28(1)] **Directions:** From Forks, follow US Highway 101 south for 15 miles to the Hoh River Road. Turn left and follow the road 3 miles to Willoughby Creek.

Activities: Camping, hiking, fishing, wildlife and plant spotting.

Facilities: Campsites, outhouses, picnic area.

Dates: Open year-round, weather and funding permitting.

Fees: Fees are charged for camping.

Closest town: Forks, 32 miles.

For more information: Washington State Department of Natural Resources Olympic Regional Headquarters, 411 Tillicum Lane, Forks, WA 98331. Phone (360) 374-6131.

MINNIE PETERSON DEPARTMENT OF NATURAL RESOURCES CAMPGROUND

[Fig. 27(5), Fig. 28(2)] **Directions:** From Forks, follow US Highway 101 south for 15 miles to the Hoh River Road. Turn left and follow the road and 6.5 miles to Minnie Peterson Campgrounds.

Activities: Camping, hiking, fishing.

Facilities: Campsites, outhouse.

Dates: Open year-round, depending on weather and funding.

Fees: Fees are charged for camping.

Closest town: Forks, 35.5 miles.

HOH CAMPGROUND

[Fig. 28(3)] The Hoh Campground is part of Olympic National Park and is situated at the end of the Hoh River Road. It has 88 camping spaces, many located right next to the river. Roosevelt elk occasionally roam through the campground, and river otter can be spotted by those willing to get up early enough. So can the occasional cougar. The visitor center has a small but excellent museum with displays of animals and birds. Dried samples of wildflowers are fun and informative, if a little faded. The campground is 19 miles from the main road, and 10 miles from the nearest store.

The trailhead for the Hoh River Trail is located next to the visitor center. There also are two nature trails located there. The Hall Of Mosses Nature Trail (0.75 mile long) goes through stands of Douglas fir, hemlock, and spruce, but the highlight is the groves of bigleaf maples (*Acer macrophyllum*) shrouded with mosses, ferns, and Wallace's selaginella *(Selaginella wallacei)*. The Spruce Nature Trail (1.25 miles) is tucked between the Hoh River Trail and the river itself. Some parts of the Spruce Nature Trail flood periodically; alders and maples predominate on the floodplain and elk feed in the grassy meadows that grow beneath the trees. Be sure to watch the river for a small, grayish bird, the American dipper *(Cinclus mexicanus)*. It sits on the river rocks, bobbing its head rhymically before diving into the water where it searches for food on the river bottom. Sitka spruce *(Picea sitchensis)* hold sway in the upper portions of the trail, mixed in with western redcedar *(Thuja plicata)*, hemlocks and Douglas firs.

Directions: From Forks, go 15 miles on US Highway 101 south to the Hoh River Road. Turn left and follow the road 19 miles to its end. The campground is located just to the south of the Hoh Rain Forest visitor center.

Activities: Tent and RV camping, hiking, interpretative trails, fishing, wildlife and plant spotting, ranger programs.

Facilities: Tent and RV sites, museum and visitor center, drinking water, garbage service and restrooms, picnic area, visitor center and phone, RV dump.

Dates: Open year-round, weather and funding permitting.

Fees: Fees are charged for camping and overnight backpacking permits.

Closest town: Forks, 32 miles.

For more information: Olympic National Park, Wilderness Information Center, 600 East Park Avenue, Port Angeles, WA 98362. Phone (360) 452-0330.

HOH RIVER TRAIL

[Fig. 28(4)] Although there are more isolated and luxurious rain forests than this, the Hoh Rain Forest somehow seems like the jewel of them all. This is considered by many to be a contender for the most beautiful trail in the United

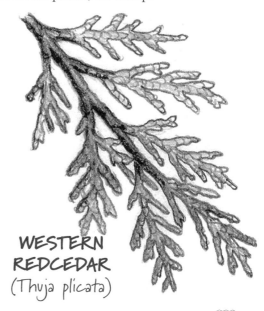

WESTERN REDCEDAR
(Thuja plicata)

States. One hiking magazine voted it the second most beautiful trail in the world several years ago. The trail follows the Hoh River to its source, Mount Olympus, and is the main route for those climbing Mount Olympus. It passes through all of the climatic zones, from alpine meadows on Mount Olympus's upper slopes down to the rain forests, where the river braids channels through the flat bottomlands.

Less ambitious visitors can enjoy the trail's lower campsites or day hike. The first camping area is at Happy Four Shelter, 5.6 miles and an elevation gain of only about 200 feet from the trailhead. The most popular camping destination is Olympus Guard Station, at 8.6 miles and an elevation gain of 350 feet total from the trailhead. The trail does continue beyond Olympus Station another 9.5 miles, with camping along the way. It ends at the snout of Blue Glacier and Mount Olympus.

Those wishing to backpack on the trail should check at the Wilderness Information Center, as permits are required for overnight stays.

Directions: From Forks, follow US Highway 101 south for 15 miles to the Hoh River Road. The trailhead is located by the visitor center.

Activities: Hiking, backpacking, mountain climbing.

Dates: Open seasonally, depending on weather.

Fees: Fees are charged for overnight permits.

Closest town: Forks, 32 miles.

For more information: Olympic National Park, Wilderness Information Center, 600 East Park Avenue, Port Angeles, WA 98362. Phone (360) 452-0330.

Trail: 18 miles, one-way.

Elevation: 5,000-foot elevation gain.

Degree of difficulty: Strenuous.

DOUGLAS FIR
(Pseudotsuga menziesii)
In coastal areas, the Douglas fir grows tall and straight, reaching 180 to 250 feet and rivaling the redwood tree in height.

SOUTH FORK CAMPGROUND

[Fig. 28(5)] The South Fork River parallels the Hoh River before it flows into the Hoh north of Huelsdonk Ridge. Its source is Mount Olympus's Hubert Glacier, however, and not the three big glaciers that feed the Hoh. The South Fork Trail begins at the end of Road 1000. The South Fork Campground is undeveloped, with only three sites and an outhouse, but it is tucked against the river and is very pleasant—and free! Like the Hoh, strong runs of salmon and steelhead return to the South Fork River, and the fishing is good. The only source of water is the river; be prepared to boil or otherwise purify water, or bring some in.

Directions: From Forks, follow US Highway 101 south for 17 miles. About 1 mile past the Hoh Oxbow Campground, turn left on Road 1000 at the Clearwater Honor Camp sign. The road branches at about 4 miles; take the left branch to the east. The campground is about another 4 miles.

Activities: Hiking, camping, fishing in season.

Facilities: Campsites, outhouse, no potable water.

Dates: Open year-round.

Fees: None.

Closest town: Forks, about 15 miles.

For more information: Olympic National Park, Wilderness Information Center, 600 East Park Avenue, Port Angeles, WA 98362. Phone (360) 452-0330.

SOUTH FORK TRAIL

[Fig. 28(6)] The trail begins at the end of Road 1000, 2 miles from the campground, and about 800 feet in elevation. The trail gains about 50 feet in elevation, but as it tends to go uphill and down over and over again, this is somewhat deceptive. The rain forest is thick and lush along this trail and elk can be seen browsing the meadows. After the first 0.4 mile the rain forest begins. There is good camping near the river at the far side of a wide, grassy bottom area known as Big Flats, 1.3 miles, and about 725 foot elevation. Big Flat is surrounded by stands of deciduous vine maples, bigleaf maple, and spruce trees, and is an attractive place to camp. The next camping area is another 1.2 miles in at Camp Stick-in-Eye, so-called because in 1978 a camper accidentally did just that. Note the alder, spruces, western hemlock, and Douglas fir trees along the trail. Although the trail used to go all the way to the base of Hoh Peak, it now vanishes entirely about 1 mile after Stick-in-Eye, and that mile is in a bad state of disrepair.

Trail: 6.5 miles, one-way.

Elevation: 50-foot elevation gain.

Degree of difficulty: Moderate.

▨ LAKE QUINAULT RAIN FOREST

[Fig. 29(1)] Lake Quinault Rain Forest is the farthest south of the major rain forest river valleys located on the western slopes of the Olympic Peninsula. Both the National Park Service and the U.S. Forest Service manage different sections of the

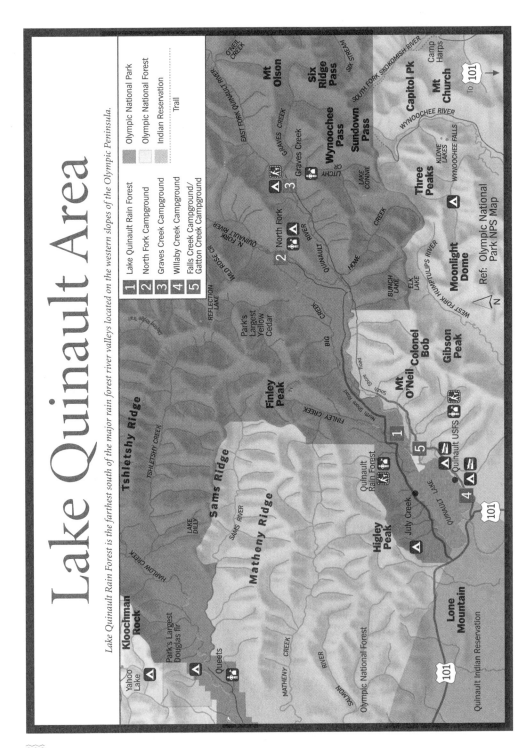

Lake Quinault Area

Lake Quinault Rain Forest is the farthest south of the major rain forest river valleys located on the western slopes of the Olympic Peninsula.

Olympic National Park
Olympic National Forest
Indian Reservation
Trail

1 Lake Quinault Rain Forest
2 North Fork Campground
3 Graves Creek Campground
4 Willaby Creek Campground
5 Falls Creek Campground/Gatton Creek Campground

Ref: Olympic National Park NPS Map

lakeshore and river valley, and the forests around them. The Quinault Indian Reservation owns the lake's actual water. Lake Quinault Rain Forest is the ideal spot for visitors coming from the south end of Puget Sound desiring to visit both a major rain forest and see the Pacific Ocean. Besides its easily accessible freshwater beaches, Lake Quinault has all the usual rain forest features: towering moss-draped trees, dense undergrowth, and torrents of rain, plus a gorgeous recreational lake. It also offers both campgrounds and a number of privately owned resorts, as well as Lake Quinault Lodge (*see* Lake Quinault Lodge page 202.), another of Olympic National Park's concessionaire-run resort facilities. The ocean beaches that run between Kalaloch and the Queets River are within about a 40-minute drive.

NORTH FORK CAMPGROUND

[Fig. 29(2)] This seven-site campground offers access to the Big Creek and North Fork trails, among others.

Directions: From Hoquiam, follow US Highway 101 north for 40 miles to Amanda Park. Go 1.6 miles north of Amanda Park, and turn right onto North Shore Road on Lake Quinault. Go 17 miles. The campground is at the end of the road.

Activities: Camping, hiking, fishing, picnicking, hunting.

Facilities: Tent sites, restrooms, picnic tables.

Dates: Open year-round.

Fees: Fees are charged for camping.

For more information: Olympic National Park, Wilderness Information Center, 600 East Park Avenue, Port Angeles, WA 98362. Phone (360) 452-0330.

GRAVES CREEK CAMPGROUND

[Fig. 29(3)] Located on the East Fork Quinault River, this 30-unit campground is the jumping off place to some good hiking, including Enchanted Valley. The campground is undeveloped, with no running water. It is 13 miles to Enchanted Valley. It is possible to hike the Enchanted Valley Trail all the way from the Quinault River Valley to Dosewallips on the eastern side of the mountain range, a total of 30.7 miles.

Directions: From Hoquim, travel US Highway 101 north 39 miles to the intersection with Old State Route 9. Turn right onto Old State Route 9 and go about 1 mile to the junction with South Shore Road. Graves Creek is at the end of South Shore Road, 17.5 miles.

Activities: Camping, hiking, fishing, picnicking.

Facilities: Campsites, outhouse, picnic tables.

Dates: Open year-round except when the road is closed by slides in the winter.

Fees: Fees are charged for camping.

For more information: Olympic National Park, Wilderness Information Center, 600 East Park Avenue, Port Angeles, WA 98362. Phone (360) 452-0330.

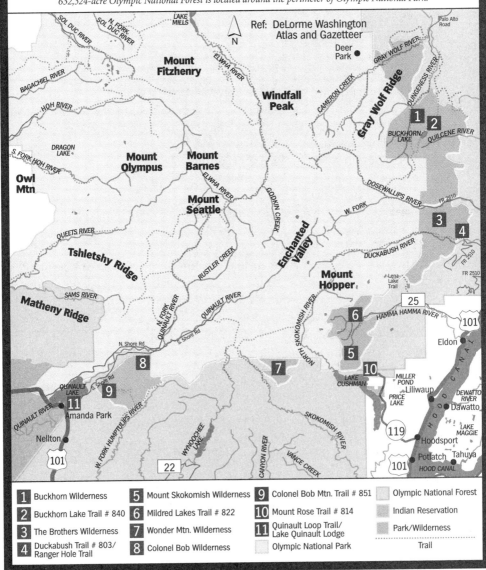

Olympic National Forest Area

632,324-acre Olympic National Forest is located around the perimeter of Olympic National Park.

1	Buckhorn Wilderness	**5**	Mount Skokomish Wilderness	**9**	Colonel Bob Mtn. Trail # 851	Olympic National Forest
2	Buckhorn Lake Trail # 840	**6**	Mildred Lakes Trail # 822	**10**	Mount Rose Trail # 814	Indian Reservation
3	The Brothers Wilderness	**7**	Wonder Mtn. Wilderness	**11**	Quinault Loop Trail/ Lake Quinault Lodge	Park/Wilderness
4	Duckabush Trail # 803/ Ranger Hole Trail	**8**	Colonel Bob Wilderness		Olympic National Park	Trail

Olympic National Forest

[Fig. 30] This 632,324-acre national forest is located around the perimeter of the Olympic National Park. The natural features and habitat are the same in both park and forest, and there are few ways to tell where one stops and the other begins. The main sign the visitor can see is the logged areas that occur in the national forest. Second growth forest probably belongs to the Forest Service, but for the most part passage from park land to forest land is seamless. The boundaries belong to humans, not nature.

The national forest includes some high mountains that offer a challenge for hikers and climbers, as well as 24 campgrounds with a total of more than 500 campsites with a wide variety of facilities. There are five wilderness areas with a total of some 88,265 acres of rugged, mountainous grandeur in the forest.

The forest is managed by the U.S. Forest Service, a part of the U.S. Department of Agriculture. The park is managed by the National Park Service, a part of the U.S. Department of Interior. The policies and programs of the two agencies are similar, but there are some differences of interest to visitors. The forest does not require a permit to stay overnight in the wilderness, while the park does. The forest allows firearms and hunting under state regulations; the park does not. The forest allows motorized trail bikes on some trails; the park does not. The forest allows pets on trails; the park does not. The forest allows visitors to collect plants and cut firewood with a permit, while the park does not. It is wise for visitors to ask a ranger for the full regulations in either jurisdiction.

The national forest was created as a forest reserve in 1897 by a proclamation signed by President Grover Cleveland. That set aside 1,500,000 acres in the center of the Olympic Peninsula. Eight years later the name was changed to the Olympic National Forest, and in 1909, President Theodore Roosevelt issued a proclamation designating the center of the forest as the Mount Olympus National Monument. The monument was transferred to the Park Service in 1933, and the national park was created in 1938 during the administration of President Franklin D. Roosevelt. The lands around the perimeter of the park remain as the national forest.

Climactic conditions in the forest are similar to those of the park it surrounds. Weather conditions vary widely between places short distances apart. This is mainly because of the prevailing wet, ocean winds carrying moisture from the Pacific and meeting the mountains. As the air rises it cools, and the moisture condenses and falls as rain or snow on the western flank. As the air continues over the mountains' summit and descends the slopes on the other side of the mountains, it warms and dries, leaving a relatively dry climate. Thus, within a short 50 miles, the vegetation can change from the lush temperate west side rain forest of the Quinault Valley, where rainfall measures in the hundreds of inches during a year, to the east side's Hood Canal Ranger District, where less than 25 inches of rain may fall annually. In the winter an average of about 10

Common Loon

Common loons (*Gavia immer*) are much like ducks that dive in the water for food. They eat primarily fish, but also take reptiles, leeches, insects, and even aquatic plants. They use both their webbed feet and their wings to swim and can dive as deep as 300 feet. Sometimes they become trapped on small lakes with a rim of high trees that don't provide room to gain enough speed to become airborne. When that happens loons must wait patiently, sometimes for weeks, for a strong wind that will provide their wings with enough lift to get out of the trap.

inches of snow falls in the warm valleys while in the cold high elevations of the mountains the snow depths can be as much as 250 inches.

The national forest is divided into two ranger districts. Each is managed by a crew under the direction of a district ranger and each has two offices where information, permits, and other services may be obtained. One of the districts is the Pacific Ranger District. One of its offices is in Forks at 437 Tillicum Lane, Forks, WA 98331, phone (360) 374-6532. The other office is in Quinault. The address is PO Box 9, 353 South Shore Road, Quinault, WA 98575, phone (360) 288-2525. That ranger district serves primarily the west side of the Olympic Peninsula. The east side is under the jurisdiction of the Hood Canal Ranger District. One of that district's offices is in Quilcene. The address is PO Box 280, 295142 Highway 101 South, Quilcene, WA 98736, phone (360) 765-2200. The other office is in Hoodsport at PO Box 68, 150 North Lake Cushman Road, Hoodsport, WA 98548, phone (360) 877-5254.

The national forest is almost entirely inland, but it touches salt water for a short distance on Hood Canal at Seal Rock (*see* Seal Rock Campground, page 205). There are, however, numerous lakes and streams to attract anglers. Fishing in forest waters is regulated by the state, which establishes seasons and conditions for fishing. State fishing and hunting licenses can be obtained from sporting goods stores throughout the state. The Quinault Indian Reservation regulates fishing on Lake Quinault. Among the andromous fish that frequent the forest's waters are steelhead, sea-run cutthroat trout, and Pacific salmon. Freshwater fish include Dolly Varden, Eastern brook, and rainbow trout.

The forest teems with wildlife, ranging from tiny mice that weigh a few ounces to the Roosevelt elk which often weighs more than 600 pounds. There are an estimated 5,000 to 7,000 elk on the Olympic Peninsula, the largest elk population in America. The elk run in herds that wander back and forth between the national forest and the national park, and, since hunting is banned in the park, they attract large numbers of hunters to the forest during the fall hunting season.

Deer, too, are in abundance in the forest, and they also attract numerous hunters during the hunting season. Hunting, like fishing, is regulated by the State Fish and Game Department, and state licenses are required.

Smaller mammals in the forest include several that are so rare or so shy that humans seldom see them. Those include the marten (*Martes americana*), bobcat (*Lynx rufus*), mink (*Mustela vison*), porcupine (*Erethizon dorsatum*), opossum (*Didelphis virginiana*) and otter (*Lutra canadensis*). The otter is a dark brown, long-tailed, playful member of the weasel family that has been heavily hunted, both for its fur and because it is suspected of depleting the trout population. Otters are seen most often on riverbanks, where they seem to enjoy sliding down steep slopes of mud or snow on their bellies.

Perhaps seen more often are less shy animals such as chipmunks, marmots, squirrels, and black bears, which will be glad to relieve a camper of any food available in a campsite. Bats, lizards, and snakes are also abundant, but no poisonous snakes are native to the Olympic Peninsula.

Congress has set aside five places in the forest as designated wilderness, where the land management is guided by the Wilderness Act of 1964, which defines wilderness as "an area where the earth and its community of life are untrammeled by man, where man himself is a visitor who does not remain." The Forest Service takes those words literally. It manages the wilderness areas so that people are simply visitors who pass through, leaving no sign they have been there, and using only their own muscle or that of animals for transportation. There are no roads in the wilderness; indeed, one of the wildernesses doesn't even have trails. Nor are machines of any kind allowed to enter the wilderness areas. Except during emergencies, landing a helicopter or dropping supplies from an airplane are outlawed. Bicycles, all other wheeled vehicles, hang gliders, and chainsaws are banned. Storing supplies, equipment, or other property for 24 hours or more, a practice called caching, is prohibited. Parties of visitors are limited to 12 persons and/or head of livestock. Fires are banned above 3,500 feet in elevation and so is gathering wood for a fire at that elevation. Livestock

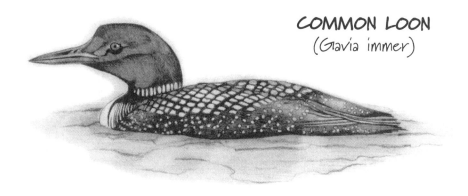

COMMON LOON
(*Gavia immer*)

may not be tethered to trees or other vegetation for more than 30 minutes at a time. Visitors should check with a ranger before entering the wilderness to make certain they understand the limitations.

There are 57 trails in the forest, covering a total of 216 miles and ranging from 0.3 to 12 miles in length. They vary from short, easy, interpretive walks to long, steep hikes through lowland forests and into the high country. Hikers are permitted to leave the trail and hike cross-country, but that is not recommended for people who are not in good physical condition, and who don't have extensive experience in the forests and mountains. There are no restrictions on where hikers can camp, but visitors should be careful not to unduly disturb the natural setting, especially in the wilderness areas. Many of the trails are closed to motorized vehicles. Some are closed to mountain bikes, and a few are closed to livestock. Check with the ranger on which trails are closed for specific uses at any given time.

Directions: The forest consists of islands of land around the Olympic National Park. The islands can be reached from US Highway 101, which circles the perimeter of both the forest and the park.

Activities: Hiking, camping, fishing, hunting, mountain climbing, boating, horseback riding, mountain biking.

Facilities: Trails, campgrounds, boat launches, lodging.

Dates: Open year-round.

Fees: A trailhead fee may be charged.

For more information: Olympic National Forest Headquarters, 1835 Black Lake Boulevard Southwest, Olympia, WA 98512. Phone (360) 956-2300.

BUCKHORN WILDERNESS

[Fig. 30(1)] This 44,258-acre wilderness is both the largest in the Olympic National Forest, and one of the most rugged, with steep terrain that begins at approximately 1,000 feet in elevation, and ranges up to the top of 7,134-foot Mount Fricaba on the western border of the wilderness. At 6,988-feet, Buckhorn Mountain, which gives the wilderness its name, is the second highest peak in the wilderness. The other major peaks include Iron Mountain, 6,950 feet and Tyler Mountain at 6,350 feet. The backcountry features numerous steep, rocky cliffs and ridges that are kept barren by the strong winds and cold weather of the high country. The wilderness is divided into two parts by the Dungeness River, with both parts adjacent to the eastern border of the Olympic National Park. Some of the wilderness's trails give access to the park.

A little below the barren high ridges, the high country features meadows of brightly colored flowers such as Indian paintbrush (*Castilleja miniata*), the most common of the paintbrush species in these parts. It blooms from May to July. The Makah Indians used it as a lure to trap hummingbirds, which tribal whale hunters used as a charm.

Mixed with the meadows are stands of high country trees such as subalpine fir (*Amies amabilis*) and western white pine (*Pinus monticola*). The western white pines in the United States are under attack from white pine blister rust disease, which was imported with a shipment of seedlings from a French nursery in 1909. The American trees lack a natural resistance to the disease and have been seriously affected. Genetic strains that resist the disease are being bred, and scientists hope they will restock the species.

The lowlands of the wilderness are populated by stands of tall, stately old-growth Douglas fir, western redcedar, and western hemlock.

A half dozen trails, ranging from 2.5 miles to 8.6 miles in length, go into the wilderness. Most of them are open to use with livestock, but visitors should check with a ranger for closures.

Directions: This large wilderness area can be reached by several roads. The southern, larger segment can be reached by going about 2.5 miles east from Sequim on US Highway 101 and turning south on the Palo Alto Road. Then go about 7.5 miles, and bear to the left onto Forest Road 28. Take that road for 8.5 miles, and turn right onto Forest Road 2860. The trailhead to Trail 833 is on the right side of the road about 18.9 miles from US Highway 101.

Activities: Hiking, camping fishing, hunting.

Facilities: None.

Dates: Open year-round.

Fees: A trailhead fee may be charged.

Closest town: Sequim, 25.5 miles.

For more information: Quilcene Ranger Station, 20482 US Highway 101 South, PO Box 280, Quilcene, WA 98376. Phone (360) 765-2200.

BUCKHORN LAKE TRAIL NUMBER 840

[Fig. 30(2)] This 6-mile wilderness trail goes steeply up into the glaciated valley on the east side of the Olympic Mountains, where there is less rain to contend with. It passes through a 216-acre island of private land where the Tubal Cain Mine site is located, then veers to the left on a side trail that goes to Buckhorn Lake. The main trail Number 840 goes on over Buckhorn Pass and Marmot Pass to meet several other trails that lead to various places in the high country, including the interior of the Olympic National Park that is adjacent to the wilderness. Camping at Buckhorn Lake provides a good base for exploring the trails. It also is a good place for anglers to try their luck and photographers to record the magnificent scenery.

The hike begins in a forest of Douglas fir and western hemlock reaching high overhead, while the ground bears numerous understory plants such as Oregon grape (*Berberis nervosa*), which has a small, blue berry that pioneers made into jelly and wine, but is too sour for most modern palates. Indians combined Oregon grapes with sweeter berries, mashed them, dried them, and stored them for use during the winter. The Indians also used the roots to make yellow dye and to brew a tea to cure stomach trouble. The trail also passes wild rhododendron *(Rhododendron macrophyllum)*, the Washington state flower, which paints the forest with brilliant pink flowers in the spring.

The trail passes a side trail to an old mine shaft in the lower part of the Tubal Cain Mine. About 0.5 mile farther, the trail enters an area burned by a forest fire. Look for meadowlike slopes of grasses and flowers. As the trail rises, Puget Sound and the San Juan Islands come into view in the northeast, while high mountain peaks dominate the scene to the south. At 5.5 miles from the trailhead, a fork to the left goes to Buckhorn Lake. There are campsites there as well as elsewhere along the trail. The right fork goes on to Buckhorn Pass and beyond.

Directions: Go about 2.5 miles east from Sequim on US Highway 101, and turn south on the Palo Alto Road. Then go about 7.5 miles and bear to the left onto Forest Road 28. Take that road for 8.5 miles and turn right onto Forest Road 2860. The trailhead to Trail 840 is on the right side of the road, about 23 miles from US Highway 101.

Activities: Hiking, fishing, hunting.

Facilities: None.

Dates: Open July to mid-Oct.

Fees: A trailhead fee may be charged.

Closest town: Sequim, 25 miles.

For more information: Quilcene Ranger Station, 20482 US Highway 101 South, PO Box 280, Quilcene, WA 98376. Phone (360) 765-2200.

Trail: 6 miles, one-way.

Elevation: 3,250-foot elevation gain.

Degree of difficulty: Moderate.

THE BROTHERS WILDERNESS

[Fig. 30(3)] This 16,682-acre wilderness is mostly in the Hood Canal Ranger District, but the northern end extends into the Quilcene District, and it is separated from that district's Buckhorn Wilderness by little more than Forest Road 2610, which runs between them. Like the Olympic National Forest's other wildernesses, it is adjacent to the Olympic National Park, and trails lead from one entity to the other.

The terrain is steep throughout the wilderness except for a relatively level area along the East Fork of Lena Creek. The wilderness is named after its highest peak, Brothers Mountain, 6,866 feet in elevation, directly on the border of the national park. The other major peaks include Mount Jupiter Ridge, 5,701 feet in elevation, and St. Peter's Dome, 4,490 feet in elevation. The low point of the wilderness is a spot 699 feet in elevation on the Dosewallips River valley.

The wilderness is largely forested, with Pacific silver fir and mountain hemlock in the high country, and Douglas fir, western hemlock, and western redcedar on the lower reaches. The highest parts of the wilderness, where frigid temperatures and high winds inhibit vegetation, either feature bare rock or are covered with meadows and subalpine fir. There are numerous small streams, but the Duckabush River, which rises in the national park and cuts through the middle of the wilderness, is the only major stream. The Jupiter Lakes, lying below Jupiter Ridge, offer both camping and fishing.

The view from high country spots looks across Puget Sound to Mount Rainier, Mount St. Helens, Mount Adams, and lesser mountains in the Cascades Range. It also includes the towers of Seattle nestled beside the sound.

Directions: One route to the wilderness is to turn west off US Highway 101 approximately 13 miles north of Hoodsport onto Forest Road 25. Then go about 8 miles to the trailhead of the Lena Lake Trail Number 810. The trail leads to Lena Lake then forks, with the left fork, Trail Number 111, going along the northern edge of the wilderness toward Upper Lena Lake. The right fork, Trail Number 821, enters the wilderness and goes toward The Brothers Mountain where the trail ends.

Activities: Hiking, camping, fishing, hunting.

Facilities: None.

Dates: Open during the summer.

Fees: A trailhead fee may be charged.

Closest town: Hoodsport, 21 miles.

For more information: Olympic National Park/National Forest Information Center, 150 North Lake Cushman Road, PO Box 68, Hoodsport, WA 98548. Phone (360) 877-5424.

DUCKABUSH TRAIL NUMBER 803

[Fig. 30(4)] This trail follows the Duckabush River through the Brothers Wilderness, and then goes beyond into the Olympic National Park. There, it interconnects with numerous other trails, including the route over Anderson Pass, through the fabulous Enchanted Valley, and down the Quinault River Trail to Quinault on the other side of the Olympic Range. That is a major undertaking and most hikers are content with a day hike or overnight backpack.

The trail meanders easily for about 2.5 miles, then goes upward, first over Little Hump, a 400-foot climb, then over Big Hump, a 1,000-foot climb. It leads past some magnificent old-growth forest in the Duckabush Valley. Some very nice campsites are beside the river just west of Big Hump. The national park border is 6.2 miles from the trailhead.

Directions: Turn west off US Highway 101 onto Forest Road 2510 about 22 miles north of Hoodsport. The trailhead, complete with a place to unload horses, is about 6 miles from the highway.

Activities: Hiking, camping, fishing, hunting, mountain climbing, horseback riding.

Facilities: None.

Dates: Open during the summer.

Fees: There may be a trailhead fee.

Closest town: Hoodsport, 28 miles.

For more information: Olympic National Park/National Forest Information Center, 150 North Lake Cushman Road, PO Box 68, Hoodsport, WA 98548. Phone (360) 877-5424.

Trail: 6.7 miles, one-way.

Elevation: 1,475-foot elevation gain.

Degree of difficulty: Moderate.

MOUNT SKOKOMISH WILDERNESS

[Fig. 30(5)] This 13,015-acre wilderness is on the southeastern corner of the national forest, and features very steep terrain that goes from 800 feet in elevation near its southern edge to its high point on the peak of 6,612-foot Mount Stone. Five other peaks reach to 6,000 or more feet in elevation. The valleys are largely covered with old-growth forests of the Douglas fir, western hemlock, and western redcedar that are well known in this part of the land. Subalpine pine and western white pine stretch across the middle elevations, while the high country consists of scattered alpine vegetation among the bare rocks.

The wilderness offers streams and lakes for fishing, including the Hamma Hamma River that runs through the wilderness on its way to Hood Canal. There are 13 miles of trail that lead to the fishing spots, and the scenery is awesome.

Directions: One route to the wilderness is to take US Highway 101 about 9 miles north from Hoodsport, and turn west onto Forest Road 24. Take that road about 10 miles to the trailhead of Trail 814 that goes to Mount Rose (*see* Mount Rose Trail Number 814, page 201). The wilderness border is about 0.5 mile from the trailhead.

Activities: Hiking, camping, fishing, mountain climbing.

Facilities: None.

Dates: Open during the summer.

Fees: A trailhead fee may be charged.

Closest town: Hoodsport, 20 miles.

For more information: Olympic National Park/National Forest Information Center, 150 North Lake Cushman Road, PO Box 68, Hoodsport, WA 98548. Phone (360) 877-5424.

MILDRED LAKES TRAIL NUMBER 822

[Fig. 30(6)] This is a rough trail that even the Forest Service describes as a primitive route with extremely steep slopes. It gains 2,100 feet in elevation in its 4.5-mile length. The Forest Service considers it a "way trail" so it gets only a little maintenance, and the route is likely to include numerous downed trees and rockfalls that not only make it tough going, but also leave the trail hard to follow in some places. At the end of the long, hard trail, there are mountains to be climbed and three alpine lakes to be fished.

All three lakes have good campsites. The view includes the rocky, awesome Sawtooth Mountain Range, as well as the sparkling lakes. A side trail from the highest lake goes to Mount Lincoln, where there is an extended view.

Directions: Take US Highway 101 approximately 14 miles north from Hoodsport, and turn west on Forest Road 25, which goes to the Hamma Hamma Recreation Area. Follow that road for 14 miles to the trailhead at the end of the road.

Activities: Hiking, camping, mountain climbing, fishing.

Facilities: None.

Dates: Open during the summer.

Fees: A trailhead fee may be charged.

Closest town: Hoodsport, 28 miles.

For more information: Olympic National Park/National Forest Information Center, 150 North Lake Cushman Road, PO Box 68, Hoodsport, WA 98548. Phone (360) 877-5424.

Trail: 4.5 miles, one-way.

Elevation: 2,100-foot elevation gain.

Degree of difficulty: Strenuous.

WONDER MOUNTAIN WILDERNESS

[Fig. 30(7)] This little wilderness hangs down from the southern border of the Olympic National Park like laundry on a clothesline. At 2,349 acres, it is one of the smallest designated wilderness areas in the western part of the nation. Its major feature is Wonder Mountain, 4,758 feet in elevation. The lowest spot is in the McKay Creek valley at 1,740 feet in elevation. There are no major streams in the wilderness, but Wonder Mountain forms the headwaters of McKay Creek, which drains into the nearby national park, and there are several ponds along the higher reaches of the stream.

There are no trails in or to the wilderness, and the only way to get there is to go cross-country. That, obviously, makes for hard going, but it increases the likelihood that visitors will not meet anyone else in the rugged forests and massive rock outcrops of the wilderness. The lower slopes are densely covered with stands of Douglas fir, Pacific silver fir, and western hemlock.

No road leads directly to the wilderness, and those that go closest are closed from Oct. 1 to May 1 to benefit wildlife.

Directions: One route

MARTEN
(Martes americana)

to the wilderness is to take US Highway 101 about 9 miles north from Hoodsport, and turn west onto Forest Road 24. Take that road about 12 miles, with Lake Cushman on the left for the last 3 miles. Near the end of the lake, turn left onto Forest Road 2451, and go about 2 miles. Then bear right onto Forest Road 2451-100, and go about 3 miles to the end of the road. The wilderness is about 0.5 mile to the west of the road. Note: Forest Road 2451 is closed for the benefit of wildlife from Oct. 1 to May 1.

Activities: Cross-country hiking, fishing, mountain climbing, camping under primitive conditions.

Facilities: None.

Dates: Open during the summer.

Fees: There may be a trailhead fee.

Closest town: Hoodsport, about 26 miles.

For more information: Hood Canal Ranger Station, 150 North Lake Cushman Road, PO Box 68, Hoodsport, WA 98548. Phone (360) 877-5254.

COLONEL BOB WILDERNESS

[Fig. 30(8)] This 11,962-acre wilderness is in the Quinault Ranger District on the Quinault Valley side of the Olympic Mountains. That means it is the only one of the national forest's five wildernesses that drains into the Pacific Ocean instead of Hood Canal.

The wilderness is east of Lake Quinault on the southwestern corner of the national forest, and its topography is steep and rugged. Since it is on the west side of the mountains, it gets the full benefit of the wet, prevailing ocean winds, and compared to the wildernesses on the eastern side it gets much more precipitation, as much as 150 inches a year. That means the vegetation is different from that of the east-side wildernesses. The lush temperate rain forest has considerable numbers of sitka spruce in addition to the Douglas fir, western hemlock, Pacific silver fir, and western redcedar. The understory is crowded with mosses, lichens, ferns, and shrubs that give the forest an enchanting green hue. On the slopes above the forest, the rugged peaks and gray rock outcrops are mixed with subalpine and alpine vegetation and green meadows, with their brightly colored flowers that change as different species bloom one after the other during the season.

The highest spot in the wilderness is 4,509 feet in elevation and is located near the southeastern corner of the wilderness. Colonel Bob Mountain, at the center of the wilderness, rises to 4,492 feet in elevation. The lowest spot in the wilderness is 300 feet in elevation in the Quinault Valley, but most of the wilderness is above the 1,500-foot level.

In the wilderness, there are 12 miles of trail, many of them very steep and very difficult. There are no major lakes or rivers in the wilderness so visitors are attracted largely by the scenery and hunting.

Directions: From Hoquiam, go north about 43 miles on US Highway 101 and turn east on the South Shore Lake Quinault Road. The road goes beside the lake for several miles, then parallels the wilderness' northwestern border. The trailhead to the Colonel Bob Mountain Trail Number 851 is about 2 miles east of the lake. The trailhead to the Fletcher Canyon Trail Number 857 is about 5 miles farther up the road.

Activities: Hiking, camping, hunting, and mountain climbing.

Facilities: None.

Dates: Open during the summer months.

Fees: There may be a trailhead fee.

Closest town: Hoquiam, 49 miles.

For more information: Quinault Ranger Station, 353 South Shore Road, PO Box 9, Quinault, WA 98575. Phone (360) 288-2525.

COLONEL BOB MOUNTAIN TRAIL NUMBER 851

[Fig. 30(9)] This difficult wilderness hike goes to the top of Colonel Bob Mountain in a long, arduous 6.3 miles. The reward is the peak of the mountain, which was once the site of a forest fire lookout station, and commands a terrific view that extends to the Pacific Ocean to the west and the magnificent mountains of the interior of the Olympic Range to the north.

The trail begins in the wet, coniferous forest of the Quinault River valley and goes up for a time, then down, then up again, leaving hikers with the problem of gaining the same elevation twice. There are campsites at Moonshine Flats, about 5.5 miles from the trailhead. The forest on this part of the mountain has changed from the Douglas fir, western hemlock, and western redcedar of the lowland to Alaska yellow cedar (*Chamaecyparis nootkatensis*), mountain hemlock, and silver fir, all designed to cope with the heavy snow that arrives here during the winter. Alaska cedars grow very slowly, but they live for many centuries, allowing some specimens to grow to more than 100 feet high. The ground cover includes red heather (*Phyllodoce empetriformis*) and white heather (*Cassiope mertensiana*), beargrass (*Xerophyllum tenax*), and blueberries (*Vaccinium* spp.), which are also called huckleberries because they resemble an eastern genus, *Gaylussacia,* which bears the common name of huckleberry. By either name, the western berry is delicious whether eaten by the handful on the trail or taken home for pie. Northwest Indians used to start fires in the forest to keep

MOUNTAIN
HEMLOCK
(*Tsuga mertensiana*)

the blueberry fields from being taken over by other plants.

Directions: See Colonel Bob Wilderness, page 198.

Activities: Hiking, camping.

Facilities: None.

Dates: Open during summer months.

Fees: There may be a trailhead fee.

Closest town: Hoquiam, 51 miles.

For more information: Quinault Ranger Station, 353 South Shore Road, PO Box 9, Quinault, WA 98575. Phone (360) 288-2525.

Trail: 6.3 miles, one way.

Elevation: 4,280-foot elevation gain.

Degree of difficulty: Strenuous.

RANGER HOLE TRAIL

[Fig. 30(4)] This short trail goes to a fishing hole in the Duckabush River where there aren't as many fish as there used to be. It is a level trail, except for the last 500 feet, which lead steeply down to the fishing hole. In the early part of the twentieth century, forest rangers stationed in the nearby Interrorem Cabin, about 0.75 mile from the fishing hole, depended on it for much of their fresh food. It was just a matter of hiking to the fishing hole, putting in a line, and pulling out a large trout or steelhead for dinner.

The fishing hole was so good that it attracted large numbers of anglers, and the Forest Service now has a maintained trail to the hole. The 1907 Interrorem Cabin, where the lonely rangers once lived, is for rent now through the Forest Service Cabin Rental Program. The abundance of large fish, however, has been reduced considerably, although it is possible to come up with a small specimen.

Numerous people use the short, level trail in all seasons. One reason for its popularity is that it meanders through delightful, large, second-growth Douglas fir trees, and large maple trees along the way turn vivid colors during the fall. Another is that the fishing hole pool is just below a waterfall that provides moving whitewater to make the scene immensely beautiful.

The Interrorem Nature Trail Number 804 is an interesting 0.25-mile interpretive trail that loops through the forest, beginning about 100 feet from the trailhead of the Ranger Hole Trail. It makes a nice addition to the main trail.

Directions: Some 22 miles north of Hoodsport on US Highway 101, turn west on Forest Road 2510 and go 4 miles to the picnic area at the end of the pavement. The trailhead is on the left side of the road next to the Interrorem Cabin.

Activities: Hiking, fishing.

Facilities: There are a historic rental cabin and picnic area at the trailhead.

Dates: Open year-round.

Fees: There may be a trailhead fee.

Closest town: Hoodsport, 26 miles.

For more information: Olympic National Park/National Forest Information Center, 150 North Lake Cushman Road, PO Box 68, Hoodsport, WA 98548. Phone (360) 877-5424.

Trail: 0.8 mile, one-way.

Elevation: 320-foot elevation gain.

Degree of difficulty: Easy.

MOUNT ROSE TRAIL NUMBER 814

[Fig. 30(10)] This trail goes steeply uphill from the beginning, gaining 0.6 mile in elevation in its 3.2-mile length. The trail is maintained only for about 2.5 miles, then becomes a scramble to the top of the mountain, and in some places the route is difficult to find.

Some of the trail goes through old-growth forest, but the summit is mostly rock. The view from there is wide and long. Among the sights is Lake Cushman, directly below. In the distance loom Mount Ellinor, Mount Washington, Mount Pershing, and Bear Gulch. It is a terrific view for those who survive the climb.

Directions: On US Highway 101 about 9 miles north of Hoodsport turn west onto the Lake Cushman Road (State Route 119), and go about 10 miles to the trailhead.

Activities: Hiking, climbing.

Facilities: None.

Dates: Open during the summer.

Fees: A trailhead fee may be charged.

Closest town: Hoodsport, 19 miles.

For more information: Olympic National Park/National Forest Information Center, 150 North Lake Cushman Road, PO Box 68, Hoodsport, WA 98548. Phone (360) 877-5424. For cabin rental, National Recreational Reservation Service, PO Box 281470, Atlanta, GA 30384-1470. Phone (877) 444-6777.

Trail: 3.2 miles, one-way.

Elevation: 3,500-foot elevation gain.

Degree of difficulty: Strenuous.

QUINAULT LOOP TRAIL

[Fig. 30(11)] This easy trail is a delightful 4-mile walk through magnificent old-growth rain forest that includes the Big Tree Grove of huge, 500-year-old Douglas firs. This trail is less frequently hiked than some other trails through the Washington coast's rain forests. It is likely that people who hike it will be pretty much alone with the natural beauty that abounds everywhere.

Beginning at the west end, near the Willaby Campground, the trail goes about 0.3 mile, then offers a 0.5-mile side loop over an interpretive trail with signs telling about the rain forest ecosystem. The interpretive trail loops back to the main trail, giving people a choice of returning to the trailhead or continuing on the much longer loop through the rain forest and past Lake Quinault.

Those who take the long route follow a nearly level but somewhat undulating trail that passes through classic rain forest of huge Douglas firs, western redcedars, sitka spruce, and western hemlocks. The frequent rain throughout the year combines with the nearly constant mild temperature to grow everything large here. The trailside is littered with huge ferns and devil's club (*Oplopanax horridum*), which bears innumerable mildly toxic thorns that make it painful to hold. Even the large, attractive leaf is covered on the underside with needle-like thorns. Here, devil's club grows to as much as 10 feet tall.

The thick canopy of the forest shades the ground, but nevertheless the lower story is thick with mosses, ferns, and wood sorrel (*Oxalis oregana*), which folds its large, clover-like leaves into half their size, possibly to conserve moisture when conditions are dry. The branches of the trees are draped with clubmosses (*Lycopodium* spp.) that add to the lush green atmosphere of the rain forest. The trail passes a junction with the Willaby Creek Trail, then goes over cedar planking and through a swamp that features gaunt, gray cedar snags that brood over the marsh.

A little way east of the cedar swamp, the trail crosses Cascade Creek, turns north, crosses the South Shore Lake Quinault Road, and reaches the shore of the lake. It follows the lake and leads hikers past Quinault Village, where the Forest Service ranger station and the Lake Quinault Lodge are located, and back to the trailhead in a landscape that is very different from that just across the road. The beautiful turquoise lake gives hikers a wide view and may offer them a sight of water wildlife such as the common loon (*Gavia immer*) that eat fish, reptiles, frogs, leeches, insects, and aquatic plants they find in the lake. Loons are champions among diving birds and can go as much as 300 feet deep. The black-and-white or brown-gray-and-white birds look a lot like oversized ducks. They swim well but fly poorly and, on land, they walk even more poorly. They are easily identified from a distance by their piercing, loud, maniacal cry that sounds like the laugh of someone who has gone "loony."

Directions: Drive 40 miles north from Hoquiam on US Highway 101 and turn east on the South Shore Lake Quinault Road. Go about 1.5 miles to the trailhead on the right side of the road.

Trail: 4 miles, one-way.

Elevation: There is no significant elevation gain.

Degree of difficulty: Easy.

LAKE QUINAULT LODGE

[Fig. 30(11)] This pleasant lodge on the shores of Lake Quinault began as a log hotel built in the 1880s, years before the national forest that surrounds it was created. That building was destroyed by fire in 1921 and, under an agreement with the national forest, replaced first by a temporary building, then by a permanent structure that now is called The Annex. The main lodge was built in 1926.

The lodge, which is expensive, now is a full-service hotel with 92 guestrooms, some with fireplaces. There is a large, well-equipped lobby, an auditorium, a swimming pool, saunas, and a large dining room with windows that look out over the lake at forest-covered mountains. The lake belongs to the Quinault Indian Reservation that extends in a wide triangle westward to the ocean. The forest-covered mountains on the other side of the lake are part of the Olympic National Park.

The manicured grounds offer a gazebo and lawn games such as croquet and horseshoes. There is a dock on the lakeshore for fishing, as well as for landing boats and canoes. Beyond the grounds there are hiking, fishing, and bicycling. Elk and deer are among the wildlife nearby. If it rains, and in a rain forest it probably will, there is a large, brick fireplace in the lobby and chairs suitable for reading and talking.

Directions: From Hoquiam, go north on US Highway 101 for about 40 miles to milepost 125. Turn east on South Shore Lake Quinault Road and go 2 miles to the lodge.

Activities: Hiking, boating, fishing.

Facilities: Lodging, restaurant, boat/fishing dock, swimming pool, sauna, Jacuzzi, game room, boat rental.

Dates: Open year-round.

Fees: Fees are charged for lodging, services, and rentals.

Closest town: Hoquiam, 42 miles.

For more information: Lake Quinault Lodge, PO Box 7, Quinault, WA 98575-0007. Phone from Washington and Oregon (800) 562-6672. From elsewhere, (360) 288-2900.

LAKE QUINAULT CAMPGROUNDS

The Forest Service has three campgrounds near Lake Quinault Lodge. They are located within walking distance of the small community that has built up around the lodge.

WILLABY CREEK CAMPGROUND

[Fig. 29(4)] **Directions:** From Kalaloch, continue south on US Highway 101 for approximately 30 miles. From Hoquiam, continue north on US Highway 101 for approximately 34 miles. At milepost 125, turn east onto South Shore Road. Willaby Creek Campground is about 1 mile from Highway 101.

Activities: Camping, fishing, boating, swimming, picnicking.

Facilities: 34 RV and tent sites, boat ramp, restrooms, running water, picnic tables.

Dates: Open year-round.

Fees: Fees are charged for camping.

Closest town: Hoquiam, 35 miles.

For more information: Olympic National Park/U.S. Forest Service, 551 South Fork Avenue, Forks, WA 98331. Phone (360) 374-7566.

FALLS CREEK CAMPGROUND

[Fig. 29(5)] **Directions:** 1 mile east of Willaby Creek, just beyond the ranger station and Quinault Lodge.

Activities: Camping, fishing, swimming, hiking, boating, picnic area.

Facilities: RV and tent sites, boat ramp, RV dump.

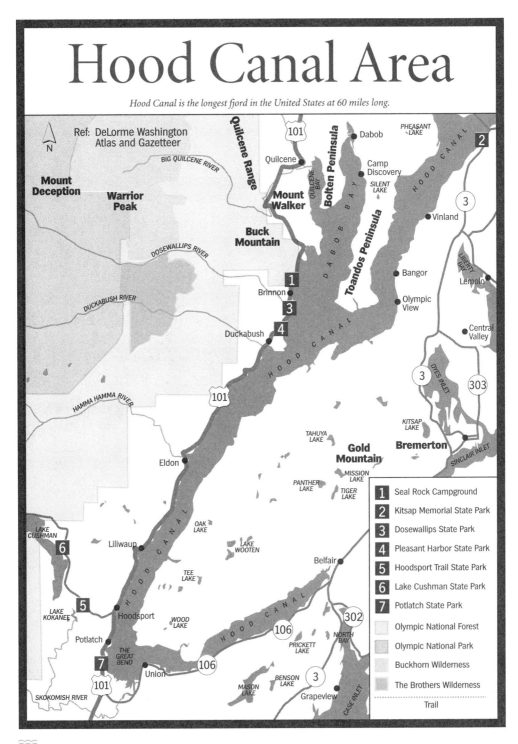

Hood Canal Area

Hood Canal is the longest fjord in the United States at 60 miles long.

Ref: DeLorme Washington Atlas and Gazetteer

1	Seal Rock Campground
2	Kitsap Memorial State Park
3	Dosewallips State Park
4	Pleasant Harbor State Park
5	Hoodsport Trail State Park
6	Lake Cushman State Park
7	Potlatch State Park
	Olympic National Forest
	Olympic National Park
	Buckhorn Wilderness
	The Brothers Wilderness
	Trail

Dates: Open year-round.

Fees: Fees are charged for camping.

Closest town: Hoquiam, 35 miles.

For more information: Olympic National Park/U.S. Forest Service, 551 South Fork Avenue, Forks, WA 98331. Phone (360) 374-7566.

GATTON CREEK CAMPGROUND

[Fig. 29(5)] **Directions:** About 0.3 mile from Falls Creek Campground.

Activities: Tent sites, fishing, swimming.

Facilities: Outhouse, no running water.

Dates: Open year-round.

Fees: Fees are charged for camping.

Closest town: Hoquiam, 35 miles.

For more information: Olympic Nation Park/U.S. Forest Service, 551 South Fork Avenue, Forks, WA 98331. Phone (360) 374-7566.

SEAL ROCK CAMPGROUND

[Fig. 31(1)] This nice, full-service campground is the Olympic National Forest's only facility on salt water. It sits on Dabob Bay, an arm of Hood Canal, and has 42 campsites, with the maximum size for trailers being 21 feet. The shore is rocky but suitable for wading and swimming. There is no official boat launch, but it is possible to put small, portable boats and canoes in the water.

The campground has a nature trail, fishing, and swimming. Visitors will sometimes see seals on the beach and bald eagles in the air.

Directions: The campground is on the east side of US Highway 101 about 8 miles south of Quilcene.

Activities: Camping, boating, swimming, fishing, oyster hunting.

Facilities: Restrooms, piped-water system with potable water, picnic tables, nature trail, garbage service.

Dates: Open during the summer only.

Fees: Camping fees are charged.

Closest town: Quilcene, 8 miles.

For more information: Quilcene Ranger Station, 20482 US Highway 101 South, PO Box 280, Quilcene, WA 98376. Phone (360) 765-2200.

Hood Canal

[Fig. 31] Although the long, straight arm of Hood Canal digs deeply into the east side of the Olympic Peninsula, the only spot where it actually touches the border of the national forest even briefly is at Seal Rock Beach. When Captain George Vancouver was exploring the Puget Sound region in 1792, he thought it looked like a canal so that's what he called it. Actually, it is the longest fjord in the United States, but Vancouver's name stuck and it has been called Hood Canal ever since. It is 60 miles long, the first 45 miles running in a straight southwesterly direction down from Puget Sound's Admiralty Inlet. Then it does a nearly complete U turn to the northeast and runs up to Belfair where it comes to an abrupt end. The fjord is in the Olympic Mountains' rain shadow and enjoys the weather benefits of that. The land on the east side, between Hood Canal and Puget Sound, is fairly heavily settled, but on the west side, the canal nestles up against the mountains and government land and is relatively open. One result of that is a string of state parks along US Highway 101, from where the highway starts near Olympia in the south and goes along Hood Canal to the canal's confluence with Puget Sound where Highway 101 turns west and follows the Strait of Juan de Fuca.

The fjord is a popular place for fishing, clamming, and hunting oysters. Wildlife includes raptors, shorebirds, and marine mammals. The water is fairly shallow and warms more quickly than the ocean and most places along Puget Sound, so a lot of swimming takes place there, as well as boating, canoeing, and kayaking.

KITSAP MEMORIAL STATE PARK

[Fig. 31(2)] This 57-acre park is a little south of the Hood Canal Bridge. It has a saltwater beach and grassy playfields where various ball games can be played. A trail goes through second-growth timber, where pileated woodpeckers and flickers (*Colaptes auratus*) use their chisel-like beaks to tunnel into the trees in search of the delicious insects that make up 90 percent of their diet. Another short trail goes down to the rocky beach where tidepool creatures can be found, but the rocks make shellfish hunting difficult. There is a mooring buoy for boaters.

Directions: From the Kingston ferry landing in Kingston, go west for 8 miles on State Route 104 to Port Gamble, then go south 3 miles on State Route 3 from the Hood Canal Bridge.

Activities: Camping, boating, fishing, picnicking, team games.

Facilities: 18 RV campsites, 25 tent sites, group camp, picnic sites, community hall for up to 200 persons, restrooms, showers, trailer dump station, horseshoe pits, volleyball court, mooring buoy.

Dates: Open year-round.

Fees: Fees are charged for camping.

Closest town: Kingston, 11 miles.

For more information: Kitsap Memorial State Park, 202 Northwest Park Street, Poulsbo, WA 98370. Phone (360) 779-3205.

DOSEWALLIPS STATE PARK

[Fig. 31(3)] This 425-acre park, with 1 mile of shoreline on Hood Canal, is situated on both sides of US Highway 101 at the mouth of the Dosewallips River, which rushes down from the Olympic Mountains. It has 137 individual campsites for RVs, and tents, plus group camping. There are also three platform tents with electricity and heat; all campers need to supply are sleeping bags and food. Camping reservations are available during the summer by contacting Reservations Northwest, PO Box 500, Portland, OR 97207-0500, phone (800) 452-5687.

A trail leads past a wildlife-viewing platform to the beach. The combination of salt and fresh water attracts a wide variety of wildlife including seals, oysters, and clams. A loop trail goes through evergreen forest where elk can be seen during the winter.

Several miles of the tidelands south of the park are owned by the State Parks and Recreation Commission and are open below mean high tide level to beach walking, scuba-diving, and shellfish hunting. Most of the tidelands are accessible only by boat.

Directions: Go 1 mile south of Brinnon on US Highway 101.

Activities: Camping, picnicking, hiking, fishing.

Facilities: 4 RV sites, 88 standard campsites, 3 primitive campsites, 3 platform tents, 2 group camps, 40 picnic sites, 3 restrooms, 2 showers, trailer dump station, 4 miles of trail for hiking and biking, wildlife viewing platform.

Dates: Open year-round.

Fees: Camping fees are charged.

Closest town: Brinnon, 1 mile.

For more information: Dosewallips State Park, PO Box Drawer K, Brinnon, WA 98320. Phone (360) 796-4415.

PLEASANT HARBOR STATE PARK

[Fig. 31(4)] This little park consists mainly of a dock and a float in a protected cove, where boaters can tie up without worrying about storms on Hood Canal. The park has a picnic table, and a marina in the cove where fuel, water, and moorage are available.

Directions: The harbor is behind Black Point on the west side of Hood Canal. By road, take US Highway 101 approximately 1.25 miles south of Brinnon and turn east on a narrow road that goes 0.2 mile to the harbor.

Facilities: Dock, moorage float, picnic table and restrooms.

Dates: Open year-round.

Fees: Fees are charged for docking.

Closest town: Brinnon, 1.5 miles.

For more information: Contact Dosewallips State Park, PO Box Drawer K, Brinnon, WA 98320, Phone (360) 796-4415.

HOODSPORT TRAIL STATE PARK

[Fig. 31(5)] This 80-acre park essentially is a 2-mile trail that loops through second-growth forest of mostly Douglas fir and western redcedar. The new forest grows beside Dow Creek amidst the huge stumps of the harvested forest. There are picnic tables and vault toilets at the trailhead.

Directions: Take State Route 119 (the Lake Cushman Road) for 3.1 miles north from Hoodsport.

Activities: Hiking, picnicking.

Facilities: Picnic tables, vault toilets.

Dates: Open during the summer months.

Fees: None.

Closest town: Hoodsport, 3.1 miles.

For more information: Contact Lake Cushman State Park, North 7211 Lake Cushman Road, Hoodsport, WA 98548. Phone (360) 877-5491.

LAKE CUSHMAN STATE PARK

[Fig. 31(6)] This 600-acre park is on a large lake some 7 miles into the forest from Hoodsport, the major town on Hood Canal. The park occupies some 8 miles of the lake's shoreline and lies between Big Creek and the lakeshore. The lake is popular with anglers. The park has 4 miles of trail, a boat launch, a swimming beach, an amphitheater, and horseshoe pits, as well as campsites, restrooms, showers, and picnic sites. Camping reservations are available by contacting Reservations Northwest, PO Box 500, Portland, OR 97207-0500, phone (800) 425-5687.

Directions: Take State Route 119 (the Lake Cushman Road) for 7.2 miles north from Hoodsport.

Activities: Camping, hiking, swimming, boating, water skiing, fishing, and swimming.

Facilities: 30 RV sites, 50 standard campsites, 2 primitive campsites, group camp, 40 picnic sites, restrooms, showers, and a trailer dump station.

MULE DEER
(Odocoileus hemionus)
This deer species, named for its large, mulelike ears, avoids areas of human activity.

WESTERN GRAY SQUIRREL
(Scivrus griseus)

Dates: Open during summer months.
Fees: Fees are charged for camping.
Closest town: Hoodsport, 7 miles.
For more information: Lake Cushman State Park, North 7211 Lake Goodwin Road, Hoodsport WA 98548. Phone (360) 877-5491.

POTLATCH STATE PARK
[Fig. 31(7)] This 57-acre park, with well over 1 mile of Hood Canal shoreline, is located where local Indian tribes once held regional celebrations called potlatches. The park lies on both sides of State Route 101 and has a forested campground and a 0.5-mile loop trail. The mud and stone beach has a large tidal area where oysters and clams can be hunted. Canoes and kayaks can be carried across the beach to the water. Larger craft tie up at mooring buoys in deep water.

Seals often frequent the waters off the beach and waterfowl include species of loon (*Gavia* spp.) Squirrels, deer, and rabbits are among the wildlife in the park's cedar forest.

Directions: Take US Highway 101 for 3 miles south from Hoodsport.
Activities: Camping, hiking, boating, picnicking, scuba-diving, fishing, shellfish hunting.
Facilities: 18 RV campsites, 17 standard campsites, 2 primitive campsites, 81 picnic sites, horseshoe pits, sheltered kitchen, 81 picnic sites, restrooms, showers, trailer dump station.
Dates: The day-use area is open year-round. The campground is open during the summer.
Fees: Fees are charged for camping.
Closest town: Hoodsport, 3 miles.
For more information: Potlatch State Park, PO Box 1051, Hoodsport, WA 98548-1051. Phone (360) 877-5361.

WA Ocean Beaches And Columbia River

Large portions of the Willapa Bay and Grays Harbor have been set aside as national wildlife refuges.

N

33 109 101 W A S H I N G T O N

Shelton

PUDGET SOUND

Tacoma

Lakes District

Fort Lewis

Ocean City

Ocean Shores

GRAYS HARBOR

Hoquiam

Aberdeen

CHEHALIS RIVER 12

Olympia

Lacey

5

Westport 101

Tenino 507

Oakville

34 105 35

Raymond

South Bend 6

Peel

6

Centralia

Chehalis

WILLAPA BAY

103 101

Winlock

Vader 5 505

411

504 504 504

Long Beach

Ilwaco

103 101

401 4 36

Hammond

COLUMBIA RIVER

Astoria

Warrenton

30

Castle Rock

Longview Kelso

Ocean Beach

Kalama

Gearhart

Seaside

O R E G O N

47

Woodland

St. Helens

Battle Ground

Cannon Beach

101 53

NEHALEM RIVER

26

Scappoose

5

30 **Vancouver**

37

Parkrose

Wheeler

6

Bay City

TUALATIN RIVER

Portland

205

Tigard

Lake Oswego

Tillamook

101

FIGURE NUMBERS

33	Ocean Shores Area
34	Westport Area
35	Willapa Bay Area
36	Fort Columbia State Park Area
37	Portland Area

Washington Ocean Beaches And Columbia River

South of the Olympics, the country becomes more hospitable to people. The land is comparatively level and the elevation low. Sandy beaches and rolling surf are major attractions and many facilities for visitors have been established to accommodate visitors.

In many ways this portion of the coast is a beachcomber's paradise. Miles-long stretches of sandy beach collect the "treasures" that float in from places across the ocean. The much-prized glass floats that break loose from Japanese fishing craft have been found here. The mineral sediments that make up the beach are tiny pieces of rock that have broken away from the mother rock, probably because of wave action. They may very well be quartz and feldspar, but whatever their composition, they form a sandy place where crustaceans, polycheate worms, mollusks, and other interesting creatures can be found by an enterprising beachcomber.

[*Above:* Wave action wears away softer rock first, leaving strange formations]

But there is more to the south coast of Washington than resorts and beaches. The shoreline area is host to innumerable birds and sea mammals, especially on the islands, rocks, and reefs of the Copalis National Wildlife Refuge, which is off the Quinault Indian Reservation shoreline and the beaches south of the reservation. It is one of four such refuges on the Washington coast that are set aside for the protection of wildlife and are closed to the public, but the birds can be seen from afar, and they can be watched as they fly to and from the refuges. Some of the rocks and reefs are simply rock outcroppings that are underwater at high tide. Others are permanently above the tide, and support plants such as salmonberry (*Rubis spectabilis*), which grows 1-inch red or fuchsia flowers that become edible red or yellow berries in midsummer. The rocks also grow salal (*Gaultheria shallon*), and in some places, stunted evergreen trees manage to find a foothold on their rocky perch.

The Copalis refuge is primarily a nesting place for innumerable seabirds such as the tufted puffin (*Fratercula cirrhata*), a gaudy black bird with summer plumage that is mostly black, except for the face, which is mostly white with long, white feathers curling back over the head and down the nape. It has a gray and orange beak. Orange legs and feet complete this sartorial wonder. This puffin nests in colonies. Other birds in the refuge include the common murre (*Uria aalge*) that, with a black back and a white front, looks a little like it is wearing a tuxedo. Then, too, there are rhinoceros auklets (*Cerohinca monocerata*), Cassin's auklets (*Ptchoramphus aleuticus*), pelagic cormorants (*Phalacrocorax peligicus*), Brandt's cormorant (*Phalacrocorax penicillatus*), and black oystercatcher (*Haematopus bachmani*). In addition to the seabirds the refuge attracts species such as the bald eagle and peregrine falcon, as well as multitudes of migrating birds and sea mammals.

A little to the south of the Copalis National Wildlife Refuge, the long Copalis Spit is separated from the mainland's spruce forest by the narrow Copalis River. The spit offers a sandy beach where beachcombers may see bald eagles and numerous beach creatures. A little south of that are the large bays of Grays Harbor (*see* Grays Harbor, page 213) and Willapa Bay (*see* Willapa Bay, page 225). Large portions of both bays have been set aside as national wildlife refuges for well over 1 million shorebirds and their visitors.

The surf and beaches of the area have spawned a number of towns and cities that cater to visitors, and there are several state parks strategically scattered along the coast. Two of the larger towns, Aberdeen, population about 17,000 and Hoquiam, population about 9,000, are adjacent to each other on the shore of Grays Harbor, the only deep-water harbor on the West Coast north of San Francisco. The two cities were founded in the mid 1800s and developed as commercial centers, largely depending on forests, forest products, and shipping. That economic foundation has declined in recent years, but the two cities remain interesting places to visit, with early twentieth century, mill-town architectural flavor. They are busy places, with the business section on the flat harbor area below a wooded bluff. The other larger community along this coast is Ocean Shores, which was founded with resorts, recreation, and visitors in mind, (*see* Ocean Shores, page 217).

Grays Harbor Area

GRAYS HARBOR NATIONAL WILDLIFE REFUGE

[Fig. 33(1)] This 1,500-acre bay consists of tidal flats, salt marsh, freshwater ponds, and deciduous forests. It is the major seaport on Washington's Pacific coast and the state's two largest coastal communities, Aberdeen and Hoquiam are on its northeastern edge.

The huge bay also is a refuge for as many as 1 million shorebirds, and is a major stopover for western sandpipers (*Calidris mauri*), which pause here in their annual migration, beginning in about mid-April each year. The western sandpipers flock to the mud flats on their way north. They return on their way south from June through October, but in smaller numbers. Up to 500,000 may be on hand at a time, and they number about 85 percent of the shorebirds here in the spring.

The bay bears the name of Robert Gray, the American navigator, explorer, and trader who sailed into this part of the coast in 1792 in the 230-ton ship, the *Columbia Rediva*. He discovered the bay and also was the first to take his ship over the treacherous bar at the mouth of the Columbia River, which he named after his ship.

The estuary is one of four large-scale staging areas for North American shorebirds, and provides a place where they can rest and store energy to complete their annual migration to and from their northern breeding grounds. They come from as far south as Argentina and end their migration as far north as southern Alaska. Some travel as many as 15,000 miles. The estuary is managed by the U.S. Fish and Wildlife Service, and is so important to the environment that it has been named a Western Hemisphere Shorebird Reserve Network Site of Hemispheric Significance. And that is why it is sometimes is referred to as a birder's paradise.

The refuge consists of 1,500 acres of salt marshes, uplands, and mud flats. The mud flats are the last part of Grays Harbor to be flooded by the tide and the first part to be exposed when it goes out, giving the shorebirds additional time to feed. The birds use long, pointed beaks to probe and peck for invertebrates in the mud. Vegetation in the nearby salt marshes gives birds cover when they roost.

Shorebirds found at the refuge include the semipalmated plover (*Charadrius semipalmatus*), dunlin (*Calidris alpina*), short-billed dowitcher (*Limnodromus griseus*), long-billed dowitcher (*Limnodromus scolopaceus*), and black-bellied plover (*Pluvialis squatarola*).

But shorebirds are only part of the attraction. There also are ponds that attract various species of ducks, swallows, and gulls. Open areas bring species such as the common yellowthroat (*Geothlypis trichas*) and Savannah sparrow (*Passerculus sandwichensis*). Birds of prey may include peregrine falcons (*Falco peregrinus*), red-tailed hawks (*Buteo jamaicensis*), and northern harrier (*Circus cyaneus*). When these birds appear, huge clouds of shorebirds take off. Mammals that frequent the refuge include coyotes and mule deer, and visitors may also find salmon, oysters, shrimp, clams, and crabs.

Parking is available at designated places, and long-range shorebird viewing is popular here during high tide. A 1-mile, one-way, level trail goes to a closer viewing area but the trail is wet and muddy, and boots are highly recommended. It rains frequently here, and wet weather gear is also advisable. The best viewing time is the two hours before high tide. Boats, including kayaks, are not permitted.

There are no lodging or food services in the refuge, but the adjacent cities of Hoquiam and Aberdeen have numerous restaurants and hotels.

Directions: From Hoquiam, take State Route 109 west. Turn left onto Paulson Road, then right on Airport Way and proceed to where the road ends. Then walk 1 mile to the tip of the peninsula.

Activities: Wildlife viewing, hiking.

Facilities: Trail, parking lot, chemical restrooms, viewing area. There are plans for future development of a visitor center, boardwalks, and educational exhibits.

Dates: Open year-round but the shorebird season peaks during the spring migration from mid-April through early May.

Fees: None.

Closest town: Hoquiam, adjacent to the refuge.

For more information: The refuge is administered from the Nisqually National Wildlife Refuge, 100 Brown Farm Road, Olympia, WA 98516. Phone (360) 753-9467.

▨ PACIFIC BEACH STATE PARK

[Fig. 33(2)] This beachside park is a few miles south of the large Quinault Indian Reservation and in the southern portion of the Copalis National Wildlife Refuge (*see* Copalis National Wildlife Refuge, page 212). The nearby community of Pacific Beach offers food, lodging, groceries, gasoline, a post office, and a bank with an ATM.

Pacific Beach has been a tourist attraction since the Northern Pacific Railroad arrived in town in the early 1900s. A one-time Navy base has dwindled, but still offers a rest and recreation facility for military personnel and Department of Defense employees. It has 28

WESTERN GULL
(*Larus occidentalis*)

cabins, 44 RV spaces, and four suites. For reservations, phone (360) 276-4414.

The state park is only a little more than 10 acres, but it has 2,300 feet of shoreline and a rock breakwater. It offers 31 RV campsites, 31 standard campsites, two primitive campsites, and 10 picnic sites. Wheelchair-accessible campsites are available.

The major activities are on the broad, sandy beach, which is closed to vehicles. They include beachcombing, bird-watching, shell fishing, surf fishing, and boating. Joe Creek, near the south edge of the park, is a good place for bird-watching. Sometimes, the gulls and pelicans beat their wings on the water surface to round up fingerling fish for dinner. A nearly constant north wind makes the beach a prime place for flying kites. And sandcastle building on the beach sometimes takes on the look of an art form. Camping reservations are accepted year round.

Directions: Take State Route 109 west, and then travel north from Hoquiam for 29 miles to the park entrance at the end of Second Street in Pacific Beach.

Activities: Camping, picnicking, surf fishing, shellfishing, bird-watching, beach-combing, boating, whale watching.

Facilities: Campsites, restrooms, showers, trailer dump stations.

Dates: Open year-round.

Fees: There are camping fees.

Closest town: Pacific Beach, adjacent to park.

For more information: Ocean City State Park, 148 State Route 115, Hoquiam, WA 98550. Phone (360) 389-3553 or (800) 233-0321. For reservations, phone (800) 452-5687.

OCEAN CITY STATE PARK

[Fig. 33(3)] This wooded 170-acre park has well over 0.5 mile of ocean beach as well as several ponds that attract a variety of wildlife. There are 29 RV sites, 149 standard sites, and 3 primitive campsites, as well as a group campsite for up to 40 persons.

A small creek at the edge of the beach nurtures an abundance of algae and shore plants, including red clover (*Trifolium pratense*), and seacoast lupine (*Lupinus*

Deer Slotting

Usually deer have strict limits on how close they want humans to come. When someone gets closer than that, deer disappear into what appears to be a solid wall of vegetation. On occasions, however, they become overly friendly, actually getting into people's camps and upsetting things. When an enemy startles them, they flee, often with a long, graceful, leaping gait called slotting. In rough terrain, the slotting gait allows deer to change directions from one leap to the next, leading the pursuer to stumble over obstacles. On open terrain they may simply run all out, attempting to outdistance whatever is behind them.

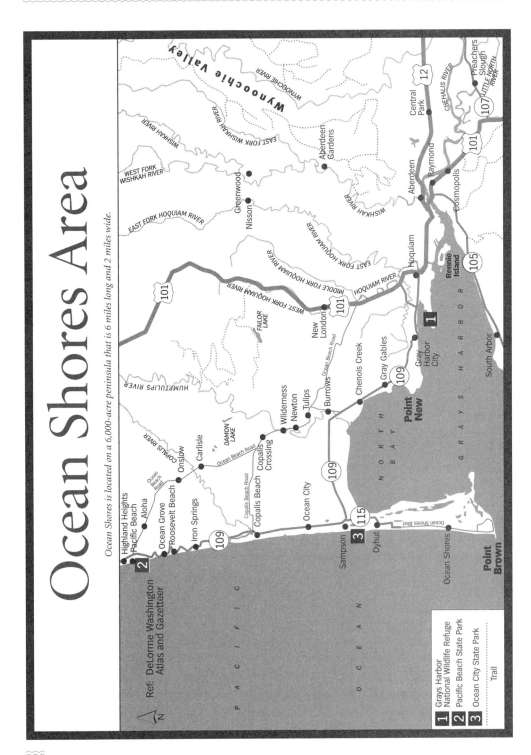

Ocean Shores Area

Ocean Shores is located on a 6,000-acre peninsula that is 6 miles long and 2 miles wide.

Ref: DeLorme Washington Atlas and Gazetteer

Legend:
1 Grays Harbor National Wildlife Refuge
2 Pacific Beach State Park
3 Ocean City State Park
Trail

littoralis), which sports clusters of blue-purple flowers.

The campsites are protected by stands of pine and kinnikinnick (*Arctostaphylos uva-ursi*). There are freshwater ponds and marshes adjacent to mixed stands of deciduous and pine trees. Ducks populate the ponds. Trails to the ponds pass through a profusion of native plants, including rhododendron, salal and skunk cabbage.

A day-use area offers a parking lot near a short, level, sandy trail. The trail leads through tall shrubbery and shore grasses to the beach, which, in the proper season, may have a large number of people looking for clams.

Wheelchair access is available at the campsites. Camping reservations are available during the summer

Directions: Take State Route 109 west from Hoquiam for 15 miles and turn south onto State Route 115 for 1 mile.

Activities: Camping, beachcombing, picnicking, shellfishing, kite flying, surfing, surf fishing, canoeing, bird-watching, horseback riding.

Facilities: Campsites, trails, picnic shelters, wheelchair-accessible restrooms, showers, trailer dump station.

Dates: Open year-round.

Fees: Camping fees are charged.

Closest town: Ocean Shores, about 3 miles.

For more information: Ocean City State Park, 148 State Route 115, Hoquiam, WA 98550. Phone (360) 389-3553 or (800) 233-0321. For reservations, phone (800) 452-5687.

OCEAN SHORES

[Fig. 33] This city with a population of about 3,000 was conceived, designed, and built for people who want to enjoy the ocean and its attractions. Founded in 1960 and incorporated in 1970, it has become a major attraction for vacationers from far away places, as well as a home away from home for people who have holiday residences.

It is situated on a 6,000-acre peninsula that is 6 miles long and 2 miles wide. It was formed by accretion of sand washed along the northern edge of Grays Harbor. The sand sheltered the harbor from the ocean surf and, at the same time, left the city with 6 miles of beach to enjoy. That beach gives Ocean Shores magnificent saltwater scenery on both its west and east sides. The city also has some 23 miles of interconnected canals and freshwater lakes served by boat launches in city parks. The major launch is in North Bay Park on Duck Lake. There is a launch for sea-going boats at the Ocean Shores marina on the southern end of Point Brown Avenue. Boats and canoes can be rented at a shop on the Grand Canal near the sea-going launch.

The accretion process that built the peninsula has continued into modern times. Part of what now is the city was an island 100 years ago. Historically, the peninsula attracted Native Americans who gathered here to trade and to hunt clams and other delicacies. Like much of the rest of this coast, it was first charted by Robert Gray, the American sea captain who traded along the West Coast.

The story of both the natural and human history of the peninsula is told in the **Ocean Shores Environmental Interpretive Center** at the intersection of Catala Avenue Southeast and Discovery Avenue Southeast (Take Point Brown Avenue south from the city center to Discovery Avenue Southeast. Turn left and go about a block to Catala Avenue). The interpretive center is a good place to gain an insight into the surroundings as an early step in a visit.

Some of the property in Ocean Shores is used as homes by retired people, or as second homes by people who live elsewhere. There also are numerous people who work in the city. But at any given time, a considerable percentage of the people here are visitors who come to enjoy the natural beauty of the coast. And the community has gone all out to make them welcome.

The city has, for instance, a large number of hotels and motels, some of them facing the beach where you can see, and hear, in the distance the breakers rolling in. Those tend not to be the less expensive places, however. There are numerous restaurants, ranging from fast food to pleasant dining.

In addition to the miles of boating waterways, the city has 120 miles of roads that are paved, level, and carry a minor amount of traffic, making this a good place to be explored on bicycles. Those who walk on the beach may discover beach creatures as well as "treasures" from far away places deposited by the tide. With nearly constant ocean breezes, the community promotes itself as a site for world-class kite flying on the beach. Frequently, two or more kite flyers engage each other in kite dances that are fascinating to watch. There is surf fishing, especially at the town's North Jetty on the south end of town, and crabbing is popular at Damon Point. A paved road to Damon Point goes through vast fields of shore grasses and stunted spruce to a parking lot at the end of the road. There, the quiet water of Grays Harbor Bay laps against a beach of smooth sand and there is a profusion of driftwood and seashells. It is a pleasant place for a picnic. Nearby, Duck Lake offers freshwater fishing. A summer-only passenger ferry runs across the mouth of Gray's Harbor from Ocean Shores to Westport on the beach to the south (*see* Westport, page 221). Shops sell and/or rent equipment for most of the activities, reducing the necessity for packing large amounts of gear.

Between Damon Point and North Jetty, the state maintains the 1,100-acre **Oyehut Wildlife Preserve.** Wildlife to be seen here include deer, black bears, beavers, foxes, coyotes, and river otters. There also are multitudes of migrating birds in the spring and fall. Brown pelicans arrive in the summer. Raptors that frequent the preserve include peregrine falcons, bald eagles, and red-tailed hawks. Geese, ducks, gulls, egrets, songbirds, and owls also contribute to making this a birder's Shangri-La.

Storm watching and whale watching are popular pastimes, and both demonstrate that nature is both fascinating and immensely powerful. The North Jetty is a good place for storm watching, but 25-foot seas and strong winds can be dangerous. Contact the Ocean Shores Police Department for specific information.

Directions: Take State Route 109 west from Hoquiam for 16 miles and turn south onto State Route 116 for 3 miles.

Activities: Hiking, boating, beachcombing, clamming, fishing, kite flying, sandcastle building, agate hunting, wildlife watching, storm watching, shopping, swimming.

Facilities: Lodging, docks, trails, restaurants, equipment rental, charter boats, interpretative center.

Dates: Activities continue year round.

Fees: Fees are charged for goods and services. None for the Ocean Shores Environmental Interpretive Center and Oyehut Wildlife Preserve.

For more information: Ocean Shores Visitor Center, PO Box 382, Ocean Shores, WA 98569. Phone (800) 762-3224.

RESTAURANT IN OCEAN SHORES

Home Port Restaurant. 857 Point Brown Avenue. This family restaurant offers steak, seafood, and hamburgers, as well as a salad bar. There is a cocktail lounge. Reservations recommended. *Inexpensive.* *(360) 289-2600.*

LODGING IN OCEAN SHORES.

Ocean Shores is a tourist-oriented community with a large selection of good places to stay.

The Nautilus. 835 Ocean Shores Boulevard. This three-story condominium with beach access has 22 guest rooms with kitchens, fireplaces, and decks. All rooms have an ocean view. There is a whirlpool. *Moderate to expensive.* *(800) 221-4541 or (360) 289-2722.*

The Canterbury Inn. 643 Ocean Shores Boulevard. This three-story condominium motel on the oceanfront has beach access. The 45 units have balconies or patios, most have fireplaces, and all have kitchens. Twelve of the units have two bedrooms. There is an exercise room, a heated swimming pool, and whirlpool. *Moderate to expensive.* *(800) 562-6678 or (360) 289-3317.*

WESTHAVEN STATE PARK

[Fig. 34(1)] This day-use only park is one of four state parks on the south side of the mouth of Grays Harbor, all of them within easy distance of the town of Westport. The park has about 80 acres on the northwestern tip of the peninsula that separates the bay from the ocean. It started as a rock jetty built in the 1940s to prevent silting in the harbor. Sand accretion around the rocks eventually built up to the point that dune plants sprouted. They blocked the wind, which dropped its sand and created

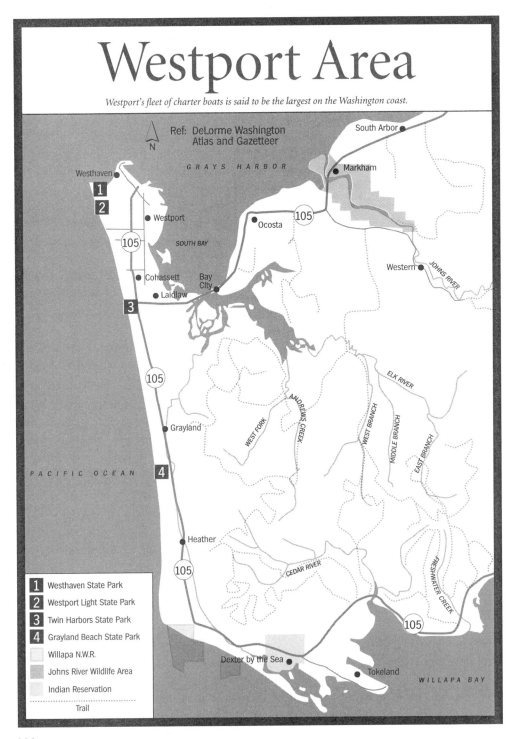

Westport Area

Westport's fleet of charter boats is said to be the largest on the Washington coast.

Ref: DeLorme Washington Atlas and Gazetteer

N

GRAYS HARBOR

South Arbor

Markham

Westhaven

1
2

Westport

105

Ocosta

105

SOUTH BAY

Western

JOHNS RIVER

Cohassett

Bay City

Laidlaw

3

105

ELK RIVER

Grayland

WEST FORK

ANDREWS CREEK

WEST BRANCH

MIDDLE BRANCH

EAST BRANCH

PACIFIC OCEAN

4

Heather

CEDAR RIVER

FRESHWATER CREEK

105

1 Westhaven State Park
2 Westport Light State Park
3 Twin Harbors State Park
4 Grayland Beach State Park

Willapa N.W.R.
Johns River Wildlife Area
Indian Reservation
.... Trail

105

Dexter by the Sea

Tokeland

WILLAPA BAY

dunes. There is a broad, sandy shore that invites breaking waves, which, in turn, invite surfers and sea kayakers. It is said to be the state's most popular surfing beach, with low, incoming tides producing the best rides. The water temperature is usually less than 60 degrees Fahrenheit, so wet suits are needed.

The beach also is a popular place for sandcastle building, surf fishing, crabbing, and hunting for agates that are rolled onto the beach by the surf.

There is a 1.4-mile paved trail between this park and the nearby Westport Light State Park (*see* Westport Light State Park, page 222). There are viewing platforms with interpretive displays along the way. The trail passes along the dunes, just inland from the roaring surf. At the turn of the twentieth century this area had little vegetation, but settlers planted grasses to keep the sand from blowing. That resulted in the formation of shallow marshes, making it possible for native plants to move in. Now, the area inland from the beach bears sitka spruce, pine, and willow trees, as well as shoregrasses, blueberries, and crabapple, while wild strawberry plants creep along the ground, staying low to escape the constant wind off the ocean. The plant life has attracted numerous animals, including black-tailed deer, coyotes, bear, elk, raccoons and pocket gophers (*Thomomys mazama*). Birds include different species of owl, swallows, thrushes, warblers, and peregrine falcons. The intertidal area offers clams, crabs, and worms, while the rocks provide anchors for mussels, goose barnacles, and kelp. Offshore, sometimes whale spouts indicate the presence of those large creatures of the deep sea.

Directions: From Westport go north on South Forest Street, which becomes East Wilson Avenue. After a little more than 1 mile, turn northwest on North Montesano Street and go about 0.2 mile to the park entrance road, which reaches the park in about 0.5 mile.

Activities: Beachcombing, surfing, kayaking, surf fishing, kite flying, hiking, picnicking, sandcastle building, scuba-diving, horseback riding, crabbing.

Facilities: Picnic sites, water, wheelchair-accessible restrooms, shower.

Dates: Open year-round.

Fees: None.

Closest town: Westport, 1 mile.

For more information: Contact Twin Harbors State Park, Westport, WA 98595. Phone (360) 268-9717, or (800) 233-0321.

WESTPORT

[Fig. 34] This little community is on the other side of the mouth of Grays Harbor from Ocean Shores (*see* Ocean Shores, page 217) and, like its neighboring community, Grayland, it is older than Ocean Shores and maintains a somewhat different atmosphere that is related more toward the ocean and its attractions. That is no great surprise; in the early days of the twentieth century Westport was an important whaling port. Harpooning whales is banned now, but charter boats still make their way out to sea to hunt for whales. Today, however, they go to admire the magnificent animals, rather than to kill them.

Westport's fleet of charter boats is said to be the largest on the Washington coast. The boats and the related businesses are the major means of support for the community of some 2,000 persons. The town seems to be full of motels, restaurants, trailer parks, resorts, charter boat offices, and other places that specialize in giving visitors a good time. Nearby Westport Light, Twin Harbors, and Grayland Beach state parks are also attractions. The **Westport Maritime Museum** (2201 Westhaven Drive, phone (360) 268-1990) provides interesting insight into the community for visitors who take a break from fishing or whale watching. A bike/pedestrian trail passes along the community's waterfront, past a harbor full of colorful charter boats, fishing boats, and pleasure boats. The boats go after, among others, coho and chinook salmon, while the waterfront offers fishing from boardwalks, groins, and jetties for perch, cod, sole, rockfish, and other bottom fish. There are viewing towers, including one that is three stories high, along the waterfront, providing wide views of the mouth of Grays Harbor.

Directions: From Aberdeen, go some 20 miles west on State Route 105 and turn right on the highway spur to the north. Go about 3 miles to Westport at the end of the peninsula.

Activities: Fishing, boating, whale watching, beachcombing.

Facilities: Lodging, restaurants, boat harbor, charter boats, tackle shops, cold storage.

Dates: Fishing is in season. Other activities are year-round.

Closest town: Aberdeen, 23 miles.

For more information: Westport/Grayland Chamber of Commerce, PO Box 306, Westport, WA 98595. Phone (800) 345-6223.

LODGING IN WESTPORT

Chateau Westport. 710 West Hancock. This large, four-story motel has 108 rooms, including some with fireplaces and balconies. There are two executive suites with saunas. Eleven of the units have kitchens. Amenities include a view of the ocean, playground with sports equipment, whirlpool, and heated swimming pool. Breakfast is free. *Moderate to expensive.* (800) 255-9101 or (360) 268-9101.

Windjammer Motel. 461 East Pacific Avenue. This motel has 12 rooms and three two-bedroom units. Four units have kitchens. *Inexpensive to moderate.* (360) 268-9351.

WESTPORT LIGHT STATE PARK

[Fig. 34(2)] This is one of four state parks within a short distance of the town of Westport. It has 210 acres and 3,400 feet of saltwater shoreline on the Pacific Ocean. A major attraction is the Westport Lighthouse, which still uses its original 1895 Fresnel lens to send a beam to sailors up to 25 nautical miles at sea. The 107-foot tower makes it the tallest lighthouse on the U.S. West Coast. The original oil lamps have been replaced with a 1,000-watt lamp.

Inland of the beach are dunes covered by pine trees and grass. The blacktop Westport Light Trail that connects this park with Westhaven State Park wanders along the dunes, past the three viewing platforms that have interpretive displays (*see* Westhaven State Park, page 219).

The facilities, including picnic tables with wind screens, are grouped near the access road on the south end of the beach, where the access road leads through the dunes onto the beach.

Directions: From Westport, go west on West Ocean Avenue for about 1 mile to the park parking lot.

Activities: Hiking, picnicking, shelling, surf fishing, beachcombing, sandcastle building, kite flying, and surfing.

Facilities: Picnic sites, trail, restrooms.

Dates: Open year-round.

Fees: None.

Closest town: Westport, 1 mile.

For more information: Contact Twin Harbors State Park, Highway 105, Westport, WA 98595. Phone (360) 268-9717 or (800) 233-0321.

▨ TWIN HARBORS STATE PARK

[Fig. 34(3)] With some 240 acres, this is the largest of the four state parks in the immediate vicinity of the town of Westport and the only one with camping. As many as 500,000 people a year visit the campground, and its 300 campsites are often filled during the warm weather of summer and during the razor clam seasons in the spring and fall. Several loop roads on both sides of State Route 105 lead to the campsites and trails lead to the beach. There is a children's play area and the park has nearly 6,500 feet of shoreline.

A separate, 0.75-mile loop nature trail threads through the scrub pine forest to the beach. A pamphlet distributed by the park describes the ecological processes at some 20 numbered stations along the trail. Plants here include black twinberry (*Lonicera involucrata*), huckleberry (*Vaccinium ovatum*), and kinnikinnick (*Arctostaphylos uva-ursi*). Animals include various species of mice, as well as brush rabbits (*Sylvilagus bachmani*) and an occasional deer.

Vehicles can reach the beach by taking Bonge Avenue on the south side of the park.

Directions: The park is on State Route 105 about 1 mile south of Westport.

Activities: Camping, beachcombing, kite flying, sandcastle building, shellfish hunting, surf fishing, horseback riding.

Facilities: Some 250 standard campsites, 50 RV campsites, 5 primitive campsites, 12 picnic sites, group camp for up to 80 persons, day-use area, 6 restrooms, showers, trailer dump station, children's playground.

Dates: Open year-round.

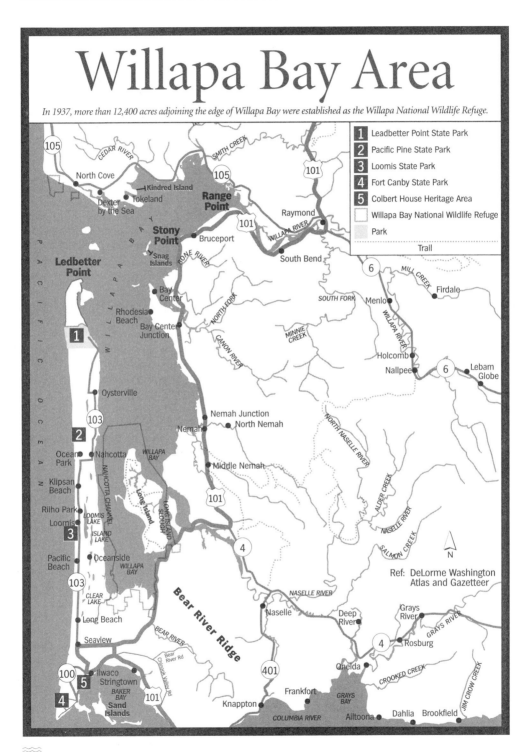

Willapa Bay Area

In 1937, more than 12,400 acres adjoining the edge of Willapa Bay were established as the Willapa National Wildlife Refuge.

1	Leadbetter Point State Park
2	Pacific Pine State Park
3	Loomis State Park
4	Fort Canby State Park
5	Colbert House Heritage Area
	Willapa Bay National Wildlife Refuge
	Park
	Trail

Ref: DeLorme Washington Atlas and Gazetteer

Fees: Camping fees are charged.

Closest town: Westport, 1 mile.

For more information: Twin Harbors State Park, Highway 105, Westport, WA 98595. Phone (360) 268-9717 or (800) 233-0321. For reservations, contact Reservations Northwest, PO Box 500, Portland, OR 97207-0500. Phone (800) 425-5687.

GRAYLAND BEACH STATE PARK

[Fig. 34(5)] As State Route 105 skirts the Pacific Ocean shoreline it passes through Grayland about 3 miles south of Westport and then continues for about 5 miles before it turns east to get around Willapa Bay. About 1 mile past Grayland, it passes the entrance road for the Grayland Beach State Park, a full-service, 435-acre park with 7,750 feet of ocean shoreline. Campsite reservations are available in the summer. There are no designated facilities for day use, but the beach is fully equipped with driftwood suitable for sitting on while eating a sandwich.

The campsites are nestled in scrub pine and kinnikinnick. A 0.25-mile trail leads through dense shrubbery to the beach, where strong winds often lure kite flyers, including those who participate in occasional kite festivals here that sometimes attract thousands of people.

Razor clams can be taken from the beach during the season, and an 8-mile length of the beach is open to motorized vehicles, horses, and beachcombers.

Directions: Take State Route 105 south about 6 miles from Westport, and turn west for 0.2 mile on the road to the park entrance.

Activities: Camping, beachcombing, beach driving, horseback riding, sandcastle building, fishing, shellfish hunting, and kite flying.

Facilities: 60 RV campsites, 3 primitive campsites, wheelchair accessible restrooms, and showers.

Dates: Open year-round.

Fees: There is a camping fee.

Closest town: Grayland, 1.2 miles.

For more information: Twin Harbors State Park, Highway 105, Westport, WA 98595. Phone (360) 268-9717 or (800) 233-0321.For reservations, Reservations Northwest, PO Box 500, Portland, OR 97207-0500. Phone (800) 452-5687.

Willapa Bay

[Fig. 35] About 10 miles directly south of Grays Harbor, the huge Willapa Bay is another of the places that, from time immemorial, have provided a haven for numerous migratory birds. The bay is the estuary of the Willapa River. The wide valley of the river's mouth filled with water when the ice sheets melted some 15,000 years ago, raising the level of the sea. The ocean built a 25-mile long peninsula across the southern side of the estuary, dividing it from the sea and forming the bay.

In 1937 some 12,400 acres adjoining the edge of the bay were established as the **Willapa National Wildlife Refuge** to provide a sanctuary for both migrating and wintering populations of waterfowl, shorebirds, and their habitats. That area is in 10 separate units that are largely set aside for the use of the birds and other wildlife, but people are encouraged to come to the wild habitat, to admire the wildlife and to take part in activities such as photography, fishing, hunting, and environmental education.

The habitat varies from sand dunes, to sandy beaches, to grasslands, to mud flats, to coniferous forests, to both freshwater and saltwater marshes. On 275 acres of the Long Island Unit, there is even a stand of old growth western hemlock and western redcedar, a rarity in this vicinity. With that kind of habitat variety one would expect a large diversity of wildlife, and that is exactly what there is.

The harbor is one of several places along the coast of Washington and Oregon where an accidental change in the environment has taken place. Smooth cordgrass (*Spartina alterniflora*), a native of the Atlantic and Gulf coasts, apparently was brought to Willapa Bay shortly before or after the turn of the twentieth century. Some say it arrived as packing material in shipments of Eastern oysters (*Crassostera virginica*). Another theory is that the seeds arrived mixed in the solid ballasts of ships. Either way the plants found their way into the bay and flourished, spreading to other marshy places along the coast. From that meager beginning, the seeds and rhizomes of smooth cordgrass have spread not only through Willapa Bay, but also up and down the coast by riding on the tides. The spread was apparently assisted when *Spartina* was planted deliberately in San Francisco Bay during the 1970s, perhaps as wetland mitigation. The seed production and germination rate of smooth cordgrass is higher than that of the native cordgrasses, and after it is established it grows six times faster. By 1989 it covered some 5 percent of the Willapa Bay mud flats, making it possible that the accidental change in the environment may crowd out native species that rely on mud flats such as Dungeness crab (*Cancer magister*), juvenile chum salmon (*Oncorhynchus keta*), and English sole (*Pleuronectes vetulus*). Commercial production of pacific oysters (*Crassostrea gigas*) may be affected, as well as forage for shorebirds and other animals.

The land animals of the bay include deer, elk, black bear, coyote, and beaver. The salt marshes support large areas of American glasswort (*Salicornia virginica*). The glasswort, along with other attractions, lure large numbers of migrating shorebirds that have toes, and waterfowl that have webbed feet and thick bills, which they use to filter

PACIFIC OYSTER
(*Crassostrea gigas*)

small organisms from the water or take hold of invertebrates or underwater vegetation. Among the species here are black brant (*Branta bernicla*), American wigeon (*Anas americana*), Canada goose (*Branta canadensis*), and the trumpeter swan (*Cygnus buccinator*), which was nearly extinct in the early part of the twentieth century. It has increased its numbers since it was given protection in 1918, and is now so common that it is not on either the threatened or endangered list.

Other species in the refuge include the brown pelican (*Pelicanus occidentalis*), sooty shearwaters (*Puffinus griseus*), and snowy plover (*Charadrius alexandrinus*), which can be found by walking on the sandy trails that lead to the ocean over dunes covered with hardy salal and kinnikinnick. Some of the birds in the refuge are permanent residents, but many are just stopping over during their annual migrations between the far south and far north. Summer is the best season for finding large numbers of birds here.

The refuge is divided into separate units along the shore of the huge Willapa Bay that is formed by the sandy, 25-mile-long North Beach Peninsula. The extreme northern 3 miles or so of the peninsula is the Leadbetter Unit of the refuge, one of the major units. It can be reached by taking the Sandridge Road north from Seaview, an unincorporated hamlet at the intersection of State Routes 101 and 103 that serves as a gateway to the North Beach Peninsula. The north end of the Sandridge Road is also known as Stackpole Road and ends at the parking lot in the Leadbetter Point State Park, adjacent to the wildlife refuge. The Lewis Unit, another major unit, is at the southern end of the bay. A third major unit is the Long Island Unit, which is on a large island in the east-central segment of the bay, and can be reached only by boat. US Highway 101 skirts much of the eastern shore of the bay and gives access to the Lewis Unit and a boat launch that gives access to the Long Island Unit.

The human population in this part of the country is sparse. There are only three small towns along the edge of Willapa Bay. **Tokeland** is on a peninsula that juts down into the northern shore. The others, on the inland shore of North Beach Peninsula, are Nahcotta and Oysterville. **Nahcotta** has oyster farms and the Port of Peninsula, which includes a boat launch and toilets. A boat harbor and an oyster works dominate the waterfront, and huge piles of oyster shells, the size of a small house, are scattered around the community. The town faces a public oyster bed on Willapa Bay. Many of the bay's other oyster beds are privately owned. **Oysterville**, founded in 1854, once prospered by supplying oysters to the early boomtown of San Francisco. The quaint little village is on the National Register of Historic Places. The oyster business declined in the 1880s, but it revived in the 1930s after entrepreneurs imported oysters from Japan. Now oyster farming and sales are a major feature of the community. The community is a pleasant, spacious place with a multitude of quaint houses. Oysterville is on State Route 103, about 16 miles north of Long Beach. Nahcotta is on State Route 103 a few miles south of Oysterville.

The North Beach Peninsula has 28 miles of beach, and local folk proudly call the flat, compact sand stretching along its shores the world's longest beach. The peninsula is served by State Route 103, which leads off US Highway 101 through the town of Seaview toward Stackpole Road, the Leadbetter Unit of the Willapa National Wildlife Refuge, and the Leadbetter Point State Park.

The southern edge of the peninsula is the Columbia River, which offers the views and habitats of freshwater sites in contrast to the ocean shores and the estuarine habitats of the bay. The peninsula is a center for growing cranberries, with well over 450 acres in production.

Hunting and fishing are permitted in designated places on the refuge for persons with state licenses, but a presidential proclamation has closed part of the bay to waterfowl hunting. Hunters should contact the wildlife refuge headquarters for information.

Much of Willapa Bay is a mud flat. It is easy for an inexperienced person to become mired and stranded in the thick, sticky mud at low tide. The incoming tide can, and has, drowned victims who could not extricate themselves. Refuge officials highly recommend that people venture into the tideflats in groups of two or more, are aware of the tides and the mud, and have proper equipment such as maps and tide tables.

Directions: The bay is skirted by US Highway 101 beginning about 23 miles south of Aberdeen; by State Route 105, which leads westward from US Highway 101, 23 miles west of Aberdeen; and by State Route 103, which leads westward from US Highway 101 beginning about 14 miles north of Astoria, OR.

Activities: Beachcombing, kite flying, bike riding, wildlife viewing, whale watching, fishing, clam digging, crabbing, hunting, horseback riding. Note: Some activities are restricted on the refuge but allowed off of it. Check with a ranger.

Facilities: Lodging, restaurants, shops, state parks, wildlife refuge observation points, camping.

Dates: Accessible year-round.

For more information: Willapa National Wildlife Refuge, HC 01 Box 910, Ilwaco, WA 98624-9707. Phone (360) 484-3482, or Long Beach Peninsula Visitor's Bureau, PO Box 562, Long Beach, WA 98631. Phone (360) 642-2400.

WILLAPA NATIONAL WILDLIFE REFUGE

[Fig. 35] **Leadbetter Unit**—This is one of the major separate parts of the Willapa National Wildlife Refuge and is at the extreme north end of the North Beach Peninsula. Visitors may reach it by taking the Sandridge Road north from Seaview to where it joins State Route 103 south of Nahcotta, and following that past Oysterville then turning right onto Stackpole Road. The parking lot is at the end of the road, which reduces to one lane near the end. The unit has a broad area of saltwater marsh and there are stands of coniferous forest. The northern tip of the peninsula is a sandy dune area.

The varied landscape provides habitat for a variety of wildlife, including numerous migrating shorebirds, such as pelicans and several species of plover. Leadbetter Point is the northern limit of the breeding range of the snowy plover (*Charadrius alexandrinus*), which nests on the upper ocean beach from April through the summer. The tiny shorebird is a threatened species and a large part of the northern tip of the peninsula is closed to visitors during its nesting period. Visitors should watch for signs designating the closed areas. Trails lead to other vantage points in the state park and wildlife refuge, where many of the wildlife species can be visited. There are pit toilets, but no camping. At high tide, boating is available along the shore, but to launch a boat here it must be carried some 100 yards over the beach vegetation.

The end of the Stackpole Road is the trailhead for an assortment of trails designated by colored markings on posts along the way and which lead to places where the wildlife may be. The green trail goes 1.1 miles through largely sitka spruce and alder forest that regenerated naturally after a major forest fire burned off the old forest in the 1850s. It is a good example of a forest healing itself after a catastrophe. The green trail, which is populated by wildlife including deer, leads to a salt marsh within sight of the bay. Turn left there and go 1.25 mile toward the ocean beach. The trails may be flooded as much as hip high during the fall, winter, and spring. Another trail begins just before the end of the Stackpole Road and leads about 100 yards to the beach.

Lewis Unit—The entrance to this major unit of the wildlife refuge is on US Highway 101 between mile posts 18 and 19, at the mouth of the Bear River. The unit is reached by a 1-mile-long entrance road that skirts the mouth of the Bear River at the southern extreme of Willapa Bay and ends at a small parking lot with a pit toilet and a trail on the Dike Road leading into the unit. The unit includes large areas of marshland.

Wildlife may include the Virginia rail (*Rallus limicola*), a small, brown bird that feeds in the marshes but is so rare that it is a lucky visitor who actually sees one. There may be numerous garter snakes (*Thamnophis sirtalis*) along the trail during the summer, and northern river otters (*Lutra canadensis*) may be hunting for fish, frogs, snakes, and turtles in the river and marsh channels beside the entrance road. Occasionally elk and bear can be seen here and sometimes peregrine falcons (*Falco peregrinus)* perch on old electric poles where they watch the marsh for something to eat. Northern harriers (*Circus cyaneus*), great blue herons (*Ardea herodias*), mallards (*Anas platyrhynchos*), and cinnamon teal (*Anas cyanoptera*) may also be seen.

Long Island Unit—A major attraction of this 5,000-acre forested island is the Cedar Grove, a 275-acre stand of old-growth forest that is one of the few survivors of the thick forest that once covered much of this part of the coast. This is the largest estuarine island on the U.S. Pacific Coast. It lies off the eastern, inland shore of Willapa Bay near the bay's southern end. It is accessible only by boat at high tide when the mud flats are covered.

On the mainland, the wildlife refuge headquarters on US Highway 101 between mileposts 24 and 25 has information, toilets, and maps. Across the highway from the headquarters there is a public boat launch. An adjacent boat dock is for use only by the U.S. Fish and Wildlife Service. The boat launch is just a short boat ride across the channel to Long Island. The tide, currents, and mud flats can make boating tricky and/or dangerous here, so it is necessary to have a tide table and a map that provides tide levels required to reach various parts of the island.

There are five primitive campgrounds with a total of 24 campsites on the island. They can be reached only by boat. Camping is permitted only in the designated sites, and the campsites may be full, especially during the hunting season and on holidays and weekends during the summer. Camping is on a first-come, first-served basis. There is no camping fee. The beach and several gravel roads that are closed to private vehicles can be hiked to reach many parts of the island. The 0.75-mile Trail of Ancient Cedars goes through the old-growth forest, as well as second-growth areas that were logged during the 1930s and 1960s.

Parts of the island were logged beginning in 1900 and, in 1867 a shanty town called Diamond City was built on the northern tip of the island to provide shelter for oyster harvesters. The oyster business declined by 1878, but logging continued until the 1990s. Much of the island now has second-growth forest in various stages of growth, but the wildlife refuge set aside 275 acres of mostly western redcedar and western hemlock old growth in the Cedar Grove. Those trees stand as a reminder of how the island looked hundreds of years ago when Chinook Indians hunted, fished, and harvested clams and oysters here. Individual cedar trees may live as long as 1,000 years, and the hemlocks that grow interspersed among the cedar sometimes live for 500 years. Scientists estimate the grove has succeeded, generation after generation, for 4,000 years.

The ground of the grove is littered with fallen logs that may last as many as 500 years, slowly releasing their nutrients into the soil for new generations. When seeds fall on the logs some germinate, and the logs become "nurse trees" where the young grow on the log, eventually sending their roots to the ground. When the dead log finally rots away, the living tree remains, standing on its roots. Sometimes a number of trees grow on a single log, forming a straight line, standing on their roots above where the log once was.

Above ground, the canopy of the forest spreads out to capture light and moisture. Even the thin gray shade of the winter sun and the light moisture of ocean fog are enough to maintain the life functions of the trees. The upper story also provides habitat for creatures that live their lives high off the ground. Plants, birds, and insects, for instance, find living space on the thick branches of the high forest.

The island also grows sitka spruce, and salal, blueberry, and salmonberry bushes. The west side has intertidal meadows of non-native eelgrass (*Zostera japonica*), while the meadows grow native grasses such as *Spartina* that provide nursery grounds for young salmon and other fish, as well as food for black brant and other waterfowl.

Tidal marshes on the east side of the island provide a home for shorebirds and ducks. When the marsh plants die and decay, they become covered with bacteria and algae, which is consumed by young fish, worms, and clams, which become food for birds, fish, and seals. Other wildlife on the island includes black bear and an estimated 80 to 100 elk. Smaller animals include raccoon (*Procyon lotor*), Townsend's chipmunk (*Tamias townsendi*), Douglas squirrel (*Tamiasciurus douglasi*), and deer mouse (*Peromyscus maniculatus*). In addition to shorebirds and waterfowl there are birds in the trees such as pileated woodpecker (*Dryocopus pileatus*), dark-eyed junco (*Junco hyemalis*), golden kinglet (*Regulus satrapa*), the gaudy, blue and black Steller's jay (*Cyanocitta stelleri*). And above the trees a bald eagle (*Haliaeetus leucocephalus*) may be soaring in search of something delicious below such as the blue grouse (*Dendragapus obscuras*) and ruffed grouse (*Bonasa umbellus*) that live near the ground.

A presidential proclamation has closed the island to hunting migratory birds, but the island is open to hunting elk, deer, bear, and grouse and other species only with bow and arrow. The hunting season is in the late autumn and early winter. Check with the State Fish and Wildlife Department for specific times. Phone (360) 902-2200.

Directions: The wildlife refuge headquarters is on US Highway 101 approximately 13 miles north of Illwaco. Maps, information, and directions to the separate units are available there.

Activities: Wildlife observation, camping, hiking, fishing, hunting, boating.

Facilities: Wildlife observation and interpretive stations, trails, campsites, boat launches, restrooms.

Dates: Open year-round, except the dunes at the north end of the Leadbetter Unit which are closed to visitors during the snowy plover nesting period—usually Mar. through Sept. Check with the refuge for current dates.

Fees: There is a fee for goose hunting from a blind.

Closest town: Ilwaco, 13 miles to the refuge headquarters.

For more information: Willapa National Wildlife Refuge, HC 01, Box 910, Ilwaco, WA 98624-9707. Phone (360) 484-3482.

LEADBETTER POINT STATE PARK

[Fig. 35(1)] This 1,185-acre park is near the northern end of the North Beach Peninsula, adjacent to the Leadbetter Unit of the Willapa National Wildlife Refuge, and has beach frontage on both its western, ocean side and the eastern, bay side, a total of some 3 miles of saltwater beach. It is a day-use park with more than 6 miles of hiking trails, including 1 open to bicycling.

The trails lead to the beaches of both the ocean and the bay. The longest trail is the 2.1 mile Loop Trail that circles through open shore pine growth beginning at the parking lot at the end of the Stackpole Road, and leads hikers to the Stackpole Slough, then takes them back to another parking lot on Stackpole Road about 1 mile south of the end-of-the-road parking lot. The road is adjacent to the bay, and the flat, sandy trail gets so close to the ocean that the breakers can be heard, but it does not actually go to the ocean beach. Visitors may access the ocean via the 1.3-mile Ocean Beach Trail, which forks off the Loop Trail about 0.75 mile from the end-of-the-road parking lot. From October through May both the Loop Trail and the Ocean Beach Trail can be deeply flooded.

The 1.8-mile Beach Trail begins at the end-of-the road parking lot, winds its way a short distance to the beach on Willapa Bay, and leads to the Willapa Bay Wildlife Refuge. The 0.5-mile Bay Trail circles between the Ocean Beach and Beach trails, and is the park's only trail that is open to bicycles.

In their short distances, the trails pass through a surprising variety of habitats. The beach is bordered by low growth such as blackberries, blueberries, and kinnikinnick. A little way inland that growth merges into a forest of deciduous alder and evergreen spruce, cedar, and hemlock. The marshes bear sprawling patches of American glasswort (*Salicornia virginica*). The dunes are stabilized by low plants such as gorse (*Ulex europaeus*), a dense shrub with spiny branches and, in the spring, yellow flowers. The dunes also have creeping sand verbena (*Abronia latifolia*) and seacoast lupine (*Lupinus littoralis*). During the summer the lupine bears little clusters of purple to blue flowers on short stalks that grow upright on prostrate stems.

Directions: Take the Sandridge Road north from Seaview to where it joins State Route 103 south of Nahcotta. Follow State Route 103 past Oysterville and then turn right onto Stackpole Road. The parking lot is at the end of the road, which narrows to one lane near the end.

Activities: Hiking, beachcombing, wildlife viewing, shellfish hunting, bicycling, picnicking, fishing.

Facilities: Trails, wheelchair accessible restrooms.

Dates: Open year-round.

Fees: None.

Closest town: Seaview, 24 miles.

For more information: Contact Fort Canby State Park, PO Box 488, Ilwaco, WA 98624. Phone (360) 643-3078 or (800) 233-0321.

PACIFIC PINE STATE PARK

[Fig. 35(2)] This little 10-acre, day-use park has 590 feet of saltwater shoreline, and a short trail that leads from the paved parking lot through the shore pine trees to the beach. There are eight picnic sites behind some trees for people who don't want to eat their sandwich in the wind on the beach.

Directions: Take State Route 103 about 0.5 mile north from Ocean Park, and then go west about 0.2 mile on 274th Place.

Activities: Beachcombing, shellfish hunting, kite flying, surf fishing, picnicking.

Facilities: Picnic tables, wheelchair-accessible restrooms, paved parking lot, horseshoe pits.

Dates: Open during the summer.

Fees: None.

Closest town: Ocean Park, about 0.7 mile.

For more information: Contact Fort Canby State Park, PO Box 488, Ilwaco, WA 98624. Phone (360) 643-3078 or (800) 233-0321.

LOOMIS LAKE STATE PARK

[Fig. 35(3)] About 13.5 acres of this 295-acre park are on the ocean beach and developed for use. The remaining portion of the park is on the 2.5-mile-long lake in the middle of Long Beach, and is left undeveloped to preserve it as habitat for trumpeter swans and other waterfowl that use the lake. There is no lake access from the park but the State Department of Fish and Wildlife stocks the lake with rainbow trout and has a public fishing pier, boat launch, and pit toilet on the west shore. That facility can be reached by driving on State Route 103 north about 0.33 mile from the park entrance road and then going east on the short access road to the Fish and Wildlife facilities.

Lewis and Clark

Lewis and Clark achieved a major goal of their extraordinary, three-year venture through more than 2,000 miles of uncharted wild lands when they reached the mouth of the Columbia River. Their exploration provided the United States with scientific information about the land of the Louisiana Purchase that President Thomas Jefferson had bought from France. It also established, once and for all, that there was no Northwest Passage that would make it possible to travel from coast to coast by water. At the same time, the Lewis and Clark journey established the route of the Oregon Trail that led to the American immigration to the Northwest beginning in the 1840s. That immigration overwhelmed the settlements of the British Hudson's Bay Company, and established that the land that is now Washington and Oregon belongs to the United States.

The part of the park on the beach has 425 feet of shoreline. A wheelchair accessible, paved path leads from the parking lot to a viewing platform on a sand dune above the beach. A sand trail leads from there to the beach, where the nearly constant wind invites kite flying, and the sandy beach invites shellfish hunting and surf fishing. A thick forest of sitka spruce covers much of the park.

Directions: Take State Route 103 north from Seaview for about 10 miles and turn left on an unmarked road between 179th Street and 188th Street.

Activities: Beachcombing, kite flying, shellfish hunting, fishing, wildlife viewing, picnicking.

Facilities: Wheelchair-accessible restrooms, viewing platform, 7 picnic tables with wind screens and fireplaces.

Dates: Open year-round.

Fees: None.

Closest town: Long Beach, about 10 miles.

For more information: Contact Fort Canby State Park, PO Box 488, Ilwaco, WA 98624. Phone (360) 643-3078 or (800) 233-0321.

Long Beach/Seaview

These adjacent communities near the bottom of the North Beach Peninsula offer food and lodging for people intending to explore up the peninsula. Seaview is unincorporated. Long Beach, has about 1,400 people.

Lodging and food establishments are scattered along State Route 103, which bisects both communities (*see* The Shelburne Inn, page 235).

The communities face the beach and offer many beach activities such as picnicking and beachcombing. At the west end of Bolstad Street, Long Beach has a high, bridgelike boardwalk that overlooks the surf. Trails lead through the sand dunes.

Directions: On State Route 103, 3 miles north of Ilwaco.

Activities: Hiking, picnicking, surfboarding, beachcombing, shopping, kite flying.

Facilities: Food, lodging, shops, picnic sites, trails.

Dates: Open year round.

For more information: Long Beach Peninsula Visitor's Bureau, PO Box 562, Long Beach, WA 98631. Phone (360) 642-2400.

▨ RESTAURANTS IN LONG BEACH

A meal is not hard to find in Long Beach.

Milton York Restaurant. 107 Pacific Street. This family restaurant was founded as a candy shop in 1882 and still sells homemade ice cream and candy. The dinner menu offers steak, and prime rib, as well as fresh seafood. *Inexpensive.* (*360*) *642-2352.*

The Lightship Restaurant. 410 Southwest Tenth Street. This restaurant with an American cuisine has a wide view of the ocean. The menu features beef and fresh local seafood and a children's menu is available. There is also a cocktail lounge. A feature is the Sunday brunch. *Inexpensive.* (*360*) *642-3252.*

▨ LODGING IN LONG BEACH

There is a multitude of places to stay in Long Beach.

Edgewater Inn. 409 Tenth Street Southwest. This motel has 84 rooms in two buildings. It faces the ocean and has access to the beach. Many of the rooms have an ocean view and there are six suites. *Moderate.* (*800*) *561-2456* or (*360*) *642-2311.*

Scandinavian Gardens Inn Bed and Breakfast. 1610 California Avenue. This bed and breakfast has 5 guest rooms in a two-story home. It is near the beach and has a sauna, whirlpool, and private baths. Breakfast is free. *Moderate to expensive.* (*800*) *988-9277* or (*360*) *642-8877.*

🎑 THE SHELBURNE INN

The Shelburne Inn, in Seaview, is a historic hostelry that was built by Charles Beaver in 1896 as a combination home and boarding house for tourists from Portland. In 1911 it was moved across the street and joined to another building. Guests arrived on the narrow-gauge Clamshell Railroad after taking a ferry from Astoria on the Oregon side of the Columbia River. The inn was a major stop for the railroad. Since then State Route 103 has replaced the railroad, and the building has been refurbished and expanded four times.

Now it is a three-story, 15-room Victorian hotel that features many antiques and the charm of days long gone. There is no elevator, but all rooms have bath and/or shower and some have balconies.

The inn is especially proud of the complimentary "country style breakfast" it serves family style at the large oak table in the lobby. The Shoalwater Restaurant at the inn serves meals based on fresh, locally produced harvests, and emphasizes Northwestern wines. The adjacent Heron and Beaver Pub serves drinks and light meals.

Directions: Shelburne Inn is located at 4415 Pacific Way, in Seaview.

Dates: Open year-round.

For more information: Shelburne Inn, PO Box 250, 4415 Pacific Way, Seaview, WA 98644. Phone (360) 642-2442 or (800) 466-1896.

Ilwaco Area

🎑 FORT CANBY STATE PARK

[Fig. 35(4)] This 1,900-acre park with some 8 miles of shoreline is where the Columbia River currents meet the Pacific Ocean breakers with considerable historical consequences. It also is where overland explorations, most notably those of the epic Lewis and Clark Expedition, discovered that the Columbia was part of a route across the continent to the Pacific coast which, until then, had been accessible only by sea. At the mouth of the Columbia, Lewis and Clark reached the land that sailing adventurers, most notably Robert Gray and George Vancouver, had discovered only a few years earlier after sailing around the southern tip of South America through the treacherous Strait of Magellan. That conjunction of land and sea routes began the process of European settlement of the Pacific Northwest.

Gray left the name of his ship, *Columbia Rediva*, on the river. Vancouver gave names to many of the landmarks in the new country, and Lewis and Clark used his maps to find their location as they came down the river. But, perhaps, it is the Lewis and Clark journey that most captures the imaginations of Americans.

The two army officers, Meriweather Lewis and William Clark, were assigned by

President Thomas Jefferson to explore the land Jefferson had obtained in the Louisiana Purchase, and to go beyond that to hunt for the long-sought water route to the Pacific. They started from a camp in Illinois across the Mississippi River from the mouth of the Missouri River in the summer of 1804. In the beginning, they had 43 companions they called the Corps of Discovery. They spent the winter with the Mandan Indians in the Dakotas. In the spring they sent some of their companions home with the scientific information they had gathered thus far.

The land beyond the Dakotas was completely unknown, but the explorers continued their epic journey by boat, afoot, and on horseback. They traveled up the Missouri, across the rugged Rocky Mountains, and down the Columbia until November 1805, when they finally saw the breakers of the Pacific Ocean from a camp a few miles up the river from where Fort Canby State Park is now (*see* Lewis and Clark Campsite Heritage Area , page 242). The men stayed at that campground for a few days, but it wasn't a good campsite and local Indians told them the hunting was better on the south side of the Columbia. They went across the river and built a rudimentary frontier fort where they stayed the winter before starting home in the spring (*see* Fort Clatsop, page 264). The party spent the winter hunting elk and deer for food, exploring the countryside, and writing long, detailed reports on their scientific findings. The exploration took them near and far. Clark left his name carved on a tree in what is now Fort Canby State Park. They sent a party some 15 miles down the Oregon Coast to where Seaside is now to make salt by boiling pots of sea water until they were dry then scraping the salt off the bottom of the pots. They used the salt to preserve meat for the trip home. The site of the fires is still on exhibit in Seaside (*see* Lewis and Clark Salt Works, page 270).

The Corps of Discovery's trip established that there was no water route to the Pacific, and the explorers gathered immense amounts of scientific information about the environment, the people, and the wildlife west of the Mississippi. Perhaps most importantly to present day Americans, their journey gave America a strong claim for the land against the Spanish and English.

A lot has happened at the mouth of the Columbia since it was discovered, so much of it of historical importance that Cape Disappointment, where the river's fresh water meets the oceans salt water has been named a National Historic District. The cape is on the northern shore. John Meares, captain of a fur trading vessel, named it in 1788. He was attempting to find a major river that had been vaguely reported in the vicinity. He sailed close enough to see the cape and thought it gave promise, but he failed to find the river so he named the cape after his disappointment. Four years later the American Captain Robert Gray had better luck, or better eyesight, and named the river after his ship.

In 1852, just 46 years after the Corps of Discovery left, a military reservation was established on 584 acres where Fort Canby State Park is now. It was established to protect the Columbia River from invasion, and was the first American fortification north of San Francisco. It eventually became part of a complex of forts that commanded both sides of the river's mouth. After the Civil War began in 1862, smooth bore cannon were emplaced in the fort, and early in the twentieth century the defenses were improved with gun batteries and mortars, as well as mines that were emplaced off the shore. During World War II, long-range, rapid-fire guns were installed, but by the end of that war, forts had been made obsolete by modern armaments and the land was turned over to the state for use as a park.

The bluffs on the southern tip of the North Beach Peninsula, where the park is located, look out over the Columbia River Bar. Treacherous currents have brought many vessels of all kinds to trouble here, so many that the bar is known as the Graveyard of the Pacific. To help ships navigate over these waters, the government built a lighthouse on Cape Disappointment in 1856, just four years after the fort was established and a half century after Lewis and Clark left Fort Clatsop. The light could not be seen from ships approaching from the north so a second one was built on the other side of the cape, at North Head in 1898. The two lighthouses are major features of the park.

Lewis and Clark's Corps of Discovery is commemorated in the Lewis and Clark Interpretive Center, which sits high on a bluff of pillow lava from an ancient volcanic eruption near the Cape Disappointment Lighthouse. The exhibit features information panels telling the story of the explorers' journey, and how the Corps of Discovery achieved its principal objective when it arrived here at the Pacific Ocean. The panels spiral down then up for two flights. Programs are presented in a multimedia theater on the lower level. The upper level has picture windows that look out on awesome views of the river, the ocean, and the Cape Disappointment Lighthouse. Just behind the interpretive center the heavy, concrete fortifications of Battery Harvey Allen still seem threatening a century after they were built.

A road on the southern, river side of the park ends at the north jetty, a rock wall that controls erosion and waves at the mouth of the river. The jetty extends some 800 feet beyond the end of the headland, and is a popular place for anglers seeking rockfish and perch. Just to the north of the jetty, along the ocean shore, Benson Beach is where anglers go for surf fishing. Lake O'Neil, northwest of Cape Disappointment, is also a popular fishing spot, and a boat launch just north of the cape gives access to both the river and the sea.

A variety of trails, covering a total of 5.5 miles, lead to interesting places, such as a World War II, 6-inch gun emplacement. The guns have been removed, but the concrete fortifications are as solid as ever and beg to be explored. The underground portion of the battery, however, is far too dark to be entered without a flashlight. Another interesting trail to explore is the 1.5-mile loop through a forest of sitka spruce that was 300 years old when Lewis and Clark first saw it. Several trails lead to and along the ocean beach, and in the northern part of the park a side road leads off Robert Gray Drive to the North Head Lighthouse, which looks far out to the Pacific,

Osprey

Osprey (*Pandion haliaetus*) hunt by diving from as high as 100 feet in the air to grab a fish as deep as 3 feet in a natural or manmade lake. The bird, with a 54-inch wingspan, then surfaces and immediately struggles to get airborne, grasping its prey that may weigh as much as the bird.

beyond the waves crashing into the shore. A short trail from the end of the road to the lighthouse goes through a typical beach growth of sitka spruce and kinnikinnick.

From the parking lot near Mackenzie Head, the North Head Trail goes north for about 1.8 miles, and then it crosses the North Head Lighthouse Road at the lighthouse trailhead parking lot. It continues for another mile or so to connect with a 1-mile trail to an old quarry called Beard's Hollow. Second-growth fir, alder, and oak now thrive in the vicinity of the quarry, and nearby are some dead cedars that grew beside freshwater marshes that formed behind dunes built by waves pounding in from the sea. Salt water breached the dunes and flowed into the marshes, killing some of the cedars.

Numerous birds populate the park, including red-throated loons (*Gavia stellata*), pelagic cormorants (*Phalacrocorax peligicus*), and great blue herons (*Ardea herodias*). Mammals include black-tailed deer, black bear, and raccoon.

The park has 190 standard campsites, 60 campsites with utilities, and 4 primitive sites, as well as permanent lodging such as cabins and yurts. The yurts are interesting, circular, domed, tentlike structures similar to those used by nomadic people in Central Asia. There is a concession that sells groceries and fishing gear. Numerous restrooms are scattered through the park. Day users have a choice of 50 picnic sites. The park is very popular, and has been host to as many as 1 million visitors a year.

Directions: In Ilwaco, take Spruce Street, which becomes Robert Gray Drive and in about 2 miles reaches a point where it parallels the park, just outside the boundary. Side roads lead to Beards Hollow and North Head Lighthouse. Robert Gray Drive enters the park about 3.5 miles from Ilwaco.

Activities: Camping, picnicking, fishing, hiking, beachcombing, clamming, boating, wildlife watching.

Facilities: Campsites, picnic sites, cabins, yurts, store, interpretive center, restrooms, boat launches, trails, lighthouses, showers.

Dates: Open year-round.

Fees: There are fees for camping, lodging, and boat launch.

Closest town: Ilwaco, 3.5 miles.

For more information: Fort Canby State Park, PO Box 488, Ilwaco, WA 9862. Phone (360) 642-3078 or (800) 233-0321. For camping reservations (summer only), Reservations Northwest, PO Box 500, Portland, OR 97207-0500. Phone (800) 452-5687.

🐚 ILWACO

[Fig. 35] This town of some 800 people was established in 1868 near Cape Disappointment as a fishing village. Some of the fishermen used traps to catch the prized salmon. Others used gillnets. Their disagreements over which method would prevail evolved into a battle, and by 1896 the militia was called out to separate the combatants, while an armed launch patrolled the bay to keep the peace. The battle ended in a draw, and the participants went back to whatever fishing method they chose.

The town became a stop for tourists from Portland, who arrived by boat to take a train to Long Beach. The boats could land only when the tide was in, so the train schedule varied with the tide.

Protected by tall headlands to the west, today Ilwaco is a haven for small vessels, and the community attracts commercial and sport fishermen, as well as pleasure boaters. Fish, crab, and shellfish processing are major industries in the town, which ships seafood as far as Europe and Asia.

The town is a good base for exploring the North Beach Peninsula, Fort Canby State Park, Fort Columbia State Park, and other nearby attractions. There are restaurants, motels, and bed and breakfast houses. The **Ilwaco Heritage Museum** at 115 Southeast Lake Street displays the history of the Long Beach Peninsula.

Directions: From the Astoria Bridge over the Columbia River, go 11 miles northwest on U. S. Highway 101.

Activities: Fishing, clam digging, boating, shopping.

Facilities: Boat harbor, charter fleet, shops, restaurants, lodging.

Dates: Open year-round.

For more information: Long Beach Peninsula Visitor's Bureau, PO Box 562, Long Beach, WA 98631. Phone (360) 642-2400.

COLBERT HOUSE HERITAGE AREA

[Fig. 35(5)] This rambling, two-story historical house with a porch that looks out over the bay is operated by the state park system and is a well-maintained example of a middle class Victorian home in Ilwaco. Fred Colbert and his wife Catherine built the house nearby in Chinookville in 1871. It was moved to its present location in 1883. Colbert was a Swedish immigrant who prospered in fishing and owned a fishnet manufacturing business, livery stable, and carriage house. Swedish immigrants who lived there made the fishnets in the loft of the house. Twelve members of the Colbert family also lived in the rambling, two-story house.

Directions: The house is on the corner of Lake and Quaker streets.

OSPREY
(Pandion haliaetus)

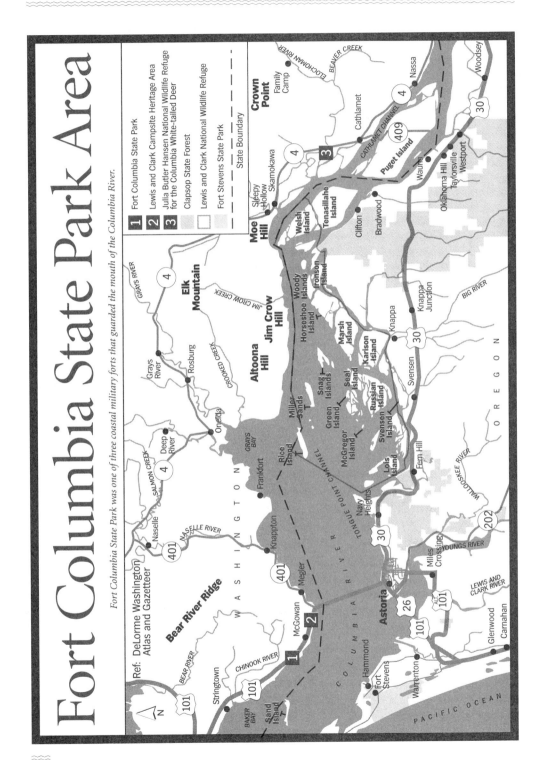

Fort Columbia State Park Area

Fort Columbia State Park was one of three coastal military forts that guarded the mouth of the Columbia River.

Ref: DeLorme Washington Atlas and Gazetteer

1 Fort Columbia State Park
2 Lewis and Clark Campsite Heritage Area
3 Julia Butler Hansen National Wildlife Refuge for the Columbia White-tailed Deer
  Clapsop State Forest
  Lewis and Clark National Wildlife Refuge
  Fort Stevens State Park
  State Boundary

Dates: Open weekends during the summer.

Fees: A tour fee is charged.

For more information: Contact Fort Canby State Park, PO Box 488, Ilwaco, WA 9862. Phone (360) 642-3078 or (800) 233-0321.

Columbia River Area

▨ FORT COLUMBIA STATE PARK

[Fig. 36(1)] This 592-acre park was one of the three coast artillery forts that guarded the busy mouth of the Columbia River from potential invaders. The other two, Fort Canby on the Washington side and Fort Stevens on the Oregon side (*see* Fort Canby State Park, page 235 and Fort Stevens, page 266), are situated on the headlands where the Columbia meets the Pacific. Fort Columbia is a few miles inland, making any marauding ships the center of a triangular target area.

The park was built on what had been the site of a village of a band of Chinook Indians led by the famous Chief Comcomly. The park is heavily devoted to history, rather than the conventional, largely recreational and ecological functions of many parks. Much of the fortification was built during the 1885-1905 period, when forts with big guns and strong emplacements could be depended on to defend the nation's shores. Battery 246, however, was built during the era of World War II when the attack on Pearl Harbor left the U.S. Pacific Fleet in shambles, and there was concern that the enemy might bring its ships to raid or invade. That battery was composed of shielded 6-inch guns, and two of them are still in place, even though the forts along the coast were abandoned after the war.

The fort's commanding officer's home, called the Columbia House, is in the residential area, and has been restored and period furniture installed. The enlisted men's barracks on the other end of the compound has been converted to a historical display with the squad room, mess hall, and kitchen much as they were when the building was home to the soldiers who manned the fort's guns. The squad room has cots and foot lockers, a mess hall table is set with dishes for a meal, and a display in the kitchen includes a tape describing the room and its equipment.

Other rooms in the building contain displays of the fort emplacements, local Indian artifacts, and the history of the area. A walk leads from the barracks, past the Columbia House, to the powerhouse, and down to the gun emplacements, then along old roads to the fire control post on Scarborough Hill, and then back down to the Columbia House. A leg of the walk goes behind the barracks to the quartermaster's storehouse, where a room displays a replica of the office of the *Chinook Observer*, a local newspaper, as it looked early in the twentieth century.

Tall spruce and bigleaf maple (*Acer macrophyllum*) help beautify the fort's landscape making a stroll there a pleasure, and there are some 25 picnic tables. The grounds front on well over a mile of the Columbia river bank, but high bluffs make it difficult to reach the water, just as it would have made it difficult for enemy troops to reach the fort.

Directions: The fort is on US Highway 101 about 2.5 miles west from the north end of the Columbia River Bridge to Astoria.

Activities: Viewing historical fortifications, hiking, picnicking.

Facilities: Historical displays, picnic sites, restrooms.

Dates: Open June 1 to Sept. 30.

Fees: None.

Closest town: Chinook, 1 mile.

For more information: Contact Fort Canby State Park, PO Box 488, Ilwaco, WA 9862. Phone (360) 642-3078 or (800) 233-0321.

LEWIS AND CLARK CAMPSITE HERITAGE AREA

[Fig. 36(2)] This little spot next to US Highway 101 is where Lewis and Clarks' Corps of Discovery camped from November 16 to 25, 1805. They could see breakers of the Pacific Ocean and knew they had reached their destination. "Ocian (sic) in view! O! the joy," Clark wrote in his field notes.

The party agreed this was not a good campsite and local Indians told them the hunting was better on the other side of the river so they moved across the river and built a rudimentary, frontier fort (*see* Fort Clatsop, page 264). They stayed there until spring, when there was hope the winter snow in the Rocky Mountains had melted sufficiently so they could cross them safely on their way home.

A commemorative statue and a roadside sign mark the site, just a few feet from the north bank of the Columbia River. There are a few picnic tables and little else to designate it as the site of an important piece of the nation's history.

A few feet to the east of the campsite is the quaint, weathered, gray building of the St. Mary's McGowan Church built in 1902, nearly a century after Lewis and Clark stayed here.

Directions: The site is on US Highway 101, about 1.9 miles west of the bridge that crosses the Columbia River to Astoria, Oregon.

Facilities: Picnic tables.

Dates: Open year-round.

Fees: None.

For more information: Contact Fort Canby State Park, PO Box 488, Ilwaco, WA 98624. Phone (360) 642-3078 or (800) 233-0321.

JULIA BUTLER HANSEN NATIONAL WILDLIFE REFUGE FOR THE CO-LUMBIAN WHITE-TAILED DEER

[Fig. 36(3)] This refuge has some 4,750 acres of Columbia River floodplains on the mainland and several Columbia River islands specifically set aside in 1972 as a safe place for a population of some 230 Columbian white-tailed deer (*Odocoileus virginianus leucurus*), an endemic subspecies that is on the endangered species list.

The Columbian white-tailed deer is found only in a small area on both sides of the Columbia River and on three islands in the Columbia. By the mid 1970s the subspecies had dwindled to only about 400 deer. An island and a portion of land on the mainland on the Washington side of the river was set aside as the refuge in an effort to save the species. The deer are not given supplemental food but the land is managed to improve the nutritional value of the browse and to provide a safe haven where the animals may live without being hunted or harassed. Since the refuge was created, the number of deer has fluctuated over the years and by the end of the 1990s the herd had increased to some 1,000 head.

The refuge also is home to other species, including the Canada goose (*Branta canadensis*), mallard (*Anas platyrhynchos*), wigeon (*Anas americana*), and pintail (*Anas acuta*), among the wintering birds. There also are water birds, bald eagles, and osprey. Mammals include elk, as well as the deer for which the refuge was established. Salmon (*Oncorhynchus* sp.), sturgeon (*Acipenser transmontanus*), and trout (*Oncorhynchus* sp.) are among the fish in the nearby waters of the Columbia River.

The mainland section of the refuge lies between the Columbia River and a 4-mile stretch of State Route 4, between Skamokowa and Cathlamet. It can be seen from the highway and an interpretive display near the east end includes a great deal of information, as well as blinds where visitors can see the animals without disturbing them. The one-lane Brooks Slough Road runs through the refuge between Skamokawa and a point 0.25 mile west of the interpretive display.

Directions: The refuge is on State Route 4 between Skamokawa and Cathlamet. The islands are accessible only by boat.

Activities: Wildlife observation, bird hunting, fishing

Facilities: Interpretive display, wildlife viewing blinds.

Dates: Open year-round

Fees: None.

For more information: Julia Butler Hansen National Wildlife Refuge, PO Box 566, Cathlamet, WA 98612. Phone (360) 795-3915.

Vancouver

[Fig. 37] This city of 132,000 people is on the Washington side of the Columbia River across from Portland, Oregon, the metropolis of the Columbia. Despite being considerably smaller than its neighbor across the river is, it is prosperous and a major player in the area. It has many amenities, including 55 parks totaling 549 acres, the Columbia Way Promenade that parallels the Columbia's bank for more than 1 mile, and trails that meander through miles of thick forests and grasslands on treads ranging from gravel to asphalt. There is a tennis center with both outdoor and indoor tennis courts, as well as racquetball courts, and the city's swimming pool has won major awards. Food and lodging are available on both sides of the river.

It all began in 1825 when George Simpson, governor of the Hudson's Bay Company became dissatisfied with Astoria as the Hudson's Bay Company's Columbia Department headquarters and decided to move. The company built a fort on the north bank of the Columbia near Government Island, Oregon. That spot did not work out, so the company moved the fort to a site closer to the river near the place British Lieutenant William Broughton had named Vancouver. The fort there originally was square and relatively small, but it was expanded to a larger rectangle, containing more than two dozen buildings inside a strong wooden stockade. More buildings were built outside the stockade, and nearby acreage was cultivated to raise food for the company's people. Docks and wharves were erected on the riverbank west of the fort for ships from Europe and America, including the *Beaver,* the first steamship in the Northwest.

Dr. John McLoughlin, chief factor of the company's Columbia Department, supervised the fort that became the hub of the company's department which covered what are now Washington, Oregon, British Columbia, Idaho, Western Montana, and Hawaii. The fort functioned as a fur trading post and as a supply depot for the company's 24 other forts and posts in the department. For some 20 years it was the most important European settlement in the Pacific Northwest (*see* Fort Nisqually, page 50). Several hundred men worked in the department, including Europeans, Indians, French Canadians, and Hawaiians. The fort, to a large extent, was in the beaver-hat business. Its brigades of trappers ranged over the territory trapping beavers, or trading for them with Indians. The pelts were sent to Europe where they were sold to other firms that transformed the beaver hair into the top hats that were extremely popular there, and which commanded a good price.

By the 1840s American settlers arrived in such numbers that they overwhelmed the company, and in 1846 the American and the British governments agreed to make the 49th parallel of latitude the Canadian border. The company continued to operate Fort Vancouver as a trading post until the trade diminished, and in 1860, the company moved its few remaining employees to Victoria, British Columbia, abandoning what it called the "Oregon Country" to the Americans.

In 1849, the U.S. Army moved into the area adjacent to Fort Vancouver and established Columbia Barracks, later changing the name to Vancouver Barracks. It was a neighbor to an American settlement, called Columbia City, which changed its name to Vancouver.

Directions: Vancouver is on I-5 at the north side of the Columbia River.

For more information: City Hall, 210 East Thirteenth Street, PO Box 1995, Vancouver, WA 98668. Phone (360) 696-8121.

▒ FORT VANCOUVER

[Fig. 37(1)] Fort Vancouver was the headquarters for the army in much of the Pacific Northwest and grew to a major military installation, starting with a log structure that was built as the commanding officer's home. That building, much changed, is still here under the name of the Ulysses S. Grant House. Grant, a West Point graduate, was an unhappy lieutenant at the barracks, but resigned from the army to live a civilian life in Illinois. He did poorly as a civilian and rejoined the army early in the Civil War, going on to become the commanding general of all the Union Armies. He accepted Confederate General Robert E. Lee's surrender at Appomattox Courthouse on April 9, 1865, and was elected president in 1869. He never lived in the commanding officer's home but he revisited the barracks in 1879, and the building was named for him then.

From 1936 to 1938, General George C. Marshall was the commanding officer of Vancouver Barracks. He went on to become the Army Chief of Staff during World War II and directed the American Army forces in that war. He later became the secretary of state and secretary of defense, and was the author of the Marshall Plan, which rebuilt Europe after the war and halted the spread of the Soviet Union through that continent. He was awarded the Nobel Peace Prize in 1952. The house he lived in during his term at the barracks was built in 1886, and is named after him.

Another stately old home on what has become known as Officers' Row was built in 1879 and is named after General O.O. Howard who won the Congressional Medal of Honor during the Civil War, and was the commanding officer at the barracks from 1874 to 1880.

In 1904, the year after the Wright brothers made the first flight in a heavier than air machine, a rudimentary, pioneer flying field was opened on land where the Hudson's Bay Company had raised crops to feed its people, and where the barracks had had an ammunition dump. In 1911, the field was the scene of the first biplane flight in the Northwest, and in 1937 it was the landing field for Soviet aviator Valeri Chaklov when he made the first nonstop transpolar flight. He traveled 5,288 nautical miles in 63 hours and 16 minutes from Moscow, Russia to Vancouver. Many other pioneers in aviation history used the field, including Jimmy Doolittle, who led the air raid on Tokyo in the early days of World War II, and Eddie Rickenbacker, the leading American Ace in World War I.

In 1925, the field was officially named for Army Lieutenant Alexander Pearson, who had lived in Vancouver as a child and became one of the best pilots in what was known then as the Army Air Service. He won the first cross-country air race in 1919 and made the first air survey of the Grand Canyon, but was killed in 1924. Pearson Field now is one of the oldest continuously operating airfields in the nation. It was declared surplus and sold to the city of Vancouver after World War II. The field continues to operate as a civilian airfield. It also contains the Pearson Air Museum (*see* Pearson Air Museum, page 246).

The barracks continued as a military reservation through World War II. Then it was closed piece by piece and turned over to agencies that have made it one of the nation's major historical reservations. Officers' Row was placed on the National Register of Historic Places in 1974.

Vancouver has multiple sites of major significance in the history of European development in the Northwest, all adjacent to each other and within easy walking distance. Separate efforts by different agencies to preserve, study, and display those sites have been going on for years, but they were given a measure of cooperation in 1996 when Congress created the Vancouver National Historic Reserve. The goal of the Reserve was to establish a partnership for cooperative management of the historic sites in a 366-acre area within the Vancouver city limits. Listed here are the four segments of the reserve:

The Fort Vancouver National Historic Site was established in 1948, and is managed by the National Park Service. The site includes the area where the fort was located, the Parade Ground of the Vancouver Barracks, and a portion of the Columbia River waterfront. Archaeologists have performed numerous studies in and near the site of the fort, which was destroyed by fire a few years after the Hudson's Bay Company moved out. Based on those studies, the National Park Service has reconstructed the large, elegant, comfortable Chief Factor's House, Indian Trade Shop, blacksmith shop, bake house, fur storage building, and others. A circa 1845 period garden grows just outside the fort's entrance. A visitor center on the slope above the fort has a museum with a large assortment of artifacts and displays depicting the fur trade, and the living style of the people of the fort. There also is a video about the fort, and restrooms. The site is open to visitors year-round.

Officers' Row is owned and operated by the city of Vancouver, which began to rehabilitate the magnificent, Victorian structures in 1980 after the army declared them surplus and sold them to the city for $1. The site consists of 51 residential units. Parts of the buildings are rented to public and private agencies, but parts also are open to the public, including the steepled George C. Marshall House, the porticoed Ulysses S. Grant House, and the stately General O.O. Howard House. The Howard and Marshall buildings are multistory, nineteenth century mansions that now house museums depicting their times and history. Entry is free, but donations are accepted.

The City of Vancouver owns Pearson Field. This operating airfield is managed under a long-term agreement with the National Park Service that calls for the transition of the field from a dominant use for general aviation to aviation history by 2022.

Pearson Air Museum is operated on the airfield under an agreement between the city and the National Park Service. This fascinating little museum exhibits carefully rebuilt old planes that are crammed into every corner of an old hangarlike building. There is also a computer center, audio presentations, photographs, and historic aviation films. A glassed-in section allows visitors to watch people working to restore old planes.

Directions: Take I-5 Exit 1C, and go east on Mill Plain Road then turn right on Fort Vancouver Way and go a short distance to the historic complex.

Activities: Viewing historical sites.

Facilities: Original and reconstructed historical structures and museum displays.

Dates: The Grant House and Pearson Air Museum are open Tuesday through Sunday year-round. Fort Vancouver and the O.O. Howard House are open daily except Thanksgiving and December 24 and 25. The Marshall House is open daily year-round unless reserved for special use.

Fees: Fees are charged at Fort Vancouver during the summer, and year-round at Pearson Air Museum. Donations are accepted at Officers' Row.

For more information: Fort Vancouver National Historic Site, 612 East Reserve Street, Vancouver, WA 98661-3897. Phone (360) 696-7655 or (800) 832-3599. Officers' Row, contact the Marshall House, 1301 Officers' Row, Vancouver WA 98661. Phone (360) 693-3101. Pearson Air Museum, 1115 East Fifth Street, Vancouver WA 98661. Phone (360) 694-7026. Pearson Field, 1115 East Fifth Street, Vancouver, WA 98661. Phone (360) 694-7066.

RESTAURANTS IN VANCOUVER

Billyjan's. 13200 Northeast Highway 99. This restaurant with a decidedly informal atmosphere specializes in entrees grilled over mesquite wood fire. There is a cocktail lounge and a children's menu. *Inexpensive. (360) 573-2711.*

Who-Song & Larry's Restaurant. 111 East Columbia River Way. This establishment on the Columbia River features Mexican dishes. There is a cocktail lounge, children's menu, and Sunday brunch. *Inexpensive. (360) 695-1198.*

LODGING IN VANCOUVER.

With a network of major highways, Vancouver has a wide range of places to stay.

The Heathman Lodge. 7801 Northeast Greenwood Drive. This motel has 143 rooms, including 22 suites. Some units have balconies or patios, fireplaces, and whirlpools. There are four two-bedroom units. The motel has a heated swimming pool, sauna, whirlpool, and restaurant. *Expensive. (888) 475-3100 or (360) 254-3100.*

Sleep Inn. 9201 Northeast Vancouver Mall Drive. This three-story motel on the road to Vancouver's shopping mall has 63 rooms. There is a heated swimming pool. *Moderate. (800) 753-3746 or (360) 254-0900.*

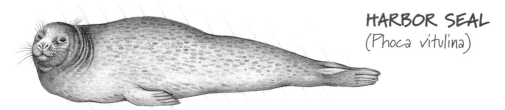

HARBOR SEAL
(*Phoca vitulina*)

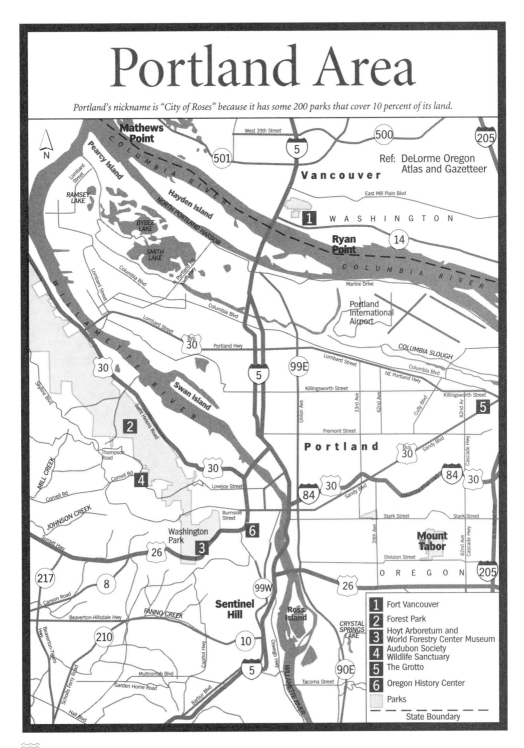

Portland Area

Portland's nickname is "City of Roses" because it has some 200 parks that cover 10 percent of its land.

Ref: DeLorme Oregon Atlas and Gazetteer

1 Fort Vancouver
2 Forest Park
3 Hoyt Arboretum and World Forestry Center Museum
4 Audubon Society Wildlife Sanctuary
5 The Grotto
6 Oregon History Center
⬜ Parks
--- State Boundary

Portland

[Fig. 37] When Lewis and Clark led the Corps of Discovery down the Columbia River on the last leg of their epic journey to the Pacific, they made note of an Indian village of about five houses on the south bank. The village was located a few miles upriver from the place where the Willamette River flows into the Columbia. That village of some 200 people has been replaced by a bustling modern city of some 500,000 people.

But bustling and modern doesn't just mean concrete, asphalt, and automobiles. The city also has forests, enough gardens to earn the nickname City of Roses, and some 200 parks that cover more than 10 percent of its land. Indeed, in 1904 when most of the city was forest and meadow, it hired the Olmsted Brothers of Brookline, Massachusetts, renowned park planners, to propose a park plan. The brothers worked out a dream of developing a 40-mile trail circling the city. They called their dream "the 40-mile loop." Portlanders not only embraced the fantastic dream, but also they extended it to 140 miles to serve the metropolitan area beyond the city limits. They still are working on it, but many of the trails are complete and in use as part of the city's system of scores of parks, including the 4,800-acre Forest Park, which consists of several smaller, interconnected parks. Together, they make Forest Park, the nation's largest urban wilderness park.

Portland began in 1843 when Asa Lovejoy and William Overton built a cabin and filed a land claim on a clearing on the banks of the Willamette River, near its confluence with the Columbia. Overton sold his half in 1844 to Francis W. Pettygrove, and the new partners platted a town on the west side of the river. Lovejoy wanted to name the city after his home town of Boston. Pettygrove, who was from Maine, held out for Portland. They tossed a coin and Pettygrove won. The coin still is on display at the Oregon History Center (*see* Oregon History Center, page 253).

Lovejoy and Pettygrove chose their site well. Two major rivers served it in a time when rivers were the major means of transportation and commerce. The Columbia River was the largest west of the Mississippi, and was a route between the newly settled land and both the United States and the rest of the world, albeit in the early days it was a treacherous place to sail a ship. The Willamette, the longest north-flowing river in the nation, served the rich agriculture lands of the Willamette Valley where pioneers were building farms.

By 1880 the city had grown to 20,000 population. By the turn of the twentieth century, there were nearly 100,000. By the turn of the twenty-first century, the city's population was about 500,000, and the metropolitan area counted well over 1.5 million people.

Now the city is a major hub of commerce served by railroads, highways, an airport, and ocean-going ships. It also is a cultural center of parks, theaters, museums, arts, and gardens. There are scores of hotels and motels, and dozens of restaurants ranging from fast food to gourmet.

Directions: Portland is on I-5, directly south of the Columbia River.

For more information: Portland Visitors Association, 26 Southwest Salmon, Portland, OR 97204. Phone (503) 222-2223 or (877) 678-5263.

RESTAURANTS IN PORTLAND

This full-sized city has a multitude of restaurants.

Couvron. 1126 Southwest Eighteenth Avenue. This dressy restaurant features seasonal menus and French cuisine. Reservations and more formal dress required. *Expensive. (503) 225-1844.*

Couch Street Fish House. 105 Northwest Third Avenue. This restaurant in a renovated historic building serves lamb, steak, veal, and chicken dishes, as well as its featured fresh Northwest seafood. There is a cocktail lounge. Reservations are recommended. *Inexpensive to moderate. (503) 223-6173.*

Pazzo Ristorante. 627 Southwest Washington. This establishment features regional Italian dishes such as a fresh seafood and pasta. There is a cocktail lounge and children's menu. *Inexpensive. (503) 228-1515.*

LODGING IN PORTLAND

This big city has a multitude of chain-operated lodging places but it also has some independents.

The Benson Hotel. 309 Southwest Broadway. This historic 13-story hotel has 287 rooms and nine suites, including two with whirlpools and fireplaces. There is a dining room and grill. *Expensive. (888) 523-6766 or (503) 228-2000.*

Fifth Avenue Suites Hotel. 506 Southwest Washington Avenue. This 10-story hotel has 221 rooms and suites. The rooms have speaker phones, iron and ironing board, and video games. Four of the suites have whirlpools. There is a dining room and cocktail lounge. *Expensive. (800) 711-2071 or (503) 222-0001.*

The Lion and the Rose Victorian Bed and Breakfast. 1810 Northeast Fifteenth Street. This historic bed and breakfast in a three-story, 1906 Queen Anne style home is on the National Register of Historic Places. There are 7 guest rooms and period furnishings. *Expensive. (800) 955-1647 or (503) 287-9245.*

FOREST PARK

[Fig. 37(2)] This 4,800-acre park is one of more than 200 parks in Portland, and it is the largest wilderness park within a city limits in the nation. It is located on the eastern slope of Portland's Northwest Hills and parallels the Willamette River. It is 8 miles long and about 1.5 miles at its widest point. The park is crisscrossed by roads that began as trails farmers once used to take their produce to the river for shipment.

The park, which consists of several interconnected parks, has some 70 miles of trails, including the Wildwood Trail that extends for 23 miles and is a major part of the city's 40-mile loop trail system. As they hike the trails, visitors pass second-

WESTERN HEMLOCK

(Tsuga heterophylla) This species has longer cones than other hemlocks and thrives on cool, moist slopes.

growth Douglas fir, ponderosa pine (*Pinus ponderosa*), western redcedar, western hemlock, red elderberry (*Sambucus racemosa aborescens*), and common horsetail (*Equisetum arvense),* the prolific enemy of Pacific Northwest gardeners. More than 100 species of birds and 50 species of mammals have been identified in the park.

In a somewhat confusing arrangement, Forest Park includes five other parks that connect to form Forest Park. Four of the interconnected parks are outside the city. They are all wild lands, left pretty much to the whims of nature. In addition to that, Forest Park is adjacent to Washington Park, at the head of Park Place, which offers more highly developed attractions such as the Hoyt Arboretum, Japanese Gardens, International Rose Test Gardens, and the World Forestry Center that tells the story of Oregon's forests.

Directions: Forest Park is between Northwest Skyline Road and St. Helens Road south of Newberry Road.

Activities: Hiking, jogging, picnicking, biking.

Facilities: Trails, restrooms, picnic sites.

Dates: Open year-round.

For more information: Portland Bureau of Parks and Recreation, 1120 Southwest Fifth Avenue, #1302, Portland, OR 97204. Phone (503) 823-7529.

HOYT ARBORETUM

[Fig. 37(3)] Some 10 miles of trails wander through 850 varieties of trees, including maples, magnolias, and spruce in this 175-acre arboretum. There is a visitor center, and self-guiding tours take visitors through the trees. Guided tours are available on Saturday and Sunday afternoons.

Directions: The arboretum is located at 4033 Southwest Canyon Road in Washington Park.

Activities: Hiking, picnicking.

Facilities: Trails, some suitable for wheelchairs, visitor center, picnic shelter.

Dates: Open year-round.

Fees: None, but donations are accepted.

For more information: Portland Bureau of Parks and Recreation, 1120 Southwest Fifth Avenue, #1302, Portland, OR 97204. Phone (503) 823-7529.

WORLD FORESTRY CENTER MUSEUM

[Fig. 37(3)] This museum is part of the World Forestry Center, a forest education complex that traces its roots to the American Pacific Exhibition the city held in 1905, and includes several buildings and the Magnuss Memorial Tree Farm near Wilsonville, Oregon. The museum, in an imposing wooden structure, focuses on forests, trees, and their products. The exhibits cover many parts of the world, with an emphasis on the Pacific Northwest forests that played a major part in the development of the region.

A highlight is a 70-foot "talking tree" that tells about the forest. One major exhibit depicts the old-growth forests of the Northwest and another displays specimens of petrified wood some 300 million years old.

Directions: The museum is at 4033 Canyon Road in Washington Park.

Dates: Open year-round, except Christmas.

Fees: There is an admission charge.

For more information: The World Forestry Center, 4033 Southwest Canyon Road, Portland, OR 97221. Phone (503) 228-1367.

AUDUBON SOCIETY WILDLIFE SANCTUARY

[Fig. 37(4)] This 160-acre wildlife sanctuary has several miles of trails leading to places where native birds and animals can be seen in their natural environment. There also is a Wildlife Care Center where injured birds are cared for. The injured animals are kept indoors or out, depending on species, and are on display for visitors.

An educational exhibit displays stuffed birds, nests, and eggs, with information on how to identify them.

Directions: The sanctuary is located at 5151 Northwest Cornell Road.

Activities: Hiking, on trails through bird, and mammal habitat.

Dates: Open year-round.

Fees: None.

For more information: Audubon Society of Portland, 5151 Northwest Cornell Road, Portland, OR 97210. Phone (503) 292-0304.

THE GROTTO

[Fig. 37(5)] The full name of this pleasant, natural, 62-acre retreat is the National Sanctuary of Our Sorrowful Mother, and as the name implies, it is a Catholic religious sanctuary for people of all faiths. It is a natural gallery with paths that wander through flowers and towering firs at the bottom of a 100-foot cliff. Founded in 1924, it is maintained by the Servite Friars and Sisters, and offers a reflection pond and sculptured shrines of bronze, wood, and marble. During the Christmas season each year, a popular Lighting and Choral Music Festival takes place.

An elevator takes visitors to the top of the cliff where there are manicured lawns and sweeping views of the Columbia River valley and the Cascade Mountains, including the diminished hulk of Mount St. Helens. The volcano lost its 0.25-mile top in the spring of 1980 when it exploded in the worst volcanic eruption in United States history.

Directions: The Grotto entrance is at the intersection of Northeast Sandy Boulevard and Northeast Eighty-Fifth Avenue.

Activities: Nature walks.

Facilities: Restrooms, visitor center, cafe.

Dates: Open year-round.

Fees: Admission fees are charged during the Christmas Lighting and Choral Music Festival. At other times, admission to the plaza level is free but there is a charge for the elevator.

For more information: The Grotto, PO Box 20008, Portland, Oregon, 20008. Phone (503) 254-7371.

OREGON HISTORY CENTER

[Fig. 37(6)] This fascinating museum, incorporated in 1898, portrays Portland from the beginning, starting with the coin its founders tossed to decide on a name for their new city.

The displays begin outside, with eight-story-high murals of the Lewis and Clark expedition and the earliest European contact. An optical illusion makes the murals seem three-dimensional.

Touring the museum is a good way to become acquainted with Oregon and its largest city. Especially informative is a permanent exhibit that follows the development of the city from the beginning to the present.

Directions: The address is 1200 Southwest Park Avenue.

Dates: Open year-round, except Mondays.

Fees: There is an admission charge.

For more information: Oregon History Center, 1200 Southwest Park Avenue, Portland, OR 97205. Phone (503) 222-1741.

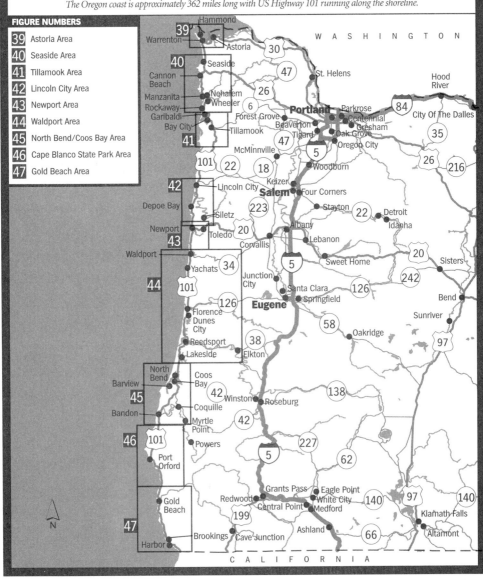

US Hwy. 101 in Oregon

The Oregon coast is approximately 362 miles long with US Highway 101 running along the shoreline.

FIGURE NUMBERS

39	Astoria Area
40	Seaside Area
41	Tillamook Area
42	Lincoln City Area
43	Newport Area
44	Waldport Area
45	North Bend/Coos Bay Area
46	Cape Blanco State Park Area
47	Gold Beach Area

U.S. Highway 101
In Oregon

The Oregon coast is some 362 miles long and its width is tucked between the Coast Range Mountains and the sparkling ocean. In some places the mountains tower directly above the surf. In other places they are a short distance inland. Either way, the coast is a place of awesome beauty, with wide, sandy beaches punctuated by frothy white surf. There are forests of tall trees. Grass and flowers grow in meadows. Animals range from tiny forest creatures that are weighed in ounces to gigantic whales that are weighed in tons.

The land here does not lend itself to large-scale industry. Once, logging and its associated industries provided an economic basis, but that has decreased. Some people still make a living in the woods, and at fishing, farming, and a few other occupations, but the economic foundation of the coast is welcoming visitors and seeing that they are comfortable and having a good time.

[*Above:* Sea stacks and rocky islands add character to the Northwest beaches]

US Highway 101 threads its way along the shoreline from one end of the state to the other. The highway rises near Olympia, Washington, skirts along the eastern and northern edges of the Olympic Peninsula, then parallels the Washington coast until it crosses the Columbia River to Astoria, Oregon. From there, it hugs the beach in a nearly straight line to California.

The highway has a different aspect in Oregon, however. In Washington it courses, for the most part, inland, often a dozen or more miles from the ocean and only occasionally running close enough to the ocean for travellers to see the water. In Oregon, the right-of-way snuggles against the coast. Only in a few places does it go inland more than a few miles, and in many places it is within sight of the beach and the water. Oregon has taken advantage of that by providing innumerable parks, recreation areas, heritage areas, natural areas, scenic viewpoints, and waysides, which it defines as small, isolated pieces of roadside land usually with parking, restrooms, and picnic tables. The state facilities are dotted all along the coast, sometimes so close that they adjoin each other. They provide a steady succession of opportunities for visitors to get off the highway to relax, eat a sandwich, and see the view, which very often is magnificent. The parks perform a more elaborate function, offering over-night camping and similar amenities. Any of the state facilities is likely to have access to the beach, either directly or over a trail. For more information contact the Oregon State Parks and Recreation Department, 1115 Commercial Street, Northeast, Salem, OR 97310-1001. Phone (503) 378-6305.

An unusual feature of Oregon State Parks are the yurts that are offered at many of the parks where camping is available. The yurts are domed tents similar to the shelters used over the centuries by natives in Mongolia. They have structural supports, plywood floors, lockable doors, and beds with mattresses. There is electricity, lighting, and heat. Cooking in the yurts is banned, but there are fire rings and picnic tables just outside

In addition to the state facilities, two national forests, the Siuslaw (*see* Siuslaw National Forest, page 325) and Siskiyou (*see* Siskiyou National Forest, page 341) offer attractions. Both have campgrounds and wilderness areas and the Siskiyou forest, in the far southwestern corner of the state, also has the Oregon Dunes National Recre-ation Area, a 32,000-acre area covering some 40 miles of beach. It is covered with sand dunes as high as a 400 feet (*see* Oregon Sand Dunes, page 327).

The route has innumerable services for visitors. For more sophisticated lodging the highway features a large assortment of motels and resorts that offer accommoda-tions ranging from just comfortable to luxurious.

US Highway 101 is not a high-speed freeway. For the most part it is a two-lane road with curves and hills. This is a route for people who have time to wander along at less than interstate highway speeds and enjoy the scenery. It is not necessary, however, to drive the entire distance on US 101. Along the way, there are at least eight state and national highways that connect US 101 with I-5, some 50 miles to the east on the other side of the Coast Range Mountains. That makes it relatively easy to get to and from the high-speed freeway and the low-speed highway. And those roads pass through some magnificent scenery, too.

Visitors can travel US 101 in a car in one day, but that makes for a hurried trip and forces travellers to skip many of the rewards the coastline has to offer. Two days allows drivers more opportunities to see, enjoy and learn about the coast; but to get the full benefit of the coast, it might be better to plan for at least a week of exploring by car.

But the automobile isn't the only means for traveling on the Oregon coast. An alternative is the **Oregon Coast Bike Route**. Much of it runs on the shoulder of US Highway 101 that is marked off specifically for bicycles. Where it is practical, the route veers off to less traveled roads that parallel the highway. The route totals 370 miles from Astoria on the Columbia River to Brookings near the California border and is marked by white-on-green signs. Campgrounds, restaurants, and commercial lodging are available along the way. Bicycles take more work and more time, obviously, but they also offer a more leisurely trip that gives a close-up view of the coast. For maps and pamphlets of the bike route, contact the Bikeway Program Manager, Oregon Department of Transportation, Transportation Building, Salem, OR 97310. Phone (503) 986-3556.

The Oregon Coast Trail, a hiking trail planned to go 360 miles from the Columbia River to California, the full length of the coast, is partly completed in segments along the coast. The completed portion crosses some 20 coastal state parks and recreation areas. For more information, contact the Oregon State Parks and Recreation Department, 1115 Commercial Street, Northeast, Salem, OR 97310-1001. Phone (503) 378-6305.

People

Modern Americans are not the first people to be attracted to the Oregon coast. Archeologists have tracked Indian occupation to between 8,000 and 9,000 years ago. When Europeans put in their appearance on the coast, they found diverse cultures with different languages and a variety of systems for coping with the environment. The people lived in small villages of a few houses on the beach or rivers, supporting themselves by the produce of the forest and the sea.

When the Europeans arrived, there was a serious culture clash, which led to the Rogue Indian Wars of the 1850s. The Indians were thoroughly defeated and left at the mercy of the new culture.

Rather than annihilate the defeated tribes or leave them to starve, the government created the 1 million acre Coast Reservation in 1855 for 24 different bands and tribes in the area between the Cascade Mountains and the coast from northern California to southern Washington. The 1860 census showed more than 3,000 Indians living on the reservation. The people of those groups, with many different languages and cultures, organized into a single organization called the Confederate Tribes of Siletz Indians and remained on the reservation under the jurisdiction of the Bureau of Indian Affairs while they became accustomed to the European culture.

Tribal members adopted the European's culture, many of them going into farming or logging, and in 1954 Congress, believing the members had been assimilated, terminated the Confederate Tribes of Siletz. After the termination, some of the reservation land was sold. Much of the rest of it became liable to taxation and eventually was lost to the Indians.

Members of the tribe remained in poverty and leaders petitioned Congress for help. In 1977 a law recognizing the Siletz as the Confederated Tribes of Siletz Indians was approved. In 1980 the government created a 3,666-acre reservation. With 3,000 enrolled members, the tribe is governed by an elected nine-member Tribal Council which controls tribal programs and funds. The council provides services from a central office in Siletz, Oregon and satellite offices in Portland, Salem, and Springfield. The service area is spread to tribal members in 11 counties of Western Oregon. Services include housing, health care, education, and job opportunities.

Among the businesses operated by the tribe are a hardwood lumber mill and a gambling casino. Cultural activities include powwows that feature competition Indian dancing, and displays of Native American arts and crafts. The largest of the powwows is held annually in Siletz during the second weekend in August. For more information, contact the Confederated Tribes of Siletz Indians, 201 Southeast Swan Avenue, Siletz OR 97380. Phone (800) 922-1399.

The mouth of the Columbia River, at the northern extreme of the Oregon Coast, actually was the center of the early European history of the Pacific Northwest. The first European to see the river was the Spanish explorer Bruno de Heceta, who sailed past the mouth in 1775. He was prevented from entering the river by the treacherous bar at its mouth, but he put it on his charts. In 1788 Captain John Meares became the last of a long list of seafarers who sailed past the Columbia River without finding it. He, however, did get close enough to name Cape Disappointment at the mouth. He chose that name because he decided the river he was looking for wasn't there.

Four years later Captain Robert Gray, the American seaman, explorer, and fur trader, found the river and actually crossed the treacherous bar to sail a short distance up the river, trading with the Indians as he went. Later that same year, English Navy Captain George Vancouver sent his lieutenant, William Broughton, to chart the lower 100 miles of the river. Vancouver published the charts and in 1805, 13 years after Broughton left, Lewis and Clark used his charts as they moved down the Columbia on the last leg of their epic journey across the continent by land. Lewis and Clark spent the winter a few miles from where Astoria is now. In 1811, John Jacob Astor's Pacific Fur Company established Astoria on the Columbia's southern bank. That was the first permanent European settlement west of the Mississippi River. Astoria is still here, a thriving little city where US Highway 101 enters Oregon, and where the Oregon coast begins.

Europeans' exploration on the lower part of the Oregon coast occurred at a much slower pace. In 1542 Captain Juan Rodriguez sailed up from Spain's Mexican settlements into what is now the southern portion of the Oregon coast. After that, a series of English, American, Spanish, and Russian seafarers made their way along the coast, seeking knowledge as well as fur, and the ever elusive Northwest Passage between Europe and Asia. A minor gold rush in the early 1800s brought some settlers to the Rogue River, near the southern end of the Oregon coast, but the California gold rush in 1849 had an even greater effect on Oregon. The gold hungry people who flocked to the San Francisco area during that bonanza created a heavy demand for lumber, food, and other commodities that Oregon, like Washington, was only too glad to fill.

The impetus of the 49er Gold Rush created an economic base that brought settlers to the coast. By 1913 the coast was becoming fairly well settled, so much so that the settlers began to affect the beauty and seclusion of the shoreline. To counter that development, Governor Oswald West and the state legislature adopted a measure declaring the beach to be a state road, thus restricting development. In the mid-twentieth century, someone fenced off a portion of the beach in front of his or her property. That raised such an outcry that Governor Tom McCall and the legislature adopted the Oregon Beach Bill in 1967 to declare that the beach is public property up to 16 feet above sea level. That means the entire, magnificently beautiful coast is open to be enjoyed by everyone for its entire, 362-mile length, from the Columbia River to the California border.

Whale Diet

Whale species differ in how and what they eat. Some are odontocetes, which means they have teeth. They feed primarily on fish, squid, and marine mammals. Others are baleen whales that, instead of teeth, have baleen plates or whalebones that hang down from their upper jaw. The plates overlap in the mouth and have stiff hairs, which sift thousands of tiny, shrimplike crustaceans and small fish out of the water to be swallowed for dinner.

Plants and Animals

The coast is free and open to nature, too. Fish, whales, and other sea animals swim in the offshore waters, just as they have for untold eons. Tidepools are filled with creatures such as Troschel's sea star (*Evasterias troschellii*) and strawberry anemone (*Corynactis califonica),* waiting for the incoming tide to bring them renewed sustenance. The creatures range from ugly to beautiful, but they all are fascinating, and

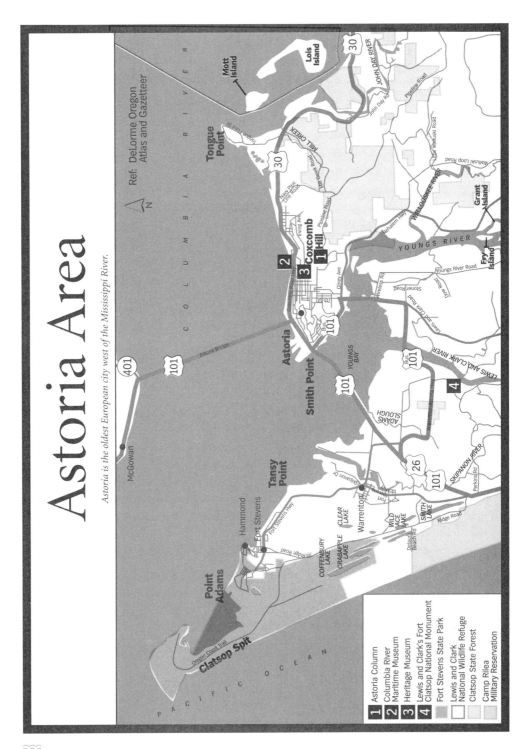

Astoria Area

Astoria is the oldest European city west of the Mississippi River.

Ref: DeLorme Oregon
Atlas and Gazetteer

1 Astoria Column
2 Columbia River
Maritime Museum
3 Heritage Museum
4 Lewis and Clark's Fort
Clatsop National Monument

Fort Stevens State Park

Lewis and Clark
National Wildlife Refuge
Clatsop State Forest
Camp Rilea
Military Reservation

when they are trapped in their tidepools, they are easy to find. Many forms of life including mole crabs (*Emerita analoga*) and California beach fleas (*Orchestoidea californiana*) inhabit the beaches. A little higher on the beach the sand may be home to plants such as yellow abronia (*Abronia latifolia),* beach silvertop (*Glenhia leiocarpa),* and the silky beach pea (*Lathyrus littoralis*).

Above the beach plants the forest begins, first, usually, with stately stands of sitka spruce, and inland from there, the classic Northwestern forest of western hemlock, Douglas fir, western redcedar and red alder. Meadows in the forest may display colorful flowers such as blue lupine, snowberry, fireweed, and beargrass. And the land here has residents such as elk, deer, cougar, bear, and coyote.

Astoria/Warrenton

[Fig. 39] These two closely neighboring towns mark where European-style civilization first arrived in the Pacific Northwest. Astoria, with 10,000 people, is the oldest city west of the Mississippi. It is near Fort Clatsop, the rudimentary fort where Lewis and Clark's Corps of Discovery stayed the winter of 1805-06 to wait for spring to open the snow-clad passes of the Rocky Mountains so they could go home.

Five years after Lewis and Clark left, John Jacob Astor sent two parties, one by sea around Cape Horn, the other by land, to open up the fur trade in the Northwest interior. They founded Astoria, which in a few years traded hands from American, to Canadian, and finally, to British fur companies. Nevertheless the fur companies sent fur traders deep into the interior of the new land to bring back not only furs but also detailed information on the geography, flora, and fauna of the new land. Astoria remained the headquarters of the fur trade, and thus, of the European culture in the Pacific Northwest until 1825, when George Simpson, governor of the Hudson's Bay Company, moved the company's headquarters 100 miles up the river and founded Fort Vancouver (*see* Fort Vancouver, page 245). The site of the original Fort Astoria is at the intersection of Fifteenth and Exchange streets in Astoria.

Astoria sits on the bank of the Columbia River, which flows softly toward the Pacific Ocean a few miles away. Where the river touches the ocean is the infamous Columbia Bar, which has the reputation of being the most dangerous river bar in the world. Some 200 vessels have been destroyed as they attempted to get over the bar on their way between the river and the ocean, leading sailors to call it the "Graveyard of Ships." Now there is a marked channel 600 yards wide and 5 miles long that guides vessels safely over the bar. Some 340 to 360 ships cross the bar each year as they go to and from ports along the Columbia. They go upriver as far as Portland, Oregon and Vancouver, Washington, but Astoria has always been closely associated with the sea, and many vessels call here, too.

Directions: Astoria/Warrenton are on US Highway 101, on the south side of the Columbia River.

For more information: Astoria-Warrenton Area Chamber of Commerce, PO Box 176, 111 West Marine View Drive, Astoria, OR 97103-0176. Phone (503) 325-6311.

ASTORIA COLUMN

[Fig. 39(1)] For a bird's eye view of Astoria, the endless ocean in front of it, the river beside it, and the hills of the land behind it, climb the stairs to the top of this landmark column high above the city. The column was built by the Great Northern Railroad and descendants of John Jacob Astor as a memorial to a 1926 cross-country railroad excursion. It is a 125-foot tall, thin, round structure at the top of Coxcomb Hill, 595 feet in elevation. A frieze on the outside depicts area history. Inside, the building is just wide enough to contain a circular iron staircase that is reminiscent of the stone stairs in Europe's ancient castles. The stairway goes up 164 steps to the lookout. From here the view includes a wide section of the gray Pacific Ocean that reaches to the far horizon. Below is a panoramic view of the town, nestled in its peninsula and looking out at the river where seagoing ships anchor.

Behind the town, the mountains and foothills are covered with evergreen forests, young trees in the foreground and more mature giants in the background. The view from the top of the Astoria Column is every bit as breathtaking as the 164 steps it takes to get there.

Directions: From downtown Astoria, turn off Marine Drive and go south on Sixteenth Street. Follow the signs to the tower at the top of the hill.

Activities: Scenic viewing.

Facilities: Parking lot, souvenir shop, landscaped garden.

Dates: Open year-round.

Fees: None.

For more information: Astoria/Warrenton Area Chamber of Commerce, 111 West Marine Drive, PO Box 176, Astoria, OR 97103-0176. Phone (800) 875-6807 or (503) 325-6311.

COLUMBIA RIVER MARITIME MUSEUM

[Fig. 39(2)] This fascinating museum explores some 200 years of nautical history in Oregon's coastal area. It covers lighthouses and shipwrecks, whaling, fishing, the merchant marine, and the U.S. Navy during the eras of sail, steam, and diesel. The exhibits inside the attractive modern building include the conning tower of the USS *Rasher*, a World War II submarine that was credited with sinking 22 enemy ships during its first five cruises. There are old fishing and U.S. Coast Guard vessels, and the bridge of a World War II destroyer. The "A Ship Named Astoria" exhibit traces the histories of three U.S. Navy ships that bore that name.

The Spanish history on Oregon's coast is depicted in a full-size model of the 52-foot schooner *Sonora*, which explored the coast in 1775. The model shows her construction, and contains murals depicting the hard life of the sailors who manned her. Smaller displays include porcelain that was traded in China for furs bought from Northwest Indians. Indian artifacts include a dugout canoe made by the Cathlamet Indians. An honored place in the museum is reserved for "Shark Rock" which is inscribed by the survivors of two shipwrecks, The *Shark* (*see* Cannon Beach, page 271) in 1846 and the *Industry* in 1865.

Outside the building, the retired 128-foot Coast Guard Lightship *Columbia* is tied up at a pier, looking much as she did when she was commissioned in 1950. She spent her career stationed off the mouth of the Columbia River, where her light and foghorn warned of the dangerous waters, until she was decommissioned and replaced by an automated navigational buoy in 1979. The *Columbia* now is a National Historic Landmark and much of it, both above and below deck, is open to the public.

Directions: From US Highway 30, also known as Commercial Street, in downtown Astoria, turn north on Seventeenth Street. Go 1 block and turn east on Marine Drive and enter the parking lot.

Activities: Historic studies and viewing museum exhibits.

Facilities: Wheelchair-accessible exhibits, research library, museum store, restrooms.

Dates: Open year-round.

Fees: An entrance fee is charged.

For more information: Columbia River Maritime Museum, 1792 Marine Drive, Astoria, OR, 97103. Phone (503) 325-2323.

HERITAGE MUSEUM

[Fig. 39(3)] This is one of three museums within a few blocks that are operated in conjunction with each other. It is housed in an impressive, two-story, Neoclassic building that once was Astoria's city hall. It is devoted to the history of the region, beginning with the Native Americans and going on to the early explorers, the pioneers, and the immigrants and settlers who contributed to the development of the community, each in their own turn. It provides a pleasant way to learn about the area's history and the people who lived it.

Directions: From US Highway 30, also known as Commercial Street, in downtown Astoria, turn south on Sixteenth Street and go about two blocks to the museum.

Activities: Historic studies and viewing museum exhibits.

Facilities: Historic exhibits, gift shop, restrooms.

Dates: Open year-round.

Fees: An entrance fee is charged.

For more information: Heritage Museum, 1618 Exchange Street, Astoria, OR 97103. Phone (503) 325-2203.

RESTAURANTS IN ASTORIA

Astoria is close to the sea both geographically and emotionally, so it is natural that its restaurants tend to feature seafood, but the visitor's choices also extend to meat, pastas, salads, and other items that appeal to American tastes.

Pier 11 Feed Store. 77 Eleventh Street. This restaurant occupies the building of a former feed store on a dock beside the Columbia River, and has views overlooking the river. The menu features seafood, steak, chicken, pasta, sandwiches, and salad. Reservations recommended. *Inexpensive. (503) 325-0279.*

Ship Inn. One Second Street. This seafood restaurant is popular for its sandwiches and fish and chips. It also features salads and English cuisine specialties. There is a view of the Columbia River. There is a cocktail lounge and special menus for children and senior citizens. *Inexpensive. (503) 325-0033.*

Cafe Uniontown. 218 West Marine Drive. This American cuisine café offers a menu with a wide variety, including seafood, pasta, and meat entrees. There is a cocktail lounge and children's menu. Reservations welcomed. *Inexpensive. (503) 325-8708.*

LODGING IN ASTORIA

Astoria offers places to stay ranging from large chain motels to small independents and bed and breakfasts.

Astoria Dunes Motel. 288 West Marine Drive. This modern, two-story motel has 58 rooms, some with views of the Columbia River. The rooms have coffee makers. There is a heated swimming pool and whirlpools. *Moderate. (503) 325-7111*

Crest Motel. 5366 Leif Erickson Drive. This 40-room motel is situated on a hillside overlooking the Columbia River, 4 miles east of the Columbia River Bridge on US Highway 30. The rooms are of various sizes, and there are two two-bedroom units. Most rooms have decks and views of the river. There is a patio, hot tub, and free continental breakfast. *Moderate. (503) 325-3141, or for reservations (800) 421-3141.*

Bayshore Motor Inn. 555 Hamburg Avenue. Some of the 77 rooms in this four-story motel have views of the bay. There is a heated swimming pool, whirlpools, and a sauna. Continental breakfast is free. *Moderate. (503) 325-2205.*

Clementine's Bed and Breakfast. 847 Exchange Street. This two-story, 1888, Italianate Victorian bed and breakfast on a downtown hillside has five guest rooms. It has attractive gardens and is within walking distance of the waterfront. Breakfast is free. *Moderate. (800) 521-6801. (503) 325-2005.*

LEWIS AND CLARK'S FORT CLATSOP NATIONAL MONUMENT

[Fig. 39(4)] When Lewis and Clark reached the camp on the north side of the Columbia in November 1804, they could see the breakers of the Pacific Ocean, and they knew they had reached their goal of finding a way across the continent from the Mississippi River. But they still faced the matter of getting back home with the information they had gathered. And before they could even start the journey back, they had to wait until spring cleared the snow from the Rocky Mountain passes they had to negotiate.

They stayed in the camp for 10 days, finding so little game that they were hungry all the time. Some Indians told them there was better hunting on the other side of the Columbia, so they went across and explored about 3 miles up the Lewis and Clark River where they found a place just above the riverbank. There they built Fort Clatsop, a 50-square-foot structure, with walls for security and rooms for shelter.

They arrived on December 8, and completed the fort on December 30. They stayed there until April 7, 1805. When they left they gave the fort to Chief Coboway of the Clatsop tribe, who had befriended them during their stay. The fort slowly deteriorated over the years, and when settlers reached the area they destroyed whatever was left.

The federal government established the location as the Fort Clatsop National Memorial in 1958, and the National Park Service built a replica of the fort on the original site, closely following the drawings and descriptions left by members of the Corps of Discovery. The 50-foot-square log stockade is located in a thick stand of pine trees. It consists of two rows of rooms that face each other. At each end there are log walls with gates, making a secure fort that could be defended against attack by either the elements or marauders.

The memorial includes a visitor center that has a theater, with movies and slide shows that depict the Corps of Discovery, its people, and what they discovered. There also are video presentations, and displays of the men and what they found on their long trip to this place and back.

Outside the visitor center, there is a trail past signs that point out some of the plants that Lewis and Clark described in the journals of their trip. Flora includes salmonberry (*Rubus specabilis*), Oregon crabapple (*Pyrus fusca)*, vine maple (*Acer cirinatum*), and thimbleberry (*Rubus parviflorus*), which Lewis and Clark described as "a shrub of which the natives eat the young sprouts."

The trail leads a few yards to the fort. By modern standards it is dank and uncomfortable, but to the Corps of Discovery, it was a haven that kept them warm and dry through the long winter. On March 23, 1806, two weeks before the explorers left the fort for the last time, Clark wrote, "At this place...we wintered and remained from the 7th Decr. (sic) 1805 to this day and have lived as well as we had a right to expect."

The structure has three rooms for the troops on one side of the tiny parade ground. On the other side is the room where Lewis and Clark lived and worked on their journals and reports. Next to their room were the guard shack and the meat room where the corps cured food for the long journey home. To the south of the captains' room is the room of Tousaint Charbonneau, his Shoshone Indian wife, Sacagawea, and their baby, Jean Baptiste. Charbonneau had been hired to guide the party, but his wife turned out to be a more important source of information and advice. During the summer, park staff members in period costume present living-history programs which portray the clothing, lifestyle, skills, and equipment of the Corps of Discovery.

At the rear of the fort, a small door opens on a trail to a nearby spring that probably was the major source of water for the fort. Beyond the spring, the trail leads a short distance to the river and a small cove where the party's five canoes were kept. From there, the trail loops a few hundred yards through a thick evergreen forest to a picnic area and the parking lot.

Directions: The entrance road to the national memorial is on US Highway 101, 5 miles southwest of Astoria.

Activities: Historical studies, short hike, picnicking.

Facilities: Historical displays, visitor center, restrooms, picnic sites.

Dates: Open year-round.

Fees: An admission fee is charged.

Closest town: Astoria.

For more information: Fort Clatsop National Monument, Route 3, Box 604-FC, Astoria, OR 97103. Phone (503) 861-2471.

FORT STEVENS STATE PARK

[Fig. 39] This large state park includes the remains of Fort Stevens, which originally was built during the Civil War when the army feared England might enter the war on the side of the Confederates and invade the Columbia River. The British in the Northwest had been pushed back to Canada by the influx of American settlers, and it seemed likely they would like to retake that territory.

The British never came, but there were other threats, and the fort grew over the years into a major coast artillery fortification with concrete emplacements and large guns. It was manned by the army until the end of World War II, when it was decommissioned because modern technology made that kind of installation obsolete. One indication of that obsolescence was that, despite the nearby guns of Fort Stevens, the beach south of the jetty became the first place in the United States to be shelled by an enemy since the War of 1812. The shell was fired by a Japanese submarine far out at sea during World War II and landed harmlessly just inland of the beach, near the intersection of Ridge Road and Ocean View Cemetery Road. The fort did not return fire because the submarine was beyond the range of its largest guns.

After the war the land was turned over to the Oregon State Park system, which maintains it in much of its original condition. A museum on the grounds tells the story.

In addition to the remains of the fortifications and hundreds of campsites, there are 14 miles of pedestrian/bicycle trails with wildlife viewing areas. The rim of the park includes many miles of beach, where the rolling waves of the Pacific Ocean meet the currents of the Columbia River, and a major feature of the beach is the remains of the *Peter Iredale*, a four-masted, steel sailing ship. On October 25, 1906 it became one of the hundreds of vessels to run afoul of the treacherous breakers of the Columbia Bar. All hands escaped to safety, but the ship lodged high on the beach just a few feet from where the road is now. Part of it was dismantled for scrap, and the rest is pretty well rusted, but the skeleton is still there, telling the story of the treacherous bar sailors call the Graveyard of Ships.

A feature of the park is the 8-mile-long jetty, which was built to extend the spit that protects the mouth of the Columbia from the ocean's currents. The jetty was built by bringing huge rocks from a quarry on the Washington side of the river and dumping them into the ocean. Railroad cars moved on tracks built over the top of the jetty, carrying rocks to the end, and dumping them into the ocean. When the rocks reached the right elevation, the rails were extended over the new addition, and the process began all over again. The tracks are gone now, but at high tide the ocean still smashes against the rocks in an awesome display of spray and foam.

The jetty is covered by stands of evergreen trees that are stunted by the harsh, seaside growing conditions, but grow so thickly that it is difficult to walk through the stands. The forest is interspersed by profuse growths of beach grass and shrubs. There are several places to access the jetty and the beach, from the park's Ridge Road.

Directions: Take US Highway 101 approximately 10 miles west of Astoria to the park at the mouth of the Columbia River.

Activities: Historic viewing, hiking, biking, camping, boating, swimming, wildlife viewing, beachcombing, picnicking, fishing.

Facilities: Campsites: 171 with full hookup, 304 with electrical connections, 43 tent, 15 yurts, 4 group tents, 7 hiker/biker, restrooms, showers, picnic sites, boat basin, trails.

Dates: Open year-round.

Fees: Fees are charged for camping and day use.

Closest town: Astoria, 10 miles.

For more information: Oregon State Parks Information Center, 2501 Southwest First Avenue, Suite 100, Portland, OR 97201. Mailing address, PO Box 500, Portland, OR 97207. Phone (800) 551-6949 or Fort Stevens State Park, phone (503) 861-1671. For reservations, phone Reservations Northwest, (800) 452-5687.

RED ALDER
(Alnus rubra)

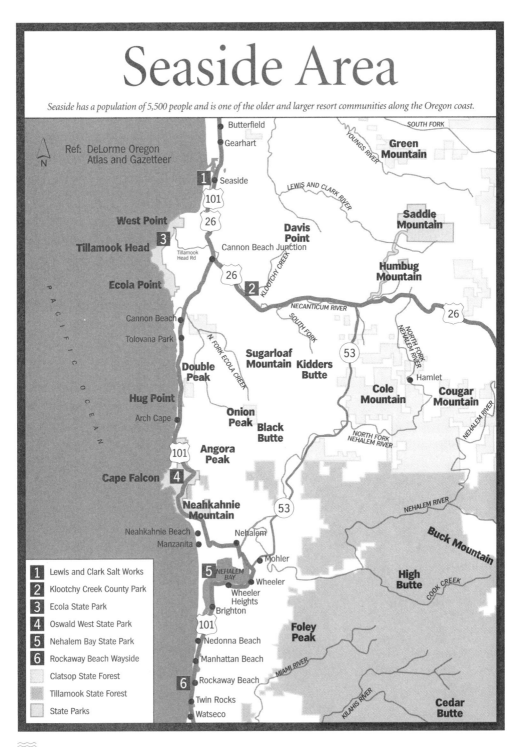

Seaside Area

Seaside has a population of 5,500 people and is one of the older and larger resort communities along the Oregon coast.

Ref: DeLorme Oregon Atlas and Gazetteer

N

Butterfield
Gearhart

SOUTH FORK

YOUNGS RIVER

Green Mountain

1 Seaside

101

26

West Point

Tillamook Head

26

LEWIS AND CLARK RIVER

Davis Point

Cannon Beach Junction

Tillamook Head Rd

Saddle Mountain

KLOOTCHY CREEK

2

Humbug Mountain

Ecola Point

Cannon Beach
Tolovana Park

NECANTICUM RIVER

SOUTH FORK

53

26

NORTH FORK NEHALEM RIVER

Sugarloaf Mountain

Kidders Butte

Double Peak

N. FORK ECOLA CREEK

Hamlet

Cole Mountain

Cougar Mountain

Hug Point

Arch Cape

Onion Peak

Black Butte

NORTH FORK NEHALEM RIVER

NEHALEM RIVER

101

Angora Peak

Cape Falcon **4**

Neahkahnie Mountain

53

NEHALEM RIVER

Buck Mountain

Neahkahnie Beach
Manzanita

Nehalem

Mohler

5 NEHALEM BAY

Wheeler

Wheeler Heights
Brighton

High Butte

COOK CREEK

101

Foley Peak

Nedonna Beach

Manhattan Beach

MIAMI RIVER

6 Rockaway Beach

Twin Rocks

Watseco

KILAHIS RIVER

Cedar Butte

PACIFIC OCEAN

1 Lewis and Clark Salt Works
2 Klootchy Creek County Park
3 Ecola State Park
4 Oswald West State Park
5 Nehalem Bay State Park
6 Rockaway Beach Wayside
　 Clatsop State Forest
　 Tillamook State Forest
　 State Parks

Seaside

[Fig. 40] This city of some 5,500 people is one of the older and larger resort communities along the Oregon coast. It has historically been involved with tourism, because it is only about 100 miles from heavily populated Portland, and US Highway 26 makes it easy for Portlanders to travel down to enjoy the ocean.

The attractions for tourists are largely tied to the broad, sandy beach that fronts the town, and that is the location of many of its tourist amenities. A wide, paved walkway called the Promenade runs for 1.6 miles along the beachfront, and is a popular place for strolling, jogging, and bicycle riding beside the Pacific. Kite flying is a popular activity on the beach, as are beachcombing and admiring the interesting creatures left stranded in the tidepools when the tide recedes. Among those creatures are giant green anemones (*Anthopleurav xanthogrammica*), hermit crabs (*Pagurus* spp.), purple sea urchins (*Strongylocentrotus purpuratus*), black turban snails (*Tegula funebralis*), and checkered periwinkle (*Littorina scutulata*).

Other activities include crabbing, fishing, golf, horseback riding, swimming, and, in the cove at the south end of town, surfing.

The small **Seaside Aquarium** at Second Avenue and the north end of the Promenade has numerous displays of the creatures that inhabit the ocean a few feet to the west. Among the features is a 30-foot tank of seals that cavort in their pool while they wait for a handout from visitors. Near the end of the tank there is a waterspout and a towel dispenser where visitors can rinse their hands when they finish feeding the seals. Other displays at the aquarium include California moray (*Gymnothorax mordox)* and blue perch (*Embiotoca lateralis)*. Blue perch can be caught by surf fishing, using marine worms as bait.

The small **Seaside Museum** at 570 Necanicum Street displays some of the history of Seaside and the surrounding area. Exhibits include items from the Clatsop Indians that once lived in this area, as well as a working Linotype type setting machine from the 1920s. The restored 1912 **Butterfield Cottage** behind the main building depicts a typical beach cottage of the era.

Directions: Seaside is on US Highway 101, 17 miles south of Astoria.

Activities: Strolling, jogging, and bicycle riding on the Promenade, kite flying, beachcombing, crabbing, fishing, golf, horseback riding, swimming, and surfing.

Facilities: Food, lodging, museum, aquarium and theater.

Dates: Open year-round.

Fees: Fees are charged for goods and services.

For more information: Seaside Convention and Visitors Bureau, 415 First Avenue, Seaside, OR 97138. Phone (888) 306-2326 or (503) 738-3097.

▨ RESTAURANTS IN SEASIDE

Restaurants in Seaside cater to the tourist trade as well as to local tastes.

Shilo Inn Restaurant. 30 North Prom. This restaurant in the Shilo Inn Resort on the oceanfront offers seafood, beef, and chicken dishes and features a Sunday brunch. There is a cocktail lounge. Reservations recommended. *Inexpensive.* *(503) 738-8481.*

Doogers Seafood and Grill. 505 Broadway. This popular family restaurant offers a wide selection of seafood as well as other dishes, sandwiches, and salads. There is a children's menu, and beer and wine are available. *Inexpensive.* *(503) 738-3773.*

LODGING IN SEASIDE

As a resort town, Seaside has a large selection of lodging places.

Seashore Resort Motel. 60 North Prom. This three-story, 54-room motel is on the Promenade, one block from downtown, and most rooms have ocean views. There is a heated swimming pool, whirlpool, and sauna, and access to the beach. Four of the units have two bedrooms. *Moderate to expensive.* *(503) 738-6368.*

The Inn at the Shore. 2275 South Prom. With 18 rooms, this three-story inn on the Seaside Promenade has rooms and suites. There are oversized jetted Jacuzzi tubs, gas fireplaces, patios, balconies, ocean views, bike rentals, and an espresso bar. Six of the units have two bedrooms. *Moderate to expensive.* *(800) 713-9914* or *(503) 738-3113.*

Riverside Inn Bed and Breakfast. 430 South Holladay Drive. This bed and breakfast has 11 guest rooms, and features a front deck facing the Necanicum River. The rooms have private baths and private entrances. *Moderate.* *(800) 826-6151* or *(503) 738-8254.*

Gilbert Inn Bed and Breakfast. 341 Beach Drive. This 1892 Queen Anne Victorian home is decorated in antique, period furnishings and has 10 guest rooms, each decorated in period style. Baths are private. The home is one block from either the beach or downtown shops. *Moderate.* *(503) 738-9770.*

LEWIS AND CLARK SALT WORKS

[Fig. 40(1)] One of the major tasks of Lewis and Clark's Corps of Discovery while they spent the winter of 1805-06 at Fort Clatsop was to preserve meat the hunters provided for the long journey back to civilization. To do that, they needed salt. The captains assigned a crew of three men, Joseph Fields, George Gibson, and William Brattan, to obtain the salt from sea water. The three hiked about 10 miles from Fort Clatsop to where Seaside is now and built a rock structure to hold five iron pots. They built a fire under the pots, filled them with sea water, and boiled it until there was nothing left but a residue of salt in the bottom of the pots. They started on January 2, 1806, and kept the pots boiling until February 20 when they had five bushels of salt.

The original rock structure disappeared after the Corps of Discovery left the area, but Jenny Michel, whose Indian father had watched the boiling process when he was a boy, identified the site in 1900. He pointed it out to her when she was a child.

A reproduction based on Lewis and Clark's description of the rock structure is now located on the site. It is based in concrete and obviously has little relationship to the original, but it, nevertheless, is an illustration of the explorers' ingenuity.

Directions: The salt works is a few feet from the beach at the foot of Lewis and Clark Way in Seaside.

Dates: Open year-round.

Fees: None.

For more information: Seaside Convention and Visitors Bureau, 415 First Avenue, Seaside, OR 97138. Phone (888) 306-2326 or (503) 738-3097.

KLOOTCHY CREEK COUNTY PARK

[Fig. 40(2)] US Highways 26 and 101 run together from Astoria to about 3 miles south of Seaside, where 101 goes straight to parallel the coastline to the other end of Oregon and 26 veers to the east to head toward Portland. On Highway 26, about 2 miles from where the highways separate, is Clatsop County's Klootchy Creek Park. A few feet off the north side of the highway, a short boardwalk leads to the base of the largest sitka spruce tree (*Picea sitchensis*) in the United States. This 750-year-old giant is 216 feet high and 17 feet in diameter, with a circumference of 56 feet and a crown spread of 93 feet.

If this giant were harvested, it would yield enough material to make 100 tons of paper, or enough lumber for six homes. Sitka spruce is a light, strong wood that is valued for building boats, and during the World War I era it was used extensively in manufacturing aircraft.

The giant tree is surrounded by the stumps of its siblings that were cut down many years ago. The area is now covered with mature alder that has grown up to replace the old spruces.

Directions: Klootchy Creek Park is on the north side of US Highway 26, about 2 miles east of US Highway 101.

Activities: Nature study, fishing.

Facilities: Boardwalk trail, drinking water, toilets.

Dates: Open year-round.

For more information: Seaside Convention and Visitors Bureau, 415 First Avenue, Seaside, OR 97138. Phone (888) 306-2326 or (503) 738-3097.

Cannon Beach

[Fig. 40] On September 10, 1846, the 300-ton U.S. Navy schooner *Shark* grounded on the Columbia River Bar as she was trying to leave the river. The vessel stuck fast and began to break up so the crew abandoned the ship and went to shore in small boats, with all hands saved. On the beach one of the sailors engraved a record of the shipwreck on a large rock. Nineteen years later, the same rock also was engraved by one of the seven survivors of the *Industry*, which was wrecked on the same shoals. The rock now is on display in the Columbia River Maritime Museum in Astoria (*see* Columbia River Maritime Museum, page 262).

When the *Shark* broke up, part of the deck carrying the capstan and a cannon floated south on the currents until it beached, and the cannon was deposited on the shore. Over the years a community grew at that spot and became known as Cannon Beach. A duplicate cannon, made of moldings of the original, is now displayed beside US Highway 101 just south of Hug Point, which is just south of Cannon Beach.

The city of Cannon Beach, with about 1,200 people, is probably best known for its beautiful, wide beach and for Haystack Rock, which, at 235 feet high, is one of the world's largest monolithic rocks. It lies off the beach with several smaller rocks, called the Needles, nearby. Brooding Haystack Rock is dark brown. Its sheer cliffs rise out of the sea to an off-center, pointed top, which is covered with bright green growth. It is a natural wonder that attracts viewers from many distant places.

At the Cannon Beach there is 9 miles of wide, walkable surface. Kite flying is a popular activity here. Wildlife includes shorebirds such as tufted puffins (*Fratercula cirrhata*), pelagic cormorants (*Phalacrocorax pelagic*), pigeon guillemots (*Epphus columba*), and herring gulls (*Larus argentatus*). Tidepools are home to limpets, starfish, crabs, anemones, and sculpins.

Downtown, the town carefully cultivates an earth-toned, rustic look that is designed to encourage strolling among the quaint shops, which include glass blowing and crafts. The community's **Cannon Beach Coaster Theater**, 108 North Hemlock, (503) 436-1242, offers concerts, stage plays, and other entertainment year-round

Les Shirley City Park at the foot of Fifth Street is reputedly the place where William Clark and 11 men of the Lewis and Clark expedition went to look for a whale that local Indians told them had been stranded on the beach. If the men came here, the park is the southernmost point reached by the Corps of Discovery. The carcass of the whale had been stripped by the time Clark's party arrived, but he bought 300 pounds of blubber from the natives. When he returned to Fort Clatsop with it, there was a feast, and Lewis wrote that he "thanked the hand of Providence" for

LIMPET
(Diodora aspera)

being kinder to them than He was to Jonah for "having sent this monster to be swallowed by us in stead (sic) of swallowing of us as jonah's (sic) did." The park also has signs explaining the interaction of the sea water and fresh water in the nearby Ecola Creek estuary.

Directions: Cannon Beach is on US Highway 101, about 25 miles south of Astoria.

HERMIT CRAB
(Pagurus samuelis)

Activities: Beach walking, shopping, kite flying, tidepool observation.

Facilities: Food, lodging, beach, viewpoints.

Dates: Open year-round.

For more information: Cannon Beach Information Center, 207 North Spruce Street, PO Box 64, Cannon Beach, OR 97110. Phone (503) 436-2623

RESTAURANTS IN CANNON BEACH

There are a variety of places to eat among the shops in downtown Cannon Beach.

Bistro. 263 North Hemlock. This restaurant maintains the town's rustic atmosphere, and offers a menu featuring pasta and seafood. Reservations recommended. *Inexpensive. (503) 436-2661.*

Heather's. 271 North Hemlock. This little restaurant is located off Hemlock Street behind a mini mall, and serves gourmet lunches of exotic soups and sandwiches. *Inexpensive. (503) 436-9356.*

LODGING IN CANNON BEACH

Stephanie Inn. 2740 South Pacific. With 50 rooms this beachfront inn has an atmosphere reminiscent of New England. Nicely decorated rooms and suites have views of the ocean or mountains. Rooms have fireplaces, decks, and whirlpools. The dining room serves breakfast in the morning. Dinner is by reservation only. Cocktails are available. *Expensive. (800) 633-3466 or (503) 436-2221.*

Hallmark Resort Cannon Beach. 1400 South Hemlock. This full-service resort on a bluff overlooking the ocean has 136 rooms and suites. Most have fireplaces and balconies with views, some have kitchens, and 36 have spas. There are two heated swimming pools and a gift shop. *Moderate to expensive. (888) 448-4449* or *(503) 436-1566.*

Schooner's Cove. 188 North Larch. This two-story, 30-unit motel fronts the beach and offers one-and two-bedroom units. There are kitchens, balconies, and hot tubs. *Moderate to expensive.* *(800) 843-0128* or *(503)* 436-2300.

ECOLA STATE PARK

[Fig. 40(3)] This pleasant park boasts a 6-mile segment of the Oregon Coast Trail (*see* Oregon Coast Trail, page 257), as well as a hike-in camp. There are nice views, including the spectacular Tillamook Rock Lighthouse on a small island off the shore. There is access to the beach over several trails through thick stands of conifer trees. During the spring and summer, sea lions can be seen on rocks off the coast and whales can be seen at sea. A short distance from the park Ecola Point provides spectacular, and much photographed, panoramic views of Cannon Beach, Haystack Rock, and the Coast Range Mountains.

Directions: The park is 2 miles north of Cannon Beach on the road to Tillamook Head.

Activities: Hiking, beach walking, picnicking, fishing.

Facilities: Trails, picnic tables, viewpoints and group picnic facilities.

Dates: Open year-round.

Fees: A day-use fee is charged.

Closest town: Cannon Beach, 2 miles.

For more information: Oregon State Park Information Center, 2501 Southwest First Avenue, Suite 100, Portland, OR 97201. Mailing address, PO Box 500, Portland, OR 97207. Phone (800) 551-6949. Or Nehalem Bay State Park, phone (503) 368-5943. Group picnic facilities may be reserved by calling Reservations Northwest, (800) 452-5687.

OSWALD WEST STATE PARK

[Fig. 40(4)] This large state park lies on both sides of US Highway 101. On the west side, there is a parking lot that gives access to a mildly undulating but reasonably straight 0.5-mile trail through typical, very beautiful forest to the beach. Near the end, the trail forks, with the right fork going down to the Cape Falcon Beach and the other fork leading to a pleasant cove with a sandy beach. Both places are beautiful.

On the east side of the highway, the park has 28 walk-in campsites on short trails. Wheelbarrows are provided for carrying camping gear to the campsites.

Directions: The park is on US Highway 101 approximately 35 miles south of Astoria.

Activities: Hiking, camping, fishing, beach walking, picnicking.

Facilities: Campsites, trails, picnic tables, viewpoints.

Dates: Open year-round.

Fees: Fees are charged for camping.

Closest town: Manzanita, 5 miles.

For more information: Oregon State Park Information Center, 2501 Southwest

First Avenue, Suite 100, Portland, OR 97201. Mailing address PO Box 500, Portland, OR 97207. Phone (800) 551-6949.

NEHALEM BAY STATE PARK

[Fig. 40(5)] This large park is in the shadow of Neahkanie Mountain, and also has access to a long stretch of ocean beach. There are 277 electrical campsites, 12 yurts, a hiker/biker camp, 17 horse campsites with corrals, and six primitive campsites in a fly-in camp next to an airstrip. There is a large meeting hall, a 2-mile loop bicycle trail, a 6-mile horse trail, and 1.5 miles of hiking trail. The beach is popular for kite flying, beachcombing, fishing, and wind surfing.

The park is close to Manzanita, population 450, and Nehalem, population 250, both of which are charming places where the 1920s architecture is reminiscent of earlier, quieter times.

Directions: On Highway 101, about 10 miles south of Manzanita Junction.

Activities: Camping, picnicking, fishing, hiking, bicycling, horseback riding, beach walking, boating.

Facilities: Yurts, wheelchair-accessible restrooms, showers, picnic tables, view-points airstrip, campsites, corrals, meeting hall, trails.

Dates: Open year-round.

Fees: Fees are charged for camping and for day use.

Closest town: Manzanita, 10 miles.

For more information: Oregon State Park Information Center, 2501 Southwest First Avenue, Suite 100, Portland, OR 97201. Mailing address, PO Box 500, Portland, OR 97207. Phone (800) 551-6949. Or Fort Stevens State Park, phone (503) 861-1671. For reservations, phone Reservations Northwest, (800) 452-5687.

ROCKAWAY BEACH WAYSIDE

[Fig. 40(6)] This little wayside has a place to park and a short trail leading to the beach. It is a good place to pause and enjoy the beach before following US Highway 101 as it veers inland for a time to pass through Tillamook.

Directions: On Highway 101 about 10 miles south of Nehalem.

Activities: Beach walking, picnicking.

Facilities: Trail to beach, picnic sites.

Dates: Open year-round.

Fees: None.

Closest town: Nehalem, 10 miles.

For more information: Oregon State Parks and Recreation Center, 2501 Southwest First Avenue, Suite 100, Portland, OR 97201. Mailing address, PO Box 500, Portland, OR 97207. Phone (800) 551-6949.

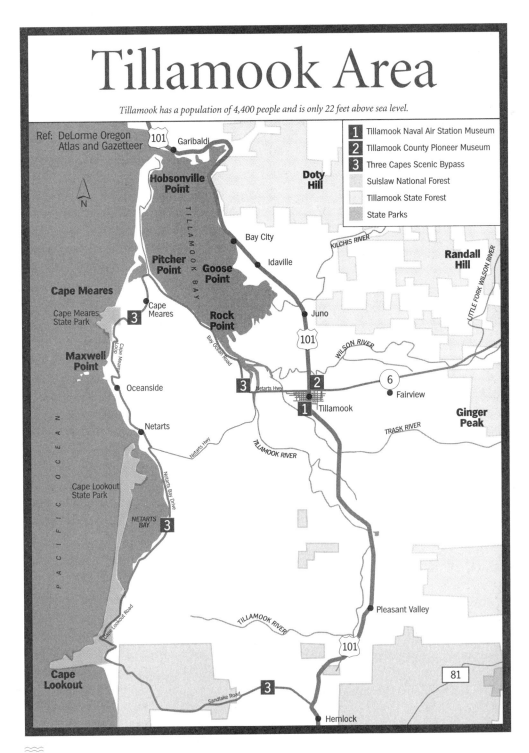

Tillamook Area

Tillamook has a population of 4,400 people and is only 22 feet above sea level.

Ref: DeLorme Oregon Atlas and Gazetteer

1	Tillamook Naval Air Station Museum
2	Tillamook County Pioneer Museum
3	Three Capes Scenic Bypass
	Suislaw National Forest
	Tillamook State Forest
	State Parks

Tillamook

[Fig. 41] With some 4,400 people, this little town has more of an agrarian atmosphere than most communities on the Oregon section of US Highway 101. It is only 22 feet in elevation, but it is back away from the beach, and the character of the land changes from the coastal forest to rolling green farmland. The economy here is based on agriculture, as well as tourism. Tillamook County, with 1,115 square miles, has about 149 dairy farms where large numbers of cows graze peacefully in pleasant, green pastures. It is not unusual to see wild elk grazing beside the cattle during the winter, when the elk are forced out of the mountains by the weather.

Much of the milk given by those cows is destined for the community's cheese makers, such as the **Tillamook County Creamery Association Cheese Factory,** 4175 US Highway 101, phone (503) 842-4481. The factory welcomes visitors who can watch the cheese making process through windows to the factory work area.

For more information: Tillamook Chamber of Commerce, 3705 Highway 101 North, Tillamook, OR 97141. Phone (503) 842-7525.

RESTAURANTS IN TILLAMOOK:

Tillamook Cheese Factory and Visitors Center. 4175 Highway 101 North. This nook in the Tillamook County Creamery Association Cheese Factory Building is popular for its ice cream straight from the source, as well as the accompanying cafe-style snack bar. *Inexpensive. (800) 542-7290 or (503) 815-1300.*

Wee Willie Restaurant. 6060 Whiskey Creek Road West. This place is popular with visitors and local folk alike, partly for its hamburgers and sandwiches but also for its fresh baked bakery goods. *Inexpensive. (503) 842-6869.*

LODGING IN TILLAMOOK

There are lodging facilities for tourists in and near Tillamook.

MarClair Inn. 11 Main Avenue. This 47-unit motel is nicely decorated. There are six suites with full kitchens, and there is a sauna and whirlpool. *Moderate. (503) 842-7571.*

Western Royal Inn. 1125 North Main. A two-story motel with 40 rooms, this establishment also offers 12 two-bedroom units. *Moderate. (800) 624-2912 or (503) 842-8844.*

TILLAMOOK NAVAL AIR STATION MUSEUM

[Fig. 41(1)] After a Japanese submarine shelled Fort Stevens on the northwest corner of Oregon early in World War II, the U.S. Navy began patrolling the water off the coast in earnest. Airplanes were fine for surveying the area, but slow-moving blimps were even better, so the Navy established five bases for them along the coast. One was on the airport just outside of Tillamook. The huge airships here were responsible for patrolling the ocean between Northern California and the Strait of Juan De Fuca.

The two huge hangars that were built to house the blimps are said to be the largest all-wood, clear-span structures ever built. The base was decommissioned in 1946. One of the hangars, 1,000 feet long and 296 feet wide, still stands and is used as an aviation museum. Exhibits include blimps and some 40 World War II aircraft, such as the American P-51 Mustang, the German Messerschmidt ME-109, and the English Spitfire MK-8, all in operating condition. Photographs and material dealing with World War II air history also are on display.

Directions: On Highway 101, 2 miles south of Tillamook, the entrance is at a flashing light, where an A-4 airplane is displayed on a pole.

Activities: Aviation history studies.

Facilities: Aviation displays, restrooms.

Dates: Open year-round.

Fees: An admission fee is charged.

Closest town: Tillamook, 2 miles.

For more information: Tillamook Naval Air Station Museum, 6040 Hangar Road, Tillamook, OR 97141. Phone (503) 842-1130.

TILLAMOOK COUNTY PIONEER MUSEUM

[Fig. 41(2)] This museum has three floors of exhibits depicting the natural and human history of the region. Among them are wildlife dioramas, a mineral and rock collection, and exhibits illustrating military, pioneer, and logging history. A donkey steam engine, used to move harvested logs, is on exhibit in the building, and a logging railroad steam engine is on display outside.

Directions: Located at 2106 Second Street.

Dates: Open year-round.

Fees: An admission fee is charged.

For more information: Tillamook County Pioneer Museum, 2106 Second Street, Tillamook, OR 97141. Phone (503) 842-4553.

THREE CAPES SCENIC BYPASS

[Fig. 41(3)] This 25-mile bypass loops off US Highway 101 from Tillamook to some magnificent shoreline and, eventually, back to US Highway 101. It begins by running through some back roads of Tillamook, then parallels the broad expanse of Tillamook Bay. At 3 miles from Highway 101, it reaches the **Bayocean Spit Dike**. A 1-mile, gravel road on the dike goes to a recreation site where crabbing, clamming, and fishing are permitted, but the 200 species of birds that frequent this quiet nook are protected by game laws.

Beyond the Bayocean Spit Dike, the Three Capes Scenic Bypass Road passes a forest of tall western red alder trees and reaches Cape Meares and the **Cape Meares**

State Scenic Viewpoint, about 10 miles from Tillamook. The cape is named after Captain John Meares, who charted it in 1788 during his voyage of discovery for the newly independent American nation. A national wildlife refuge offshore does not have recreational or educational facilities but, nevertheless, thousands of birds can be seen and admired from the mainland as they pass through on their spring migrations.

In the spring and summer, look for pigeon guillmots (*Cepphus columba*), common murres (*Uria aalge*), tufted puffins (*Fratercula cirrhata*), and several species of cormorants (*Phalacrocorax* spp.). In the summer and fall the area is likely to be visited by California brown pelicans (*Pelecanus occidentalis*), sooty shearwaters (*Puffinus griseus*), Heermann's gulls (*Larus heermanni*), and Caspian terns (*Sterna caspia*). During the winter the cape may play host to surf scoters (*Mellanitta perspicillata*), black scoters (*Melanitta nigra*), Pacific loons (*Gavia pacifica*), red-throated loons, (*Gavia stellata*), horned grebes (*Podiceps auritus*), and red-necked grebes (*Podiceps grisegena*).

The waters here also attract marine mammals such as seals, sea lions, porpoises, and orcas or killer whales.

Wildlife is not the only natural attraction here. A 650-foot trail goes up to a bluff high above the ocean, where there are magnificent views of the white surf rushing to shore. A few feet from the bluff, the Octopus Tree testifies to the effect ocean winds have on growing things. The tree, an old sitka spruce, does not grow straight up like ordinary spruces. Instead, six immense branches grow horizontally out of the huge base several feet above the ground for as much as 30 feet before turning upward. The result is a tree with an strange octopus-like shape. Unusual wind currents coming over the bluff a few feet away apparently caused the strange shape.

The State Scenic Viewpoint's other trail goes a short distance down to the Cape Meares Lighthouse, which is perched on a high bluff that juts out above the sea. The lighthouse was commissioned on January 1, 1890, decommissioned in 1963, and opened to the public in 1980. Inside, there are steep circular stairs that go up 15 steps to the bottom of the light, then another 10 steps to the light itself. There visitors can look out the windows at the vast ocean that the light once made a little less dangerous. Below the light, the waves batter the shore and the rocks off the cape. The battering has eroded a hole completely through one of the house-sized rocks, so you can see daylight on the other side. There are picnic tables at the scenic viewpoint, but that is about all the amenities available.

About 3 miles farther on, the Three Capes Bypass Road reaches the little community of Oceanside, and just to the west of the downtown area a side road leads to the **Oceanside Beach Wayside**. The wayside is beside a rocky beach, and provides good views of the ocean in front and the village houses perched on steep slopes to the rear.

About 8 miles south of Oceanside, the Three Capes Bypass Road passes the **Cape Lookout State Park**, which offers camping—38 full hookup sites, 1 electrical

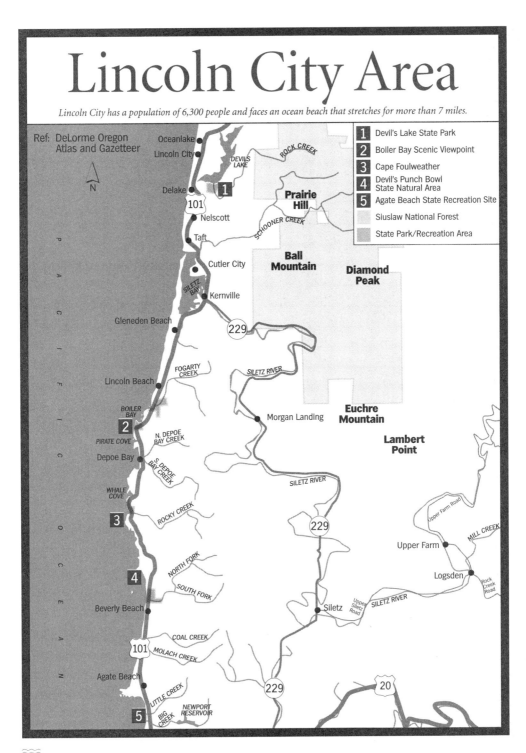

Lincoln City Area

Lincoln City has a population of 6,300 people and faces an ocean beach that stretches for more than 7 miles.

Ref: DeLorme Oregon Atlas and Gazetteer

N

1 Devil's Lake State Park
2 Boiler Bay Scenic Viewpoint
3 Cape Foulweather
4 Devil's Punch Bowl State Natural Area
5 Agate Beach State Recreation Site
Siuslaw National Forest
State Park/Recreation Area

Oceanlake
Lincoln City
ROCK CREEK
DEVILS LAKE
Prairie Hill
Delake
101
Nelscott
SCHOONER CREEK
Taft
Ball Mountain
Diamond Peak
Cutler City
SILETZ BAY
Kernville
Gleneden Beach
229
FOGARTY CREEK
SILETZ RIVER
Lincoln Beach
BOILER BAY
Morgan Landing
Euchre Mountain
2
PIRATE COVE
N. DEPOE BAY CREEK
Lambert Point
Depoe Bay
S. DEPOE BAY CREEK
WHALE COVE
SILETZ RIVER
3
ROCKY CREEK
229
Upper Farm Road
MILL CREEK
Upper Farm
4
NORTH FORK
SOUTH FORK
Logsden
Rock Creek Road
Beverly Beach
Siletz
Upper Siletz Road
SILETZ RIVER
COAL CREEK
101
MOLACH CREEK
229
20
Agate Beach
LITTLE CREEK
NEWPORT RESERVOIR
5
BIG CREEK

PACIFIC OCEAN

connection site, 176 tent sites, 10 yurts, 4 group campsites, and a hiker/biker camp. There is a 2.5-mile trail to the tip of the cape, where, with a little luck, whales can be seen, especially by people who brought good optical equipment. There are restrooms available in the park. For more information about the park, contact the Oregon State Park Information Center, PO Box 500, Portland, OR 97207. Phone (800) 452-6949. For campground reservations, phone (800) 452-4687.

About 5 miles past the Cape Lookout State Park facilities, the Three Capes Bypass Road goes past some sand dunes, then a side road that leads westward to the **Sand Lake Recreation Area** and dune buggy riding. The bypass road continues to Cape Kiwanda and the **Cape Kiwanda State Natural Area**, where there is more whale watching, as well as wave-frazzled cliffs, sand dunes, and tidepools.

From there, the bypass road veers eastward and rejoins US Highway 101.

Directions: In Tillamook, go west on Third Street (State Highway 6) then north on Bayocean Street to the Three Capes Bypass Road.

Activities: Wildlife viewing, lighthouse visit, camping, picnicking, hiking, dune buggy riding, beach walking, crabbing, clamming, fishing.

Facilities: Scenic viewpoints, lighthouse, trails, campground, picnic tables, restrooms.

Dates: Open year-round.

Fees: Fees are charged for camping and day use at Cape Lookout State Park.

For more information: Tillamook Chamber of Commerce, 3705 Highway 101 North, Tillamook, OR 97141. Phone (503) 842-7525.

Lincoln City

[Fig. 42] This city of 6,300 people faces an ocean beach that stretches for more than 7 miles. There is a wealth of places to go and things to do. One way to get to the beach is to turn off US Highway 101 onto Logan Road, which leads to the **Roads End State Recreation Site**, where there is a large parking lot, grand views of the ocean, and the nearby green and brown headlands. The recreation area offers access to the beach and its rolling white breakers. Beachcombing and long walks on the sand are among the possibilities here. Picnic tables and restrooms are available near the parking lot.

Near the south end of the city, a right turn off US Highway 101 onto Southwest Fifty-First Street leads 0.3 mile to the **D River Wayside** and a parking lot, with a view to the opposite bank where sea lions gather. The wayside has restrooms and access to the beach.

A wide beach at Lincoln City is popular for examining tidepools, beachcombing, watching shorebirds, kite flying, and whale watching.

A long shopping area along US Highway 101 includes the Factory Stores at

Lincoln City where more than 60 manufacturing outlets offer their goods at steep discounts. Other stores along the highway include specialty shops that offer items such as beach bikes, antiques, kites, and handicrafts. A casino operates near the intersection of US Highway 101 and Logan Road.

Directions: Lincoln City is on US Highway 101, 39 miles south of Tillamook.

For more information: Lincoln City Visitor and Convention Center, 801 Southwest US Highway 101, Lincoln City, OR 97367. Phone (800) 452-2151.

RESTAURANTS IN LINCOLN CITY

There is a large assortment of food choices available to visitors in Lincoln City.

Kyllo's Seafood and Grill. 110 Northwest First Court. This seafood specialty house also serves chicken and beef dishes, as well as sandwiches. There is an ocean view and a patio. Cocktails and a children's menu are available. *Inexpensive. (541) 994-3179.*

Dory Cove. 5819 Logan Road. The menu here emphasizes seafood, but it also offers hamburgers and sandwiches. Beer and wine are available, and there are special menus for children. *Inexpensive. (541) 994-5180.*

Kernville Steak and Seafood House. 186 Siletz Highway. This restaurant with a rustic atmosphere and a river view offers generous dishes of American cuisine. There is a cocktail lounge. Reservations recommended. *Inexpensive. (541) 994-6200.*

LODGING IN LINCOLN CITY

There are many choices of places to sleep in this tourist-oriented community.

Siletz Bay Lodge. 1021 Southwest Fifty-First Street. A four-story hotel with 44 units, this lodge faces the Siletz Bay beach. All rooms have bay or ocean views and some rooms have balconies. Three rooms have whirlpools. Continental breakfast is free and there is a gift shop. *Expensive. (888) 430-2100 or (541) 996-6111.*

Ashley Inn. 3430 Northeast Highway 101. A three-story motel with 74 large rooms, Ashley Inn has a swimming pool, and offers choices such as whirlpools and suites. *Moderate. (541) 996-7500.*

Inn at Spanish Head. 4009 Southwest Highway 101. This large, 10-story, oceanfront condominium has 120 rooms. There is an ocean view, beach access, and varied accommodations. A heated swimming pool and whirlpool are available, and there is a gift shop and a dining room where cocktails are available. *Expensive. (800) 452-8127 or (541) 996-2161*

DEVILS LAKE

[Fig. 42] This 682-acre lake, on the inland side of Lincoln City, was formed when sand dunes and beach debris dammed the D River not far from where it enters the ocean. Ancient Indians believed that a huge creature in the lake devoured people who attempted to cross in canoes. There are parks along the shore offering boat launches, fishing, camping, swimming, picnicking, and restrooms. Fish in the lake include rainbow trout (*Oncorhynchus mykiss*).

The lake is frequented by many species of birds, such as American coot (*Fullica americana*), gadwall (*Anas strepera*), American wigeon (*Anas americana*), mallard, (*Anas platyrhynchos*), and fish-eating birds such as the bald eagle (*Haliaeetus leucocephalus*) and cormorant (*Phalacrocorax spp.*).

Directions: In Lincoln City, on US Highway 101.

Activities: Fishing, swimming, boating, picnicking.

Facilities: Parks, boat launch, beach, picnic tables, restrooms.

Dates: Open year-round.

Fees: There are fees at the parks.

For more information: Lincoln City Visitor and Convention Bureau, 801 Southwest US Highway 101, Lincoln City, OR 97367. Phone (800) 452-2151 or (541) 994-8378.

DEVIL'S LAKE STATE PARK

[Fig. 42(1)] This park on Lincoln City's Devils Lake has 29 full hookup campsites, 3 electrical sites, 55 tent sites, 10 yurts, and a hiker/biker camp. Aside from offering visitors opportunities for camping, boating, and fishing, the park features outstanding opportunities for seeing waterfowl, especially from designated places in the day-use area.

Directions: In Lincoln City, go east on Northeast Sixth Drive from US Highway 101.

Activities: Camping, boating, fishing, wildlife viewing, picnicking.

Facilities: Campground, picnic sites, wheelchair-accessible restrooms, showers, trailer tank dump, boat moorage slips, fishing dock, boat launch.

Dates: Open year-round.

Fees: There are fees for camping and day use.

For more information: Oregon State Park Information Center, 2501 Southwest First Avenue, Suite 100, Portland, OR 97201. Mailing address PO Box 500, Portland, OR 97207. Phone (800) 551-6949. For reservations, phone Reservations Northwest (800) 452-5687.

Depoe Bay

[Fig. 42] This little town of about 1,000 people has its business district directly on the ocean, where a little 6-acre natural harbor provides a haven for small vessels. The harbor is said to be the smallest natural navigable harbor in the world. Natural tubes, called Spouting Horns, in the volcanic rocks of the intertidal area jut out from the mainland. During stormy weather the waves of incoming tides shoot up the tubes and erupt out of fissures in fountains of spray that sometimes shoot as high as 60 feet in the air, and have been known to reach US Highway 101.

Charter boats based on Depoe Bay's docks take passengers out to sea for whale watching cruises of varying lengths. A resident pod of gray whales stays nearby for 10 months of the year. Fishing charters also are available. Several state waysides on US Highway 101 near Depoe Bay provide magnificent scenic views, picnicking, fishing, and whale watching.

A seawall along the waterfront provides downtown businesses with spectacular ocean views.

Directions: On US Highway 101, about 10 miles north of Newport.

For more information: Depoe Bay Chamber of Commerce, 70 Northeast Highway 101, PO Box 21, Depoe Bay, OR 97341. Phone (541) 765-2889.

RESTAURANTS IN DEPOE BAY

Sea Hag Restaurant and Lounge. 58 East Highway 101. This popular and long-established restaurant offers seafood and steak dishes, and a salad bar. There are children's and senior citizen's menus, and a cocktail lounge. *Inexpensive. (541) 765-2734.*

LODGING IN DEPOE BAY

Despite its small size, visitors can find a place to sleep in Depoe Bay.

Gracie's Landing Bed and Breakfast Inn. 235 Southeast Bay View Avenue. This B&B has the flavor of nineteenth century inns in the eastern sections of the country. There are 13 guest rooms with a patio or balcony; nine of them have fireplaces and four have whirlpools. There is a library, parlor, and breakfast room with a view of the waterfront. *Expensive. (800) 228-0448* or *(541) 765-2322.*

BOILER BAY STATE SCENIC VIEWPOINT

[Fig. 42(2)] This is one of many state waysides scattered along US Highway 101 in Oregon. They are small, attractive places, some with little more than a view of the ocean, others with amenities such as trails to the beach, picnic tables, or restrooms. Boiler Bay State Scenic Viewpoint is especially interesting because it has a history. In 1910, the steam schooner *J. Marhoffer* exploded off the coast, killing one person. The ship's boiler drifted to shore here and can still be seen at very low tide where it is caught up on the rocks. That wreckage gives the wayside its name.

The wayside is on a pleasant, grassy headland beside a tiny bay, where breakers smash against rocky outcrops sending spray high into the air. A small waterfall cascades into the sea. This is a fine place for a picnic lunch, but be careful about what you take from the beach. This is an intertidal research area, where a special permit is required to collect certain marine invertebrates.

Directions: On Highway 101, 1 mile north of Depoe Bay.

Activities: Scenery viewing, beach walking, picnicking, whale watching.

Facilities: Picnic tables, restrooms.

Dates: Open year-round.

Fees: None.

Closest town: Depoe Bay, 1 mile.

For more information: Oregon State Park Information Center, 2501 Southwest First Avenue, Suite 100, Portland, OR 97201, mailing address PO Box 500, Portland, OR 97207. Phone (800) 551-6949.

CAPE FOULWEATHER

[Fig. 42(3)] Captain James Cook who explored the world for the British named this cape. On March 1, 1778, he was sailing east from the Sandwich Islands (Hawaii) in a storm, and this was his first sighting of the American mainland he called New Albion. He and one of his crew members, John Ledyard, a corporal of Marines, both published reports on the land, and that led other sailors to venture here in search of furs. That was the beginning of European influence on the Northwest Pacific Coast.

The name Cape Foulweather is apt. Winds of 100 miles an hour are not unusual here. There is a trail to a gift shop on the bluff above the sea where the view is especially spectacular and the winds blow freely.

Directions: About 5 miles south of Depoe Bay on the Otter Crest Highway, off US Highway 101.

Activities: Scenery viewing.

Facilities: Gift shop.

Dates: Open year-round.

Fees: None.

Closest town: Depoe Bay, 5 miles.

For more information. Depoe Bay Chamber of Commerce, 70 Northeast Highway 101, PO Box 21, Depoe Bay, OR 97341. Phone (541) 765-1889.

DEVIL'S PUNCH BOWL STATE NATURAL AREA

[Fig. 42(4)] This wayside on a bluff above the ocean offers a spectacular view down to where part of the roof of a large cave collapsed, leaving a gaping hole where waves wash in. A trail to the beach begins at the north end of the parking lot. The beach has a large intertidal area, rich in marine plants and animals. Here, breakers smash against the rocky shore, sending white spray high into the air.

Directions: West of Highway 101, 8 miles north of Newport.

Activities: Viewing scenery, beachcombing, picnicking.

Facilities: Trail to beach, picnic tables, restrooms.

Dates: Open year-round.

Closest town: Newport, 8 miles.

Fees: None.

For more information: Oregon State Parks and Recreation Center, 2501 Southwest First Avenue, Suite 100, Portland, OR 97201. Mailing address, PO Box 500, Portland, OR 97207. Phone (800) 551-6949.

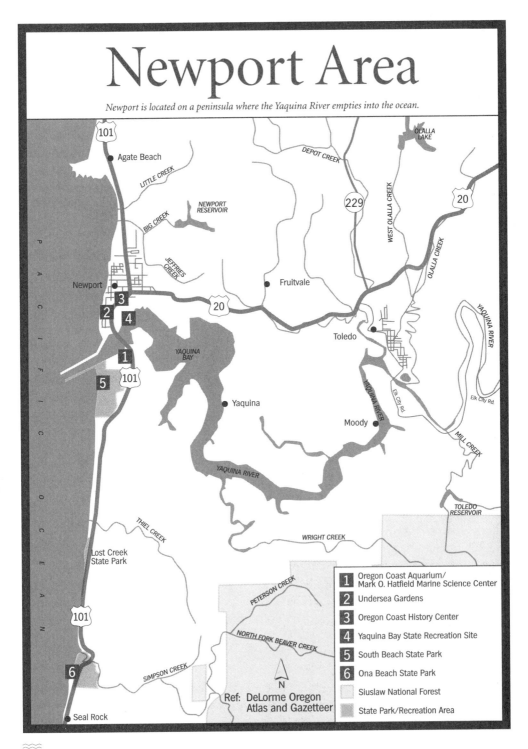

Newport Area

Newport is located on a peninsula where the Yaquina River empties into the ocean.

1 Oregon Coast Aquarium/
Mark O. Hatfield Marine Science Center

2 Undersea Gardens

3 Oregon Coast History Center

4 Yaquina Bay State Recreation Site

5 South Beach State Park

6 Ona Beach State Park

Siuslaw National Forest

State Park/Recreation Area

Ref: DeLorme Oregon
Atlas and Gazetteer

▩ AGATE BEACH STATE RECREATION SITE/YAQUINA HEAD OUTSTAND-ING NATURAL AREA

[Fig. 42(5)] The major attraction of this recreation site is the view of the Yaquina Head Lighthouse, which is on a headland that juts a mile or so into the ocean. The recreation site offers an awesome view of the headland and its lighthouse. At 93 feet, the lighthouse tower is higher than any other on the Oregon coast. It stands on a bluff, putting it 162 feet above sea level. It was illuminated for the first time in 1873. Now automated, it still sends out a beam to aid navigation of vessels at the entrance to Yaquina Bay, as well as those along the coast.

The lighthouse is part of the **Yaquina Head Outstanding Natural Area** which is 0.25 mile from the recreation area and is managed by the federal Bureau of Land Management. The natural area also features views of resident harbor seals, nesting shorebirds, and wildflowers. With a little luck, visitors may see migrating gray whales. There also are trails to tidepools, and during the spring, BLM interpreters provide information about tidepools and the creatures that live there. More than 500,000 people visit the natural area and its interpretive center each year.

Directions: The recreation area is off US Highway 101, 1 mile north of Newport. The natural area entrance is on US Highway 101, about 0.25 mile north of the recreation area parking lot.

Activities: Fishing, beach walking, nature study.

Facilities: Lighthouse, nature exhibits, picnic sites.

Dates: Open year-round.

Fees: There is an entry fee at the lighthouse.

Closest town: Newport, 1 mile.

For more information: Oregon State Park Information Center, 2501 Southwest First Avenue, Suite 100, Portland, OR 97201. Mailing address PO Box 500, Portland, OR 97207. Phone (800) 551-6949. Or Yaquina Head Outstanding Natural Area, (541) 574-3100.

Newport

[Fig. 43] This city of some 10,200 persons is one of the larger communities on the Oregon coast. It has been in the tourist business for more than a century and has become expert at it. Located on a peninsula where the Yaquina River empties into the ocean, the city is the location of institutions that specialize in ocean sciences, as well as art and history (*see* Hatfield Marine Science Center, page 289; Oregon Coast Aquarium, page 289; Undersea Gardens, page 290; and Oregon Coast History Center, page 290.

Commercial fishing is a traditional industry in Newport, and the eastern end of the community's bay front is the mooring place for a quaint fishing fleet. The bay front stretches along a three-block area of Bay Boulevard, and is part of a picturesque business district of early twentieth century buildings that house shops and services. There are charter boats for fishing and whale watching. Among the bay front attractions are the *Ripley's Believe it or Not* show, a wax museum, docks, oddity shops, and an immense old waterwheel.

Winter storms expose agates on the beach in the Newport area, especially along the beach called, appropriately, Agate Beach. Agates are quartz stones formed naturally when oxides, silicas, and metals combine. The chamber of commerce provides free pamphlets on agate hunting.

Fresh seafood is available in fish markets at **Nye Beach** on the west side of US Highway 101, about a mile north of the bay front. Also at Nye Beach is the city's performing arts center, which attracts audiences to performances such as plays, concerts, and ballets by both local and visiting performers. For information on performances, phone (541) 265-2787.

Directions: Newport is at the intersection of US Highway 101 and US Highway 20.

Activities: Fishing, whale watching, shopping, agate hunting, boating, crabbing, clamming, bird-watching, beach walking.

Facilities: Boat harbor, food, lodging, performing arts center, educational facilities.

For more information: Greater Newport Chamber of Commerce, 555 Southwest US Highway 101, Newport, OR 97365. Phone (541) 265-8801 or (800) 262-7844.

RESTAURANTS IN NEWPORT

Restaurants tend to offer seafood in this little city, where fishing and tourism are a major part of the history.

Canyon Way. 1216 Southwest Canyon Way. This popular, informal restaurant's menu offers a wide variety including pasta, steak, fresh seafood, chicken, and prime rib. Cocktails and a children's menu are available, and there is a patio. Reservations recommended. *Inexpensive. (541) 265-8316.*

The Whale's Tale. 452 Southwest Bay Boulevard. Fresh seafood and shellfish are among the dishes served at this comfortable little restaurant that is decorated with the work of local artists. Beer and wine are available. *Inexpensive. (541) 265-8660.*

LODGING IN NEWPORT

With more than 100 years experience caring for visitors, Newport has a wide variety of lodging choices.

The Whaler Motel. 155 Southwest Elizabeth Street. This three-story motel has 73 rooms. There is an ocean view and beach access. Six rooms have fireplaces, refrigerators, and microwaves, and 12 have refrigerators and microwaves only. There is a heated swimming pool. Continental breakfast is free. *Moderate to expensive. (541) 265-9261 or for reservations, (800) 433-9444.*

Embarcadero Resort Hotel and Marina. 1000 Southeast Bay Boulevard. This three-story inn has 85 guest rooms and condos on Newport's historic bay front. Fifty of the units have kitchens, and some have fireplaces and balconies overlooking Yaquina Bay. There is a heated pool, saunas, whirlpools, and a restaurant. The marina offers fishing, crabbing, and charter boats, as well as a bait shop. *Moderate to expensive. (800) 547-4779 or (541) 265-8521.*

OREGON COAST AQUARIUM

[Fig. 43(1)] This large institution provides visitors with a comprehensive understanding of Oregon's sea and shore. It consists of a large structure with specific rooms for traditional aquarium displays such as wetlands, sandy shores, rocky shores, and coastal waters, each with live specimens of the creatures that live in those habitats. The building, which once housed Keiko, the whale that starred in the movie *Free Willy*, also has a Whale Theater, a gift shop, a book store, and a cafeteria.

Outside the building are four outdoor exhibits of creatures that live where the sea meets the land. They include separate exhibits of seals, sea lions, sea otters, and a giant octopus. There is an open ocean exhibit, and one of the largest aviaries of seabirds in the nation. There also is a nature trail with viewing platforms above Yaquina Bay and, at the end of the trail, a children's playground.

Directions: On the south side of the Yaquina Bay Bridge in Newport, turn west off US Highway 101 at the South Beach exit and follow the signs to the aquarium.

Activities: Wildlife studies, hiking.

Facilities: 40,000 square feet of exhibits with 2,000 species of fish, birds, and mammals from the Pacific Northwest, cafe, restrooms, and gift shop.

Dates: Open year-round.

Fees: An entrance fee is charged.

For more information: The Oregon Coast Aquarium, 2820 Southeast Ferry Slip Road, PO Box 2000, Newport, OR 97305. Phone (541) 867-3474.

MARK O. HATFIELD MARINE SCIENCE CENTER

[Fig. 43(1)] This research-teaching institution provides facilities for more than 300 researchers from state and federal institutions. They study a multitude of subjects such as fisheries, aquaculture, water quality, marine biology, botany, microbiology, zoology, and oceanography.

But fascinating exhibits and displays for the lay public accompany the academic features of the center. Subjects include shellfish, demonstrations of scientific methods, evolution, and recordings and interpretation of the sounds whales make to communicate with each other. There are many videos and a movie theater. The exhibits and programs make science seem both human and interesting. This is a great place for children, and buses full of them come.

Directions: On the south side of the Yaquina Bay Bridge in Newport, turn west off US Highway 101 at the South Beach Exit, and go to the end of OSU Drive.

Activities: Wildlife and scientific studies.
Facilities: Exhibits, theater, restrooms.
Dates: Open year-round.
Fees: None, but donations are accepted.
For more information: Hatfield Marine Science Center, Marine Science Drive, Newport, OR 97365. Phone (541) 867-0100.

UNDERSEA GARDENS

[Fig. 43(2)] This establishment in downtown Newport is popular with families and provides close-up views of marine plants and animals through large, underwater windows. It is oriented toward tourists, with more emphasis on entertainment and less on education than the nearby Oregon Coast Aquarium. Underwater exhibits are seen through subsurface windows in their natural setting. Scuba-diving shows are presented through the day.
Directions: 250 Southwest Bay Boulevard in Newport.
Activities: Close-up viewing of underwater marine life.
Dates: Open year-round.
Fees: An entrance fee is charged.
For more information: Undersea Gardens, 250 Southwest Bay Boulevard, Newport, OR 97365. Phone (541) 265-2206.

OREGON COAST HISTORY CENTER

[Fig. 43(3)] This museum is operated by the Lincoln County Historical Society and is housed in a log cabin, which contains exhibits of native American objects, early maritime, farming, logging activities, and shipwrecks in the Newport area. Adjacent to the museum is the 1895 Victorian Burrows House, which contains furniture and clothing of the era.
Directions: 545 Southwest Ninth Street in Newport.
Dates: Open year-round.
Fees: None.
For more information: Oregon Coast History Center, 545 Southwest Ninth Street, Newport, OR 97365. Phone (541) 265-7509.

YAQUINA BAY STATE RECREATION SITE

[Fig. 43(4)] This pleasant and interesting site is located where the north bank of Yaquina Bay meets the Pacific Ocean. It is an attractive area of expansive green lawn at the edge of a high bluff above both the bay and the sea. It looks down on the side of a breakwater that marks the jetty on the north side of the ships' channel to the bay. Beyond the channel is the graceful shape of US Highway 101's long Yaquina Bay Bridge. On the west side, the view is past the frothy white breakers far out to sea. Boats shuttle through the ships' channel on their way between bay and sea.

High on a second bluff above the recreation site is the historic Yaquina Bay Lighthouse, which is the second oldest standing lighthouse on the Oregon coast. The lighthouse has had an on again off again career. It was built in 1871, then replaced by a brighter Yaquina Head Lighthouse 4 miles to the north in 1873. The original light was closed then and largely abandoned for 14 years. Then in 1888, it became living quarters for members of the U.S. Army Corps of Engineers who were building the north jetty at Yaquina Bay. In 1906, it became living quarters for a crew of the U.S. Life Saving Service, which later became the U.S. Coast Guard. The crew stayed until 1933. Eventually, the structure was turned over to the state, which restored the building in the 1970s. In 1975, the lighthouse was opened to the public as a museum, and in 1996 it was relighted to shine a low-intensity beam some 5 miles out to sea, resuming the function for which it was built well over a century earlier.

The lighthouse structure includes the stately, beautiful, 1880s Cape Cod-style home where the lightkeeper, Charles H. Pierce, lived with his wife and seven of their nine children. Because the light operated for only three years, the Pierces were the only people to live there until the lighthouse became quarters for the Corps of Engineers, except, perhaps, for a ghost that is said to be a resident.

The light is in a 40-foot tower above the two-story living quarters that now is a museum of household items from the 1880s. The downstairs includes a kitchen with a coal stove and a hand pump that took water from a cistern that collected rain water from the roof. The upstairs has four bedrooms. Narrow, iron, circular stairs go up from the second floor to a tiny office and to the light itself. Both are closed to the public. The basement has a gift shop and a video room.

Directions: The entrance to the Yaquina Bay State Recreation Site is on the west side of US Highway 101 just north of the Yaquina Bay Bridge.

Activities: Beach walking, fishing, picnicking, hiking.

Facilities: Picnic sites, trails, historic lighthouse, hiking trails, restrooms, and picnic tables.

Dates: Open year-round.

Fees: None, but donations are accepted at the lighthouse.

For more information: Oregon State Park Information Center, 2501 Southwest First Avenue, Suite 100, Portland, OR 97201. Mailing address, PO Box 500, Portland, OR 97207. Phone (800) 551-6949.

SOUTH BEACH STATE PARK

[Fig. 43(5)] This interesting park has facilities for team sports such as volleyball and basketball courts, in addition to the trails and campsites that are the primary attractions of most state parks. But that doesn't mean there is a shortage of the usual facilities. The campground has 232 electrical hookup sites, six primitive sites, 16 yurts, hiker/biker camping, and three areas for tent-camping groups. A 1.75-mile nature trail has signs with descriptions of the local natural features, which include a

Elk

Elk (*Cervus elaphus*) can be seen in many places along the coast of the Pacific Northwest. They are magnificent, cow-sized animals some 7 to 8 feet long plus a tail of 4 to 6 feet. Adults are mostly solid brown or tan while fawns have white spots that help with camouflage. Elk can sometimes be seen on farm pastures, grazing beside the cattle.

thick forest of sitka spruce and other evergreen trees that have been stunted and misshapen by the strong prevailing winds of the ocean. The Yaquina Bay Jetty can be reached by a 2.75-mile trail through the vegetation. The jetty offers nice views of Yaquina Bay and the Yaquina Bay Lighthouse.

Directions: The campground is on US Highway 101, 176 miles south of Astoria and 2 miles south of Newport.

Activities: Camping, hiking, beach walking, picnicking, biking, fishing.

Facilities: Campsites, yurts, showers, trails, trailer dump station, wheelchair accessible restrooms.

Dates: Open year-round.

Fees: Fees are charged for camping.

Closest town: Newport, 2 miles.

For more information: Oregon State Park Information Center, 2501 Southwest First Avenue, Suite 100, Portland, OR 97201. Mailing address, PO Box 500, Portland, OR 97207. Phone (800) 551-6949.

ONA BEACH STATE PARK

[Fig. 43(6)] This pleasant, grassy state park is adjacent to tidewater flats and also to Beaver Creek, where there is a boat launch on the east side of US Highway 101. There is no camping, but boating, swimming, and picnicking are popular here. There is access to the ocean beach.

Directions: On US Highway 101, 8 miles south of Newport.

Activities: Boating, fishing, picnicking, swimming, beach walking.

Facilities: Boat launch, picnic tables.

Dates: Open year-round

Fees: None.

Closest town: Newport, 8 miles.

For more information: Oregon State Park Information Center, 2501 Southwest First Avenue, Suite 100, Portland, OR 97201. Mailing address, PO Box 500, Portland, OR 97207. Phone (800) 551-6949.

SEAL ROCK STATE RECREATION SITE

[Fig. 44(1)] This wayside is adjacent to the town of Seal Rock and its small business district, which offers jewelry, ceramics, and wooden sculptures carved with chain saws. In the 1880s the town was the terminus for the Corvallis and Yaquina Bay

Wagon Road. The townsite was platted in 1887, and a large hotel beckoned beach-loving tourists, but the wagon road gave way to more modern means of transportation, depriving Seal Rock of its position as a terminal for visitors.

The state recreation site has nice views of large offshore rock formations, and on the beach there are tidepools whose occupants can be examined at low tide. A trail through wind-stunted evergreens leads to the beach.

Directions: On US Highway 101, 10 miles south of Newport.

Activities: Fishing, beach walking, tidepool study, fishing, picnicking.

Facilities: Picnic sites, trail.

Dates: Open year-round.

Fees: None.

Closest town: Seal Rock.

For more information: Oregon State Park Information Center, 2501 Southwest First Avenue, Suite 100, Portland, OR 97201. Mailing address, PO Box 500, Portland, OR 97207. Phone (800) 551-6949.

ELK
(Cervus elaphus)
The Northwest coast is home to the largest elk population in North America. An estimated 5,000 to 7,000 live on the Olympic Peninsula.

Waldport Area

Waldport is on the south shore of Alsea Bay and has a population of 1,600 people.

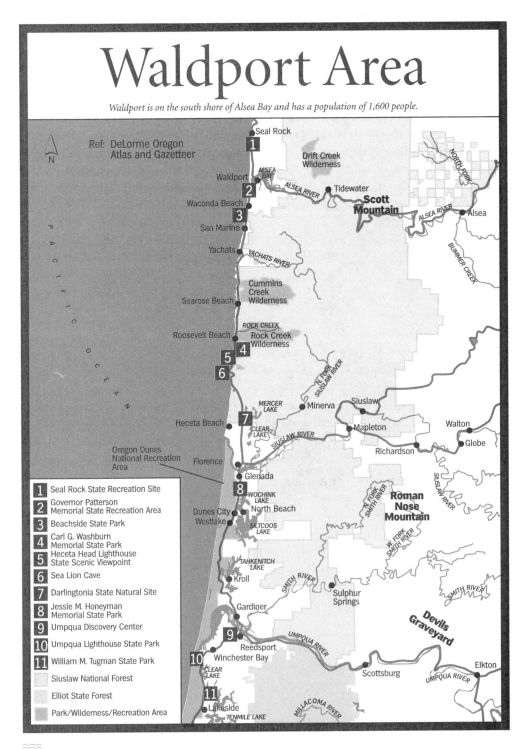

Ref: DeLorme Oregon
Atlas and Gazetteer

N

Seal Rock
1
Drift Creek
Wilderness

NORTH FORK

Waldport
ALSEA
BAY
2
ALSEA RIVER
Tidewater
**Scott
Mountain**

Waconda Beach
3
ALSEA RIVER
Alsea

San Marine

BUMMER CREEK

Yachats
YACHATS RIVER

Cummins
Creek
Wilderness

Searose Beach

ROCK CREEK

Roosevelt Beach
4
Rock Creek
Wilderness

5
6
N. FORK
SIUSLAW RIVER

MERCER
LAKE
Minerva
Siuslaw

Walton

Heceta Beach
7
CLEAR
LAKE
SIUSLAW RIVER
Mapleton
Globe

Oregon Dunes
National Recreation
Area
Florence
Richardson

Glenada
8
WOCHINK
LAKE
N. FORK
SMITH RIVER
SIUSLAW RIVER
**Roman
Nose
Mountain**

Dunes City
Westlake
North Beach

SILTCOOS
LAKE

W. FORK
SMITH RIVER

TAHKENITCH
LAKE

Kroll
SMITH RIVER
Sulphur
Springs
**Devils
Graveyard**

Gardiner

9
UMPQUA RIVER
Reedsport
10
Winchester Bay
CLEAR
LAKE
Scottsburg
UMPQUA RIVER
Elkton

11
Lakeside
TENMILE LAKE
MILLACOMA RIVER

1 Seal Rock State Recreation Site

2 Governor Patterson
Memorial State Recreation Area

3 Beachside State Park

4 Carl G. Washburn
Memorial State Park

5 Heceta Head Lighthouse
State Scenic Viewpoint

6 Sea Lion Cave

7 Darlingtonia State Natural Site

8 Jessie M. Honeyman
Memorial State Park

9 Umpqua Discovery Center

10 Umpqua Lighthouse State Park

11 William M. Tugman State Park

Siuslaw National Forest

Elliot State Forest

Park/Wilderness/Recreation Area

PACIFIC OCEAN

Waldport

[Fig. 44] This little town of 1,600 people once was the location of thriving wood products and fish-canning industries, but now it is primarily a low-key tourist attraction. It is on the south shore of Alsea Bay, and the shore on both sides of the bay offers a choice of sandy or rocky beaches. The beach is popular for agate hunting, crabbing, and clamming. The business district includes the ranger station of the U.S. Forest Service's Waldport Ranger District and the Drift Creek Wilderness (see Siuslaw National Forest, page 325). The bay is popular for saltwater fishing, and the streams and lakes attract freshwater anglers.

Directions: On US Highway 101, 15 miles south of Newport.

Activities: Fishing, crabbing, clamming, agate hunting, hiking, shopping.

Facilities: Shops, forest ranger station.

For more information: Waldport Chamber of Commerce, 280 Alsea Way, Waldport, OR 97394. Phone (541) 563-2133.

LODGING IN WALDPORT

Alsea Manor Inn. 190 Southwest US Highway 101. This two-story motel has 16 units, including one with two bedrooms. *Inexpensive to moderate. (888) 700-0503 or (541) 563-3249.*

Cliff House. 1450 Adahi Road. This bed and breakfast in a two-story, rustic, restored home is located on a bluff above the shore and has spectacular views of the ocean, the Coast Range Mountains, and Alsea Bay. There are four guest rooms with early period furnishings and private baths. Some rooms have wood-burning stoves and balconies. *Expensive. (541) 563-2506.*

GOVERNOR PATTERSON MEMORIAL STATE RECREATION AREA

[Fig. 44(2)] This pleasant recreation area near the mouth of Alsea Bay is named after a former governor of Oregon. The recreation area is directly beside the beach, amidst wind-stunted sitka spruce and other evergreen trees. It has hiking trails as well as beach access.

Directions: On US Highway 101, approximately 2 miles south of Waldport.

Activities: Hiking, beachcombing, picnicking.

Facilities: Trails, beach access, picnic sites.

Dates: Open year-round.

Fees: None.

Closest town: Waldport, 2 miles.

For more information: Oregon State Park Information Center, 2501 Southwest First Avenue, Suite 100, Portland, OR 97201. Mailing address PO Box 500, Portland, OR 97207. Phone (800) 551-6949.

🎋 BEACHSIDE STATE PARK

[Fig. 44(3)] A major feature of this little park is that all the campsites are within a few feet of the broad, sandy beach. Thirty-three of the campsites have electrical hookups, and 49 are for tent camping. There is also a hiker/biker campground and two yurts. South of the park the Siuslaw National Forest land (see Siuslaw National Forest, page 325) extends from the Coast Range Mountains to the coastline. The Forest Service manages recreation features along that stretch of the beach, unlike much of the coast where the Oregon Parks and Recreation Department manages most of the recreation facilities.

Directions: On US Highway 101, 4 miles south of Waldport.

Activities: Camping, beach walking, fishing, picnicking.

Facilities: Campsites, yurts, restrooms, showers, picnic sites.

Dates: Open year-round.

Fees: Fees are charged for camping.

Closest town: Waldport, 4 miles.

For more information: Oregon State Park Information Center, 2501 Southwest First Avenue, Suite 100, Portland, OR 97201. Mailing address, PO Box 500, Portland, OR 97207. Phone (800) 551-6949. For camping reservations, phone (800) 452-5687.

🎋 CARL G. WASHBURNE MEMORIAL STATE PARK

[Fig. 44(4)] This full-service park has a 6-mile loop trail to Heceta Head and the Heceta Head Lighthouse, which lie to the south of the campground. The campground is divided and has entrances on both sides of US Highway 101. There are 58 full-hookup campsites, seven walk-in tent sites, two yurts, and hiker/biker campsites.

The beach here is unobstructed for 5 miles, and there are cliffside tidepools, which may be home to creatures such as Troschel's sea star (*Evasterias troschellii*) and strawberry anemone (*Corynactis califonica*).

Directions: On US Highway 101, 14 miles north of Florence.

Activities: Camping, fishing, hiking, tidepool hunting, picnicking.

Facilities: Campground, yurts, wheelchair-accessible restrooms, showers, trails, picnic sites.

Dates: Open year-round.

Fees: Fees are charged for camping.

Closest town: Florence, 14 miles.

For more information: Oregon State Park Information Center, 2501 Southwest First Avenue, Suite 100, Portland, OR 97201. Mailing address, PO Box 500, Portland, OR 97207. Phone (800) 551-6949.

HECETA HEAD LIGHTHOUSE STATE SCENIC VIEWPOINT

[Fig. 44(5)] This scenic viewpoint also is the location of the historic Heceta Head Lighthouse, which was built in 1894 for a reported $180,000. Builders used construction stone from the Clackamas River near Oregon City, bricks and cement from San

Francisco, and wood that came by sea as rafts from mills in Oregon. The lighthouse can be reached by a trail from the state scenic viewpoint parking lot. Now automated, the light can be seen 21 miles out on the ocean, and is rated as the brightest on the Oregon coast.

The 56-foot lighthouse tower and its accompanying buildings sit on a shoulder of Heceta Head some 205 feet above the sea. Heceta Head is named after Bruno de Heceta, the Spanish explorer who sailed these waters in the mid-1770s. The white buildings with bright red roofs can be seen from many miles away, at sea and along the coast. Conversely, the view from Heceta Head is magnificent, looking down the coast and out to sea, where there may be whales.

Below the lighthouse bluff, Devils Elbow Beach offers tidepools where, in the lower part of the intertidal area, there may be creatures such as the purple sea urchin (*Strongylocentrotus purpuratus*). The urchins hide in rounded pits or depressions, which, scientists believe, they dig by using their spines and a five-jawed chewing mechanism, called Aristotle's lantern. The urchin remains in its pit as long as there is enough plant material drifting by for it to eat.

Offshore rocks and headlands provide nesting sites for seabirds, which can be seen from Heceta Head.

The assistant lightkeeper's house, built in 1893, has bed-and-breakfast rooms, and facilities for group meetings. Phone (541) 547-3696 for information. During the summer, tours of the lighthouse are available.

Directions: The state scenic viewpoint is on US Highway 101, 13 miles north of Florence, beside a small cove and under a highway bridge that crosses adjacent Cape Creek. A side road leads down to the beach. A short trail leads to the lighthouse.

Activities: Hiking, beach walking, tidepool hunting, wildlife viewing, fishing, picnicking.

Facilities: Lighthouse and bed and breakfast, picnic sites.

Dates: Open year-round.

Fees: There is a day-use fee.

Closest town: Yachats, 11 miles.

For more information: Oregon State Park Information Center, 2501 Southwest First Avenue, Suite 100, Portland, OR 97201. Mailing address, PO Box 500, Portland, OR 97207. Phone (800) 551-6949.

SEA LION CAVES

[Fig. 44(6)] This is where bull sea lions stay in their off-season. It is a huge, 1,500-foot long, privately owned, cavern with two large entrances open to the sea. Inside, a rocky island and rocks on the side of the cavern are covered with multitudes of bellowing sea lion bulls, which can be seen from a viewing place that is within the cavern but far above the surface where the sea lions rest. This is the West Coast's only mainland rookery for California sea lions (*Eumetopias jubata*). A bull weighs about

1,200 pounds, compared to the cow's 500 to 700 pounds. California sea lions live about 20 years.

Parking is available on both sides of US Highway 101 in front of the building that is the entrance to the caves. There is a gift/souvenir shop inside and a booth that sells tickets to an elevator that goes 208 feet down through solid rock to the cavern. The route to the elevator from the gift shop is a paved walkway carved out of a sheer cliff. The walkway, a dizzying distance above the sea far below, goes several hundred feet to the right of the shop building to reach the elevator door. A similar walkway to the left goes to a lookout above a rock ledge, where dozens more sea lions lie about in the open. Both walkways have coin-operated binoculars that are especially useful when there are whales nearby. The air above the walkways is filled with shorebirds, including cormorants and pigeon guillemots.

The stroll along the walkways may take considerable time, considering the view out to sea and the abundant wildlife to be watched. At the bottom of the elevator ride, the door opens in the cavern. A short walk from the elevator leads to an upper opening that was the entrance before the elevator was installed in 1961. Visitors walked down the stairs to reach it. From that opening there is a magnificent view of the Heceta Head Lighthouse (*see* Heceta Head Lighthouse State Scenic Viewpoint, page 296) and the surf pounding the rocky cliff beneath the lighthouse. That view gives some idea of the force of the pounding waves that carved out the cavern along a fracture in an ancient lava flow.

Directions: On US Highway 101, 8 miles north of Florence.

Activities: Wildlife viewing, shopping.

Facilities: Elevator, viewpoints, gift shop.

Dates: Open year-round.

Fees: An entrance fee is charged.

Closest town: Florence, 8 miles.

For more information: Sea Lion Caves, 91560 US Highway 101, Florence, OR 97439. Phone (541) 547-3111.

DARLINGTONIA STATE NATURAL SITE

[Fig. 44(7)] This boggy wayside has a botanical area where unusual, carnivorous cobra lilies (*Darlingtonia californica*) grow in large masses. The plants' leaves form hollow tubes with hairs that point downward. An unwary insect that enters the tube in search of dinner can crawl over the hairs going down, but is caught when it tries to go back up. Eventually, it falls to the bottom of the leaf, which contains juices that digest animal matter, and instead of finding dinner, the insect is dinner.

There is a hiking trail with interpretive signs through the sphagnum bog where the plants grow. Cobra lilies are native to the southwestern part of Oregon and the northwestern part of California. The flowers bloom in May and June.

The natural site also has picnic sites.

Directions: The natural site is on US Highway 101, 5 miles north of Florence.
Activities: Hiking through a unique natural area.
Facilities: Interpretive trail, picnic tables.
Dates: Open year-round.
Fees: None.
Closest town: Florence, 5 miles.
For more information: Oregon State Park Information Center, 2501 Southwest First Avenue, Suite 100, Portland, OR 97201. Mailing address, PO Box 500, Portland, OR 97207. Phone (800) 551-6949.

Florence

[Fig. 44] This pleasant town of some 6,700 people is a short distance from the ocean, but it borders the Siuslaw River, one of the larger rivers along the Oregon coast. It is on US Highway 101 but also is the terminus for State Route 126, which goes east through the Coastal Range Mountains for 61 miles to Eugene, Springfield, and the I-5 corridor.

The town was first settled along the riverbank, and some of the original buildings from the 1800s still stand in what natives call the Old Town district. Old Town has numerous quaint shops, including a kite shop, art galleries, and gift shops. More stores and services are in the newer part of the city along US Highway 101. There are two golf courses just north of the business district, and horseback riding is popular both on the beach and in the mountains during the summer. There is easy access to clamming and crabbing on the ocean beaches. The Forest Service's **Mapleton Ranger Station**, 2635 Highway 101 North, phone (541) 902-8526 can provide information about the forest and mountains, as well as the sand dunes on the beach just west of Florence (*see* Siuslaw National Forest, page 325).

Directions: Florence lies on both sides of US Highway 101 at the Siuslaw River, about 185 miles south of Astoria.
Activities: Hiking, kite flying, horseback riding, biking, fishing, crabbing, clamming, shopping.
Facilities: Lodging, dining, stables, golf courses, beaches, forest trails.
For more information: Florence Chamber of Commerce, 270 Highway 101, PO Box 26000, Florence OR, 97439. Phone (800) 524-4864 or (541) 997-3128.

▨ RESTAURANTS IN FLORENCE

There are restaurants in Florence both on and off the major highways.

Windward Restaurant. 3757 Highway 101 North. The menu here includes seafood, chicken, and steak, as well as soup, salad, and sandwiches. There is a cocktail lounge and menus for children and senior citizens. Reservations recommended. *Inexpensive.* (541) 997-8243.

Lotus Seafood Palace. 1150 Bay Street in Old Town. This restaurant with a bay view offers Northern Chinese dishes as well as American cuisine especially seafood selections. There is a cocktail lounge and children's menu. Reservations recommended. *Inexpensive. (541) 997-7168.*

LODGING IN FLORENCE
Lodging options here range from large to small establishments.

Driftwood Shores Resort and Conference Center. 88416 First Avenue. This four-story establishment fronts the ocean and has 136 units, including 23 large, three-bedroom suites with fireplaces. All rooms have ocean views and balconies or patios, and/or kitchens. There is a restaurant with an ocean view. *Moderate to expensive.* *(800) 422-5091* or *(541) 997-8263.*

Edwin K Bed and Breakfast. 1155 Bay Street in Old Town. This bed and breakfast is in an early twentieth century woodcrafter's home with carefully landscaped grounds opposite the Siuslaw River. There are six guest rooms, antique furnishings, and whirlpools. *Moderate to expensive. (541) 997-8360.*

JESSIE M. HONEYMAN MEMORIAL STATE PARK
[Fig. 44(8)] This large, attractive state park is adjacent to the north end of the U.S. Forest Service's 47-mile-long Oregon Dunes National Recreation Area (*see* Siuslaw National Forest, page 325). The park has three freshwater lakes with year-round fishing, and sand dunes hundreds of feet high, with direct access for off-road vehicles from the campground. There are concessions with food and supplies, as well as rental paddle boats. The park has 44 full-hookup campsites, 122 electrical sites, 191 tent sites, 10 yurts, six group-campsites, and hiker/biker camping.

Directions: On US Highway 101, 3 miles south of Florence.

Activities: Camping, dune buggy riding, fishing, picnicking, boating, swimming, hiking.

Facilities: Campsites, yurts, concession store, wheelchair-accessible restrooms, showers, picnic sites.

Dates: Open year-round.

Fees: Fees are charged for camping and day use.

Closest town: Florence, 3 miles.

For more information: Oregon State Park Information Center, 2501 Southwest First Avenue, Suite 100, Portland, OR 97201. Mailing address, PO Box 500, Portland, OR 97207. Phone (800) 551-6949. For camping reservations, phone Reservations Northwest, (800) 452-5687.

Reedsport

[Fig. 44] Reedsport, with 4,800 people, and Winchester Bay, with 600, are neighbors at the mouth of the Umpqua River that share not only some unique and beautiful recreation possibilities but also their chamber of commerce and visitor information bureau.

State Route 38, which goes through the Coastal Mountain forest some 58 miles to the I-5 corridor, terminates at Reedsport. Three miles east of the city, on Route 38, the 1,000-acre **Dean Creek Elk Viewing Area** often has herds of elk grazing peacefully in the meadows of a former ranch, which has been converted to a public game preserve. There sometimes are scores of the magnificent animals within a short distance of the highway.

Once this area was a center of industry, but now the emphasis is on recreation, and the Forest Service's Oregon Dunes National Recreation Area is where much of that recreation takes place (*see* Siuslaw National Forest, page 325). The headquarters for the recreation area is at 855 Highway Avenue, phone (541) 271-3611.

Reedsport has public tennis courts in **Highland Park** at the intersection of Longwood Drive and Ranch Road, a public swimming pool at **Highland School**, 2605 Longwood Drive, and **The Forest Hills Country Club public golf course** at One Country Club Drive.

Winchester Bay has the **Salmon Harbor Marina**, the largest public marina on the Oregon coast with 900 moorage slips, as well as boat launches, campgrounds, and docks. The bay is popular for fishing, and the marina is headquarters for charter boats that go whale watching, and also fishing in both the Pacific Ocean and the Umpqua River. Salt-water fish include chinook salmon (*Oncorhynchus tshawytscha*), steelhead (*Oncorhynchus mykiss*), and smallmouth bass (*Micropterus dolomieu*). The

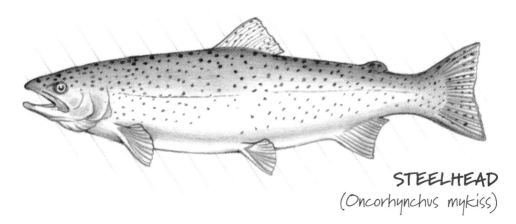

STEELHEAD
(*Oncorhynchus mykiss*)

Umpqua River has chinook salmon, striped bass (*Morone saxatilus*), and steelhead trout.

Directions: On US Highway 101, 17 miles south of Florence.

Activities: Fishing, crabbing, clamming, boating, camping, dining, dune buggy riding, hiking, beachcombing, wildlife viewing, whale watching, kite flying, wind surfing.

Facilities: Boat harbor, charter boats, dunes, shops, campgrounds, trails, restaurants.

For more information: Reedsport/Winchester Bay Chamber of Commerce, 805 US Highway 101, PO Box 11, Reedsport, OR 97467. Phone (800) 247-2155 or (541) 271-3495.

RESTAURANTS IN THE REEDSPORT/WINCHESTER BAY AREA

After a busy day sampling the numerous attractions here, visitors can find a good meal and relax.

Unger's Landing Restaurant and Lounge. 345 Riverfront Way east of Reedsport. This restaurant is in the superstructure of an Umpqua River fishing vessel. The menu offers steak and seafood, with lighter fare for lunch. There is a cocktail lounge with views of the river. Reservations recommended. *Inexpensive. (541) 271-3328.*

LODGING IN REEDSPORT

Salabasgeon Inn of the Umpqua. 42509 Highway 38. This two-story motel has 12 units, four with kitchens. All rooms overlook the Umpqua River and the landscaped grounds. There is a golf chipping green, a boat dock, and a boat launch. *Inexpensive. (541) 271-2025.*

Anchor Bay Inn. 1821 Highway Avenue. This two-story motel has 21 rooms, including four kitchen units. There is a heated swimming pool. *Inexpensive. (451) 271-2149.*

UMPQUA DISCOVERY CENTER

[Fig. 44(9)] This interpretive center has interactive exhibits that explain the human and natural history of the Umpqua region. The exhibits explain the dunes, an ocean beach, and a weather station.

Directions: The interpretive center is on Reedsport's boardwalk on the Umpqua Riverfront at 409 Riverfront Way.

Facilities: Permanent and temporary exhibits explaining the scientific and historical background of the lower Umpqua area.

Dates: Open year-round.

Fees: There is an entry fee.

For more information: Umpqua Discovery Center, 409 Riverfront Way, Reedsport, OR 97467. Phone (541) 271-4816.

UMPQUA LIGHTHOUSE STATE PARK

[Fig. 44(10)] This relatively small but attractive park at Lake Maire has 20 full-hookup campsites, 42 tent sites, 2 yurts and two log cabins. It is close to the Oregon Dunes National Recreation Area (*see* Siuslaw National Forest, page 325), and the historic Umpqua River Lighthouse. The lighthouse was built originally in 1857 on the North Spit of the Umpqua River, but the sand foundation eroded away, and the lighthouse fell into the bay four years later.

The present structure, on a bluff on the south side of Winchester Bay, was built with a 65-foot tower and has been operating since 1894. The lighthouse is one of the last five to operate on the Oregon coast. Tours of the lighthouse are offered from Wednesdays through Sundays during the summer. The view of the ocean, bay, and sand dunes is awesome, and there is a whale-watching platform nearby. Blueberry bushes are available for picking in season.

The lighthouse is maintained by the Douglas County Parks and Recreation Department, phone (541) 271-4631.

Directions: The park is off US Highway 101, 6 miles south of Reedsport.

Activities: Camping, hiking, fishing, beach walking, boating, picnicking.

Facilities: Campgrounds, showers, boat facilities, trails, beach access.

Dates: Open year-round.

Fees: Camping fees are charged, and an entry fee is charged for the lighthouse.

For more information: Oregon State Park Information Center, 2501 Southwest First Avenue, Suite 100, Portland, OR 97201, mailing address PO Box 500, Portland, OR 97207. Phone (800) 551-6949. For camping reservations, Reservations Northwest, (800) 452-5687.

WILLIAM M. TUGMAN STATE PARK

[Fig. 44(11)] Located on the shore of 560-acre Eel Lake this park is some 3 miles inland from the ocean. It is in a forest consisting mostly of spruce, hemlock, cedar, and Douglas fir trees. The forest is home to many creatures, including deer, bear, elk, fox, otter, and the elusive cougar that ordinarily takes great pains to prevent being seen by humans, but sometimes allows a fleeting glimpse as it disappears into the brush.

The lake contains trout, bass, crappie, and, in the fall, coho salmon and steelhead. There is a wheelchair-accessible fishing dock and a boat launch. Speed limit on the lake is 10 miles an hour. There is a level 4-mile hiking trail on the lakeshore.

The park has 110 campsites with electrical hookups, five yurts, and hiker/biker camping. The day-use area is in an open grassy area with shade trees. It offers restrooms, a picnic shelter, and a large play area. Group picnics can be reserved by contacting Reservations Northwest.

Directions: On US Highway 101, 8 miles south of Reedsport.

Activities: Camping, hiking, boating, fishing, swimming, picnicking.

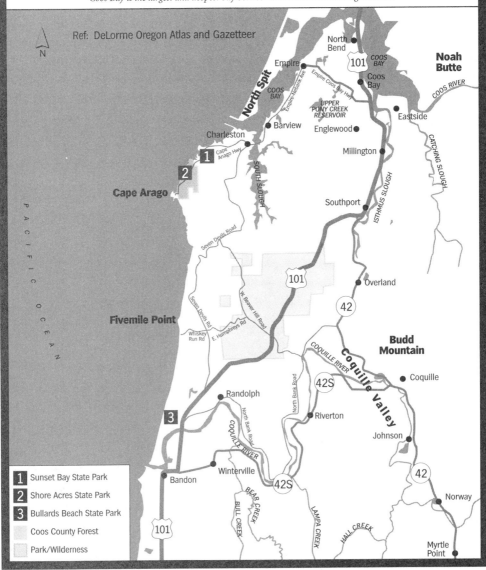

North Bend/ Coos Bay Area

Coos Bay is the largest and deepest bay between San Francisco and Puget Sound.

Ref: DeLorme Oregon Atlas and Gazetteer

1 Sunset Bay State Park
2 Shore Acres State Park
3 Bullards Beach State Park
  Coos County Forest
  Park/Wilderness

Facilities: Campsites, wheelchair accessible restrooms and fishing dock, showers, boat launch, trail, play area, picnic sites.

Dates: Open year-round.

Fees: A fee is charged for camping.

Closest town: Reedsport, 8 miles.

For more information: Oregon State Parks and Recreation Center, 2501 Southwest First Avenue, Suite 100, Portland, OR 97201. Mailing address, PO Box 500, Portland, OR 97207. Phone (800) 551-6949. For picnic reservations, phone Reservations Northwest, (800) 452-5687.

North Bend/Coos Bay

[Fig. 45] These adjacent industrial cities combine to become the biggest community along the Oregon coast. North Bend has a population of some 9,600, while Coos Bay numbers some 16,500. The cities are part of what is known as the Oregon Bay area, and share the Coos Bay, which is the largest and deepest between San Francisco and Puget Sound, and is rich in marine wildlife.

In 1854, J.C. Tolman founded Coos Bay, the larger of the cities, and named it Marshfield. Ninety years later, the city changed its name to Coos Bay. North Bend was the latecomer, being incorporated in December 1903. Now they are separate communities in a common setting.

One attraction is tours of industries peculiar to the area such as those that cut, craft, and finish items made of myrtlewood. A small area along the coast of southern Oregon is where many of the world's myrtlewood trees grow. The trees' extremely fine grain make the wood tough and durable, with large variations in color that make it both beautiful and easily workable. It is used for wood turnings, carvings, tables, and grandfather clocks. One of the myrtlewood companies, the **Oregon Connection,** 1125 South First Street in Coos Bay, phone (800) 255-5318 or (541) 267-7804, features self-guided tours.

The southern Oregon coast also is cranberry country, and during the harvest season some bogs invite visitors to watch the harvesting process. For further information, contact the Bay Area Chamber of Commerce. The chamber of commerce also has pamphlets describing self-guided tours on foot or bike. Gambling is available at the **Mill Resort and Casino**, 3201 Tremont Avenue, phone (800) 953-4800 or (541) 756-8800.

The **Coos County Historical Society Museum,** in Simpson Park on US Highway 101 has displays on local history, including a 1920s steam locomotive. The free **Marshfield Sun Printing Museum,** 1049 Front Street in Coos Bay, includes the offices of the **Marshfield Sun** newspaper that was founded in the city in 1891. The city held a referendum in 1944 to change its name from Marshfield to Coos Bay, and the Marshfield Sun went out of business. The museum has the paper's print shop on the first floor, and a collection of historical photographs and newspaper history. It is open on Mondays, Wednesdays, and Fridays during June, July, and August, and the last Sunday of the other months, except December.

The Coos Bay communities are at the southern tip of the Oregon Dunes National Recreation Area, and serve as a jumping-off place for visits to that unique area (*see* Siuslaw National Forest, page 325). The beach near Coos Bay was where the *New Carissa*, a 36,000-ton freight ship ran aground on February 4, 1999 while attempting to enter Coos Bay to pick up a load of wood chips for shipment to Japan. The surf pounded the ship until it broke in two. The forward section was towed to sea and sunk, but the after portion became stranded on the beach. The ship was set afire in an effort to burn off the fuel, but an estimated 70,000 gallons spilled, threatening shorebirds, shellfish, and other wildlife that frequent the area.

One of the shorebirds menaced by the oil was the snowy plover (*Charadrius alexandrimus*), which is protected in Oregon under the federal Endangered Species Act. The snowy plover is one of 12 subspecies of the plovers, and breeds in loose colonies along the Pacific Coast from southern Washington to Baja California in Mexico. Six of the breeding areas are along the Oregon Coast, and Coos Bay is one of the major ones. Government agencies made major efforts to control the oil leaking from the stranded after section of the ship, in an effort to protect both the snowy plover and other species that could become inundated in the oil. A year later, the U.S. Coast Guard, which coordinated the effort, announced it was ending its supervision of the program because only small pockets of oil remained on the hulk. The wreckage, however, remains on the beach, leaking small amounts of oil.

Other wildlife in the Coos Bay vicinity includes whales, seals, porpoises, sea lions, shearwaters, puffins, murres, and petrels. Charter boats take people to visit them. Contact the chamber of commerce for specific information.

Directions: These communities are on US Highway 101, 20 miles north of Bandon.

Activities: Industrial tours, sand dune tours, wildlife viewing, fishing, clamming, crabbing, boating, self guided walking and biking tours, hiking, gambling, and shopping.

Facilities: Food, lodging, casino, museums, boat launch, docks.

For more information: Bay Area Chamber of Commerce, 50 East Central Avenue, Coos Bay, OR 97420. Phone (800) 824-8486 or (541) 269-0215.

RESTAURANT IN NORTH BEND/COOS BAY

Hilltop House Restaurant. 166 North Bay Drive in North Bend. This restaurant overlooking the bay serves chicken, lamb, pasta, steak, and seafood, and the menu offers both large and small portions. There is a cocktail lounge. Reservations recommended. *Inexpensive.* (451) 756-4160.

LODGING IN NORTH BEND/COOS BAY

Edgewater Inn. 275 East Johnson Street in Coos Bay. A two-story motel with 82 rooms, this establishment has a heated indoor swimming pool, sauna, tanning bed, and game room. Some of the rooms have a river view and balcony or patio, and whirlpools. There is a suite with a whirlpool and kitchen.

SUNSET BAY STATE PARK

[Fig. 45(1)] This nice little park is at the head of a small ocean cove with a sandy beach. There are high, rocky cliffs on both sides of the cove, and the beach is protected from the surf by a reef across the mouth of the cove. Stands of sitka spruce and other evergreens are on the bluffs above the bay.

The Cape Arago Lighthouse on a tiny nearby island is not open to the public, but there are good views of the light's 44-foot-high tower from a trail in the park. The present light is the third built at this location. The first was built in 1866, the second in 1908, and the present one in 1934. Weather and erosion destroyed the first two. The light is managed by the U.S. Bureau of Land Management. For further information, phone the BLM, (541) 756-0100.

The park has 29 full-hookup campsites, 36 electrical sites, 66 tent sites, 8 yurts, 11 group tent sites, and hiker/biker camping. Reservations for group picnics are available.

Directions: West of US Highway 101, 12 miles south of Coos Bay.

Activities: Camping, boating, fishing, swimming, hiking, beach walking, picnicking.

Facilities: Campsites, trailer dump station, wheelchair-accessible restrooms, showers, picnic sites, trails, beach access.

Dates: Open year-round.

Fees: Fees are charged for camping.

Closest town: Coos Bay, 12 miles.

For more information: Oregon State Park Information Center, 2501 Southwest First Avenue, Suite 100, Portland, OR 97201, mailing address PO Box 500, Portland, OR 97207. Phone (800) 551-6949. For reservations, phone Reservations Northwest, (800) 452-5687.

SHORE ACRES STATE PARK

[Fig. 45(2)] This park is located on what once was the estate of a timber and shipping magnate. It has an 80-acre formal botanical garden, a shelter for watching the surf, and a combination interpretive center and store. There are no campsites, but there are picnic sites, as well as trails and beach access.

Directions: Off US Highway 101, 13 miles south of Coos Bay.

Activities: Picnicking, hiking, beach walking.

Facilities: Botanical gardens, sheltered ocean viewpoint, trails, picnic sites, store.

Dates: Open year-round.

Fees: A day-use fee is charged.

Closest town: Coos Bay, 13 miles.

For more information: Oregon State Park Information Center, 2501 Southwest First Avenue, Suite 100, Portland, OR 97201, mailing address PO Box 500, Portland, OR 97207. Phone (800) 551-6949. For reservations, Reservations Northwest, (800) 452-5687.

BULLARDS BEACH STATE PARK

[Fig. 45(3)] This nice park is on the ocean beach at the mouth of the Coquille River and offers visitors access to both the beach and the riverbank. It is adjacent to a bay and is grassy, with forested areas. There are 102 campsites with full hookups, 83 with electrical hookups, 13 yurts, a hiker/biker camp, and a horse camp with four corrals and eight campsites. Reservations are available. Some 7 miles of trail are available for horseback riding, and 4.5 miles of beach are suitable for exploration.

The park has a meeting hall and picnic shelter that can be reserved. The beach is popular for beachcombing and, after a storm, hunting for agates, jasper, and petrified wood. Afternoon winds invite kite flying.

Nearby, on a side road from the park, the Coquille River Lighthouse and the odd looking, octagonal building next to its 40-foot-tall tower are on the north jetty of the river. The lighthouse was built in 1896 to guide vessels across the river bar, but the channel was improved and the lighthouse was decommissioned in 1939. It was restored in 1979 as an interpretive center. Now is it open to the public year-round.

Directions: On US Highway 101, 2 miles north of Bandon.

Activities: Camping, boating, fishing, biking, horseback riding, hiking, picnicking, agate hunting.

Facilities: Campground, yurts, wheelchair-accessible restrooms, showers, picnic sites, picnic shelter, boat launch, beach access, equestrian trails, lighthouse.

Dates: Open year-round.

Fees: Fees are charged for camping.

Closest town: Bandon, 2 miles.

For more information: Oregon State Park Information Center, 2501 Southwest First Avenue, Suite 100, Portland, OR 97201. Mailing address, PO Box 500, Portland, OR 97207. Phone (800) 551-6949. For reservations, phone Reservations Northwest, (800) 452-5687.

Bandon

[Fig. 45] This attractive town of about 2,800 people is beside the sea and has both a modern business district and an Old Town district with early twentieth century architecture, shops, restaurants, and art galleries. Adjacent to Old Town are the waterfront and boat basin, where people fish and hunt crabs. Commercial fishing boats add charm to the port, and it is possible to charter a boat and go to sea.

Highway 101 in both directions from Bandon is sprinkled with cranberry bogs and small myrtlewood studios, and Bandon has its fair share of shops that offer cranberry products and myrtlewood objects. The town leads Oregon in cranberry production and is third in the nation. Cranberries are native to Oregon, and Lewis and Clark traded part of their dwindling supply of trade goods for some. Eastern growing methods were transplanted here in the 1800s, and a major agriculture business resulted.

The town has access to the beach where agates, jasper, and other semiprecious stones can be found. Kite flying and beachcombing are done here, too. A mile south of the town on US Highway 101, the **Face Rock State Scenic Viewpoint** is a good place for whale watching during the spring and in December. It also has nice views of statuesque sea stacks.

The Bandon National Wildlife Refuge northeast of Old Town attracts numerous migrating shorebirds, especially in October. Access to the refuge is via several unmarked trails along River Road. The U.S. Fish and Wildlife Service does not maintain a checklist for the specific species that stop off at the 300-acre refuge, but it is a resting and feeding place for shorebirds, wading birds, raptors, and waterfowl, and includes undisturbed salt marsh, mud flat, and beach-grass communities.

Directions: Bandon is on US Highway 101 at the mouth of the Coquille River.

For more information: Bandon Chamber of Commerce, 300 Southeast Second Street, PO Box 1515, Bandon, OR 97411. Phone (541) 347-9616.

▨ RESTAURANTS IN BANDON

Lord Bennett's Restaurant and Lounge. 1695 Beach Loop Road. The dining room here has panoramic views of sea stacks and the ocean. The menu offers fresh seafood and a variety of other entrees, as well as sandwiches and salads. There is a cocktail lounge and children's menu. Reservations recommended. *Inexpensive. (541) 347-3663.*

The Wheelhouse Restaurant. 125 Chicago Street in Old Town Mall across from the boat basin. This restaurant offers a number of unique dishes, as well as fresh seafood. There is a cocktail lounge and children's menu. Reservations recommended. *Inexpensive. (541) 347-9331.*

▨ LODGING IN BANDON.

Driftwood Motel. 460 Highway 101. A two-story motel with 22 rooms, this contemporary establishment is in the Old Town district. There is a two-bedroom unit with a kitchen. *Inexpensive to moderate. (541) 347-9022.*

Harbor View Motel. 355 Highway 101. This three-story motel has 59 units, including one with two bedrooms. It is on a bluff overlooking Old Town and the harbor, and there are balconies with views. *Moderate. (541) 347-4417.*

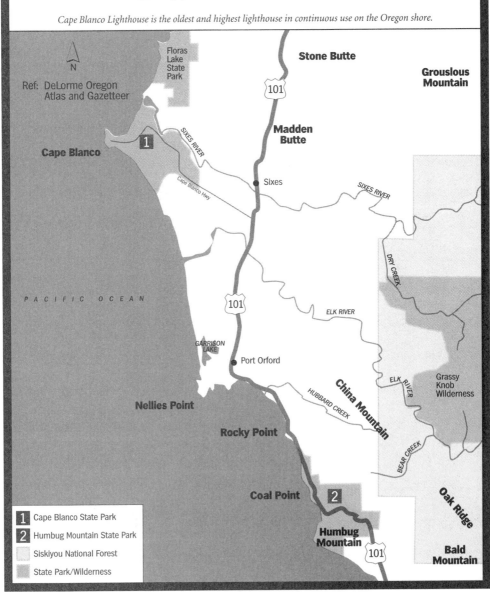

Cape Blanco State Park Area

Cape Blanco Lighthouse is the oldest and highest lighthouse in continuous use on the Oregon shore.

N

Ref: DeLorme Oregon
Atlas and Gazetteer

Floras
Lake
State
Park

Stone Butte

Grouslous
Mountain

101

Madden
Butte

Cape Blanco

SIXES RIVER

Cape Blanco Hwy

Sixes

SIXES RIVER

1

DRY CREEK

PACIFIC OCEAN

101

ELK RIVER

GARRISON
LAKE

Port Orford

ELK RIVER

Grassy
Knob
Wilderness

Nellies Point

HUBBARD CREEK

China Mountain

Rocky Point

BEAR CREEK

Oak Ridge

Coal Point

2

Humbug
Mountain

101

Bald
Mountain

1 Cape Blanco State Park
2 Humbug Mountain State Park
Siskiyou National Forest
State Park/Wilderness

CAPE BLANCO STATE PARK

[Fig. 46(1)] This park is on a bluff covered by red earth 245 feet above the sea, but the rocky cliffs below consist of white fossilized shells, so Spanish explorers named it Blanco, the Spanish word for white. The cape features the Cape Blanco Lighthouse, which has been signaling sailors since 1870 and is the oldest and highest lighthouse in continuous use on the Oregon shore. The tower stands 59 feet above the bluff. The park is on a cape that extends farther west into the sea than any other in the state, and a number of ships have been wrecked on the reefs.

The lighthouse is at the end of the road in the park, and the last part of the road is one lane. The structure overlooks a cove with a narrow beach and numerous rocks where the surf smashes and sends white spray high into the air. The view includes the coastline for many miles in both directions, and there is a large colony of sea lions on the offshore rocks.

The forest in the lighthouse area consists mostly of sitka spruce, which has been stunted and misshapen by the terrific winter storms in the area. The forest understory is largely bracken fern and salmonberry.

Nearby, the restored Victorian home built for rancher Patrick Hughes in 1898 has been converted to a state museum, which is open daily except Tuesday and Wednesday during the summer.

The park has 53 campsites with electrical hookups, four log cabins, a horse camp with eight sites and double corrals, group RV/tent sites, and hiker/biker camping. There is a 7-mile equestrian trail and 150 acres of open-riding range. Fishing is popular on the Sixes River and the black sands beach.

Directions: About 5 miles north of Port Orford on US Highway 101, turn west on the State Park Road and go about 5 miles to the park.

Activities: Camping, picnicking, fishing, horseback riding, hiking, beachcombing, lighthouse visits, whale watching.

Facilities: Campground, wheelchair-accessible restrooms, showers, trailer dump station, lighthouse.

Dates: Open year-round.

Fees: Fees are charged for camping.

Closest town: Port Orford, 10 miles.

For more information: Oregon State Park Information Center, 2501 Southwest First Avenue, Suite 100, Portland, OR 97201. Mailing address, PO Box 500, Portland, OR 97207. Phone (800) 551-6949.

HUMBUG MOUNTAIN STATE PARK

[Fig. 46(2)] Unlike most facilities along the Oregon coast, this park at the foot of Humbug Mountain and on the shore of Eel Lake has its entrance on the east side of US Highway 101, and for that reason it can easily be missed. It offers 35 electrical hookups, 73 tent sites, a group tent campsite, and hiker/biker camping. The camp is

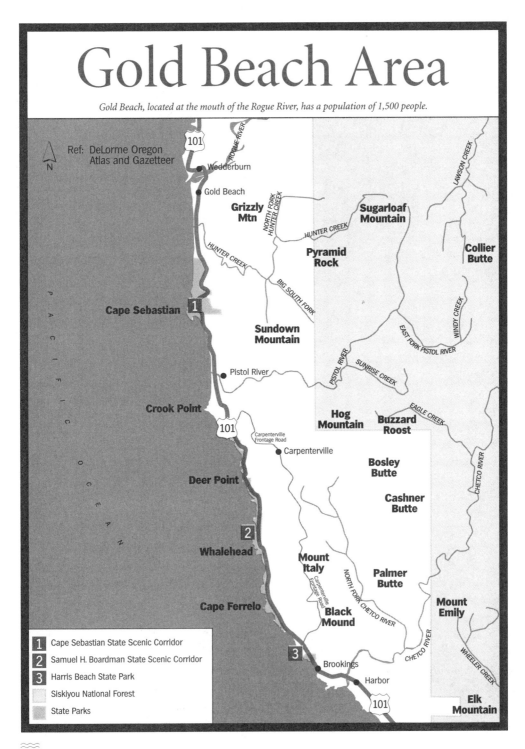

Gold Beach Area

Gold Beach, located at the mouth of the Rogue River, has a population of 1,500 people.

Ref: DeLorme Oregon
Atlas and Gazetteer

N

101

ROGUE RIVER

Wedderburn

Gold Beach

Grizzly
Mtn

NORTH FORK
HUNTER CREEK

HUNTER CREEK

Sugarloaf
Mountain

LAWSON CREEK

Pyramid
Rock

Collier
Butte

HUNTER CREEK

BIG SOUTH FORK

PACIFIC

Cape Sebastian 1

Sundown
Mountain

WINDY CREEK

EAST FORK PISTOL RIVER

PISTOL RIVER

Pistol River

SUNRISE CREEK

Crook Point

101

Carpenterville
Frontage Road

Carpenterville

Hog
Mountain

Buzzard
Roost

EAGLE CREEK

CHETCO RIVER

OCEAN

Bosley
Butte

Deer Point

Cashner
Butte

2

Whalehead

Mount
Italy

NORTH FORK CHETCO RIVER

Carpenterville
Frontage Road

Palmer
Butte

Mount
Emily

Cape Ferrelo

Black
Mound

CHETCO RIVER

WHEELER CREEK

3

Brookings

Harbor

101

Elk
Mountain

1 Cape Sebastian State Scenic Corridor
2 Samuel H. Boardman State Scenic Corridor
3 Harris Beach State Park
  Siskiyou National Forest
  State Parks

in the midst of a forest of alder, maple, and myrtlewood trees, and not far from an ocean beach.

A major feature is an easy 5.5-mile loop trail that goes from sea level to the peak of Humbug Mountain, which reaches 1,756 feet elevation. At the top there are wide, high views of the ocean and the countryside, as well as rhododendron bushes up to 20 feet high.

Directions. On the east side of US Highway 101, 6 miles south of Port Orford.

Activities: Camping, hiking, fishing, beach walking, picnicking.

Facilities: Wheelchair-accessible campground, showers, trail, trailer dump station.

Dates: Open year-round.

Fees: Camping fees are charged.

Closest town: Port Orford, 6 miles.

For more information: Oregon State Park Information Center, 2501 Southwest First Avenue, Suite 100, Portland, OR 97201. Mailing address, PO Box 500, Portland, OR 97207. Phone (800) 551-6949.

Gold Beach

[Fig. 47] This town of about 1,500 people has a full ocean view and a beach that once produced enough placer gold to bring large numbers of people to the area in the mid 1800s. The gold and the miners are long gone but it is still a nice place to visit. The town is at the mouth of the Rogue River. After the miners left, an enterpriser named Robert Hume discovered that the river's salmon were another kind of gold mine, and developed canneries that resulted in him being called the salmon king of the Rogue. Zane Grey wrote a book titled *The Rogue River Feud* about a World War I veteran's battle with a fishing monopoly in the area. The book publicized Gold Beach and visits by movie stars, presidents and other notables secured its reputation as a tourist attraction.

Its summer reputation, that is. Torrential rain and the seasonal nature of Gold Beach's industries result in a population decrease from November until spring, when the cycle begins anew.

The harbor is home to seals, birds, fishing trawlers, and jet boats that take passengers up the river that Congress has declared to be a Wild and Scenic River. The boats go past wildlife ranging from otters to black bears, deer, beavers, osprey, snowy egrets (*Egretta thula*), eagles, kingfishers (*Ceryle alcyon*), common

KINGFISHER
(Ceryle alcyon)

mergansers (*Mergus merganser*), and others. Fish include salmon and steelhead. The banks are lined with a forest of hemlock, cedar, and fir trees, dotted with myrtlewood and madrone, and sprinkled with wildflowers that change with the season, including wild beauties such as paintbrush (*Castilla* sp.), Douglas iris (*Iris douglasiana*), and large headed gold fields (*Lasthenia macrantha*), which are rare in these parts.

The longer jet boat trips enter the Siuslaw National Forest's Rogue River Wilderness where the boats slip through the rapids between high canyon walls. Running comments by the pilots cover the ecosystem, Indians, gold mining, and the history of the area. Round trips vary from 65 to 105 miles. There usually is a lunch stop at an upriver resort. An estimated 50,000 people make the trip each year.

Gold Beach is central to a wide range of attractions such as golf and horse rides on the beach, along the Rogue River, or into the green foothills. The beach invites wind surfing, whale watching, and exploring tidepools. Dozens of outfitter and guide services can be contacted through the Chamber of Commerce.

Directions: On US Highway 101, about 35 miles north of the California border.

Activities: Jet boat river tours, hiking, fishing, beach walking, tidepool hunting, whale watching, horseback riding, wind surfing.

Facilities: Food, lodging, shops, beach access, outfitter and guide services, deep sea charters.

Dates: Open year-round.

For more information: Gold Beach Chamber of Commerce, 29279 Ellensburg, Gold Beach, OR 97444. Phone (800) 525-2334 or (541) 247-7526.

RESTAURANTS IN GOLD BEACH

Nor' wester Seafood Restaurant. 10 Harbor Way. This restaurant overlooking the harbor offers entrees such as steak and fresh seafood. There is a cocktail lounge and a children's menu. *Inexpensive. (541) 247-2333.*

Spada's. 29374 Ellensburg. Italian dishes such as pizza, and seafood are on the menu here, as well as oriental dishes, sandwiches, and salads. There is a cocktail lounge and a children's menu. *Inexpensive. (541) 247-7732.*

LODGING IN GOLD BEACH

Tu Tu' Tun Lodge. 96550 North Bank Rogue Road. This resort in a picturesque area beside the Rogue River has 20 rooms in a two-story building. There is one, two-bedroom unit, and one, three-bedroom unit, as well as two, two-bedroom suites with kitchens. There also is a garden house with fireplace and deck. All rooms have a patio or balcony with a view of the river. Seven rooms have fireplaces. There is a heated swimming pool, boat ramp, and boat dock, and a pitch and putt course. A dining room is available during the summer. Activities include hiking, fishing, and jet boat rides on the Rogue River. *Moderate to expensive. (541) 247-6664.*

Gold Beach Resort. 29232 Ellensburg. This two-story motel has 39 rooms, some with balconies. There is an ocean view and beach access, as well as a heated swimming pool and whirlpool. *Moderate.* (541) 247-7066.

CAPE SEBASTIAN STATE SCENIC CORRIDOR

[Fig. 47(1)] This wayside is a feature of Cape Sebastian, a major headland some 700 feet above the sea. Sebastian Vizcaino, a Spanish explorer, named the cape in 1602. A 1.5-mile trail leads from the parking lot to the tip of the cape, where there are views that stretch 50 miles to sea.

The windswept headland is home to numerous wildflowers, including such spring beauties as Douglas iris and paintbrush. During the summer, the fields are colored by the rare, daisylike, yellow flowers called large headed goldfields, which are found only in this part of the Pacific Coast.

During World War II, a Japanese submarine surfaced here, close enough so the crew members' voices could be heard on the headland. The sub silently stole away, but it created quite a stir in the neighborhood.

From the headlands the rocks of the reef look like huge, misshapen creatures looming in the surf. There is no drinking water at the wayside.

Directions: On US Highway 101, 7 miles south of Gold Beach.

Activities: Hiking, beach walking, fishing, wildlife watching.

Facilities: Parking lot and trail.

Dates: Open year-round.

Fees: None.

Closest town: Gold Beach, 7 miles.

For more information: Oregon State Parks and Recreation Center, 2501 Southwest First Avenue, Suite 100, Portland, OR 97201. Mailing address, PO Box 500, Portland, OR 97207. Phone (800) 551-6949.

SAMUEL H. BOARDMAN STATE SCENIC CORRIDOR

[Fig. 47(2)] This is a 12-mile-long, densely forested stretch of US Highway 101, with 11 waysides and viewpoints where visitors can pause to enjoy the rocky cliffs and look down on offshore monoliths with their vegetation shining green in the sun. There are several places where trails lead to the beach, and among the beach attractions is a long stretch of the Oregon Coast Trail (*see* Oregon Coast Trail, page 257). Among the oddities along this stretch of highway are several places where there are views of sea cave remnants that form arches or natural bridges in the surf.

Directions: On US Highway 101, 5 miles north of Brookings.

Activities: Beachcombing, hiking.

Facilities: 11 highway waysides, viewpoints, and trails to the beach.

Dates: Open year-round.

Fees. None.

Closest town: Brookings, 5 miles.

For more information: Oregon State Park Information Center, 2501 Southwest First Avenue, Suite 100, Portland, OR 97201. Mailing address, PO Box 500, Portland, OR 97207. Phone (800) 551-6949.

HARRIS BEACH STATE PARK

[Fig. 47(3)] This nice park is adjacent to the inviting town of Brookings. It has a broad, sandy beach sheltered by reef rocks and Goat Island, where birds such as cormorants and pelicans rest. There are 34 campsites with full hookups, 52 with electrical hookups, 63 tent sites, 6 yurts, and hiker/biker camping. Some of the campsites have cable TV hookups.

The view from the park covers miles of rocky coastline, and there is ample opportunity to find tidepools to study. Look for crabs, sponges, and starfish, among others.

Directions: On US Highway 101, adjacent to the north side of Brookings.

Activities: Camping, beachcombing, picnicking, fishing, hiking, wildlife viewing.

Facilities: Campsites, wheelchair-accessible restrooms, showers, trailer dump station, picnic sites, beach access.

Dates: Open year-round.

Fees: Fees are charged for camping.

Closest town: Brookings.

For more information: Oregon State Park Information Center, 2501 Southwest First Avenue, Suite 100, Portland, OR 97201. Mailing address, PO Box 500, Portland, OR 97207. Phone (800) 551-949. For camping reservations, phone Reservations Northwest, (800) 452-5687.

Brookings

[Fig. 47] This town of 5,400 people and its neighbor, Harbor, have a geological/meteorological location that moderates the weather, so they are warmer than other places along the Oregon coast. The phenomenon is a result of warm air from California's Central Valley mingling with a high-pressure system that moves onto the coast from the ocean. That traps the warm air and pulls it down to the Brookings area. The town's location between Mount Emily on the east and Cape Blanco on the north shelters it from surface winds that might blow the warm air away. The result is that Brookings's average temperature is several degrees warmer than other places along the coast.

The town was founded by the Brookings Lumber and Box Company in 1914. Logging, fishing, wood products, agriculture, and tourism are its major industries today. The Port of Brookings has 281 slips for commercial boats, which provide fodder for photographers. The port also boasts seashore, a boat ramp, and a boardwalk with numerous interesting shops. There are more shops in the downtown area and along US Highway 101.

The community is especially proud of its flowering plants, and in the vicinity are numerous lily farms where some 90 percent of the nation's Easter lilies are raised.

Fishing is a year-round sport here, with both resident and migrating fish as the quarry. The town is on both the ocean and the Chetco River. The Chetco is a Wild and Scenic River, and is popular for river rafting, fishing, and wading.

On September 9, 1942 a Japanese Navy plane, launched from a submarine, dropped a bomb on Mount Emily near Brookings. It did little damage but adds history to the attraction of the magnificent mountain and the ocean views from the peak at the end of a 0.5-mile hike. To reach the trailhead, drive 6 miles from Brookings on the Wheeler Creek Road.

The **Chetco Valley Historical Society Museum** at 15461 Museum Road has displays of the area history in a house built in 1857. The largest Monterey cypress tree in Oregon grows in front of the house.

Brookings is the southernmost city on the Oregon coast, just 6 miles from the California border. It is not true that people who go beyond the border fall off the end of the earth, but there are no real attractions between Brookings and the border and there is little reason to go south of the little town on the banks of the Chetco River, except for people who are headed for California.

Directions: Brookings is on US Highway 101, about 6 miles north of the California border.

Activities: Beach walking, camping, kite flying, tidepool hunting, golf, boating, hiking, fishing, hunting.

Facilities: Food, lodging, parks, public gardens.

For more information: Brookings/Harbor Chamber of Commerce, 16330 Lower Harbor Road, PO Box 940, Brookings, OR 97415. Phone (800) 535-9469 or (541) 469-3181.

RESTAURANT IN BROOKINGS

Food is available in Brookings.

O'Holleran's Restaurant and Lounge. 1210 Chetco Avenue. This long-established restaurant with an American cuisine specializes in seafood and beef dishes. There is a children's menu. Reservations recommended. *Inexpensive.* *(541) 469-9907.*

LODGING IN BROOKINGS

Lodging choices here range from motels to bed and breakfasts.

Spindrift Motel. 1215 Chetco Avenue. This modern, two-story motel has 35 guest rooms, many with a view of the ocean. *Inexpensive.* *(541) 469-5345.*

South Coast Inn Bed and Breakfast. 516 Redwood Street. This B&B has three guest rooms in a 1917 Craftsman-style house. There also is a guest cottage with a full kitchen. All rooms have private baths and are furnished with antiques. *Moderate.* *(541) 469-5557.*

Coastal Mountains

Inland fron the Oregon beaches, the Coast Range Mountains run parallel to the coast.

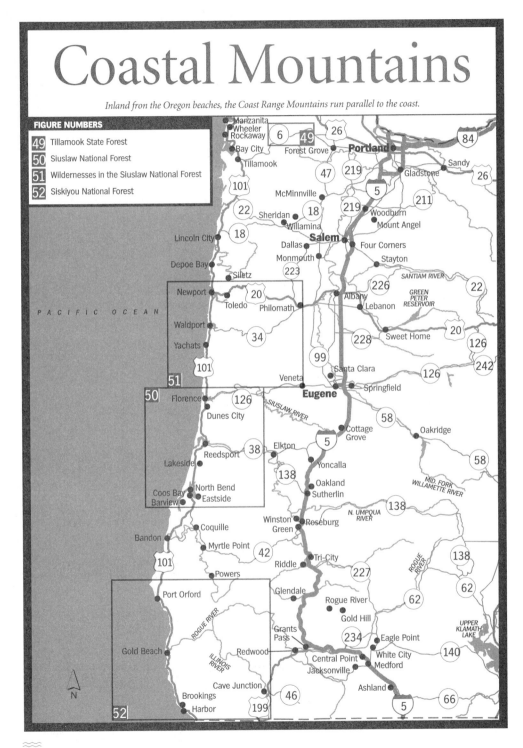

FIGURE NUMBERS

49 Tillamook State Forest
50 Siuslaw National Forest
51 Wildernesses in the Siuslaw National Forest
52 Siskiyou National Forest

Coastal
Mountains

A little way inland from the Oregon beaches the Coast Range Mountains stretch through the state—a long spine of gray rock and green forest paralleling the coast.

Geologists divide the mountains into various classifications based on their rock-types, ages, and so forth, but for most people they are a single entity of awesome natural beauty, and their divisions are a matter of governmental jurisdiction rather than scientific nomenclature.

Today, the major government agencies involved are the U.S. Bureau of Land Management Medford District, which administers an area in the south Oregon segment of the mountains, the Oregon Department of Forestry, which administers state forests, and the U.S. Forest Service, which has the Siuslaw National Forest in the northern part of the Oregon coastal area, and the Siskiyou National Forest in the

[*Above:* In mountain meadows, paintbrush (*Castilleja* sp.) ranges in color from red to yellow]

Fig. 49: Tillamook State Forest

Tillamook State Forest

A series of four fires from 1933 to 1951 burned 356,000 acres in the Tillamook State Forest.

Ref: USGS 7.5 min. Dem—Cochran, Woods Point, Roaring Creek, Timber

1	Elk Creek Campground
2	Elk Mountain Trail
	Tillamook State Forest
	Trail

southern portion. Although the land involved has different history and management systems, all of it invites exploration. For information on lodging and restaurants in the coastal mountains, see the chapter called US Highway 101 in Oregon.

Tillamook State Forest

[Fig. 49] This land of catastrophe is fascinating because of what happened during the Tillamook Burn, and even more interesting because of what has happened since. The catastrophe began in 1933 when a major forest fire blackened a huge section of the native forest in the northwestern section of Oregon. That was the first of four fires that did not end until 1951 and are collectively known as the Tillamook Burn. They left little more than blackened snags and barren land that covered some 356,000 acres where once the lush green forest stood.

Private owners abandoned much of the wasted land, and the state sold bonds to raise funds to begin a major reforestation program. Now, after six decades of cooperation between nature and science, lush new forest is growing on the devastated land.

To a large extent, it is a working forest that was regrown to provide the wood products that make homes, furniture, books, newspapers, and other things. But that doesn't mean it is not a pleasant place to be. The Tillamook Burn area gets as much as 130 inches of precipitation a year, and the new forest grows quickly. Some 95 percent of the area is forested, and some of the new forest is already nearing maturity. There are no old-growth trees, and to a large extent the forest was replanted with species of high commercial value, principally Douglas fir and western hemlock, but also western redcedar, noble fir, sitka spruce, red alder, and bigleaf maple. Beneath the trees, on the forest floor, smaller plants grow, including Oregon grape, thimbleberry, salmonberry, snowberry, blueberry, vine maple, sword fern, and salal. Flowers include trillium (*Trillium ovatum*), starflower (*Trientalis* spp.), lotus (*Lotus* spp.), and foxglove (*Digitalis purpurpea).* Foxglove, a very pretty pinkish-purple beauty, is a deadly poison that has saved the lives of untold thousands of people. It contains cardiac glycosides that affect muscle tissue and circulation. It can be fatal to people who ingest it. On the other hand, a derivative called digitalis has been used for many years to treat people with heart disease. Foxglove grows wild on roadsides and other disturbed soil and makes a very nice garden flower—just don't eat it.

Mammals in the Tillamook Forest range from large to small and include Roosevelt elk (*Cervus elaphus*), black bear (*Ursus americanus*), mule deer (*Odocoileus hemionus*), beaver (*Castor fiber*), mink (*Mustela vison*), coyote (*Canis latrans*), wood rat (*Neotoma cinerea*), and raccoon (*Procyon lotor*). The raccoon has a black band across its eyes that looks like the mask of a bandit. And that is exactly what the furry little creature is. It is perfectly capable of making its living by sneaking into your camp—or home if you live in the country—and stealing whatever good things to eat you have left where a bandit can get them. Some raccoons are fastidious, though, and have a habit of washing their food before they eat. When not stealing a camper's breakfast, they eat whatever else is available including birds, eggs, snails, fish, frogs, reptiles, and plant material such as fruit. They often find a home in a hollow tree or a burrow under the roots.

More than 70 species of birds have been identified in the Tillamook Burn area, including the western tanager (*Piranga ludoviciana*), northern flicker (*Colaptus auratus luteus*), golden crowned kinglet (*Regulus satrapa olivaceus*), rufous hummingbird (*Selasphorus rufus*), and majestic bald eagle (*Haliaeetus leucocephalus*).

The Tillamook Forest has campgrounds and trails for hiking, biking, motorcycle riding, and horseback riding. Anglers may catch trout, salmon, and steelhead. Hunters may find elk, deer, and bear. There is some logging in the forest, but most of it is what timber people call commercial thinning, in which only selected trees are logged, thus providing revenues for the state, and at the same time reducing competition for the remaining trees and allowing them to grow more vigorously.

Directions: From Portland, take US Highway 26 about 25 miles west, turn south on State Route 6, and go about 15 miles to the forest. From Tillamook, take State Route 6 east about 10 miles.

Activities: Hiking, camping, hunting, fishing, horseback riding, biking, motorcycling, and picnicking.

Facilities: Campgrounds, trails, developed trailheads, and picnic areas.

Dates: Open year-round.

Fees: Fees are charged for camping at developed campgrounds.

Closest town: Tillamook, 10 miles.

For more information: Tillamook District Office, Oregon Department of Forestry, 4907 East Third Street, Tillamook, OR 97141-2999. Phone (503) 842-2545. Or Forest Grove District Office, 801 Gales Creek Road, Forest Grove OR 97116. Phone (503) 357-2191.

ELK CREEK CAMPGROUND

[Fig. 49(1)] This rustic campground offers walk-in camping with Elk Creek on one side and the Wilson River on another. There are some swimming holes in pools

Mule Deer And Black-Tailed Deer

Once considered separate species, the mule deer (*Odocoileus hemionus*) and black-tailed deer (*Odocoileus columbianus*) are now accepted as a single species. As human populations expanded, wolf and cougar numbers went down, allowing the deer to proliferate beyond the capacity of their browse. As a result, deer suffered widespread starvation during harsh winters. Today states control the number of deer by issuing hunting permits based on the need for decreasing the deer population.

on the river, but fishing is limited to nearby locations on the Wilson River. There are no specific sites for RVs, but there are 15 walk-in tent sites near the parking area. Water is supplied from a hand-pump well, and there are vault toilets. The campground is in mostly Douglas fir forest.

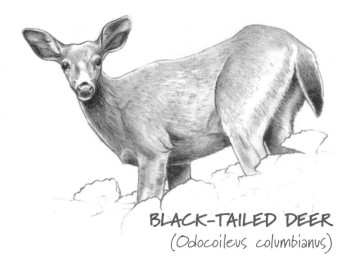

BLACK-TAILED DEER
(Odocoileus columbianus)

Directions: From Portland, take US Highway 26 about 25 miles west, turn south on State Route 6, go about 20 miles, and near milepost 28 turn north onto the Elk Creek Forest Campground Road, which leads 0.3 mile to the campground. From Tillamook, take State Route 6 east about 28 miles to the campground road.

Activities: Camping, hiking, hunting, swimming.

Facilities: Walk-in campsites, hand-pump water wells, vault toilets, trails.

Dates: Open Memorial Day through October.

Fees: Fees are charged for camping.

Closest town: Tillamook, 28 miles.

For more information: Oregon Department of Forestry, Forest Grove District Office, 801 Gales Creek Road, Forest Grove OR 97116. Phone (503) 357-2191.

ELK MOUNTAIN TRAIL

[Fig. 49(2)] The Elk Mountain trailhead is at the far end of the Elk Creek Campground. The lower section of the route goes through lush new forest, but the gray snags of the forest that burned half a century ago are still visible, displaying a stark contrast between old and new. The trail goes upward nearly its entire length.

Near the top the new forest thins out, and the gaunt snags of the old one become more prominent, while the meadows provide an ever-changing succession of flowers as the summer wears on.

The big reward is at the peak. Here, the view stretches across to the Cascades where three volcanoes—Jefferson and Hood in Oregon, and Adams in Washington—wear perpetual icy caps. Closer, the view covers miles of forest.

Activities: Hiking, horseback riding.

Dates: Open year-round.

Trail: 4 miles round-trip.

Elevation: 1,800 foot gain in elevation.

Degree of difficulty: Moderate.

Siuslaw National Forest

The Siuslaw National Forest encompasses 631,231 acres ranging from deep forest to sand dunes.

1 Horsfall Campground

2 Horsfall Beach Campground,
Bluebill Campground,
Wild Mare Horse Campground

3 Driftwood II Campground,
Lagoon Campground

Oregon Dunes National Recreation Area

Siuslaw National Forest

Elliot State Forest

Trail

Ref: DeLorme Oregon
Atlas and Gazetteer
N

Florence
126
SIUSLAW RIVER
Glenada
101
WOAHINK LAKE
Dunes City
North Beach
3
SILTCOOS LAKE
Mount Peter
Goodwin Peak
MAPLE CREEK
BEAR CREEK
FIDDLE CREEK
N. FORK SMITH RIVER
N. FORK SMITH RIVER
Roman Nose Mountain

TAHKENITCH LAKE
Henderson Peak
SMITH RIVER
WASSEN CREEK
SCARE CREEK

THREEMILE LAKE
101
SMITH RIVER
Gardiner

PACIFIC OCEAN

UMPQUA RIVER
Reedsport
38
Deer Head Point
Fern Top
Winchester Bay
SCHOFIELD CREEK
Scottsburg
38
UMPQUA RIVER

101
BLACKS CREEK
MURPHY CREEK
BIG CREEK
MILL CREEK

EEL LAKE
Lakeside
N. TENMILE LAKE
BENSON CREEK
ROBERTS CREEK
Ash Valley
LAKE CREEK
LAKE CREEK

ADAMS CREEK

Hauser
PALOUSE CREEK
101
SULLIVAN CREEK
W. FORK MILLICOMA RIVER
Horsfall Beach Rd
2
Shorewood
1

North Bend
MILLICOMA RIVER
McKeever Mountain
E. FORK MILLICOMA RIVER
Ivers Peak
Kelly Butte
COOS BAY
Coos Bay

Siuslaw National Forest

[Fig. 50] This national forest has 631,231 acres of land ranging from deep forest on the sides of the majestic Coastal Mountains to the extraordinary, graceful, and always-changing sand dunes of the seashore. It is so varied that it has two distinct vegetation zones. One is characterized by the moisture-loving sitka spruce forest of the seashore, and is near the southern extreme of the spruce's range. The stately giants of the inland Douglas fir and western hemlock forest distinguish the other.

Much of the forest in this part of Oregon was devastated by successive fires of the late nineteenth and early twentieth centuries. The natural succession began with small plants such as the fast-growing fireweed, which typically turns a blackened, burned wasteland into vast fields of purple swaying in the breeze. Plants such as fireweed would be replaced by hardier woody plants that, in turn, would give way to hardwood trees such as western red alder, and finally to evergreens such as the Douglas fir, which lives for hundreds of years and often reaches heights of more than 200 feet. Much of the forest along Oregon's Coast Range Mountains is now in maturing Douglas fir, and by all appearances the magnificent giants are the end of the forest succession. But someday they will be replaced by the western hemlock that grows in the shade at the fir's feet. An accident of nature, a lightning strike for instance, eventually will clear a hole in the forest of Douglas fir, and the hemlock will spring up in their place, eventually becoming dominant and returning the forest to what it was before the fires.

The national forest extends for 135 miles in a narrow strip parallel to the Oregon coast and the ridge of the Coast Range Mountains. The low point is sea level at the ocean shore; from there the land rises to the forest's highest point at the top of Mary's Peak, 4,097 feet in elevation (*see* Mary's Peak Trail, page 339).

The major tree species in the forest are sitka spruce, Douglas fir, western redcedar, red alder, western hemlock, and bigleaf maple. The forest has counted within its borders 69 species of mammals, 200 species of fish, 235 species of birds, and 26 species of amphibians and reptiles. Fur bearing wildlife includes the bobcat, beaver, muskrat, raccoon, mink, marten, and river otter.

The national forest has 30 natural lakes and 1,200 miles of streams where anadromous fish spawn. Anglers have a choice of freshwater fishing in the forest's rivers and lakes or saltwater fishing in the ocean, both on the same day if they choose. Fishing in the streams may produce salmon, sea run cutthroat trout, or steelhead. The lakes have species such as trout, yellow perch (*Perca flavescens*), bluegills (*Lepomis macrochirus*), and largemouth bass (*Micropterus salmoides*). Saltwater fish include seaperch and flounder, which may be caught in the surf and bays and off rocks. Clamming is a popular sport on the beaches in the spring and summer. Berry pickers in the meadows and forest clearings may find enough delicious blueberries to stave off starvation until they get home to bake a delicious pie. Hunters in the forest may find Roosevelt elk, black-tailed deer, black bear, and cougar.

Cutthroat Trout

Cutthroat trout (*Oncorhynchus clarkii*) get their name from a pink or red slash along the lower jaw. Their backs are greenish blue. They are silver on the sides and bottom and the head, sides, back, and tail have small black dots. Cutthroat trout stay in fresh water for one to four years and go to sea for one year, staying close to shore and the estuaries where they feed on small fish. They may reach 25 inches and weigh from 1 to 5 pounds. They spawn from December through May and may return to sea to begin another cycle.

During the winter, the forest's marshy areas provide a place for wading birds and shore birds, including, from October to March, tundra swans (*Cygnus columbianus*), which both nest and feed here. The other wildlife in the marshes includes species such as beavers, river otters, and muskrats.

There are three wilderness areas in the national forest (*see* Cummins Creek Wilderness, page 332; Rock Creek Wilderness, page 332; and Drift Creek Wilderness, page 331). All three are maintained in their natural condition with little or no sign of humans. One of them, Rock Creek Wilderness, doesn't even have developed trails so must be explored on a cross-country basis.

The Forest Service manages the Oregon Dunes National Recreation Area. Here the emphasis is on beach and dune recreation as well as protecting the environment and wildlife habitat (*see* Oregon Dunes National Recreation Area, page 327).

The forest has 22 campgrounds with a total of well over 850 campsites. They range from semi-primitive to developed with flush toilets, RV accommodations, and trailer dumps. All provide access to the natural wonders of the forest. The forest also has scores of trails ranging from short nature trails that interpret natural history to longer routes to mountain peaks.

Directions: The national forest is divided into numerous separate segments that can be reached along US Highway 101 between about 10 miles south of Tillamook and about 1 mile north of North Bend.

Activities: Camping, hiking, bicycle riding, hunting, fishing, clamming, beachcombing, horseback riding, sand dune play, wildlife viewing, boating, picnicking.

Facilities: Campgrounds, trails, sand dunes, stables, visitor information centers, wildlife viewing stations.

Dates: Open year-round.

Fees: Fees are charged at certain campgrounds and may be charged for camping.

For more information: The forest is managed by three ranger districts and the Oregon Dunes National Recreation Area. Hebo Ranger District, 31525 Highway 22, Hebo, OR 97122. Phone (503) 392-3161. Mapleton Ranger District, 4480 Highway 101, Building G, Florence, OR 97453. Phone (541) 902-8526. Waldport Ranger District, 1049 Southwest Pacific Highway, Waldport, OR 97394. Phone (541) 563-3211. The Oregon Dunes National Recreation Area, 855 Highway 101, Reedsport, OR

97467. Phone (541) 271-3611. The forest is managed by the Forest Supervisor's Office, 4077 Southwest Research Way, Corvallis, OR 97333. Phone (541) 750-7000.

OREGON DUNES NATIONAL RECREATION AREA

[Fig. 50] This natural wonder extends for some 40 miles along the Pacific shoreline, between the Siuslaw River on the north and the Coos River on the south. The inland boundary meanders as much as 2.5 miles from the beach. The recreation area's major feature is an uncounted number of constantly changing sand dunes that sometimes reach 400 feet in height. About 0.33 percent of the area is privately owned but about 14,000 acres are part of the national forest and open to the public. The recreation area also has lakes, forested areas, and ocean beaches.

The dunes are the result of millions of years of the natural dynamics of wind and water, and are made up of what once was sedimentary rock on the bottom of the ocean. The plate tectonics process uplifted the floor of the ocean about 12 million years ago, forming the Coast Range Mountains. Exposed to the weather, the sedimentary rock in the mountains eroded and formed vast amounts of sand, which washed down the mountain streams and back to the sea near the shore. Tide and surf washed the sand along the shoreline and back up to the dry land where it dried out, caught the wind, and blew inland along the coast.

With a stabilized shoreline over the past 6,000 years, the wind has continued to move the sand as far as 2.5 miles inland. And the wind blows under its own rules. During the summer, it comes from the north and northwest at a speed of 12 to 16 miles an hour, leaving the sand sculpted into a variety of shapes. During the winter the normal wind is lighter, but in a storm it can increase to more than 100 miles an hour, coming from the south and southwest and moving a great deal of sand. The winter also brings wet weather, raising the water table and creating marshy areas along the coastline, sometimes with water several feet deep. All that, combined with the surf and tide, brings an ever-increasing amount of sand to the shore where the heavier grains lodge on the tidelands and the wind carries the lighter grains—mostly feldspar and quartz—onto the beach. There it is caught by driftwood, forming a foredune that may be some 20 to 39 feet high.

In the early 1900s settlers planted European beachgrass (*Ammophila arenaria*) on the foredunes in the estuaries to anchor the dunes and prevent

Oregon Sand Dunes

The natural setting of sand dunes on Oregon beaches has changed since the early 1900s, when European beachgrass (*Ammophila arenaria*) was introduced to reduce blowing sand. The new grass quickly spread and prevented sand from blowing inland. But the wind still reached the inland sandy areas, blowing away the top layers down to the water table, where numerous plants that like moisture and low levels of nutrients soon invaded, changing the nature of the dunes.

them from migrating onto the inland areas. That cut off the sand that normally built the inland dunes and changed the dynamics. It caused much of the sand on the inland side of the beachgrass to blow away, exposing the water table and creating an environment for water-loving plants, which spread as the dunes moved eastward.

Wind sculpts the inland sand into various kinds of dunes. Some grow perpendicular to the wind and are called transverse dunes. They are usually from 5 to 20 feet high. Others form at an oblique angle to the wind that forms them. Those oblique dunes are parallel to each other and may be 1 mile long and 180 feet high from the base to the top. Sometimes the base is so high that the top may be more than 400 feet above sea level. The largest dunes are in the 3,000-acre Umpqua Scenic Area between the Umpqua Lighthouse and Tenmile Creek. For the most part they are accessible only on foot from the Eel Creek Campground and the Umpqua Lighthouse State Park.

WAX MYRTLE
(Myrica gale)

The environmental changes caused by the introduction of beachgrass created conditions that invited new plant communities to the beach. In places where water stands for long periods creeping buttercup (*Ranunculus repens*), and king's gentian (*Gentiana sceptrum*) may grow. Damp areas bear plants such as red fescue (*Festuca rubra*), pearly everlasting (*Anaphalins margaritace*), and coast strawberry (*Fragaria chiloensis*). In the dry areas there may be gray beach pea (*Lathyrus japonicus*), seashore lupine (*Lupinus littoralis*), and European beachgrass (*Ammophila arenaria*).

The pioneer plants are gradually replaced by shrubs such as salal (*Gaultheria shallon*), wax myrtle (*Myrica gale*), and shore pine (*Pinus contorta*), a variety of lodgepole pine. The shore variety grows from 40 to 60 feet tall on dunes, bogs, rocky hilltops, and exposed outer coast shorelines.

In a number of places the shifting sand has dammed creeks and rivers to form well over a dozen lakes, as well as wetlands. The Siuslaw, Siltcoo, Umpqua, and Smith rivers flow through the dunes. Yellow perch and cutthroat trout are among the fish in the lakes and rivers. Saltwater fishing from the rocks along the shore may produce a catch of flounder and sea perch.

More than 425 species of wildlife have been identified in the recreation area, including 79 mammals of which 50 live on the land and 29 in the ocean. Mammals include raccoon, mule deer, and beaver. Birds in large numbers are either resident or migrating visitors to the recreation area. Species include the white tailed kite (*Elanus leucurus*), downey woodpecker (*Picoides pubescens*), marsh wren (*Cistothorus palustris*), dunlin (*Calidris alpina*), Canada goose (*Branta canadensis*), common teal (*Anas cyanoptera*), and tundra swan (*Cygnus columbianus).*

When the water table rises in low, wet areas of the sand dunes, it sometimes causes light grains of sand to float on the surface, resulting in the formation of quicksand. The quicksand poses little danger to hikers, but off-road vehicles sometimes get stuck. Officials advise that ORV operators travel with others in case they need to be pulled out, and that they carry a shovel and jack.

There are numerous trails to fascinating places in the recreation area. Nearby businesses rent off-road vehicles (ORVs) and all-terrain vehicles (ATVs) to carry explorers to and through the dunes, but the federal and state prohibitions ban their use in some areas, and state permits are required for traveling off the pavement. Check for current requirements with the vendor or the Oregon Dunes National Recreation office in Reedsport. The permits may be obtained at state Department of Motor Vehicle offices throughout the state.

There are two paved roads within the dunes. One goes along the beach for 4 miles to the South Jetty Pier near the mouth of the Siuslaw River. That road begins on the west side of US Highway 101 about 0.5 mile south of the Siuslaw River. It travels west for about 2 miles then turns right and runs parallel to the beach, passing six parking lots that give access to the beach and dunes. The other road starts on the west side of US Highway 101 in the south end of the town of Winchester Bay. It winds to the west and south along the south bank of the Umpqua River, then veers to the south and follows the beach to a picnic site with wheelchair-accessible restrooms about 4 miles from Winchester Bay. There are three parking lots along the way.

In the recreation area there are 13 campgrounds with some 500 campsites and there are other campgrounds near the recreation area. Hikers, horseback riders, and people with off-road vehicles may camp in the backcountry. Officials advise that campers find a campsite in a place protected from wind and at least 200 feet from water. Drinking water should be treated, boiled, or filtered.

Directions: The recreation area extends some 40 miles along US Highway 101 between the Umpqua River and Coos Bay. There are access roads along US Highway 101. Watch for signs on the highway.

Activities: Hiking, camping, beachcombing, fishing, boating, ORV riding, horseback riding, kite flying, sand boarding.

Facilities: Campgrounds, trails, boat launches, interpretation stations, picnic sites, wheelchair accessible restrooms, beachside parking lots.

Dates: Open year-round.

Fees: Fees may be charged for parking, camping, permits, and other services.

Closest town: Several towns along US Highway 101 are within a few miles of the recreation area. The recreation area headquarters is in Reedsport, about 3 miles from the recreation area.

For more information: Oregon Dunes National Recreation Area, 855 Highway Avenue, Reedsport, OR 97467. Phone (503) 271-3611.

Wildernesses in the Siuslaw Nat. Forest

Drift Creek, Rock Creek, and Cummins Creek are the only wilderness areas in Siuslaw National Forest.

Ref: DeLorme Oregon Atlas and Gazetteer

Newport
Chitwood
Toledo
Eddyville
YAQUINA RIVER
Elk City
Yaquina
MARY'S RIVER
Burnt Woods
20
Blodgett
N
101
YAQUINA RIVER
PACIFIC
OCEAN
Harris
Mill Creek Divide
Philomath
9
Mary's Peak Road
Table Mountain
34
1
N. FORK ALSEA RIVER
2
FR 3464
Flat Mountain
Waldport
Risley Creek Rd
FR 3446
Tidewater
34
Scott Mountain
Green Pean
Dicks Ridge
7
ALSEA RIVER
34
Alsea
Bellfountain
Cannibal Mountain
NORTH FORK
Denzar Ridge
Yachats
YACHATS RIVER
FIVE RIVERS
ALSEA RIVER
6
YACHATS RIVER
Prairie Mountain
4
GREEN RIVER
5
Tenmile Ridge
101
3
Elk Mountain
57
36
Glover Ridge
Deadwood
Greenleaf
NORTH FORK SIUSLAW RIVER
Walton
Heceta Beach
SIUSLAW RIVER
Swisshome
8
Mercer Lake Road
Bailey Ridge
126
10
To Florence
126
Tiernan
Mapleton
126
Richardson
Globe

1	Drift Creek Wilderness
2	Horse Creek Trail
3	Rock Creek Wilderness
4	Cummins Creek Wilderness
5	Cummins Ridge Trail
6	Cape Perpetua Scenic Area
7	Blackberry Campground
8	Enchanted Valley
9	Mary's Peak Trail
10	Oregon Dunes National Recreation Area
	Siuslaw National Forest
	Wilderness Areas
	Trail

▓ WILDERNESS AREAS IN THE SIUSLAW NATIONAL FOREST

Congress has designated three areas in the Siuslaw National Forest as wildernesses. They are smaller than most wilderness areas in the Pacific Northwest, but are managed, like the other 473 designated wildernesses in the United States, under the Wilderness Act of 1964, which established the wilderness system. That act requires that the land be left in its original condition as "an area where the earth and its community of life are untrammeled by man, where man himself is a visitor who does not remain."

One result is strict regulations designed to eliminate indications of man's presence. Mechanical equipment of every kind, including bicycles, is banned. So is any activity that would change the landscape or harm vegetation. People who visit the wildernesses use only their strength and ingenuity to cope with the natural setting. In the Rock Creek Wilderness there is not even a developed trail to guide their steps. Another result is that the land's awesome beauty is left much as it was before machines were invented.

▓ DRIFT CREEK WILDERNESS

[Fig. 51(1)] This 5,800-acre wilderness in the central part of the Siuslaw National Forest has steep canyons that make it seem deep in the mountains even though it is only 6 miles from the ocean. The wilderness receives as much as 100 inches of rain a year, which results in lush vegetation, including large stands of old-growth western hemlock and Douglas fir trees that are hundreds of years old and as much as 200 feet tall. Other trees include bigleaf maple, spruce, and western redcedar. The forest understory has vine maple, salal, and trillium, and the meadows offer various grasses and flowers. Among the wildlife are black bear, Roosevelt elk, and black-tailed deer. The creeks have cutthroat trout, steelhead, and both coho and chinook salmon.

Directions: Go east for 7 miles from Waldport on State Route 34 and turn north on Risley Creek Road (Forest Road 3446). Go 7.4 miles and turn north on Forest Road 3464. Go to the end of the road where the Horse Creek Trail leads into the wilderness.

Activities: Hiking, camping, hunting, fishing.

Facilities: None.

Dates: Open year-round, weather permitting.

Fees: Parking fees may be charged.

Closest town: Waldport, 14.4 miles.

For more information: Waldport Ranger Station, 1049 Southwest Pacific Highway, PO Box 400, Waldport, OR 97394. Phone (503) 563-3211.

HORSE CREEK TRAIL

[Fig. 51(2)] This trail goes 5 miles across the Drift Creek Wilderness in roughly a south and north direction. It originated as a route early settlers used to travel inland. It goes through some of the Coast Range Mountains oldest old-growth forest stands.

The route requires fording Drift Creek, which is 20 feet wide and may be impassable during high water periods.

Trail: The trail goes 5 miles mostly through thick forest. Streams must be forded.

Elevation: 1,200 foot gain in elevation.

Degree of difficulty: Moderate.

ROCK CREEK WILDERNESS

[Fig. 51(3)] This 7,486-acre wilderness bears forests of mostly immature, small sitka spruce in the western portions near the ocean and young, small, immature Douglas fir and western hemlock inland. The understory is thick, with salmonberry in the lower area and salal in the higher ground. Rock Creek is the major stream. It is only about 5 miles long and never gets more than a few feet wide. It contains a few fish, such as small cutthroat trout. Mammals include Roosevelt elk, black bear, black-tailed deer, and raccoon.

Hiking, camping, hunting, and fishing are allowed in the wilderness, but understory brush is thick and tangled, making travel difficult. There are no trails so the wilderness gets only a few visitors.

Directions: Go 17 miles south from Waldport on US Highway 101 and turn east onto County Road 5082, which also is known as Rock Creek Road and becomes Forest Road 57. About 1 mile from US Highway 101 the road meets the southern border of the wilderness and continues to parallel the wilderness for about 6 miles except for a few small parcels of private property. There are no trails or trailheads, but visitors can park along the road and walk a few feet to the wilderness.

Activities: Cross-country hiking, camping hunting, fishing.

Facilities: None.

Dates: Open year-round.

Fees: None.

Closest town: Waldport, 17 miles.

For more information: Waldport Ranger Station, 1049 Southwest Pacific Coast Highway, PO Box 400, Waldport, OR 97394. Phone (503) 563-3211.

CUMMINS CREEK WILDERNESS

[Fig. 51(4)] This 9,173-acre wilderness is just east of US Highway 101 and adjacent to the Cape Perpetua Scenic Area (*see* page 334), which extends out to the ocean on the northwest corner of the wilderness. The wilderness has two primary valleys, Bob Creek and Cummins Creek. Both creeks drain directly into the sea, and both are spawning creeks for salmon runs.

One reason Congress created the wilderness in 1984 was to preserve the last remaining virgin stands of sitka spruce, Douglas fir, and western hemlock in the land along the Oregon coast. The spruces tend to dominate the forest near the ocean, while the Douglas firs thrive farther inland. The wilderness receives from 80 to 100 inches of precipitation a year, which contributes to the health of the virgin tree stands. The understory includes rhododendron (*Rhododendron macrophyllum*), sword fern (*Polystichum munitum*), elderberry (*Sambucus* spp.), and salmonberry (*Rubus spectabilis*). Wildflowers in the wilderness include yellow monkey flower (*Mimulus guttatus*), white candy flower (*Claytonia sibirica*), and the poisonous foxglove (*Digitalis purpurea*). Mammals include Roosevelt elk, black bear, and black-tailed deer.

Directions: The wilderness is just east of US Highway 101, 11 miles south of Waldport.

Activities: Hiking, camping, fishing, hunting.

Facilities: None.

Dates: Open year-round, weather permitting.

Fees: Parking fees may be charged.

Closest town: Waldport, 11 miles.

For more information: Waldport Ranger Station, 1049 Southwest Pacific Coast Highway, PO Box 400, Waldport, OR 97394. Phone (503) 563-3211.

Cummins Ridge Trail

[Fig. 51(5)] This is the only trail in the Cummins Creek Wilderness. It crosses the full length of the wilderness in an east-west direction, following the twists and turns of the summit of Cummins Ridge and ending near Cummins Peak, 2,200 feet in elevation.

The trail courses through dense Douglas fir and sitka spruce forest. The first half follows an overgrown abandoned road. The trail receives only a small number of visitors and provides people a good place to be alone in the forest but not far from civilization.

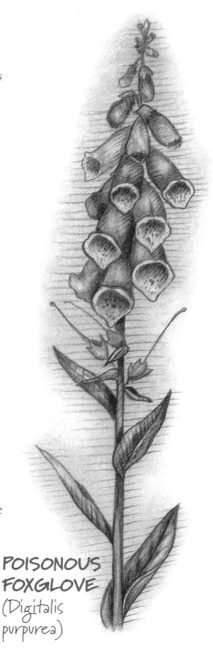

POISONOUS FOXGLOVE (*Digitalis purpurea*)

Directions: Take US Highway 101 about 15 miles south from Waldport and turn east on Forest Road 1051. Go east about 2.5 miles to a barrier across the road. The trail begins on the road on the east side of the barrier.

Activities: Hiking, camping, fishing, hunting.

Dates: Open year-round, weather permitting.

Fees: Parking fees may be charged.

Closest town: Waldport, 15 miles.

For more information: Waldport Ranger Station, 1049 Southwest Pacific Coast Highway, PO Box 400, Waldport, OR 97394. Phone (503) 563-3211.

CAPE PERPETUA SCENIC AREA

[Fig. 51(6)] The Siuslaw National Forest has recognized this 2,700 acres of rocky headland, mature sitka spruce, Douglas fir, and open meadows as an outstanding recreation area since the national forest was created in 1908. Native Americans inhabited the cape for some 8,000 years before Europeans arrived, and huge piles of fish bones mixed with the shells of clams and mussels left along the ocean shore by those early people can still be seen. And the beach still has tidepools like those that were here when the native people were. The cape was a headquarters for the Civilian Conservation Corps of the 1930s, and several of the facilities built in the area by the young CCC workers are still in use. One of them is the Cape Perpetua Campground that served as their main camp. Another is the parapet at the Cape Perpetua Viewpoint.

The cape was designated as a Recreational Reserve in 1946, and a visitor center was opened in 1967 to interpret the 8,000-year history of the cape and to explain the natural history. A network of 10 trails, ranging from 0.25 mile to 10 miles, threads through the area, providing visitors with close-up views of the natural and man-made features of the area.

Directions: The scenic area is just east of US Highway 101, about 10 miles south of Waldport.

Activities: Hiking, camping, nature walking, tidepool hunting.

Facilities: Interpretive center, campground, trails, viewpoints, interpretive facilities.

Dates: Open year-round.

Fees: Parking fees may be charged.

Closest town: Waldport, about 10 miles.

For more information: Waldport Ranger Station, 1049 Southwest Pacific Coast Highway, PO Box 400, Waldport, OR 97394. Phone (503) 563-3211.

HORSFALL CAMPGROUND

[Fig. 50(1)] This campground in the southern end of the Oregon Dunes National Recreation Area is nestled between sand dunes 2 miles from the ocean beach and is geared for people who use off-road vehicles in the dunes. There are 70 campsites suitable for either RVs or tents. The campground has piped water and showers but no electrical hookups or trailer dump station. Reservations are accepted.

Directions: Take US Highway 101 for 2 miles north from North bend, turn west on the Horsfall Beach Road, go about 1 mile, and turn right onto Forest Road 1098. Go about 0.5 mile to the campground entrance.

Activities: Camping, sand dune exploration.

Facilities: Campsites, picnic tables, piped water, wheelchair-accessible restrooms, ATV loading platform.

Dates: Open year-round.

Fees: Fees are charged for camping and may be charged for parking.

Closest town: North Bend, 2.5 miles.

For more information: Oregon Dunes National Recreation Area, 855 Highway Avenue, Reedsport, OR 97467. Phone (541) 271-3611. For reservations phone (877) 444-6777.

HORSFALL BEACH CAMPGROUND

[Fig. 50(2)] This Oregon Dunes National Recreation Area campground at the far end of Forest Road 1098 is geared toward people who use off-road vehicles in the dunes, but it also offers good access to the beach and its activities.

There are 34 campsites, including 7 for RVs, and 27 sites for either tents or RVs. There are no water or electrical hookups or trailer waste stations. Surf fishing on the beach may yield species such as yellow perch.

Directions: Take US Highway 101 approximately 2 miles north from North Bend, turn west on the Horsfall Beach Road, go about 1 mile, and turn right onto Forest Road 1098. Go about 2.4 miles to the campground entrance.

Activities: Camping, sand dune exploration, fishing, beachcombing, kite flying, horseback riding.

Facilities: Campsites, picnic tables, piped water, wheelchair-accessible rest rooms, flush toilets.

Dates: Open year-round.

Fees: Fees are charged for camping and parking.

Closest town: North Bend, 5.4 miles.

For more information: Oregon Dunes National Recreation Area, 855 Highway Avenue, Reedsport, OR 97467. Phone (541) 271-3611.

BLUEBILL CAMPGROUND

[Fig. 50(2)] This campground on Forest Road 1098 in the Oregon Dunes National Recreation Area is located in a grove of shore pine and alder trees, and off-road vehicles and all-terrain vehicles are not permitted. The nearby Bluebill Lake is actually a marsh where wildlife such as wading birds, shorebirds, beavers, and musk-rats may be found. The 1-mile Bluebill Loop Trail leads from the campground through the trees and around Bluebill Lake. The ocean beach is about 1 mile away at the end of Forest Road 1098.

Directions: Take US Highway 101 for 2 miles north from North Bend, turn west on the Horsfall Beach Road, go about 1 mile, and turn right onto Forest Road 1098. Go about 1.7 miles to the campground entrance.

Activities: Camping, sand dune exploration, beachcombing, kite flying, hiking.

Facilities: Trail, picnic tables and metal grills, eighteen campsites open for either tents or RVs, piped water, wheelchair-accessible restrooms with flush toilets. There are no hookups and no trailer dump station.

Dates: Open mid-May through mid-Oct.

Fees: Fees may be charged for camping and parking.

Closest town: North Bend, 4.7 miles.

For more information: Oregon Dunes National Recreation Area, 855 Highway Avenue, Reedsport, OR 97467. Phone (541) 271-3611.

WILD MARE HORSE CAMP

[Fig. 50(2)] This campground on Forest Road 1098 in the Oregon Dunes National Recreation Area has facilities for horse camping as well autos and RVs, but is closed to ATVs. There are 12 sites for tents or RVs, and each has its own corral. It is located in stands of shore pine trees near the beach, and both the beach and the dunes are available for serious exploration. A horse trail leads to a dune area where motorized equipment is banned. The ocean beach is about 1 mile away at the end of Forest Road 1098.

Directions: Take US Highway 101 for 2 miles north from North bend, turn west on the Horsfall Beach Road, go about 1 mile, and turn right onto Forest Road 1098. Go about 1.9 miles to the campground entrance.

Activities: Camping, sand dune exploration, beachcombing, kite flying, horseback riding.

Facilities: Campsites, picnic tables, piped water, wheelchair-accessible vault toilets, trail.

Dates: Open year-round.

Fees: Fees are charged for camping and may be charged for parking.

Closest town: North Bend, 4.9 miles.

For more information: Oregon Dunes National Recreation Area, 855 Highway Avenue, Reedsport, OR 97467. Phone (541) 271-3611.

DRIFTWOOD II CAMPGROUND

[Fig. 50(3)] This is one of several campgrounds on the Oregon Dunes National Recreation Area's Forest Road 1070, which leads from US Highway 101 to the Siltcoos Beach Parking area near the beach. The campground is designed primarily for off-road vehicles and offers access to some 4,000 acres of dunes and beach. Siltcoos Lake, about 3 miles from the campground, offers opportunities for boating and fishing. The ocean beach offers surf fishing.

Nine of the 69 campsites are designated for RVs. The others are for either tents or RVs. The campground has piped water, and there are flush toilets in the wheelchair-accessible restrooms. There are no water or electrical hookups.

Directions: Take US Highway 101 south from Florence about 7.5 miles, and turn west onto the Siltcoos Beach/Forest Road 1070. Go 1.4 miles to the campground.

Activities: Camping, dune exploration, fishing, boating, beachcombing.

Facilities: Campground, piped water, wheelchair-accessible restrooms with flush toilets.

Dates: Open year-round.

Fees: Fees are charged for camping and may be charged for parking.

Closest town: Florence, 9 miles.

For more information: Oregon Dunes National Recreation Area, 855 Highway Avenue, Reedsport, OR 97467. Phone (541) 271-3611.

LAGOON CAMPGROUND

[Fig. 50(3)] This campground in the Oregon Dunes National Recreation Area is in a stand of shore pine trees. It has no campsites designated specifically for RVs, but there are 39 sites suitable for either tents or RVs. All sites have tables and metal grills. Siltcoos Lake, about 3 miles from the campground, offers opportunities for boating and fishing. The ocean beach offers surf fishing.

The short Lagoon Trail into the nearby wetlands has viewing platforms that provide views of wildlife such as shorebirds and wading birds. Mammals such as beavers and river otters may also be found in the wetland. There is a nearby 1-mile trail to the beach.

Directions: Take US Highway 101 south from Florence for 7.1 miles, and turn west onto the Siltcoos Beach/Forest Road 1070. Go 1.4 miles to the campground.

Activities: Camping, dune exploration, fishing, boating, beachcombing.

Facilities: Campground, piped water, wheelchair-accessible restrooms with flush toilets.

Dates: Open year-round.

Fees: Fees are charged for camping and may be charged for parking.

Closest town: Florence, 9 miles.

For more information: Oregon Dunes National Recreation Area, 855 Highway Avenue, Reedsport, OR 97467. Phone (541) 271-3611.

BLACKBERRY CAMPGROUND

[Fig. 51(7)] This is one of a number of the Siuslaw National Forest campgrounds east of US Highway 101 in the Coast Mountain Range forests. It is located on a forested shoulder overlooking the Alsea River, which is popular for drifting, power boating, and fishing for steelhead, as well as chinook and coho salmon.

It has no campsites designated specifically for RVs, but there are 31 sites suitable for either tents or RVs. All sites have tables and metal grills.

Directions: From Waldport, take State Route 34 east for 17.8 miles to the campground entrance.

Activities: Camping, fishing.

Facilities: Campground, wheelchair-accessible restrooms, piped water.

Dates: Open year-round.

Fees: Fees are charged for camping and may be charged for parking.

Closest town: Waldport, 17.8 miles.

For more information: Waldport District Ranger Station, 1049 Southwest Pacific Highway, Waldport, OR 97394. Phone (541) 563-3211.

ENCHANTED VALLEY

[Fig. 51(8)] This area of lush open fields, a lake, and a creek, has wildlife, berries, and edible roots that once attracted Native Americans who traveled here to hunt game such as elk and deer, to fish for salmon, steelhead, and trout, and to gather edible plants. When Europeans arrived they used the open fields to raise livestock, which eventually became preponderantly dairy cattle. The farmers moved Bailey Creek to the edge of the valley, built dikes, and dredged the channel to provide more pasture for the livestock, inadvertently making it less desirable for the native fish.

Changes in the economy forced out the dairy industry in 1965 and the Longview Fiber Company, a forest products firm, obtained it in 1988. In 1991 Longview exchanged it for some U.S. Forest Service land. The Forest Service now is restoring the valley to its original condition.

The valley and its adjacent Mercer Lake now attract visitors interested in a wide variety of outdoor activities such as hiking, biking, bird-watching, hunting, and fishing. There are broad grassy meadows and stands of red alder, willow, and Douglas fir. Elk may frequent the valley any time of year but especially in the fall. Black-tailed deer can often be seen. Other mammals in the valley include otter, beaver, black bear, and mink. Birds include osprey and bald eagle. Steelhead and salmon swim up Bailey Creek in the winter to spawn. The creek and Mercer Lake also have rainbow and cutthroat trout, catfish, yellow perch, largemouth bass, and bluegill.

BLUEGILL
Lepomis macrochirus

The Forest Service is returning Bailey Creek to a more natural course and plans to plant trees along the bank to provide shade and shelter for fish. The agency also would like to realign the stream to form ponds that would provide habitat for more waterfowl.

Directions: On US Highway 101, 5 miles north of Florence, turn east on Mercer Lake Road and go about 3 miles to the Enchanted Valley parking area.

Activities: Hunting, fishing, bird-watching, wildlife viewing.

Facilities: Parking lot, wildlife viewing area.

Dates: Open year-round.

Fees: Parking fees may be charged

Closest town: Florence, 8 miles.

For more information: Mapleton Ranger Station, 4480 Highway 101 North, Building G, Florence, OR 97453. Phone (541) 902-8526.

MARY'S PEAK TRAIL

[Fig. 51(9)] This trail goes to the summit of Mary's Peak, which, at 4,097 feet in elevation, is the highest in the Siuslaw National Forest. Not only is Mary's Peak the highest, but it also is one of the few peaks in the forest where the nearly constant rain and unique growing conditions have resulted in lush meadows that offer a long-range view above the forest. That means that from the top, in the summer, visitors are surrounded with a riot of color from the meadow flowers, including beauties such as bleeding hearts, paintbrush, lupines, tiger lilies, and penstemons. In the distance there is a horizon full of the ocean, Coast Range Mountains, the Willamette Valley, and even the Cascade Mountain Range extending all the way to Mount Rainier in central Washington. That is a bonanza especially for people who remember to take their cameras.

There are several trails to Mary's Peak, to say nothing of a road, but a good choice of routes is the Mary's Peak Trail, which includes a section of an old sheepherder's trail. The route passes old-growth noble firs and there may be black-tailed deer along the way.

Directions: From Philomath, take State Route 34 south for 10 miles and turn north on the Mary's Peak Road. Go 9 miles to the trailhead.

Activities: Hiking.

Facilities: Trail.

Dates: Open year-round, depending on weather.

Fees: Trailhead fees may be charged.

Closest town: Philomath, 19 miles.

For more information: Waldport Ranger District, 1049 Southwest Pacific Highway, Waldport, OR 97394, phone (541) 563-3211.

Trail: 1.6 miles.

Elevation: 2,000-foot gain in elevation.

Degree of difficulty: Moderate.

Siskiyou National Forest

Siskiyou National Forest is located in southern Oregon and covers 1.09 million acres.

Ref: DeLorme Oregon
Atlas and Gazetteer

N

Langola
FLORAS CREEK
Denmark
COQUILLE RIVER
N. FORK
SALMON CREEK
WOODEN ROCK CREEK
COW CREEK
Rabbit Mountain

101
SIXES RIVER
S. FORK
SOUTH FORK COQUILLE RIVER
FOGEY CREEK

33

3

Grassy Knob Rd

Port Orford
Elk River Road
ELK RIVER
5
N. FORK
S. FORK
ROGUE RIVER
Baker Mountain

CR 375
TR 1160
4
Illahe

ROGUE RIVER

101
Ophir

Cedar Mountain

ROGUE RIVER
33
ILLINOIS RIVER
Onion Mountain

Wedderburn
Horse Sign Butte
1

Gold Beach

ILLINOIS RIVER
199

PACIFIC OCEAN
Collier Butte
Big Craggies
TINCUP CREEK

NFD 1376

CHETCO RIVER
Johnson Butte
LITTLE CHETCO RIVER

Carpenterville
Long Ridge
TR 1110
101
NFD 1909
2

CHETCO RIVER

Chetco Peak

Mount Emily
Buckskin Peak

N. Bank Chetco River Rd

Brookings
Harbor

1	Kalmiopsis Wilderness
2	Johnson Butte Trail No. 1110
3	Wild Rogue Wilderness
4	Rogue River National Recreation Trail
5	Grassy Knob Wilderness
	Siskiyou National Forest
	Rogue Wild and Scenic River
	Wilderness Areas
	Illinois Wild and Scenic River
	Trail

Siskiyou National Forest

[Fig. 52] With 1.1 million acres, this large national forest sprawls across the mountains in the southern extreme of Oregon a few miles east of the Pacific Ocean. It includes a large portion of the Siskiyou Mountain Range that is some 250 million years old and stretches in an east-west direction near the California Oregon border. The Siskiyou Range links the Coast Range Mountains, 40 to 60 million years old, to the inland Cascade Mountains, that is 2 to 60 million years old and still growing. The national forest also includes a small portion of the Coast Range Mountains and a small corner of it extends across the border into California.

The forest began its history in 1905 when President Theodore Roosevelt established the Siskiyou Forest Reserve. Two years later Congress redesignated it as the Siskiyou National Forest. The name is an Indian word for bob-tailed horse and according to legend, comes from a horse that was lost in the area. By the end of the twentieth century, Forest Service officials were considering a proposal to combine the Siskiyou with the adjacent Rogue National Forest to make it a much larger forest.

In 1852 prospectors found gold deposits in southwestern Oregon and soon small mining towns sprang up in and near where the national forest is now. The gold rush didn't amount to a great deal and most miners left to find better prospects. During World War II, miners developed chrome and nickel mines that did not last long after the war ended. Even so, there still are some 6,000 mostly dormant mining claims on the forest. The Illinois River valley is one of the places where the miners worked their claims. The river has been declared a Wild and Scenic River and still looks and feels much like it did when the gold seekers were here.

Congress has declared three areas entirely or nearly entirely within the Siskiyou Forest to be wilderness areas (*see* Kalmiopsis Wilderness, page 343; Grassy Knob Wilderness, page 347; and Wild Rogue Wilderness, page 344). Small portions of the Red Butte and Siskiyou Wilderness areas also extend into the Siskiyou Forest.

The national forest's terrain is rough, mountainous, and steep with outcrops of serpentine rock. The highest spot is the peak of Grayback Mountain at 7,055 feet in elevation. The landscape varies from timberland, to open grass and brushy areas. The Siskiyou Mountains' glossy, bright green serpentine rock contains large amounts of heavy metals, which makes the soils especially poor and affects the vegetation. Because of poor soils many of the ridges have only stunted trees and rocky meadows. Some plants, however, have adapted to these conditions.

Among the major tree species of the forest are the sugar pine (*Pinus lambertiana*), ponderosa pine (*Pinus ponderosa*), Douglas fir (*Pseudotsuga menziesii*), grand fir (*Abies grandis*), Shasta fir (*Abies magnifica shastensis*), and white fir (*Abies concolor*). The forest contains some old-growth stands. The understory includes bigleaf maple (*Acer macrophyllum*), California black oak (*Quercus kelloggii*), tanoak (*Lithocarpus densiflora*), Pacific madrone (*Arbutus menziesi*), Oregon grape (*Berberis* sp.) and bunchberry

(*Cornus canadensis*). The rare Brewer spruce (*Picea breweriana*) of this area grows in only a few other places. The *Kalmiopsis leachiana* that looks like a dwarf rhododendron also grows almost exclusively in the Siskiyou Mountains. The Kalmiopsis Wilderness was named for it (*see* Kalmiopsis Wilderness Area, page 343). An estimated 2,000 flowering plants bloom in the national forest but no checklist has been completed.

Mammals in the forest include Roosevelt elk, mule deer, black bear, Townsend chipmunk (*Eutamius townsendi*), snowshoe hare (*Lepus americanus*), porcupine (*Erethizon dorsatum*), coyote (*Canis latrans*), striped skunk (*Mephitis mephitis*), marten (*Martes americana*), and gray fox (*Urocyron cinereoargenteus*). Reptiles include several species of salamander, treefrogs, and several species of snakes including the poisonous western rattlesnake (*Crotalus viridus*). Visitors should be careful to watch for the rattlesnakes. Generally, rattlers will run from humans rather than attack, but if they fear they are being attacked, or are trapped, they will fight back. Their bite is usually not fatal to a healthy adult human, but it is extremely painful over a long period of time. Keep an eye out for rattlers and never walk in a place where you can't see the ground, such as in brush where a snake may be hidden. And don't step over a log or rock where a snake may have taken shelter. The forest also has other creatures to be wary of, such as yellow jackets, scorpions, mosquitoes, biting flies, and ticks. More than 150 species of birds are on the national forest's checklist, including the blue heron (*Ardea herodias*), red-tailed hawk (*Buteo jamaicensis*), rufous hummingbird (*Selasphorus rufus*), common merganser (*Mergus merganser*), and Steller's jay (*Cyanocitta stelleri*).

In the forest there are some 40 campgrounds, with a total of well over 250 campsites ranging from small and primitive to large and well equipped, many with wheelchair-accessible facilities. Fire lookouts with magnificent mountain views and lowland cabins no longer used for the original purpose are available for rent. For details contact the Forest Supervisor's office. In addition to the forest's 40 maintained campgrounds, there are innumerable backcountry campsites along the 600 miles of trails into the interior.

The national forest is crisscrossed with trails, including some in the lower areas that go past poison oak plants (*Toxicodendron diversilobum*). Those plants, of course, should be admired only from a distance. Many of the trails outside the wilderness areas are open to bikes or horses and other livestock. Some trails are open to motorized trail bikes.

Whitewater rafting is popular on the Illinois and Rogue wild and scenic rivers in the national forest. The Chetco, Elk, and North Fork Smith wild and scenic rivers are less popular for rafting. The Rogue and Illinois rivers are especially wild and dangerous and are not recommended for inexperienced rafters. Permits are required to raft on sections of both of those rivers from May to October. Contact the Rand Visitor Center, 14335 Galice Road, Merlin, OR 97532, phone (541) 479-3735 for information.

Steelhead, cutthroat trout, and coho and chinook salmon are among the fish in the national forest. Bird hunters look for dove and grouse. Big game animals include elk, bear, and deer.

Directions: The Siskiyou National Forest straddles the Coastal Mountain range in southern Oregon and has many access points. To reach the western portion of the forest take County Road 595 east from Gold Beach for approximately 10 miles to where the road enters the national forest. On the east side, visitors can take US Highway 199 southwest for about 10 miles from Grants Pass, then turn west on County Road 3690, and go about 2 miles to the forest border.

Activities: Hiking, camping, fishing, boating, hunting, horseback riding, trail biking, mountain biking, bird-watching, wildlife viewing, whitewater rafting.

Facilities: Campgrounds, picnic sites, trails, boat launches.

Dates: Open year-round.

Fees: There are fees for camping at many of the campgrounds and there may be a fee at trailheads.

Closest town: Brookings, 4 miles.

For more information: Forest Supervisor's Office, 200 Northeast Greenfield Road, PO Box 440, Grants Pass, OR 97526. Phone (541) 6500.

▨ KALMIOPSIS WILDERNESS

[Fig. 52(1)] At 179,800 acres, the Kalmiopsis Wilderness is by far the largest wilderness area on the Siskiyou National Forest. Geologically, the wilderness is part of the Klamath Mountain province that extends southward into California. Most of its rock was originally under the ocean and is either igneous (resulting from volcanic action), sedimentary (formed of compressed sediment), or metamorphic (igneous and sedimentary rock that has been altered by heat and pressure in the earth's interior). The rocks include serpentine, shale, sandstone, and veins of quartz that bear gold, and in the nineteenth century attracted mining, especially in the eastern part of the wilderness. The lowest valleys of the wilderness are about 500 feet in elevation, and the highest mountain is Pearsoll Peak at 5,098 feet in elevation. The landscape has deep, rough canyons, sharp, rocky ridges, and steep slopes that result in fast-flowing streams.

The Kalmiopsis Wilderness's rocks are unusually rich in heavy metals, which, in high doses, can be toxic to plants. But the flora has adapted to the harsh conditions and the wilderness is home to highly diverse plant communities with well over 300 plants growing in habitats ranging from forest, to open woods, to meadow, to moist riparian, to dry and rocky.

The Douglas fir (*Pseudotsuga menziesii*) is the dominant tree in the wilderness. This also is pine country and the trees here include ponderosa pine (*Pinus ponderosa*), lodgepole pine (*Pinus contorta*), western white pine (*Pinus monticola*), sugar pine (*Pinus lambertiana*), Jeffrey pine (*Pinus jeffreyi*), and knobcone pine (*Pinus attenuate*). There are, however considerable numbers of other coniferous species such as the white fir (*Abies concolor*), incense cedar (*Calocedrus decurrens*), and Pacific yew (*Taxus brevifolia*). Hardwood trees in the wilderness include the white alder (*Alnus rhombifolia*), red alder (*Alnus rubra*), Oregon white oak (*Quercus garryana*), canyon live oak (*Quercus chrysolepis*), and Pacific madrone (*Arbutus menziesii*). Among the other plants is the kalmiopsis (*Kalmiopsis leachiana*), a woody shrub with an attractive red flower. The wilderness gives protection to the kalmiopsis that grows almost exclusively here and is one of the world's rarest shrubs. It is a survivor of the era before the last Ice Age, is the oldest member of the heath (Ericaceae) family, and was first discovered in Gold Basin in the eastern section of the wilderness.

Directions: There are no roads open to motorized equipment but there are 13 trails into the wilderness. One of them can be reached by starting in Brookings and taking County Road 784, which becomes Forest Road 1376. Travel for about 15 miles and turn right onto Forest Road 1909. On that road, go about 13 miles, passing intersections with several other forest roads, but staying on Forest Road 1909, which leads to the trailheads of the Vulcan Peak Trail Number 1120, and Johnson Butte Trail Number 1110, both of which go into the wilderness.

Activities: Hiking, camping, fishing, hunting.

Facilities: None.

Dates: Open year-round, depending on weather.

Fees: A trailhead fee may be charged.

Closest town: Brookings, 30 miles.

For more information: Chetco Ranger Station, 555 Fifth Street, Brookings, OR 97415. Phone (541) 469-2196.

JOHNSON BUTTE TRAIL NUMBER 1110

[Fig. 52(2)] This 6.2-mile one-way trail in the Kalmiopsis Wilderness begins on an old road that once served chrome mines. After about 1.5 miles the route becomes a foot trail that passes stands of cedar, spruce, fir, and pine trees among others, and after a few miles it reaches some of the rare kalmiopsis plants that are a major attraction to the wilderness.

Views along the way include mountain peaks, ridges, and forest. Below are the Illinois River valley, creeks, and lakes. There are campsites at Salamander Lake about 5 miles from the trailhead. The route ends at Johnson Butte, 3,379 feet in elevation, but hikers may extend their trip on the Upper Chetco Trail.

Directions: From Brookings, take County Road 784 which becomes Forest Road 1376 for about 15 miles and turn right onto Forest Road 1909. Go about 13 miles, passing intersections with several other forest roads, but staying on Forest Road 1909 which leads to the trailhead to the Johnson Butte Trail Number 1110, and the Vulcan Peak Trail Number 1120 which forks off about 0.75 mile from the trailhead.

Activities: Hiking, camping.

Dates: Open spring through fall.

Fees: There may be a trailhead fee.

Trail: 6 miles, one way.

Elevation: Minor elevation gain.

Degree of difficulty: Moderate.

WILD ROGUE WILDERNESS

[Fig. 52(3)] This 36,038-acre wilderness includes 8,971 acres of U.S. Bureau of Land Management land on its northeastern end, but the remainder is part of the Siskiyou National Forest and all of it is administered by the national forest. The wilderness occupies the valley of the Rogue Wild and Scenic River (*see* below) and serves as a buffer for the river. The terrain is very steep and so brushy that cross-country travel is almost impossible.

Directions: From Gold Beach, take County Road 595, which becomes Forest Road 33, for about 32 miles. Turn right onto County Road 375, which also is called the Illahe Road. Go about 1.5 miles to the trailhead of Trail 1160, the Rogue Wild River Trail. Trail 1160 leads to short side trails that go into the wilderness.

Activities: Hiking, camping, fishing.

Facilities: None.

Dates: Open year-round depending on weather.

Fees: There may be a trailhead fee.

Closest town: Gold Beach, 34 miles.

For more information: U.S. Forest Service Gold Beach Ranger Station, 29279 Ellensburg Road, Gold Beach, OR 97444. Phone (541) 247-3600. Or BLM Medford District office, 3040 Biddle Road, Medford, OR 97504. Phone (541) 618-2273.

ROGUE WILD AND SCENIC RIVER

[Fig. 52] Congress designated some 84 miles of this magnificent river as Wild and Scenic in 1968, with the upper 47 miles administered by the BLM and the lower 37 by the Siskiyou National Forest. A central part of the Wild and Scenic River zone is adjacent to the Wild Rogue Wilderness Area but, is administered with different restrictions and is accessible by jet boat, as well as whitewater raft and a 40-mile trail that follows the north bank of the river and is closed to horses, bicycles, and all motorized equipment. Scenic areas of the river can be reached by road and have been developed.

The banks of the river are forested with vegetation such as Oregon ash (*Fraxinus latifolia*), bigleaf maple (*Acer macrophyllum*), and Pacific madrone (*Arbutus menziesii*) in the upper portion. The lower stretches have species such as Douglas fir (*Pseudotsuga menziesii*), western hemlock (*Thuja heterophylla*), and grand fir (*Abies grandis*).

Birds include kingfisher (*Ceryle alcyon*), western wood peewee (*Contopus sordidulus*), and yellow warbler (*Dendroica petechia*). Among the mammals that may be seen here are deer, bear, mink, and raccoon. Fish include salmon and steelhead.

There are 19 campgrounds along the Wild and Scenic Rogue River with a total of some 1,300 campsites. Shuttle service, which takes people and equipment to places accessible by motor vehicles, is available from some nearby communities. For information about the shuttles contact the BLM Rand Visitor Center. The river is rough and float trips require special boats and the skill to operate them safely. For a list of authorized outfitters, contact the BLM Medford District Office. Floating permits are required from May to Oct. They are issued by the Rand Visitor Center. Jet boat firms take passengers for trips of varying lengths including into the wild and scenic section of the river. They can be contacted through the Gold Beach Chamber of Commerce, 29279 Ellensburg, Gold Beach, OR 97444. Phone (800) 525-2334 or (541) 247-7526.

Directions: Take County Road 595, which parallels the Rogue River northeast from Gold Beach. Go about 11 miles to the Siskiyou National Forest border where the Wild and Scenic River designation begins.

Activities: Hiking, camping, jet boating, river rafting, hunting, fishing.

Facilities: Trail, campgrounds.

Dates: Open year-round.

Fees: A trailhead fee may be charged.

Closest town: Gold Beach, 10 miles.

For more information: U.S. Forest Service Gold Beach Ranger Station, 29279 Ellensburg Road, Gold Beach, OR 97444. Phone (541) 247-3600. BLM Medford District Office, 3040 Biddle Road, Medford, OR 97504. Phone (541) 618-2273. BLM Rand Visitor Center, 14335 Galice Road, Merlin, OR 97532. Phone (541) 479-3735.

ROGUE RIVER NATIONAL RECREATION TRAIL

[Fig. 52(4)] This 42-mile trail courses through the canyon of the Rogue National Wild and Scenic River, closely following the bank of the rushing river. A 12-mile segment of the national recreation trail is adjacent to the Wild Rogue Wilderness. The national recreation trail is closed to livestock, bicycles, and motorized vehicles. The trail is well constructed and maintained, but after a storm, landslides, fallen trees, and high water can present difficult obstructions. It takes the average hiker four to five days to complete the entire hike but a vehicle access point at Marial makes it possible to shorten the trip. Shuttle services are available for transportation to and from the access point. For information about the shuttles contact the BLM Rand Visitor Center. There are some 40 primitive campsites along the trail.

Seven lodges along the Wild and Scenic River offer lodging. All but one are accessible by trail. All are accessible by float craft. Four are accessible by powerboat. One, at Marial, is accessible by motor vehicle, and one is accessible by aircraft. All of them offer at least one meal. Prices range from moderate to expensive. For specific information contact the U.S. Forest Service Gold Beach Ranger Station or the BLM Medford District office.

The trail follows the north side of the river, wandering through the canyon carved by the rushing water over the eons. Much of the landscape is the barren rock walls of the canyon but there also are forested areas of trees such as Douglas fir, madrone, and tanoak. Deer, bear, and otters are among the mammals, and osprey hunt the river for unwary fish.

Directions: From Gold Beach take County Road 595, which becomes Forest Road 33, for about 32 miles. Turn right onto County Road 375, which also is called the

Illahe Road. Go about 1.5 miles to the trailhead of Trail 1160, the Rogue Wild River National Recreation Trail.

For more information: U.S. Forest Service Gold Beach Ranger Station, 29279 Ellensburg, Gold Beach, OR 97444, phone (541) 247-3600. BLM Medford District office, 3040 Biddle Road, Medford, OR 97504, phone (541) 618-2273. BLM Rand Visitor Center, 14335 Galice Road, Merlin, OR 97532, phone (541) 479-3735.

Trail: 42 miles.

Elevation: Minor elevation gain.

Degree of difficulty: Moderate.

GRASSY KNOB WILDERNESS

[Fig. 52(5)] This little wilderness with 17,200 acres on the northwestern corner of the national forest is characterized by rugged, forested-canyon terrain with underbrush so dense that it is difficult to penetrate. There is only one trail, an abandoned road that penetrates about a mile into the wilderness area to the former site of a fire lookout. There is nothing left of the lookout building but the foundations. The view of forests and mountain peaks, however, is still there and still awesome.

The forest in the seldom-visited wilderness includes fir, tanoak, cedar, alder, and maple. The understory contains Oregon grape, bunchberry, and salal. Deer, cougar, bobcat, and bear are among the mammals here.

Directions: Approximately 1 mile north of Port Orford on US Highway 101, take County Road 208 to the east. In about 4 miles the road enters the national forest and becomes Forest Road 5105. About 4 miles from the forest boundary, the road becomes an easy trail, which extends about 1 mile into the wilderness and the former lookout site.

Activities: Hiking.

Facilities: None.

Dates: Open year-round.

Fees: There may be a trailhead fee.

Closest town: Port Orford, 9 miles.

For more information: Powers Ranger Station, Highway 242, Powers, OR 97466. Phone (541) 439-3011.

BOBCAT
(Lynx rufus)

Appendices

A. Books and References

Agents of Chaos by Stephen L. Harris, Mountain Press Publishing Company, Missoula, MT, 1990.

Driving the Pacific Coast by Ken Oberrecht, Globe Pequot Press, Old Saybrook, CT, 1998.

Flood Tide of Empire by Warren L. Cook, Yale University Press, New Haven, CT, 1973.

Geology of the Pacific Northwest by Elizabeth Orr and William N. Orr, The McGraw Hill Companies, New York, NY, 1996.

Guide to the Geology of the Olympic National Park by Rowland W. Tabor, University of Washington Press, Seattle, WA, 1975.

Hunters of the Whale by Ruth Kirk with Richard D. Daugherty, William Morrow and Company, New York, NY, 1974.

Ice Ages Past and Future by Jon Erickson, Tab Books, Blue Ridge Summit, PA, 1990.

Indian Life on the Northwest Coast of North America by Erna Gunther, University of Chicago Press, Chicago, IL, 1972.

Marine Life of the Pacific Northwest by Thomas M. Niesen, Gulf Publishing Company, Houston, TX, 1997.

Middle Puget Sound and Hood Canal by Marge and Ted Mueller, The Mountaineers, Seattle, WA, 1990.

National Audubon Society Field Guide to the Pacific Northwest by Peter Alden and Dennis Paulson, Alfred A. Knopf, New York, NY, 1998.

Northwest Exposures by David Alt and Donald W. Hyndman, Mountain Press Publishing Company, Missoula, MT, 1995.

Northwest Trees by Stephen F. Arno and Ramona Hammerly, The Mountaineers, Seattle, WA, 1977.

100 Hikes in Oregon by Rhonda and George Ostertag, The Mountaineers, Seattle, WA, 1992.

Oregon: A Best Places Guide by Terry Richard, Sasquatch Books, Seattle, WA, 1998.

Oregon State Parks: A Complete Recreation Guide by Jan Bannon, The Mountaineers, Seattle, WA, 1993.

Outside Magazine's Adventure Guide to the Pacific Northwest by Karl Samson, Simon and Schuster, New York, NY, 1997.

Pacific Northwest Hiking by Ron C. Judd and Dan A. Nelson, Foghorn Press, San Francisco, CA, 1997.

Portland's Best Places by Kim Carlson and Stephanie Irving, Sasquatch Books, Seattle, WA, 1995.

Prehistoric Life on the Olympic Peninsula by Eric O. Bergland and Jerry Marr, Pacific Northwest National Parks & Forests Association, Seattle, WA, 1988.

Scenic Geology of the Pacific Northwest by Leonard Ekman, Binfords and Mort, Portland, OR, 1962.

The Ancient Forests of Washington by The Dittmar Family and Charlie Raines, The Mountaineers, Seattle, WA, 1996.

The Columbia River by JoAnn Roe, Fulcrum Publishing, Golden, CO, 1992.

The Last Wilderness by Murray Morgan, Viking Press, New York, NY, 1955.

The Sierra Club Guide to the Natural Areas of Oregon and Washington by John Perry and Greverus Perry, Sierra Club Books, San Francisco, CA, 1997.

Umbrella Guide to Oregon Lighthouses by Sharlene and Ted Nelson, Umbrella Books, Seattle, WA, 1994.

Umbrella Guide to Washington Lighthouses by Sharlene and Ted Nelson, Umbrella Books, Seattle, WA, 1998.

Undaunted Courage by Stephen E. Ambrose, Touchstone, New York, NY, 1996.

Vancouver's Discovery of Puget Sound by Edmond S. Meany, Binfords and Mort, Portland, OR, 1949.

Washington State Parks by Marge and Ted Mueller, The Mountaineers, Seattle, WA, 1999.

B. Washington State Parks

Washington state parks offer a wide variety of experiences and amenities. Many of the small islands that dot Puget Sound and the San Juan Islands are accessible only to people with boats and offer little more than primitive campsites with no water. Other parks, like Deception Pass, Blake Island, and Fort Worden, offer an abundance of facilities, including museums, historic displays, showers, and playgrounds, and activities such as camping, swimming, fishing, boating, and hiking.

Lack of space and the remoteness and inaccessibility of some locations precluded mention of every state park in this book. Here, however, is a list of the state parks in the areas covered in the text. There are 17 marine parks in the San Juan Islands and 24 in Puget Sound. They are designed primarily for boats and have docks, floats, and buoys where visitors may moor their vessels for a fee. Some individual parks do not have telephones. For information about them, or the park system as a whole, call Washington State Park and Recreation Department at (800) 233-0321. The Washington State Park and Recreation Department address is 7150 Clearwater Lane, PO Box 42650, Olympia, Washington 98504-2650.

Washington and Oregon share a park reservations system, Reservations Northwest, (800) 452-5687. Oregon takes reservations year-round, but Washington reservations run from May 15 to September 15, except for Fort Canby and Deception Pass, where reservations can be made year-round. Reservations can be made from two days to 11 months ahead of time.

Washington's Fort Worden State Park takes its own reservations and may be reached by calling (360) 385-4730.

OLYMPIA/TACOMA AREA

Tolmie State Park, 8 miles northeast of Olympia. Fishing, boating, beach, hiking, picnicking. There is also an underwater park for scuba-diving. **Eagle Island Marine State Park**, on Balch Passage between McNeil and Anderson Islands. Fishing, boating, beach, hiking. The tiny 10-acre island offers a sandy point to sunbathe and nearby harbor seals for company. **Jarrell Cove State Park,** East 391 Wingert Road, Shelton. Phone (360) 426-9226. Camping, fishing, boating, hiking, picnicking. Located on Harstine Island, this boater-friendly park offers car travelers an open field for camping. **Joemma Beach State Park,** 1 mile northwest of Longbranch. Phone (253) 884-1944. Camping, fishing, boating, beach, hiking, picnicking. Only 0.5 mile trail, but good crabbing and shellfish gathering are to be had here. **Hope Island Marine State Park,** near Olympia at the confluence of Pickering Passage, Hammersley Inlet, and Totten Inlet. Camping, fishing, boating, beach, hiking, picnicking. The campground on this small, heavily wooded island is situated on an old farm with trails around the island and to the beach. **Harstine Island State Park,** near Olympia, on west side of Harstine Island. Beach, hiking. Here a 1-mile long-hike leads through a small section of old-growth forest. **McMicken Island Marine State Park,** off the east side of Harstine Island. Fishing, boating, swimming, beach, hiking, picnicking. The island is accessible by foot at minus tide and has a pleasant trail and good clamming. **Stretch Point Marine State Park**, in Case Inlet on the northeast side of Stretch Island. Fishing, boating, beach, picnicking. The park's chief delight is a wonderful sandy beach. **Penrose Point State Park**, 321 158th Avenue, Lakebay. Phone (253) 884-2514. Camping, fishing, boating, swimming, beach, hiking, picnicking. Child-friendly campground with a good mix of trails, woods, and beaches. **Kopachuck State Park,** 11101 Fifty-sixth Street Northwest, Gig Harbor. Phone (253) 265-3606. Camping, fishing, boating, swimming, beach, hiking, picnicking. The shallow bay warms up quickly in the sun, and wildflowers are found in the forested campground. **Cutts Island Marine State Park**, 0.2 mile west of Kopachuck State Park. Fishing, boating, swimming, beach. This park is an easy paddle from Kopachuck State Park if the wind and tides aren't too fierce. **Dash Point State Park,** 5700 Southwest Dash Point Road, Federal Way. Phone (253) 661-4955. Camping, boating, swimming, beach hiking, picnicking. Nearly 7.5 miles of trails and a gently sloping shoreline make this park very popular. **West Hylebos Wetlands State Park**, 1 mile west of Interstate 5 Exit 142B in Federal Way. Hiking. The 1-mile boardwalk nature trail wanders through wetlands and forests. **Saltwater State Park**, 25205 Eighth Place South, Des Moines. Phone (425) 823-2992. Camping, fishing, boating, swimming, beach, hiking, picnicking. Nestled in a canyon, the park has a nice mix of beach and forest, plus a playground and swimming area.

SEATTLE AREA

Harper State Park, from Southworth ferry terminal travel 1.2 miles west on State Route 106 to Olympiad Road to reach the park. Fishing, boating. A high tide boat launch offers the nearest access to Blake

Island. **Blake Island Marine State Park**, 8 miles west of Seattle, boat access only. Phone (360) 731-8330. Camping, fishing, boating, swimming, beach, hiking, picnicking. This most popular of the state's marine parks has great views of Seattle's skyline, historic sites, and access to Tillicum Village (*see* page 58). **Fort Ward State Park**, 2241 Pleasant Beach Drive Northeast, Bainbridge Island. Phone (206) 842-4041. Camping, boating, beach, hiking, picnicking. Primitive campsites and good bird-watching coincide with World War I gun batteries.

BREMERTON/BAINBRIDGE ISLAND AREA

Square Lake State Park, 4 miles southwest of Port Orchard. Fishing, boating, swimming, hiking, picnicking. Most of this freshwater lake is undeveloped, but there are old fir groves and a short trail. **Manchester State Park**, 6 miles northeast of Port Orchard on State Route 16. Phone (360) 871-4065. Camping, fishing, boating, swimming, hiking, picnicking. Foxes and deer can be spotted along the trails or from the picnic shelter, a former torpedo storage site. **Fay Bainbridge State Park**, 15446 Sunrise Drive Northeast, Bainbridge Island. Phone (206) 842-3931. Camping, fishing, boating, beach, hiking, picnicking. The sandy beach has horseshoes, volleyball nets, and fire pits. **Illahee State Park**, 3540 Bahia Vista, Bremerton. Phone (360) 478-6460. Camping, fishing, boating, swimming, beach, hiking, picnicking. Another former military site, Illahee is forested and has a sand beach at low tide. **Scenic Beach State Park**, 12 miles northwest of Bremerton near Seabeck. Phone (360) 830-5079. Camping, fishing, boating, beach, hiking, picnicking. Views of the Olympic Mountains across Hood Canal and excellent hiking in the nearby Green Mountain Forest are the chief features here. **Old Man House State Park**, near Agate Pass. Picnicking. Historical displays commemorate the spot where an immense Indian longhouse once stood and where Chief Sealth, also known as Seattle and for whom the city is named, is said to have been born.

WHIDBEY ISLAND AREA

Fort Casey State Park, 1280 Engle Road, Coupeville. Phone (360) 678-4519. Camping, fishing, boating, beach, hiking, picnicking. Gun emplacements, Admiralty Head Lighthouse, and great views are among the attractions of this popular park (*see* page 88). **Deception Pass State Park**, 5175 North State Route 20, Oak Harbor. Phone (360) 675-2417. Camping, fishing, boating, swimming, beach, hiking, picnicking. The state's most popular park includes salt and fresh water, and beach and land activities in a stunning setting (*see* page 89). **Fort Ebey State Park,** 395 North Fort Ebey Road, Coupeville. Phone (360) 678-7636. Camping, fishing, beach, hiking, picnicking. Besides the beach, this park offers views, World War II gun battery remains, and two glacial depressions known as Ebey's Kettles (*see* page 87). **Ebey's Landing State Park**, 3 miles west of Coupeville. Fishing, beach, hiking. Pioneer property has historic markers and one of the few remaining block forts from the 1855 Indian Wars; there's no water (*see* page 86). **Hope Island State Park**, Skagit Bay, near Deception Pass State Park. Camping, boating, hiking. Primitive camping, no water, but frequently there are roosting eagles and herons. **Joseph Whidbey State Park**, 5 miles northwest of Oak Harbor. Camping, fishing, beach, picnicking. The sand-and-gravel beach is wonderful for activities such as walking and beachcombing. **South Whidbey State Park**, 4128 South Smugglers Cove Road, Freeland. Phone (360) 331-4559. Camping, fishing, beach, hiking, picnicking. The park has a nice stretch of beach, and child-friendly trails running through old Douglas fir and western redcedar forests. **Skagit Island State Park**, at the head of Skagit Bay near Deception Pass State Park. Boating, hiking. Located in the mouth of Skagit Bay, the island has offshore boat moorings and an undeveloped hiking trail.

MUKILTEO/EVERETT AREA

Mukilteo State Park, at Mukilteo on Possession Sound. Fishing, boating, beach, picnicking. This popular park, right next to the Washington State Ferry terminal and the Mukilteo Lighthouse, features a flat, pebbly beach and interpretive displays (*see* page 73). **Wenberg State Park**, 15430 East Lake Goodwin Road, Stanwood. Phone (360) 652-7417. Camping, fishing, boating, swimming, picnicking. This popular freshwater lake is located off Interstate 5 near Camano Island, Whidbey Island, and the San Juan Islands. **Camano Island State Park**, 2269 South Lowell Point Road, Camano Island. Phone (360) 387-3031. Camping, fishing, boating, swimming, beach, hiking, picnicking. Wooded campgrounds sit on the bluff above the cobblestone beach.

ANACORTES AREA

Bay View State Park, 10905 Bay View-Edison Road, Mount Vernon. Phone (360) 757-0227. Camping, fishing, swimming, beach, picnicking. Black brant, herons, eagles, and snow geese use the area to rest and feed. **Saddlebag Island State Park**, 2 miles northeast of Anacortes in Padilla Bay. Camping, fishing, boating, hiking, picnicking. Excellent crabbing exists offshore of this island, which has primitive campsites and no fresh water.

SAN JUAN ISLANDS AREA

Moran State Park, 3572 Olga Road, Eastsound, Orcas Island. Phone (360) 376 2326. Camping, fishing, boating, swimming, hiking, picnicking. There is no saltwater access here, but there are several lakes, fabulous views, and plenty of hiking, including trails on Mount Constitution. **Lime Kiln Point State Park**, 6158 Lime Kiln Road, Friday Harbor, San Juan Island. Phone (360) 378-2044. Hiking, picnicking. Whales can be spotted throughout the year as they pass through Haro Strait (*see* page 101). **Blind Island Marine State Park**, west of Shaw Island. Camping, fishing, boating, picnicking. This 3-acre rock has primitive camping with no drinking water and is open only to human-or-wind-powered boats. **Turn Island Marine State Park**, 2 miles from Friday Harbor off the northeast tip of San Juan Island. Camping, fishing, boating, beach, hiking, picnicking. Open to people with access to a boat, the campsites are primitive with no potable water; the rest of the island is a wildlife refuge, which is open to the public provided the wildlife is not disturbed. **Spencer Spit State Park**, 521A Bakerview Road, Lopez Island. Phone (360) 468-2521. Camping, fishing, boating, beach, hiking, picnicking. Visitors will find fresh drinking water on this island is scarce, but wooded paths lead to the shore and a brackish lagoon where migratory birds rest and feed. **Burrows Island**, Burrows Bay, Rosario Strait. Camping, boating, beach. This undeveloped state property, located next to the Burrows Island lighthouse, has a primitive campground and no potable water. **James Island Marine State Park**, near Anacortes, 0.2 mile east of Decatur Island. Camping, fishing, boating, beach hiking, picnicking. This campground is wooded and a short hike leads to a small beach; bring water. **Doe Island Marine State Park**, off the southeast side of Orcas Island near Doe Bay. Camping, fishing, boating, beach, hiking, picnicking. Visitors need to bring their own drinking water to this remote, underutilized island frequented by seabirds. **Clark Island Marine State Park**, 2 miles off the northeast tip of Orcas Island near Lawrence Point. Camping, fishing, boating, beach, hiking, picnicking. There's no drinking water, but good trails lead to two beaches and excellent tidepools. **Patos Island Marine State Park**, 5.5 miles north of Orcas Island. Camping, fishing, boating, beach, hiking, picnicking. The site of Patos Island Lighthouse, the park features primitive campsites, toilets, and no potable water. **Sucia Island Marine State Park**, 2.5 miles north of Orcas Island. Phone (360) 376-2073. Camping, fishing, boating, swimming, beach, hiking, picnicking. The horseshoe-shaped island has interesting geological formations and plenty of wildlife, but water is available only from April through September. **Matia Island Marine State Park**, 2.5 miles north of Orcas Island. Camping, fishing, boating, beach, hiking, picnicking. Visitors will find a primitive campground and no fresh water, but most of the island is set aside as a wildlife refuge, so there are excellent wildlife spotting opportunities. **Stuart Island Marine State Park**, 5 miles northwest of San Juan Island. Camping, fishing, boating, beach, hiking, picnicking. The park features primitive campsites and no drinking water much of the year; the island has a trail that leads out to Turn Point lighthouse and views of Haro Strait. **Posey Island Marine State Park**, 0.25 north of Roche Harbor, San Juan Island. Camping, fishing, beach, picnicking. This tiny, flat island has primitive camping, no potable water, wonderful wildflowers, and views of Vancouver Island. **Jones Island Marine State Park**, 1 mile west of the southwest end of Orcas Island. Camping, fishing, boating, beach, hiking, picnicking. The island is home to mink, eagles, and deer and potable water from April to September. **Larrabee State Park**, 245 Chuckanut Drive, Bellingham. Phone (360) 676-2093. Camping, fishing, boating, beach, hiking, picnicking. Hiking trails lead to freshwater lakes, panoramic sea views, and saltwater beaches. **Birch Bay State Park**, 5105 Helweg Road, Blaine. Phone (360) 371-2800. Camping, fishing, boating, beach, hiking, picnicking. A sandy beach with shallow water and a swampy woodland offer a variety of wildlife.

STRAIT OF JUAN DE FUCA AREA

Fort Flagler State Park, 10541 Flagler Road, Nordland. Phone (360) 385-1259. Camping, fishing, boating, beach, hiking, picnicking. This park includes an early twentieth century fort with gun batteries, the Marrowstone Lighthouse, and beaches. **Mystery Bay Marine State Park**, 1 mile south of the Fort Flagler State Park entrance. Boating, picnicking. The park offers good moorage and a boat launch. **Old Fort Townsend State Park**, 3 miles south of Port Townsend off State Route 20 on Old Fort Townsend Road. Camping, fishing, boating, hiking, picnicking. Historic interpretive center, forest trails, and views of Mount Baker are among the attractions here (*see* page 124). **Fort Worden State Park**, 200 Battery Way, Port Townsend. Phone (360) 385-4730. Camping, fishing, beach, hiking, picnicking. This early twentieth century fort houses a military museum and historic sites, playfields, and the Port Townsend Marine Science Center (*see* page 10). **Rothschild House State Park**, one block north of the intersection of Taylor and Franklin, Port Townsend. Picnicking. This restored 1868 house and its gardens are near downtown Port Townsend. **Sequim Bay State Park**, 269035 Highway 101, Sequim. Phone (360) 683-4235. Camping, fishing, boating, beach, hiking, picnicking. The park features interpretive displays, playfields, and short hiking trails. **Bogachiel State Park**, 185983 Highway 101, Forks. Phone (360) 374-6356. Camping, fishing, picnicking. The forested campground sits right next to the Bogachiel River.

HOOD CANAL AREA

Kitsap Memorial State Park, on State Route 3, 4 miles south of the Hood Canal Bridge. Phone (360) 779-3205. Camping, fishing, boating, beach, hiking, picnicking. The beach is rocky, but the park also has playfields and a play area (*see* page 206). **Dosewallips State Park**, 1 mile south of Brinnon on US Highway 101. Phone (360) 675-2417. Camping, fishing, beach, hiking, picnicking. A trail leads to the beach where there are views and, in season, good clamming. **Pleasant Harbor State Park**, 2 miles south of Brinnon on US Highway 101. Phone (360) 675-2417. Boating. The small park offers moorage in a peaceful harbor (*see* page 206). **Triton Cove State Park**, 7 miles south of Dosewallips on US Highway 101. Phone (360) 675-2417. Fishing, boating, picnicking. Primarily a boat launch, the park has picnic tables and handicapped-accessible shore fishing. **Lake Cushman State Park**, 7 miles west of Hoodsport on State Route 119. Phone (360) 877-5491. Camping, fishing, boating, swimming, beach, hiking, picnicking. The man-made lake offers activities and facilities, including a swimming beach, wooded trail, and good fishing (*see* page 208). **Hoodsport Trail State Park**, 2 miles west of Hoodsport on State Route 119. Phone (360) 877-5491. Hiking, picnicking. Visitors will find 2 miles of easy trails through second growth forest and a short interpretative trail (*see* page 207). **Potlatch State Park**, 3 miles south of Hoodsport on US Highway 101. Phone (360) 877-5361. Camping, fishing, boating, hiking, picnicking. A cobblestone-strewn beach offers good shellfish gathering at this old Indian ceremonial site (*see* page 209). **Twanoh State Park**, 12190 East Highway 106, Union. Phone (360) 275-2222. Camping, fishing, boating, swimming, hiking, picnicking. The beach water gets warm enough to swim in on sunny days. **Belfair State Park**, 410 Northeast Beck Road, Belfair. Phone (360) 275-0668. Camping, fishing, boating, swimming, picnicking. A dike at this former Indian campsite creates a small, warm, saltwater pool that is an excellent place for swimming.

WASHINGTON BEACHES AREA

Schaefer State Park, 1365 Schaefer Park Road, Elma. Phone (360) 482-3852. Camping, fishing, hiking, picnicking. Located between Olympia and the ocean, Schaefer has a shallow wading area on the bank of the Satsop River's east fork. **Lake Sylvia State Park**, off US Highway 12, 1 mile north of Montesano. Camping, fishing, boating, swimming, hiking, picnicking. In this park, a dam-created lake has plenty of waterfront campsites. **Griffiths-Priday State Park**, in Copalis; turn west on Benner Road and follow the signs. Beach, hiking, picnicking. Sandy beaches and grassy dunes make this an excellent spot for bird-watching and beach walks. **Pacific Beach State Park,** State Route 109 in Pacific Beach. Camping, fishing, beach, picnicking. The beach is excellent for beachcombing and kite flying (*see* page 214). **Ocean City State Park**, 1.5 miles north of Ocean Shores. Phone (360) 389-3553. Camping, fishing, beach, picnicking. Dunes, creek, wildlife, and plants can be found in abundance here (*see* page 215). **Ocean Shores Environmental Interpretive Center**, 1 mile from the intersection of Point Brown Avenue and Discovery Avenue Southeast in Ocean Shores. The center explains the history and nature of Point Brown. **Westhaven State Park**, 6 miles north of Twin Harbors. Fishing, beach, hiking, picnicking. The state's favorite surfboarding beach also offers good surf-fishing (*see* page 219). **Westport Light State Park**, 22 miles southwest of Aberdeen on State Route 105. Fishing, beach, hiking, picnicking. Besides the lighthouse, there are dunes and 1 mile of easy hiking (*see* page 222). **Damon Point State Park**, southeast tip of Ocean Shores Peninsula. Beach, picnicking. Over 200 different bird species can be spotted here. **Twin Harbors State Park**, 3 miles south of Westport. Phone (360) 268-9717. Camping, fishing, beach, picnicking. This popular campground has a myriad plants growing among the dunes (*see* page 223). **Grayland Beach State Park**, in Grayland on State Route 105 at Cranberry Beach Road. Camping, fishing, beach, hiking. There is no designated picnic area, but the beach is a great place for picnicking, kite flying, and shellfish gathering (*see* page 225). **Leadbetter Point State Park**, 17 miles north of Long Beach on State Route 103. Fishing, beach, hiking, picnicking. Several miles of mostly easy trails pass through shady woods to the beach (*see* page 231). **Pacific Pines State Park**, 10 miles north of Long Beach on State Route 103. Fishing, beach, hiking, picnicking. This tiny park has a sheltered picnic area and beach access (*see* page 232). **Loomis Lake State Park**, 9 miles north of Long Beach on State Route 103. Fishing, beach, picnicking.

The lake property is undeveloped, but there is access to a small ocean beach suitable for kite flying and clam digging (*see* page 233). **Fort Canby State Park**, 2.5 miles southwest of Ilwaco. Phone (360) 642-3078. Camping, fishing, boating, beach, hiking, picnicking. The park also rents cabins and yurts, and North Beach and Cape Disappointment lighthouses are nearby (*see* page 235). **Colbert House Heritage Area**, located at the intersection of Quaker and Lake streets, Ilwaco. A small pioneer home has been restored to its late 1800s glory (*see* page 239). **Fort Columbia State Park**, 1 mile from Chinook. Hiking, picnicking. Military and Indian history displays are housed in the old enlisted men's quarters. **Lewis and Clark Campsite Heritage Area**, On US Highway 101, 2 miles west of the juncture of US Highway 101 and State Route 401. Picnicking. Lewis and Clark camped and first spotted the Pacific Ocean from this commemorative park (*see* page 242). **Rainbow Falls State Park**, 4008 State Highway 6, Chehalis. Phone (360) 291-3767. Camping, fishing, hiking, picnicking. This Civilian Conservation Corps built this Chehalis River park, which has a suspension bridge where the falls can be viewed—and, under the right conditions, the rainbow spotted.

C. Oregon State Parks

Thanks to the foresight of a progressive governor, Oswald West, and the Oregon State Legislature, public access to Oregon's magnificent beaches and dunes was established in 1915. The state provides a plethora of state parks to enhance the visitor's enjoyment of this wonderful natural resource.

A year-round reservation system, which it shares with Washington State, has been set up for Oregon's state parks. Reservations may be made by calling Reservations Northwest, (800) 452-5687. Some of the individual park facilities do not have telephones. For information about them contact the Oregon State Park general information office at (800) 551-6949. The Oregon State Parks Information Center is located at 2501 Southwest Avenue, Suite 100, Portland, Oregon 97201; the mailing address is PO Box 500, Portland, Oregon, 97207.

OREGON'S NORTHERN BEACHES AREA

Fort Stevens State Park, 10 miles west of Astoria off US Highway 101. Phone (503) 861-1671. Camping, fishing, boating, swimming, beach, hiking, picnicking. This park offers the remains of a fort and the shipwrecked *Peter Ireland*, and a great beach (*see* page 266). **Del Rey Beach State Recreation Site**, 2 miles north of Gearhart off US Highway 101. Beach. It's an easy stroll from the parking lot to an excellent beach for kite flying and sandcastle building.

CANNON BEACH AREA

Ecola State Park, on Tillamook Head, 2 miles north of Cannon Beach. Fishing, hiking, beach, picnicking. Views of Tillamook Rock Lighthouse and 6 miles of the Oregon Coast Trail are among Ecola's pleasures (*see* page 274). **Tolovana Beach State Recreation Site**, 1 mile south of Cannon Beach on US Highway 101. Fishing, beach, picnicking. Enjoy the beach and views of Haystack Rock. **Arcadia Beach State Recreation Site**, 3 miles south of Cannon Beach on US Highway 101. Fishing, beach, picnicking. A shady picnic area entices beach-bound visitors. **Hug Point State Recreation Site**, 5 miles south of Cannon Beach on US Highway 101. Fishing, beach, picnicking. Natural caves can be found here.

MANZANITA AREA

Oswald West State Park, 10 miles south of Cannon Beach on US Highway 101. Phone (503) 368-5154. Camping, fishing, beach, hiking. Visitors use wooden wheelbarrows to cart their equipment to the campsites before heading to the sandy beach to play (*see* page 274). **Nehalem Bay State Park**, 3 miles south of Manzanita Junction off US Highway 101. Phone (503) 368-5154. Camping, fishing, boating, beach, hiking, picnicking. Enjoy beach activities during the day and sleep in a yurt at night (*see* page 275). **Manhattan Beach State Recreation Site**, 2 miles north of Rockaway on US Highway 101. Fishing, beach, picnicking. Spectacular 7.5-mile stretch of sandy beach offers rock formations, kite flying, and great beauty.

NETARTS AND OCEANSIDE AREA

Cape Meares State Scenic Viewpoint, 10 miles west of Tillamook on US 101. Hiking, picnicking. A short, paved trail through the woods takes visitors to Cape Meares Lighthouse and ocean views. **Oceanside Beach State Recreation Site**, 6 miles west of Tillamook off US Highway 101. Fishing, beach. Look for agates on this beach located in the center of Oceanside. **Cape Lookout State Park**, 8.5 miles southwest of

Tillamook off US Highway 101, on Three Capes Scenic Loop. Phone (503) 842-4981. Camping, fishing, beach, hiking, picnicking. Listen to the waves from oceanside campsites.

PACIFIC CITY AREA

Cape Kiwanda State Natural Area, on Three Capes Scenic Loop, 1 mile north of Pacific City off US Highway 101. Fishing, beach, hiking. Hikers will find sand dunes, tidepools, and wave-shaped cliffs. **Robert Straub State Park**, at Pacific City on Nestucca River Sand Spit off US Highway 101. Fishing, beach, picnicking. Walk along Bob Straub Beach to explore Nestucca River Sand Spit.

NESKOWIN AREA

Neskowin Beach State Recreation Site, US Highway 101, Neskowin. Fishing, beach. Long stretch of sandy beach that is great for surf fishing, sandcastle building,

LINCOLN CITY AREA

Road's End State Recreation Site, 1 mile north of Lincoln City off US Highway 101. Fishing, beach, picnicking. Tidepools display a wide variety of marine life. **D River State Recreation Site**, Lincoln City, US Highway 101 at mouth of D River. Fishing, beach. Lincoln City's spring and fall kite flying festivals are held here. **Devil's Lake State Park**, at Lincoln City, off US Highway 101. Phone (541) 994-2002. Camping, fishing, boating. Boat moorage and wonderful wildlife viewing opportunities are featured here (*see* page 282). **Gleneden Beach State Recreation Site**, 7 miles south of Lincoln City on US Highway 101. Fishing, beach, picnicking. Seals often linger in the waters off the beach at the end of a short, forested trail. **Fogarty Creek State Recreation Area**, 2 miles north of Depoe Bay on US Highway 101. Fishing, beach, hiking, picnicking. Footbridges across the creek provide access to a smooth, sandy beach. **Boiler Bay State Scenic Viewpoint**, 1 mile north of Depoe Bay on US Highway 101. Picnicking. Wild waves pound the beach, named for the stranded boiler of a wrecked ship. **Rocky Creek State Scenic Viewpoint**, 2 miles south of Depoe Bay on US Highway 101. Fishing, beach, hiking, picnicking. Picnic and fish at this quiet wayside near Cape Foulweather. **Otter Crest State Scenic Viewpoint**, 10 miles north of Newport on Cape Foulweather on US Highway 101. Beach. There are good views of Cape Foulweather from this beach. **Devil's Punch Bowl State Natural Area**, 8 miles north of Newport off US Highway 101. Fishing, beach, picnicking. Tidepools and a spectacular collapsed cave entice beach-goers.

NEWPORT AREA

Beverly Beach State Park, 7 miles north of Newport on US Highway 101. Phone (541) 265-9278. Camping, fishing, beach, hiking, picnicking. Visitors will find good views of Yaquina Head Lighthouse and a sandy beach for kite flying and sandcastle building. **Agate Beach State Recreation Site**, 1 mile north of Newport off US Highway 101. Fishing, beach, picnicking. Yaquina Head Lighthouse can be seen from the agate-strewn beach. **Yaquina Bay State Recreation Site**, on US Highway 101, north end of Yaquina Bay Bridge, Newport. Fishing, beach, hiking, picnicking. **South Beach State Park**, 2 miles south of Newport on US Highway 101. Phone (541) 867-4715. Camping, fishing, beach, hiking, picnicking. Beach hikers are rewarded with good views of Yaquina Bay Lighthouse (*see* page 291). **Lost Creek State Recreation Site**, 7 miles south of Newport on US Highway 101. Fishing, beach, picnicking. Bird watchers will spot a plethora of birds, including brown pelicans. **Ona Beach State Park**, 8 miles south of Newport on US Highway 101. Fishing, boating, swimming, beach, picnicking. Gentle, ocean-bound Beaver Creek creates a wetland and has boat moorage (*see* page 292). **Seal Rock State Recreation Site**, 10 miles south of Newport on US Highway 101. Fishing, beach, hiking, picnicking. Tidepools are a feature of the beach. **Driftwood Beach State Recreation Site**, 3 miles north of Waldport on US Highway 101. Fishing, beach, picnicking. The wide, sandy beach has picnic facilities set amid shore pines.

WALDPORT/YACHATS AREA

Gov. Patterson Memorial State Recreation Site, 1 mile south of Waldport on US Highway 101. Fishing, beach, hiking, picnicking. Excellent bird-watching, beaches, and views of the ocean and Alsea River are key attractions. **W.B. Nelson State Recreation Site**, 1 mile east of Waldport on State Route 34 on the Alsea River. Fishing, hiking, picnicking. The park features a lake and wetlands. **Beachside State Park**, 4 miles south of Waldport on US Highway 101. Phone (541) 563-3220. Camping, fishing, beach, hiking, picnicking. Ocean view campsites are just steps from the beach. **Smelt Sands State Recreation Site**, US Highway 101 at Yachats.

Fishing, beach, hiking, picnicking. Smelt Sands Wayside trail runs through interesting geological and botanical features. **Yachats State Recreation Site**, US Highway 101 at the mouth of Yachats River, Yachats. Fishing, picnicking. Visitors will find good bird-watching in this recreation site located in downtown Yachats. **Yachats Ocean Road State Natural Site**, US Highway 101 at Yachats. Beach, picnicking. The beach has tidepools and interesting rocks. **Yaquina Bay State Recreation Site,** in Newport at the north end of the Yaquina Bay Bridge. Fishing, picnicking. There is a historic lighthouse here. **Neptune State Scenic Viewpoint**, 3 miles south of Yachats on US Highway 101. Fishing, beach, hiking, picnicking. Sand-and-cobble beach stretches for nearly 3 miles. **Stonefield Beach State Recreation Site**, 6 miles south of Yachats on US Highway 101. Fishing, beach. This great whale-watching beach is easy to access.

FLORENCE AREA

Muriel O. Ponsler Memorial State Scenic Viewpoint, 16 miles north of Florence on US Highway 101. Fishing, beach, picnicking. Look for whales while hiking and picnicking along this 5-mile stretch of beach. **Carl G. Washburne Memorial State Park**, 14 miles north of Florence on US Highway 101. Phone (541) 997-3641. Camping, fishing, beach, hiking, picnicking. This five-mile-long beach has many tidepools and a 6-mile hike to Heceta Head Lighthouse (*see* page 296). **Heceta Head Lighthouse State Scenic Viewpoint**, 13 miles north of Florence on US Highway 101. Fishing, beach, hiking, picnicking. Beach activities include lighthouse tours. **Darlingtonia State Natural Site**, 5 miles north of Florence on US Highway 101. Hiking, picnicking. Carnivorous cobra lilies (*Darlingtonia californica*) thrive here.

WINCHESTER BAY/REEDSPORT AREA

Jessie M. Honeyman Memorial State Park, 3 miles south of Florence on US Highway 101. Phone (541) 997-3641. Camping, fishing, boating, swimming, hiking, picnicking. This sand dune paradise also has three lakes (*see* page 300). **Bolon Island Tideways State Scenic Corridor**, 0.5 mile north of Reedsport on US Highway 101. Fishing, hiking. A trail in this park leads to Umpqua River views. **Umpqua Lighthouse State Park**, 6 miles south of Reedsport on US Highway 101. Phone (541) 271-4118. Camping, fishing, boating, hiking. Visitors will find Umpqua Lighthouse as well as fresh and saltwater beaches and sand dunes (*see* page 303). **Umpqua State Scenic Center**, 7 miles east of Reedsport on State Route 38 on the Umpqua River. Fishing, boating, picnicking. A nice place to picnic, but there's no potable water.

LAKESIDE AREA

William M. Tugman State Park, 8 miles south of Reedsport on Eel Lake on US Highway 101. Phone (541) 888-4902. Camping, fishing, boating, swimming, hiking, picnicking. Visitors can walk the trails the freshwater lake or to the ocean beaches (*see* page 303). **Golden and Silver Falls State Natural Area**, 24 miles northeast of Coos Bay off US 101. Fishing, hiking, picnicking. Hikers wander through sections of old-growth forest on the way to two lovely waterfalls.

NORTH BEND/COOS BAY AREA

Conde B. McCullough State Recreation Site, 1 mile north of North Bend on Old Highway 101. Boating, picnicking. This undeveloped park on Harris Inlet has high tide boat moorage.

CHARLESTON AREA

Sunset Bay State Park, 12 miles southwest of Coos Bay off US Highway 101. Phone (541) 888-4902. Camping, fishing, boating, swimming, beach, hiking, picnicking. Explore the sheltered beach and view Cape Arago from this park. **Shore Acres State Park**, 13miles southwest of Coos Bay off US Highway 101. Beach, hiking, picnicking. Former estate features formal gardens (*see* page 307). **Cape Arago State Park**, 14 miles southwest of Coos Bay on US Highway 101. Fishing, beach, hiking, picnicking. Beaches and tidepools lie in three coves at the bottom of the cliff. **Seven Devils State Recreation Site**, Off US Highway 101, 10 miles north of Bandon on Seven Devils Highway. Fishing, beach, picnicking. Visitors can stroll for several miles on this out-of-the-way beach.

BANDON AREA

Bullards Beach State Park, 2 miles north of Bandon on US 101. Phone (541) 347-2209. Camping, fishing, boating, beach, hiking, picnicking. Coquille River Lighthouse is located at this park (*see* page 308). **Face Rock State Scenic Viewpoint**, 1-mile southwest of Bandon off US Highway 101. Fishing, beach, hiking, picnicking. Visitors can enjoy good bird-watching and make out the faces described in Indian stories in the unusual sea stacks. **Bandon State Natural Area**, 5 miles south of Bandon on US Highway 101. Fishing, beach, hiking, picnicking. The park has several entrances to different sections of the beach.

▨ PORT ORFORD AREA

Cape Blanco State Park, 9 miles north of Port Orford off US Highway 101. Phone (541) 332-6774. Camping, fishing, beach, hiking, picnicking. Visitors can tour Cape Blanco Lighthouse and sand beaches (*see* page 311). **Paradise Point State Recreation Site**, 1 mile north of Port Orford off US Highway 101. Beach. Walk along miles of beach, looking at the ocean and spotting whales and agates. **Port Orford Heads State Park**, in Port Orford on US Highway 101. Fishing, hiking, picnicking. Trail leads to Humbug Mountain viewpoint. **Humbug Mountain State Park**, 6 miles south of Port Orford off US Highway 101. Phone (541) 332-6774. Camping, fishing, beach, hiking, picnicking. Enjoy mountain and beach activities at this lovely park (*see* page 311).

▨ GOLD BEACH AREA

Geisel Monument State Heritage Site, 7 miles north of Gold Beach on US Highway 101. Picnicking. The gravesite of European settlers killed in the Rogue Indian War is a peaceful place to relax and picnic. **Otter Point State Recreation Site**, 4 miles north of Gold Beach off US Highway 101. Beach, hiking. Rock formations and, with luck, whales can be seen offshore from the beach. **Cape Sebastian State Scenic Corridor**, on US Highway 101, 7 miles south of Gold Beach. Fishing, beach, hiking, picnicking. Hikers along this coastal trail will be rewarded with fantastic views. **Pistol River State Scenic Viewpoint**, 11 miles south of Gold Beach on US Highway 101. Fishing, beach, hiking, picnicking. Sandy beaches draw visitors. **Samuel H. Boardman State Scenic Corridor**, this 12-mile corridor of densely forested linear park begins 5 miles north of Brookings on US Highway 101. Fishing, beach, hiking, picnicking. Forest covered cliffs and sandy beaches hidden among canyons and coves make this the most spectacular stretch of beach on the Oregon coast. **Harris Beach State Park**, north side of Brookings on US Highway 101. Phone (541) 469-2021. Camping, fishing, beach, hiking, picnicking. Bird-watching opportunities make this a birders' heaven (*see* page 316). **Alfred A. Loeb State Park**, 10 miles northeast of Brookings on Chetco River off US Highway 101. Phone (541) 469-2021. Camping, fishing, swimming, hiking, picnicking. A myrtle wood grove and access to the Redwood Nature Trail can be found here. **McVay Rock State Recreation Site**, 1 mile north of Brookings off US Highway 101. Beach. A wide lawn invites picnicking before heading to the beach to surf-fish or whale watch.

D. Lighthouses of Washington and Oregon

With the constant danger from fogs, storms, and rocks, navigational aids were a priority along the Oregon Territory Coast following the signing of the 1848 border treaty with Great Britain. By 1853, the first lighthouse, at Cape Disappointment, was under construction. It opened in 1856.

The Cape Disappointment light was the first in a system of lighthouses along the Oregon and Washington coasts. The chain of beacons eventually extended along the Strait of Juan de Fuca and into the inland waters of Puget Sound and the San Juan Islands. Eventually Oregon would be graced with 14 lighthouses. Washington, with its more complicated coastline, would boast 26 lighthouses.

Now automated or not working at all, and rendered obsolete for most ships by the advent of Global Positioning Systems, 9 lighthouses still remain standing in Oregon, and 21 in Washington, silent sentinels from another age.

LIGHTHOUSES ON THE WASHINGTON COAST
▨ PUGET SOUND

Dofflemyer Point Lighthouse, Olympia. Dofflemyer was set up as a "post" light to aid navigation through the Tacoma Narrows. Although a tower was eventually built, contract keepers always operated it. The tower and grounds are closed to the public but can be seen from Boston Harbor Town Park, 211 Northeast Seventy-third. **Browns Point Lighthouse, Tacoma.** There's been a beacon here to lead ships into Tacoma's Commencement Bay since 1887; the lighthouse was built in 1903. The grounds, located at Browns Point Lighthouse Park, are open to the public and a small museum, Northeast Points History Center, is open seasonally for limited hours. The Northeast Points Historical Society is also planning a "lightkeepers tour of duty" program. From Exit 137 on Interstate 5, the lighthouse is located on Le-Lou-Wa Place at its intersection with State Route 509. Phone (253) 927-2536. **Point**

Robinson Lighthouse, Maury Island. Although the lighthouse is closed to the public, Point Robinson Park, where it sits, is open and offers some good views of the Cascade Mountains and several small coastal towns across Puget Sound on the mainland. There are also trails to the lighthouse and the beach, picnic tables, and outhouses, but no water. The lighthouse is located at the end of Point Robinson Road, Phone (206) 463-9602. **Alki Point Lighthouse, Seattle.** This 1913 lighthouse is located near the site where Seattle's first settlers landed at Alki (*see* page 57) and is opened for tours on Saturdays and Sundays during the summer. The address is 3201 Alki Avenue Southwest. Phone (206) 217-6993. **West Point Lighthouse, Seattle.** Although closed to the public, this lighthouse is located on a wonderful beach at the bottom of Magnolia Bluff in Seattle's Discovery Park, 1500 Utah Street. Phone (206) 386-4236. **Mukilteo Lighthouse, Mukilteo.** Opened in 1906, the Mukilteo Lighthouse (*see* Mukilteo Lighthouse, page 73) adjacent to the Mukilteo ferry and Mukilteo State Park, lit the way past Point Elliot. It now has a museum and gift shop and is open for tours on weekends and holidays during the summer months. Mukilteo State Park, phone (425) 513-9602. **Point No Point Lighthouse, Hansville.** The only lighthouse on the Kitsap Peninsula and the oldest on Puget Sound, Point No Point is closed to the public but seabirds, sea lions, and whales may be spotted from the nearby beach. Located at the end of Point No Point Road. Phone (360) 337-4595.

SAN JUAN ISLANDS

Cattle Point Lighthouse, San Juan Island. Sitting on the bluff on the southernmost arm of San Juan Island, the lighthouse is closed, but there are trails to the beach as well as an interpretive center and ample opportunities to spot the whales and porpoises that travel through the area, especially in the summer months. Located at the end of Cattle Point Road. **Lime Kiln Lighthouse, San Juan Island.** The Lime Kiln Lighthouse (*see* Lime Kiln Lighthouse, page 101) tower is now a marine mammals research station and closed to the public. However, Dall's porpoise and minke, gray, and orca whales that roam Puget Sound throughout the year can often be spotted from the lighthouse grounds, now part of Whale Watch Park in Lime Kiln State Park, 6158 Lighthouse Road. Phone (360) 378-2044. **Turn Point Lighthouse, Stuart Island.** Turn Point Lighthouse, on Stuart Island, is closed but the grounds may be visited. Dock at Prevost Harbor and walk the 2 miles to the lighthouse. **Patos Island Lighthouse, Patos Island.** The lighthouse is closed to visitors, although the grounds are open. Patos Island Marine State Park (*see* page 93) is located next to the lighthouse grounds. **Burrows Island Lighthouse, Burrows Island.** Although the lighthouse is closed, the grounds can be reached from the undeveloped state property on the west tip of this island, located on the southeast corner of the San Juan archipelago. Boaters can see the lighthouse from Rosario Strait.

STRAIT OF JUAN DE FUCA

Admiralty Head Lighthouse, Coupeville. Admiralty Head Lighthouse in Fort Casey State Park near Coupeville (*see* Admiralty Head Lighthouse, page 88) like its companion, Port Wilson Lighthouse at Port Townsend, marks the passage from the Strait of Juan de Fuca into Puget Sound. Admiralty Head Lighthouse now serves as an interpretive center. Visiting hours are seasonal. Although the state park is on the opposite side of the island from Coupeville, the Fort Casey State Park's address is 1280 Engle Road, Coupeville, Whidbey Island. Phone (360) 678-4519. **Point Wilson Lighthouse, Port Townsend.** Companion to Admiralty Head lighthouse, Point Wilson is located next door to lovely Fort Worden (*see* page 119) and all its recreational opportunities. The lighthouse is opened for tours on a very limited schedule. The address is Fort Worden State Park, 200 Battery Street, Port Townsend. Phone (360) 385-4730. **Marrowstone Lighthouse, Nordland.** Located on the northern tip of Marrowstone Island, Marrowstone Lighthouse (*see* Marrowstone Lighthouse, page 122) this guardian of Admiralty Inlet is closed, although it can be seen from the beaches of Fort Flagler State Park, 10541 Flagler Road. Phone (360) 385-1259. **New Dungeness Spit Lighthouse, Sequim.** The Dungeness Spit Lighthouse (*see* page 127) is at the end of Dungeness Spit and requires a 5.5-mile hike in the Dungeness Spit Wildlife Refuge. Water, restrooms, and picnic tables are located at the lighthouse, which also has tours and a lighthouse "keeper for a week" program. Access to the spit is through Dungeness Recreation Area, 554 Voice of America Road. Phone (360) 683-9166.

OLYMPIC PENINSULA

Cape Flattery Lighthouse, Neah Bay. Located on Tatoosh Island just off Cape Flattery on the Makah Indian Reservation, the now automated lighthouse marks the entrance into the Strait of Juan de Fuca. The island is closed to the public, but both island and lighthouse can be seen from the Cape Flattery Trail (*see* page 159). Phone (360) 645-2201. **Destruction Island Lighthouse, La Push.** The lighthouse and foghorn are automated, and storm-washed Destruction Island is now a wildlife refuge, which is closed to the public (*see* Destruction Island, page 00). There is a viewpoint about 1 mile south of Ruby Beach. The beacon lens is on view at the Westport Maritime Museum, 2201 West Haven Drive, Westport. Museum phone (360) 268-0078.

SOUTH COAST

Westport Lighthouse, Westport. The Pacific coast's tallest (107 feet) tower, the Westport Lighthouse (*see* Westport Lighthouse, page 222) also is known as the Grays Harbor Lighthouse. It can be seen from Ocean Avenue, Westport, and the nearby Westport Maritime Museum conducts tours of the building. For more information contact the Maritime Museum, 2201 West Haven Drive. Phone (360) 268-0078. **North Head Lighthouse, Ilwaco.** The North Head Lighthouse (*see* North Head Lighthouse, page 237) tower, only 2 miles north of Cape Disappointment Lighthouse, was opened in 1898 to guide southbound ships to the Columbia River entrance. The lighthouse is closed, but the site is open and the assistant keeper's house can be rented for overnight stays; for information phone (360) 642-3078. The lighthouse is located near Fort Canby State Park, phone (360) 672-3078. **Cape Disappointment Lighthouse, Ilwaco.** The treacherous Columbia River bar made a lighthouse imperative, which is why Cape Disappointment Lighthouse (*see* Cape Disappointment Lighthouse, page 237) opened in 1856, is the oldest lighthouse in Washington and Oregon. The lighthouse is closed, but the views from the surrounding grounds are worth the easy, 0.75-mile hike that starts at the Lewis and Clark Interpretative Center parking lot. The lighthouse is near Fort Canby State Park, phone (360) 672-3078.

LIGHTHOUSES ON THE OREGON COAST

Tillamook Rock Lighthouse, Tillamook. Sitting on a small island just off Tillamook Head, the Tillamook Rock Lighthouse is now a privately owned columbarium and closed to the public. The closest views are from Tillamook Head, between Ecola State Park and Seaside, and from Cannon Beach along US Highway 101. **Cape Meares Lighthouse, Oceanside.** The squat tower is all that remains of the Cape Meares Lighthouse (*see* Cape Meares Lighthouse, page 279) on a high cliff in Cape Meares State Park. The lighthouse is open daily from June through Sept., and the park and nature trails are open year-round. From US Highway 101, the lighthouse is 10 miles west of Tillamook. Phone (503) 842-4981. **Yaquina Head Lighthouse, Newport.** The tallest tower, 93-feet, on Oregon's coast, Yaquina Head Lighthouse (*see* Yaquina Head Lighthouse, page 287) is situated in the Yaquina Head Outstanding Natural Area, which has seabird nests and tidepools. The lighthouse's lower floor is open seasonally. Located 3 miles north of Newport off US Highway 101. Phone (541) 574-3100. **Yaquina Bay Lighthouse, Newport.** One of the few Pacific coast lighthouses that has the tower attached to the keeper's house, Yaquina Bay Lighthouse (*see* Yaquina Bay Lighthouse, page 291) is also rumored to be haunted. The lighthouse is now a museum, open daily from May to Sept., and weekends the rest of the year. Located on Yaquina Bay Recreational Site, on US Highway 101 at the north end of the bay bridge in Newport. Phone (541) 574-3100. **Heceta Head Lighthouse, Florence.** Seabirds nest on the rocks offshore from the grounds (open year-round) around this now closed Heceta Head Lighthouse (*see* Heceta Head Lighthouse, page 297). The assistant lighthouse keeper's house, Heceta House, is a bed and breakfast. Seabirds nest in the offshore rocks. It is situated 12 miles north of Florence on US Highway 101. For more information phone Heceta House at (541) 547-3690. **Umpqua River Lighthouse, Reedsport.** At Umpqua River Lighthouse (*see* page 303), which is identical to Heceta Head Lighthouse there are tower tours, and the nearby Coastal Visitor's Center, at 1020 Lighthouse Road, houses a museum with some lighthouse artifacts. The tower is located on Umpqua Lighthouse State Park grounds. On US Highway 101, 6 miles south of Reedsport. Phone (541) 271-4631. **Cape Arago Lighthouse, Coos Bay.** Located on an island just off the cape, Cape Arago Lighthouse (*see* Cape Arago Lighthouse, page 307) is closed to the public. Nearby Sunset Bay State Park offers good views and the opportunity to hear the lighthouse's unique horn. Off US Highway 101, 12 miles southwest of Coos Bay and North Bend. Phone (541) 756-0100 or (541) 756-9214. **Coquille River Lighthouse, Bandon.** The last lighthouse built in Oregon, and in service for only 40 years, Coquille River Lighthouse (*see* Coquille River Lighthouse, page 308) is open to the public year-round, with tours of the watch room available on request. Located in Bullards Beach State Park just off US Highway 101 approximately 2 miles north of Bandon. Phone (541) 347-2209. **Cape Blanco Lighthouse, Port Orford.** The oldest lighthouse still standing in Oregon, Cape Blanco Lighthouse (*see* page 311) is closed, but there is a wildlife viewing area below it, and the surrounding Cape Blanco State Park is open year-round. Off US Highway 101, 9 miles north of Port Orford. Phone (541) 756-0100 or (541) 332-6774.

E. Conservation & Outdoor Organizations

Audubon Society of Portland. 5151 Northwest Cornell Road, Portland, OR 97210. Phone (503) 292-6855. Provides conservation advocacy and environmental education, and maintains a wildlife care facility. Publication: *The Warbler.*

Environmental Federation of Oregon. PO Box 40333, Portland, OR 97240. Phone (503) 223-9015. Promotes air and water quality monitoring, growth planning, urban parks programs, toxic chemical education, sustainable resource management, recycling, and habitat preservation, and creates partnerships to make it easier for Oregonians to support environmental groups.

Friends of the San Juans. PO Box 1344, Friday Harbor, WA 98250. Phone (360) 378-2319. Web site http://www.sanjuans.org/. For 20 years, this organization's mission has been "To protect and promote the health and future of the San Juan Islands: land, water, natural, and human communities." Publication: a quarterly newsletter.

Kalmiopsis Audubon Society. PO Box 1265, Port Orford, OR 97465. Works to protect wildlife and enhance the quality of the air, land, and water upon which all life depends.

Klamath Siskiyou Wildlands Center. PO Box 332, Williams, OR 97554. Phone (541) 846-9273. Dedicated to the preservation and restoration of biological diversity and wild places in the Klamath Siskiyou bioregion.

Northwest Ecosystem Alliance. 1421 Cornwall Avenue, Suite 201, Bellingham, WA 98225. Phone (360) 671-9950. E-mail: nwea@ecosystem.org. Aims to protect and restore Pacific Northwest wildlands. Publications: *Northwest Conservation: News and Priorities; Wild Salmon and Trout Action Plan; Of Wolves and Washington; Cascadia Wild; Protecting an International Ecosystem; Conservation Biology and National Forest Management in the Inland Northwest; A Handbook for Activists.*

Northwest Interpretive Association. 909 First Avenue, Suite 630, Seattle, WA 98104. Phone (206) 220-4140. Supports education and interpretation on public lands administered by the National Park Service, U.S. Forest Service, and various Pacific Northwest agencies.

Northwest Rafters Association. 10117 Southeast Sunnyside Road F1234, Clackamas, OR 97015. Dedicated to preserving and enhancing the whitewater experience, and promoting boating safety, equal access to streams, and river conservation. Publication: *Confluence Monthly Newsletter.*

Oregon League of Conservation Voters. 320 SW Stark, Suite 415, Portland, OR 97204. Phone (503) 224- 4011. E-mail olcv@olcv.org. Web site http://www.cnnw.net/~olcv/. OLCV is a nonpartisan organization with a diverse membership working to educate voters about how their legislators vote on the environment and to hold those legislators accountable. OLCV coordinates the Oregon Conservation Network, a statewide coalition of environmental groups that track environmental issues in the Oregon Legislature. Publication: quarterly newsletter.

Oregon Natural Resources Council. 5825 North Greely, Portland, OR 97217-4154. Phone (503) 283-6343. Promotes forest ecosystem restoration, clean water, biodiversity conservation, and salmon and river restoration. Publication: *Wild Oregon.*

Oregon Shores Conservation Coalition. PO Box 264, South Beach, OR 97366. E-mail: orshores@teleport.com. Web site http://www.teleport.com/~orshores/index.htm. Oregon Shores Conservation Coalition, founded in 1971, is Oregon's only statewide organization dedicated solely to protecting Oregon's coastal resources. Its ultimate goal is to promote, at the state and local level, laws, incentives, and enforcement mechanisms necessary for resource protection. OSCC is also dedicated to the education of Oregon citizens to enable them to participate more effectively in protecting the coastal environment.

Oregon Trout. 117 Southwest Naito Parkway, Portland, OR 97204. Phone (503) 222-9091. Protects and restores native wild fish and the ecosystems that sustain them. Publication: *The Guide to Pacific Northwest Aquatic Invertebrates.*

Pacific Northwest Trail Association. 1361 Avon Allen Road, Mount Vernon, WA 98273. Phone (360) 424-0407. Promotes the establishment of a continuous horse and foot trail from the Continental Divide to the Pacific Ocean. Publications: *Nor'wester; Pacific Northwest Trail; Blanchard Hill and Chuckanut Mountain Map.*

People for Puget Sound. 1402 Third Avenue, Suite 1200, Seattle, WA 98101. Phone (206) 382-7007. E-mail people@pugetsound.org. Web site http://www.pugetsound.org/. People for Puget Sound is a nonprofit citizens group dedicated to educating and involving people in protecting and restoring the land and waters of Puget Sound and the Northwest Straits. It seeks to eliminate contamination of the sound's waters, to halt the destruction of natural habitats, and to sustain the Sound and Straits as a healthy source of people's livelihood, enjoyment, and renewal. Publication: *Sound & Straits*, a quarterly newsletter.

Puget Sound Water Quality Action Team. PO Box 40900, Olympia, WA 98504-0900. Phone (800) 54-SOUND or (360) 407-7300. Web site http://www.wa.gov/pugetsound/index.html. The Puget Sound Water Quality Action Team—a subagency of the governor's office—brings together the heads of 10 state agencies, a city and a county representative, a representative of federally recognized tribes and ex-officio non-voting representatives of three federal agencies to lead and coordinate efforts to protect Puget Sound. Publications: The Puget Sound Water Quality Action Team produces a number of informative publications about Puget Sound. Many of these publications can be accessed online.

Puget Soundkeeper Alliance. 1415 W. Dravus, Seattle, WA 98119. Phone (206) 286-1309. E-mail pskeeper@halcyon.com. Web site http://www.pugetsoundkeeper.org/. The Puget Soundkeeper Alliance brings together concerned citizens, businesses, and government agencies to solve marine environmental issues in a responsible and balanced manner.

Sierra Club, Washington Chapter. 8511 Fifteenth Avenue Northeast, Seattle, WA 98122. Phone (206) 523-2147. Local chapter of national organization aimed at the preservation and expansion of wilderness land.

Sierra Club, Oregon Chapter. 3701 Southeast Milwaukee Avenue, Suite F, Portland, OR 97202. Phone (503) 238-0442. A nonprofit organization that promotes environmental conservation by influencing public policy decisions. Publication: *Oregon Conifer.*

The Nature Conservancy. 821 SE Fourteenth Street, Portland, OR, 97214. Phone (503) 230-1221. Works with partners to help indigenous communities buy and manage key lands.

Trout Unlimited, Washington Council. 2401 Bristol Court Southwest, Olympia, WA 98502. Phone (360) 754-2131. E-mail: kbob@halcyon.com. Works to enhance and protect coldwater fisheries in the state, with 31 local chapters. Publication: *Trout and Salmon Leader.*

Washington Environmental Council. 615 Second Avenue, Number 380, Seattle, WA 98104. Phone (206) 622-8103. E-mail: greenwec@aol.com. Dedicated to preserving, protecting, and restoring the Pacific Northwest's environment, this organization has over 100 affiliated organizations. Publications: *WEC Voices; Forest Resources News.*

Washington Recreation and Park Association. 350 South 333 Street, Suite 103, Federal Way, WA 98003. Phone (253) 874-1283. Works to enhance parks, recreation, and leisure activities in the state, and promote public support for parks and recreation. Publication: *Syllabus.*

Washington Trails Association. 1305 Fourth Avenue, Number 512, Seattle, WA 98101. Phone (206) 625-1367. Involved in trail planning, management, and maintenance in order to protect and enhance the state's trail systems. Also offers education and information programs.

Washington Wilderness Coalition. 4649 Sunnyside Avenue North, Number 242, Seattle, WA 98103. Phone (206) 633-1992. E-mail: wawild@aol.com. Offers outreach, public education, and support of grassroots conservation groups in order to preserve the wilderness areas and biodiversity of the region for future generations. Publication: *Washington Wildfire.*

Washington Wildlife and Recreation Coalition. 4001 Southwest Cloverdale, Seattle, WA 98136. Phone (206) 938-4513. Supports the acquisition of public land through public education, legislation, and research into the need for wildlife and conservation. Publication: *Land News.*

Wildlife Society, Washington Chapter. U.S. Fish and Wildlife Service, 3704 Griffin Lane Southeast, Suite 102, Olympia, WA 98501. Phone (360) 753-4325. Provides support and training for professional wildlife biologists, as well as a forum for presenting research results and management ideas. Publication: *Wildlife Society Washington Chapter Newsletter.*

F. Glossary

Algae—Simple organisms that perform photosynthetic functions that produce oxygen.

Anadromous fish—Fish that hatch in fresh water, migrate to the sea to mature, then return to breed in the freshwater site where they hatched.

Andesite—Usually gray or brown volcanic rock with a high silica content.

Archeology—The scientific study of ancient cultures.

Basalt—A fine-grained, dark, volcanic rock with a heavy content of magnesium and iron.

Bacteria—Unicellular microorganisms that may cause disease in plants or animals.

Benthos—Organisms that live on or near the bottom of a body of water.

Browse—To eat leaves or similar vegetation or the vegetation that is eaten.

Cetacea—Mammal species such as whales, dolphins, and porpoises that live exclusively at sea.

Chlorophyll—Green matter that is essential to the photosynthesis of plants.

Clear-cut—The practice of harvesting all the trees in a given area at the same time.

Cascade Mountains—An inland mountain range that parallels the Pacific Coast of America.

Coast Range Mountains—A mountain range that parallels the American coast near or adjacent to the Pacific Ocean.

Conifer—Evergreen, cone-bearing trees and shrubs.

Continental ice flow—A glacier that covers a large area of a continent.

Deciduous—Plants that lose their leaves on a seasonal basis and are leafless until they grow new leaves.

Dune—A hill or ridge of sand that is formed by the wind.

Ecology—Scientific study of the interrelationship of organisms and their environment.

Environment—The conditions and circumstances that surround organisms or groups of organisms.

Evergreen—Plants with foliage that remains green throughout the year.

Extinct—A plant or animal species that no longer exists or a volcano that no longer is active.

Fauna—Animals of a specific period or region.

Flotsam—Something that floats or drifts on open waters.

Forest canopy—The upper level of trees in a forest.

Fungi—Simple plants that lack chlorophyll.

Geography—The science that deals with the topography of the earth's surface.

Geology—The science that deals with the origin of the earth's crust and its rocks.

Glacier—A large body of ice, which is formed of compacted snow, that is forced to move by its own weight.

Glaciated valley—A valley carved or changed by glacial action.

Gneiss—A metamorphic rock consisting of light and dark bands.

Granite—Coarse igneous rock made up primarily of feldspar and quartz.

Grass—Any of many plants with jointed stems, seedlike fruit, and slender, sheathing sleeves.

Graze—To feed on living vegetation.

Habitat—The natural environment of plants or animals.

Herb—A flowering plant whose stem does not produce persistent, woody tissue.

Igneous—Rock formed when magma solidifies.

Juan de Fuca Plate—A relatively small segment of the Pacific Plate that is being subducted under the Pacific Northwest shore.

Klamath Mountains—A mountain province near the coast in the Oregon/California border area.

Lava—Magma that has been erupted onto the surface of the earth.

Lichens—Composite organisms formed by symbiotic union of fungus and algae that grow on trees or rocks.

Lithosphere—The earth's crust.

Magma—Molten rock inside the earth.

Mammals—Warm blooded, vertebrate animals that nourish their young with milk from the females' mammary glands.

Meadow—An area of land where grasses and other low growing plants predominate.

Metamorphic rock—Rock changed by heat and pressure from the earth's interior or by chemical processes.

Millennia—Periods of 1,000 years.

Outcrop—Bedrock that protrudes out of the earth.

Pangaea—A prehistoric land mass that divided and formed the continents of the present.

Pacific Plate—A tectonic plate that is being subducted beneath the Pacific Northwest coast of America.

Pelagic—Intertidal organisms that drift or swim with the tide.

Plate tectonics—A theory that large slabs of the earth's outer shell float on the molten rock beneath and are in constant motion.

Pollination—The transfer of pollen from an anther to a stigma as part of the reproductive process of flowers.

Prevailing wind—Wind that usually blows from the same direction because of atmospheric conditions.

Quartzite—A granular rock of interlocking grains of quartz.

Rapids—Part of a river that is fast moving because of a steep descent of the riverbed. Rapids are often associated with rocks and boulders that impede the flow.

Rush—Glass-like, stiff marsh herbs with hollow or pithy stems and small flowers that are used to make baskets. Also various similar plants.

Sedge—Grass-like plants that have solid stems, leaves that grow in three vertical rows, and inconspicuous flowers surrounded by scale-like bract.

Sedimentary rock—Rock formed of sediment of older rock, or the remains of plants or animals.

Shrub—A low, woody plant with multiple stems rising from the base, and lacking a main trunk.

Slate—A bluish gray sedimentary rock that divides into smooth, tabular pieces.

Snowfield—A permanent or semipermanent field of snow that lacks the characteristic movement of glaciers.

Species—A classification of organisms that ranks below genus or subgenus. Species are capable of interbreeding.

Symbiotic organisms—Organisms that live together and mutually contribute to each other's welfare.

Tidepools—Small pools of seawater in the intertidal area that provide habitat for a variety of species.

Understory—Plant life growing beneath the dominant trees of the forest.

Vent—An opening in the earth surface that emits lava, volcanic ash, or gas.

Index